Attack State Red

COLONEL RICHARD KEMP
AND
CHRIS HUGHES

PENGUIN BOOKS

PENGUIN BOOKS

Published by the Penguin Group
Penguin Books Ltd, 80 Strand, London WC2R ORL, England
Penguin Group (USA) Inc., 375 Hudson Street, New York, New York 10014, USA
Penguin Group (Canada), 90 Eglinton Avenue East, Suite 700, Toronto, Ontario, Canada M4P 2Y3
(a division of Pearson Penguin Canada Inc.)
Penguin Ireland, 25 St Stephen's Green, Dublin 2, Ireland (a division of Penguin Books Ltd)
Penguin Group (Australia), 250 Camberwell Road, Camberwell, Victoria 3124, Australia
(a division of Pearson Australia Group Pty Ltd)
Penguin Books India Pvt Ltd, 11 Community Centre, Panchsheel Park, New Delhi – 110 017, India
Penguin Group (NZ), 67 Apollo Drive, Rosedale, North Shore 0632, New Zealand
(a division of Pearson New Zealand Ltd)
Penguin Books (South Africa) (Pty) Ltd, 24 Sturdee Avenue,
Rosebank, Johannesburg 2196, South Africa

Penguin Books Ltd, Registered Offices: 80 Strand, London WC2R ORL, England

www.penguin.com

First published by Michael Joseph 2009
Published in Penguin Books 2010

003

Copyright © Richard Kemp and Chris Hughes, 2009
All rights reserved

ISBN: 978-0-141-04163-6

www.greenpenguin.co.uk

To all of the soldiers and marines of The 1st Battalion The Royal Anglian Regiment Battle Group who took the fight to the enemy in Afghanistan in 2007; in salute to the sacrifices of those who were wounded in action; and in memory of the nine Royal Anglian soldiers who laid down their lives for their comrades and their country.

Killed in Action

Corporal Darren Bonner

Lance Corporal George Davey

Private Robert Foster

Private Chris Gray

Lance Corporal Alex Hawkins

Captain David Hicks MC

Private Aaron McLure

Private Tony Rawson

Private John Thrumble

Contents

Acknowledgements

This book would not have been possible without the frankness and forbearance of the soldiers who fought as members of the Royal Anglian Battle Group in Helmand in 2007, who voluntarily gave up so much of their time in more than 300 interviews. Those who were interviewed are included in the list of battle group members at the back of this book. Without exception they told their stories willingly, in graphic detail, with great candour. And often with much emotion. The modesty of every person interviewed, and their determination to give credit to others rather than themselves, was humbling. This is their story.

Special thanks to Lieutenant Colonel Stuart Carver DSO, the Royal Anglian Battle Group Commander, who enthusiastically embraced this project from its earliest stages. He and his successor as Commanding Officer of The 1st Battalion, The Royal Anglian Regiment, Lieutenant Colonel James Woodham MC, provided the strongest support throughout the research and writing of this book, making their soldiers and battalion facilities freely available.

Thanks also for practical assistance and guidance, as well as for their interviews, to Brigadier John Lorimer DSO, Commander of Task Force Helmand, and to Lieutenant Colonel Charlie Calder, Major Mick Aston MC, Major Dominic Biddick MC, Major Tony Borgnis, Major Phil Messenger, Major Dean Stefanetti MBE, Captain Andy Buxton, Captain Tom Coleman, Captain Graham Goodey, Captain Phil Moxey, Captain Mark Nicholas, Captain Ian Robinson MBE, Captain George Seal-Coon, Captain Andy Wilde, Regimental Sergeant Major Tim Newton, Colour Sergeant Keith Nieves, Sergeant Steve Armon, Sergeant Nathan Love, Sergeant Matt Waters, Sergeant Mark Willsher, Corporal Joel Adlington, Corporal Darren Farrugia, Corporal Richard Jones, Corporal Stuart Parker, Corporal Gav Watts, Lance Corporal Tom Mann, Private Josh Hills, Private Josh Lee and Private Kenny Meighan.

The encouragement and enthusiasm of the literary professionals involved with this book has made writing it a thoroughly rewarding, edifying and above all enjoyable experience. Particular thanks to Mark

Lucas, whose expertise and guidance was absolutely invaluable in transforming the ghost of an idea into a living volume; and to his colleagues at LAW, especially Julian Alexander and Alice Saunders. Particular thanks also to Rowland White at Penguin for his vision, flexibility, understanding and guidance; to David Watson, who edited the manuscript with the most admirable skill and patience; to Alan Gilliland who also deployed great skill and patience in producing the maps; to Tom Chicken, Ana-Maria Rivera and Katya Shipster for their imagination and vigour in driving the sales and marketing process; and to Sarah Hulbert and Paulette Hearn for their unflagging energy in tying everything together and simply making it happen!

Thanks for their invaluable advice and assistance to Nick Gurr, Director General of Corporate Communications at the Ministry of Defence, and his team, including Steve Beamont and Colonel Ben Bathurst; and to the corporate communications staff at HQ Land Command.

Thanks to Ryan Alexander for his specialist advice and critical eye, and for his exceptional practical assistance; to Monica Kemp for her wise guidance and encouragement; to Lucy Christie for her outstanding interview transcriptions; to Colonel Patrick Mercer OBE and Major Chris Hunter QGM for sharing their authorial experience as well as their deep military knowledge; to Heather Millican, Colonel Nigel Burrell and Lieutenant Colonel Richard Clements OBE for their practical assistance and encouragement. Finally, thanks to Anna and Lucy – they know why.

A special word of thanks to George Davies. Although not involved with this book, his quiet generosity did a tremendous amount to ease the terrible suffering of many wounded British and Allied soldiers, including all of the Royal Anglians described in the pages that follow who were seriously wounded in action, as well as their families, and the families of Royal Anglians killed in action.

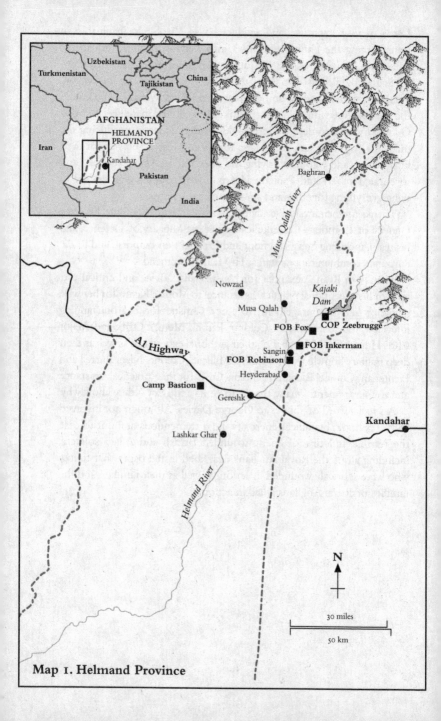

Map 1. Helmand Province

Royal Anglian Battle Group Organization

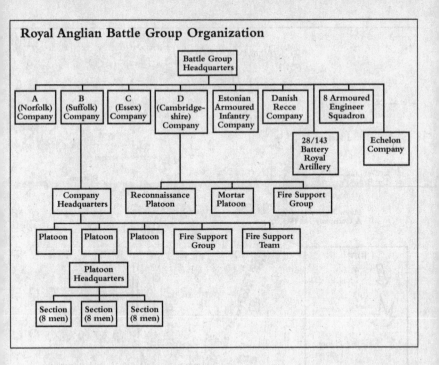

Battle Group Headquarters
- A (Norfolk) Company
- B (Suffolk) Company
- C (Essex) Company
- D (Cambridgeshire) Company
- Estonian Armoured Infantry Company
- Danish Recce Company
- 8 Armoured Engineer Squadron
- 28/143 Battery Royal Artillery
- Echelon Company

- Company Headquarters
- Reconnaissance Platoon
- Mortar Platoon
- Fire Support Group

- Platoon
- Platoon
- Platoon
- Fire Support Group
- Fire Support Team

- Platoon Headquarters

- Section (8 men)
- Section (8 men)
- Section (8 men)

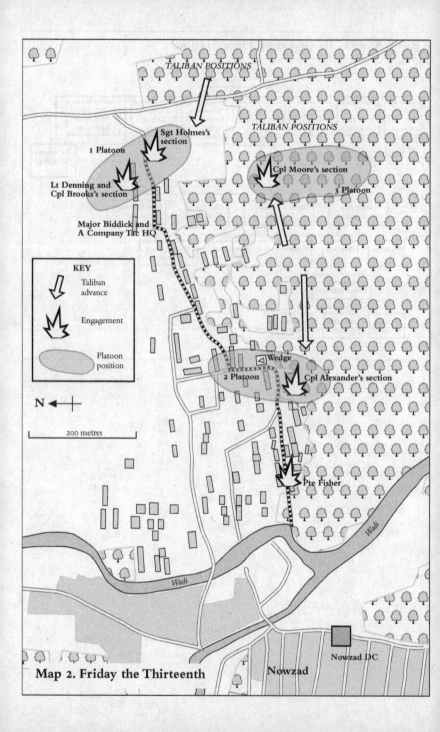

TALIBAN POSITIONS

TALIBAN POSITIONS

Sgt Holmes's section

1 Platoon

Cpl Moore's section

3 Platoon

Lt Denning and
Cpl Brooks's section

Major Biddick and
A Company Tac HQ

KEY

⇩ Taliban advance

✸ Engagement

⬭ Platoon position

N

200 metres

Wedge

2 Platoon

Cpl Alexander's section

Pte Fisher

Wadi

Wadi

Nowzad DC

Map 2. Friday the Thirteenth

Nowzad

Friday the Thirteenth: 13 April 2007

Sergeant Larry Holmes was exposed, isolated and alone. He knew he would soon be dead. But the intense, numbing fear he couldn't shake off was tempered by a deep feeling of frustration. He was a tough, aggressive infantryman and he wanted to hit back at his attackers – shoot them with his rifle, blow them apart with his grenades, get up close and thrust his bayonet into them.

But he couldn't. He couldn't move.

It could only be a matter of seconds before one of the machine-gun bullets tore him apart. When the gunfire started, moments before, Holmes threw himself straight down on to his belt buckle. He tried to force his whole body through the ground. His face was buried in the dirt and he was digging in with his eyelids. Bullets scythed past, chopping up the rocky earth next to him. Above, volley after volley of rocket-propelled grenades exploded in the air, with their deadly shrapnel scorching into the earth near by.

He'd left the section behind him, in and around a small mud hut, 30 metres back across the open field. He thought, *What the hell has happened to my lads? Are they still alive?* Slowly, carefully, he turned his head, keeping it against the ground, trying not to get it blown off.

The hut was steadily disintegrating under the endless blasting from gunfire and anti-tank rockets. *I hope to God they had the sense to get out of there, or they're probably dead already.*

Trying not to move too much, he shouted, 'Corporal Colby, can you hear me? Are you OK? Are – you – OK?'

He heard muffled yells coming from behind the low wall that ran away from the devastated hut. *At least some of them are still alive*, he thought.

He yelled back, 'Get some fire down! Get some fire going down!'

But the wall they were crouching behind was also getting hit by burst after burst of gunfire, and he doubted that any of them would be able to put their heads up to give covering fire without getting killed before they got a shot off.

What the hell am I going to do?

Thoughts of his family flashed through his mind: *I'll never see Sally or the kids again. I'm going to die here in Afghanistan. And my baby will never see her dad. Jordan and Chloe will grow up without a father and probably won't even remember me. You hear about that sort of thing, but I never for one minute thought it would happen to me or my family.*

He loved his wife and children more than anything in the world and he was overcome by sadness.

Then he got a grip of himself. *Stop thinking like that. It's not going to help. You've got to do something, get out of this – somehow.*

Mortar bombs were exploding near by, and some landed very close, lashing out jagged shards of red-hot steel in every direction. Bullets sliced through the air, and he could hear the constant short zipping noise the rounds made as they passed right by him. *Just one random shot, just one out of the thousands they are firing, and that'll be me. That's all it will take. Just one.*

His arms and face were bleeding from rocks and debris thrown up as the bullet heads hit the ground. He needed help. He hadn't been paying any attention to his radio for the last few seconds, but it had come alive with traffic. Everyone talking, cutting in, sending reports. He waited for a break and pushed down the pressel switch. 'Hello, Bronze Zero Alpha, this is Bronze One Zero Bravo. Contact. I am pinned down. I can't move. I need fire support. I cannot move. I need fire.'

He was speaking very fast, trying hard to sound calm but not succeeding, and his face was still pushed into the dirt with his radio mike in his mouth. His words were indecipherable.

'Bronze Zero Alpha, say again, say again, over.'

He took a breath, raised his face slightly and repeated his transmission.

From within the compounds of Sorkhani, 200 metres back, Major Dominic Biddick, the company group commander, spoke slowly and calmly. 'This is Bronze Zero Alpha. I need a full contact report. I need your precise location.'

'*I am pinned down!*' yelled Holmes, then calmed slightly and said, 'I cannot move. I cannot look up. I cannot see where I am. I am pinned down by highly effective enemy fire. I need support now. Over.'

Biddick's words angered him. *How the hell can I send him a full contact report? I am about to get killed.* At the same time the sound of his commander's voice gave him a glimmer of hope. With the astonishingly capable Major Biddick, the military machine, on the case, maybe – just maybe – he would get out of here. He knew that at this moment Biddick would be marshalling every conceivable resource to help him.

'Hello, Bronze One Zero Bravo, this is Bronze Zero Alpha. Stay calm. You must give me your location. Where are you? Where is the enemy? I need a target indication.'

Holmes moved his hand slowly towards his face, desperate not to move his arm a millimetre higher than he needed to. He looked at the dial of the Garmin GPS strapped to his wrist. The sweat that was stinging his eyes blurred his vision and he had to rub them to get a clear view of the numbers. He waited a couple of moments for another gap in the furious radio traffic, then read out the ten-figure grid to Biddick.

'Zero Alpha, roger, got that. What is the grid of the enemy location? Over.'

'I estimate enemy two hundred metres…bearing sixteen hundred mils from my grid. Not confirmed. I cannot see their position. I say again, that is an estimate. Over.'

Biddick responded with a clipped but calm 'Roger, understood. I will engage with mortars. Wait out.'

As the bullets and rockets continued to send chips of rock smacking into his face and arms another thought came to Holmes. He remembered that, on the way here, he had picked up Taliban chatter on his radio scanner. They had said they wanted to capture one of the soldiers advancing towards their position. *And I've got no idea where they are!* He didn't just have the bullets to worry about, but the thought that, out of a fold in the ground, enemy fighters could suddenly appear and grab him. *Then what?*

He shuddered as he remembered being told, 'If you get caught by the Taliban you've had it – you'll wish you were dead. They'll skin you alive and cut you up slowly.' Popular legend had it that hundreds of Russian soldiers captured by the mujahideen in the 1980s had been skinned alive, the skin of their stomachs pulled over their heads. Afghan soldiers caught by the Taliban had been tortured for days, then dragged around villages screaming for mercy.

Major Biddick was on the radio again: 'Bronze One Zero Bravo, Zero Alpha. Are you able to mark your forward position with smoke? Over.'

Slowly, very slowly, so as not to attract attention to himself, Holmes reached into his pouch with his left hand and pulled out a smoke grenade. He called into the radio, 'Throwing green smoke now, over.'

He pulled the pin, reached back, then lobbed the grenade as far forward as he could. The second he threw it he thought: *Mistake! Mistake!*

As the smoke started to billow, the enemy aimed straight at it. The fire intensified, growing closer and closer.

Then he just about made out Private Ian Rolph's muffled shouting from behind the wall. It sounded like: 'Firing fifty-one.'

Good lad, thought Holmes. *If he can get some 51mm mortar bombs into the enemy, I might just get a chance to pull back.*

He took out another smoke grenade, swung back his arm and launched it as far off to the left, away from him, as he could. As the smoke started to spread, again the gunfire increased, but this time directed in the area where the grenade had landed.

Holmes immediately started to edge backwards, still on his belt buckle, body pressed into the ground. He didn't dare turn round. He moved as fast as he could. Bullets flew all around him. He looked back from time to time to get his bearings. Once he saw Private Matthew Slater come up from behind the wall and fire a machine-gun burst straight over his head. Almost instantaneously, ten times as many bullets flew back at Slater, and he dropped down, avoiding certain death by a split second. *Brave lad*, thought Holmes, *not many people would try that*.

Minutes later, his arms and legs torn up on the rocky ground, he reached the wall. *How the hell am I going to get over this?*

Bullets were cutting through the air, just above his body, and just about at the height of the wall. He moved gradually down to a slight dip, where the smoking top of the wall had been torn away by a rocket-propelled grenade. He didn't know whether to slide over, keeping his body pressed against the wall, or try a dive.

He launched himself across and felt a massive jolt as a bullet thudded into the daysack on his back.

He found himself next to Slater, general-purpose machine-gun (GPMG) beside him. He sat down with his back against the wall, pouring sweat and gasping for breath. Slater reached across and put his hand on Holmes's shoulder. 'Sarge, it's really good to see you. I thought you were dead out there.'

Holmes pressed his back up against the wall, pouring sweat, heart pounding at his rib cage, mouth dry as a rock. He thought for a second. *How the hell did I get out of that? I guess it just wasn't my time to die. Wasn't my time. There is no other reason. I should be dead ten times over.* Then he grinned at Slater. 'Come on, mate, you know me better than that. It's going to take more than a bunch of spaced-out Taliban with crappy Russian machine-guns to kill the platoon sergeant.'

He looked around. Private Norman Pozo, Rolph and the other lads were spread out along the wall. He was so pleased to see they were all alive, to be back with them. He was safer now, a bit safer. At least he had some cover. And he was with his men.

But bullets were still smacking into the wall and the building beside them, which was now all but destroyed. RPG rockets were still exploding overhead. They were still isolated and cut off. And there was no way of getting back to the relative safety of the village without crossing a long stretch of very open and exposed ground – which was still under intense enemy fire.

Holmes started laughing, almost uncontrollably. Pozo and the others joined in. Nothing was funny right now, and Holmes realized it must be a nervous reaction to the horrific situation they were in.

He was jolted back to reality when he heard a radio message in his earpiece that made his blood run cold. Corporal Daz Bonner, the company signaller, said, 'All stations, this is Bronze Two One Alpha. Radio intercept from enemy forward of callsign Bronze One Zero's location as follows. Quote. Stop firing. I want them alive. We are going forward to cut them off. Unquote. Bronze One Zero Bravo, acknowledge, over.'

Immediately Holmes replied, 'One Zero Bravo, roger, out.'

He had been unable to do much out in the open, pinned down. But now there was a modicum of cover, and he was not going to lie dormant here with his men. Holmes was one of the hardest, most proactive and aggressive leaders in the battalion. He was going to defend against enemy attack, then he was going to manoeuvre to a better position, then he was going to counter-attack. He called along the wall to his men: 'OK, looks like they're coming to get us. Get your bayonets out. If they get to this wall we may have to use them.' The men stared at him in disbelief as they heard for the first time in a real situation the words 'Fix bayonets!'

2

The sniper team were moving on the left flank of the company, covering the area of open ground and providing some protection at the rear of Holmes's platoon and Tac HQ, the company commander's command team made up of indirect fire controllers and signallers. When the battle began, the snipers moved forward on to rooftops to try to get into a position to help the troops in contact.

Privates Oliver Bailey and Clay Donnachie, on top of a building, had identified a group of Taliban several hundred metres in the distance, firing at Holmes and his men.

Bailey said, 'Donnie, I've got a head shot. Can't see him clearly. I'm going for the muzzle flash. When I fire, it'll kick up so much dust they'll be straight on to us. You need to keep really low.'

Other than his lips Bailey did not move any part of his body when he shouted above the deafening racket of machine-gun fire and air-bursting rocket grenades. Peering intently through the Schmidt and Bender telescopic sight, he trained his heavy sniper rifle firmly on the target, open right eye stinging with the sweat running into it, elbows resting painfully on the unyielding mud roof. He centred the sight picture precisely over the muzzle flash, then edged it a few millimetres right, to the exact point he knew the fighter's head would be. He was ice-cool, but also concerned about the reaction his next movement was certain to provoke.

Remaining perfectly still, he took the first pressure on the trigger, inhaled, paused...and then slowly exhaled, squeezing in the second pressure. The rifle jerked back, biting at his shoulder. The .338 Lapua Magnum bullet sliced through the air at supersonic speed, forcing up a swirl of dust to his front.

The muzzle flashes had ceased. *Kill!*

Private Jimmy Long, another sniper, clambered up on to the roof and was greeted by a hail of fire as the Taliban machine-gunners trained on to the dust kicked up by Bailey's shot. The fire was intense, and the three men pressed their bodies into the sun-baked roof. For a few minutes they couldn't move: they were pinned down and expecting to be hit at any moment.

When the fire slackened slightly, they crawled to the sides and dropped down into the alleyway below.

'There's nothing for us to do down here,' said Bailey. 'We're useless in alleyways. The Taliban are obviously trying to infiltrate and split up the company. We've got to find another roof to get on to.'

Donnachie and Long headed off down to the left. Bailey slung his sniper rifle over his shoulder. It was pretty much useless in the tight complex of narrow alleys, mud walls and low buildings. He drew his 9mm Browning Hi-Power pistol, already cocked, and led the way to the right, looking for a suitable rooftop firing position. Behind him were Lance Corporal Werner van der Merwe, cover man, and Lance Corporal Jock Flight, another sniper.

The incredible din of gunfire and explosions continued, echoing and reverberating around the walls of the village, preventing any idea of where any of it was coming from or going to.

The alleyway bent hard right. Bailey was about to turn the corner when he almost walked into a tall, tan-skinned man with a huge black beard, wearing a dirty grey kurta, an AK47 assault rifle at his hip. Shocked, Bailey leapt back. As he jumped, he fired his pistol, hitting the wide-eyed fighter in the leg. Everything was happening in slow motion. He could see the man gritting his teeth with pain; his eyeballs seemed to be popping out of his head. Off-balance and reeling, the man fired wildly with his AK47. Shooting one-handed, Bailey got him in the chest with the second round, driving him back round the corner. As the man staggered backwards, Bailey continued firing and emptied his magazine at him.

Behind Bailey, van der Merwe and Flight had momentarily frozen, amazed at what they saw, and astonished they hadn't been hit by the AK47 bullets ricocheting around the narrow confines of the alleyway.

Now van der Merwe grabbed Bailey by the daysack and pulled him back behind him. Levelling his SA80, van der Merwe fired a UGL grenade, hoping to bounce it off the mud wall and kill any further Taliban waiting round the corner. But the grenade just dug in, and van der Merwe quickly lobbed a high-explosive hand grenade, blasting out lethal fragments of hot steel that would have taken care of anyone waiting to rush out at them. Van der Merwe cautiously peered round the corner, leading with his rifle. The dead Taliban fighter was sprawled awkwardly across the alley floor, one leg bent under his body.

The three men moved back down the alleyway and entered a small mud compound to get their breath. Inside was a filthy wooden table with a lukewarm tea pot and a couple of hypodermic syringes with some small open twists of white paper. This must have been where Taliban fighters had been resting when the fighting started. Or maybe just some of the village's innocent residents, who had fled when they saw the approach of the Royal Anglian soldiers.

Van der Merwe handed a water bottle to Bailey. Bailey glugged down the water, still hyped with adrenalin and speaking fast even for him, 'How didn't his shots get us? Don't want to do that again in a hurry. Amazing.'

'Yeah,' said van der Merwe, 'Thank God you got off the first shot, otherwise we'd probably all be dead. And Major Biddick too: that bloke was heading straight for his Tac.'

3

When he realized Holmes was under fire, Biddick had raced forward with his Tac HQ to get into the best position to command the three platoons and the fire support elements of A Company Group, The 1st Battalion The Royal Anglian Regiment.

Thirty-two-year-old Major Dominic Biddick had been in the Army since the age of seventeen, when he had joined the Worcestershire and Sherwood Foresters Regiment as a private. Later commissioned into the Royal Anglian Regiment, he had extensive operational experience in Northern Ireland and in Afghanistan, where he had completed two previous tours, one in Kabul as battalion operations officer, and the second as senior intelligence officer with HQ 16th Air Assault Brigade.

Biddick's thirty-man platoons were dispersed around the deserted eastern section of Nowzad town. Known as Sorkhani, it was a tightly packed area of small compounds surrounded by 2- to 3-metre-high walls. The narrow streets were compacted dusty mud tracks, flanked on either side by open sewage ditches. The whole place, ideal ground for Taliban flanking moves, infiltration and ambushes, was criss-crossed with narrow alleyways, tunnels, rat-runs and mouse-holes between buildings.

Biddick weighed up the situation. Captain Charlie Harmer, his FST commander, had already called for air support and was confident that a pair of US Air Force F15 Eagle tactical fighters would be on station within minutes. Biddick had already engaged the Taliban with mortars, and, with the weight of fire they were putting down, was confident that he was regaining the initiative. But he still needed to know exactly where the enemy were. He spoke to Lieutenant Graham Goodey, commander of 2 Platoon, who were deployed further back into Sorkhani: 'Graham, can you and maybe some of your NCOs get up on to high points and see if you can figure out where the fire is coming from? If you are able to get any weapons into a position to engage that would be even better.'

Biddick was considering how he could rebalance the company. He would need his two forward platoons to link up to form a stronger defence against the Taliban, or to assault should the opportunity present itself to move forward and attack. At the same time he was worried about enemy out-flanking teams moving around in Sorkhani, getting behind his troops. At all costs he had to secure against this potentially deadly infiltration – a speciality of the Taliban.

Biddick spoke on the company net: 'All stations, this is Bronze Zero Alpha. SITREP. Callsign Bronze One Zero is under heavy contact with the enemy on the eastern edge of the built-up area.'

He repeated the description of the enemy position given to him by Holmes, and then continued, 'I estimate Taliban in up to platoon strength. I am engaging the enemy with mortars and preparing to engage with air when I get the necessary separation and more accurate confirmation of enemy positions. I intend for Callsign Bronze One Zero to relocate and be prepared to attack the enemy if the situation allows. Bronze Four Zero Alpha, roger so far, over.'

Colour Sergeant Andy Faupel, the fire support group commander, high up on ANP Hill to the south-west, replied, 'Roger over.'

Biddick continued, 'Callsign Bronze Three Zero Alpha is to be prepared to link up with One Zero and assist them to break contact if necessary. Remain in current location at present, no move till ordered. Callsign Bronze Two Zero to remain in reserve and provide rear security from current location. All callsigns are to be aware of the possibility of enemy reinforcement and attempts to infiltrate through both our flanks and to the rear. Radio intercept indicates enemy ordering all available forces into this area. Zero acknowledge, over.'

'Roger out,' came the response from Captain Paul Steel, Biddick's 2IC and operations officer, back in their base at Nowzad District Centre.

Thirty metres east of Biddick's Tac HQ, gunfire was still pouring into Holmes's position behind the wall. He had to do something to get his men out of there and into safety, particularly if the Taliban were planning to infiltrate and capture them. With the weight of enemy fire, there was no way any of his men could even look over the wall. Raising themselves up to shoot would mean certain death. If the Taliban were skilful enough, it was certainly realistic that they could be on top of his position before he knew it. And unfortunately this group of Taliban definitely seemed to know what they were doing.

I need accurate mortar fire, and to call it in I've got to get eyes on the enemy, thought Holmes. He crawled down to the end of the wall, took a deep breath and pushed his head round, just far enough to see, but half expecting to get it blown off at any second. To his front there was a sparse green woodline. *Taliban!* He could make out nine or ten of them, only the upper half of their bodies, some static, firing, others moving up and down the position. He was astonished to see white turbans on their heads, and they all seemed to be wearing white kurtas. *Not even an attempt at camouflage.* He didn't understand it, but couldn't spend time now trying to figure it out.

He knew his own grid from his GPS, and he could estimate the distance to the woodline – about 200 metres. All he needed was a bearing and he would have enough information for a mortar fire mission. He took out his worn and scratched Silva compass and cursed when he saw a huge bubble in the needle damping oil. *That's all I need.* Wondering whether it would have a significant effect on the bearing, he lined the compass up on the enemy position, took a quick reading and ducked back behind the wall. Fourteen hundred and ten mils magnetic. Just north of east.

He hit the radio pressel switch and called the fire mission in to the company commander. Biddick flashed back: 'Zero Alpha, roger, working on it. MFC cannot observe fall of shot. Can you?'

'Bronze One Zero Bravo, er, roger, yes.'

Why did I say that? thought Holmes, just about managing to smile to himself. *Now I've got to put my head up again to adjust the mortar fire.*

Two minutes later Biddick was back on the net. 'Zero Alpha, shot over.'

'Shot out,' replied Holmes.

The word 'shot' meant that the mortars were firing their first round. This would more than likely not be on target, and the fire would have to be adjusted round by round until it was landing on the enemy position. Holmes slowly pushed his head round the wall again. Above the still-raging gunfire, he heard the whizz of the 81mm mortar and then saw it explode – 200 metres right of the enemy position and 100 metres beyond.

Pulling his head back behind the wall he said, 'Zero Alpha, One Zero Bravo, left two hundred, drop one hundred, over.'

The company commander replied, 'Zero Alpha, left two hundred, drop one hundred.'

Seconds later Biddick came back with another 'Shot over.'

Wondering when his luck would run out, Holmes again looked around the end of the wall – just in time to see the second explosion. Barely waiting till he was back in cover, he said excitedly, 'Bronze One Zero Bravo, on target. Fire for effect.'

As he crawled back to his men, Holmes heard the continuous crump-crump-crump of mortar bombs landing in and around the Taliban position. He could also make out the distinctive thump-thump of .50 cal machine-guns, the rapid crack of GPMGs and the quick-fire explosive blasts of a grenade machine-gun (GMG). Biddick must have ordered the fire support group back on ANP Hill to engage with everything they had as well. *Excellent!*

Holmes crawled up to Private Slater. The enemy fire had not stopped but was now sporadic enough to risk getting some fire down, and Holmes was desperate to do just that. The words imbued in him in basic training – *win the firefight* – had been in his mind since he first came under fire, less than half an hour earlier.

'Slater, sorry, mate, it's me and you, we've got to get some fire down. Come with me.'

The two crawled back along to the end of the wall. Without any further orders, Private Slater shoved the muzzle of his GPMG round the corner, rolling round himself, exposing his body to enemy fire. He hammered down 200 rounds, firing long bursts in rapid succession. Holmes was right beside him, equally exposed, observing over his shoulder for fall of shot. Slater was hosing tracer bullets up and down the woodline, carried away with the excitement of at last being able to give back to the Taliban some of what they had been giving out over the last thirty minutes.

Holmes grabbed Slater's helmeted head, and turned it to the Taliban position, 'There – there's your target. See them? There – there.'

Slater opened up again, concentrating his fire on the spot Holmes had indicated. Holmes tried sending a SITREP to Biddick, but his radio had stopped working. He switched to his short-range personal role radio, or PRR, and called for any station that could hear him.

To the rear, Corporal Chris Brooks, one of the section commanders in the platoon, and his point man had climbed on to the roof of a single-storey building to provide overwatch as Holmes advanced. But they had been forced back to the ground by a hail of RPG and machine-gun fire at the same time as Holmes was pinned down in the open. Now Brooks and the rest of the section were taking cover behind the compound wall, under heavy fire and in no position to support Holmes's extraction to safety. Brooks heard Holmes's transmission and answered, 'Larry, I can hear you, talk to me.'

As Brooks spoke, Holmes saw a flash of movement off to his right and, quickly turning, couldn't believe what he saw. Just 50 metres from him, two Taliban fighters ran across a clearing. Before he could turn and shoot, they had disappeared into the foliage.

'Slater, forget the front, I'll cover the front, you swing right and start gunning them there. Just fire into that woodline where they came from.'

He called into the PRR, 'Brooksy, Chris, they're flanking us. They're going round to the right, to the south, get on the net and warn the OC and Three Zero. They're coming for us…'

5

Second Lieutenant Bjórn Rose, commander of 3 Platoon, was listening to Holmes's firefight, a few hundred metres away to the north, through the thick undergrowth of the area of Sorkhani known as 'The Parks'. His platoon had gone firm, but he had told them to be ready to move immediately.

He now received orders from Biddick. 'Bronze Three Zero Alpha, this is Zero Alpha. Your callsign is to move north to assist Bronze One Zero to break clean from the enemy. You are to move now and get into a position where you can provide fire support. If you can, link up with callsign Bronze One Zero Alpha. Over.'

Bronze One Zero Alpha was Second Lieutenant Nick Denning, Holmes's platoon commander and a close friend of Rose. Rose had heard Denning on the radio in the last few minutes, trying to help Holmes and coordinate fire support for him. Denning was the same age as Rose – twenty-five – and the newest platoon commander in the company, but Rose had been amazed at how cool he had been when trying to get control over what was happening. Rose had found Denning's calmness reassuring in what was for both officers – and most of A Company – their first battle.

Rose and his section commanders had been monitoring the company net, and they realized not only was there a huge firefight going on with Holmes, but it appeared the Taliban were trying to get round the flanks and infiltrate into the middle of the company.

Rose told his section commanders, 'You heard the OC on the net. We're pushing north to help 1 Platoon. Get your lads moving. Corporal Moore, your section will lead.'

At thirty-two, Billy Moore was one of the older men in the company and an experienced soldier: he had been in the battalion for twelve years. His father had served in 7th Regiment, Royal Horse Artillery, and rarely passed up an opportunity to remind Billy that they were senior in Army precedence to the Royal Anglians. Moore's real name was Robert, but there was already a Rob in his platoon when he first arrived in the battalion, so he was immediately renamed, whether he liked it or not.

Moore's section, moving in single-file, led the way along a tree-lined alleyway towards the sound of the guns. Even in the shade, it was red-hot, and the men were dripping sweat, buckling under the immense weight of ammunition and water they had on their backs. Point man was Private Chris Gray. The job of point man was incredibly demanding and dangerous and required special qualities: good fieldcraft, excellent tactical and situational awareness, alertness ... and above all, courage – the point man was usually first to fight. Gray was nineteen and had only been in the battalion for seven months, but had proved himself to be an outstanding soldier, always keen, eager to learn and determined.

He was a Minimi gunner, and Moore, wanting heavy firepower at the front, often used Gray at point.

Moore could see that the dense vegetation opened up a few metres ahead. Aware that the Taliban could be anywhere, he told the rest of his section to go firm so that all eight men would not be exposed at the same time and pushed forward with Gray to clear the open area. They were moving along a grassy track, a dry mud wall with high brambles to the left and an orchard of low trees to the right. They could hear the incessant machine-gun fire to the front, as well as the occasional whizz of RPGs. They were now only a hundred or so metres from Holmes and 1 Platoon.

The two soldiers headed towards a lone tree and were shocked to see a line of five Taliban fighters, just 10 metres away, walking bunched up from left to right. Dressed in kurtas, carrying rifles and machine-guns, with ammunition belts draped around their shoulders and waists, the men seemed to be laughing and joking. The second he saw them Gray stopped dead, brought his Minimi up and pulled the trigger, firing a long burst of 5.56mm tracer straight at them. Moore, behind him and to the right, brought his rifle up and fired rapid, single shots, emptying his thirty-round magazine. All five fell awkwardly to the ground, dead or wounded, some screaming in agony. Moore saw one of the fighters, carrying a PKM machine-gun and strapped around with two belts of PKM ammunition, eyes wide open in horror and surprise, fall backwards, blood spurting from his chest.

Bullets started cracking around them. His brain spinning and in overdrive, Moore realized he was being fired at from a gap in the wall to his forward left, where the five fighters had come from. He could not see the enemy. The two took the best cover they could but had to stay kneeling and unprotected in the long grass to be able to observe and to shoot. Not knowing how many enemy he was facing, Moore decided to pull back to the rest of the section and then try to flank round to get at the fighters from a different position. To attempt a frontal assault, especially just the two of them, would be suicidal.

He tapped Gray with his boot. 'Chris, we're moving. You first and I'll cover.'

Gray turned to acknowledge, then slumped forward and said calmly in his low voice, 'Bill, I'm hit.'

With bullets still scything all round, Moore looked at Gray. He was not moving, and his face was pale. There was no sign of blood, but he had been shot in his left side. Moore had to get him out of here fast. He couldn't afford to get hit himself and had to do what he could to kill or suppress the enemy before he started to drag Gray back. He emptied another magazine into the enemy position, dropped his rifle and fired a full belt of 200 rounds from Gray's Minimi.

Private Terry Croft, a few metres back, realized Moore and Gray were in trouble. *They need my help*, he thought, and, heart pounding, immediately ran forward towards the enemy machine-gun fire. He hurled himself down on Moore's left, knelt up so he could see and started blasting down automatic fire with his light support weapon. All around him he saw grass chopped down by gunfire. A bullet whipped into his shirt and tore out the back, narrowly missing his shoulder. He was scared but he was fighting to save his mates and he tried to put his fear aside and focus on killing the enemy. He emptied magazine after magazine into the Taliban position. To his right, a fighter tried to move round behind, towards the rest of the section, and Croft cut him down with a burst of 5.56, firing right past Moore's head.

He glanced across at Gray, not realizing he'd been hit. Through the long grass he thought Gray was in a prone fire position and wondered why he wasn't firing.

Then Moore said, 'Chris is down.'

Gray and Croft were good friends. Shocked to the core, Croft yelled back to the rest of the platoon, 'Man down, man down.'

'Drag him back,' said Moore. 'I'll cover.'

Croft crawled to Gray. He was lying on his side, unconscious in the grass, blood lines running from his nostrils. Croft had never had to deal with a wounded comrade before – let alone his mate. He grabbed his shoulders to pull him back into cover.

Moore continued to engage the Taliban position, trying to suppress them. But as Croft struggled to drag Gray back along the grass track he had to keep throwing himself down as bullets zinged past.

Moore felt a hard punch in his right arm and swung round. *No one there*. He looked down and saw his sleeve darkening. A 7.62mm bullet had struck his upper right arm, tearing away most of his deltoid and the top half of his tricep muscles. It should be hurting but it wasn't. Adrenalin doing its job.

Moore grabbed an L109 hand grenade from his pouch, popped off the black safety clip, pulled the pin, shouted, 'Grenade!' and with his left arm hurled it into the gap in the wall. As Moore shouted, Croft instinctively hit the dirt. There was a loud explosion, and debris rained down.

Rose, the platoon commander, arrived and quickly took in the scene. Standing, he fired eighteen rounds rapid at the Taliban position and shouted to Croft, 'Get forward of Gray, get some fire down.'

Rifle in his right hand, he grabbed Gray's webbing straps with his left hand and dragged him back down the track. It was a struggle. Gray was carrying 600 rounds of belted 5.56mm ammo, a Claymore off-route anti-personnel mine and 6 litres of water. He was very heavy. Sweating and panting hard, Rose wondered how far he could get him before his arm gave out. Bullets were striking the grass around his feet and hitting the mud wall beside him. But he managed to get Gray back to the rest of the section, and then four soldiers carried him further back to a dip in the ground.

Rose went forward again. Croft and Moore were still firing. Moore said, 'Boss, I'm hit.'

Rose said, 'Move to the sarge, then. Get going.'

He called to Lance Corporal Kisby, 'Get a baseline set up and cover the rest of the platoon.'

Kisby moved forward with a fire team, just behind Croft. Croft crawled back to join the line, and they blasted into the enemy position. They were desperate to keep the Taliban back, to stop them getting round into the rear of the platoon, where Gray had been taken.

When the shooting began, Private Matt Duffy, 15 metres back, pushed out to the right, into the orchard, to get into a position where he could support Moore and Gray. As he moved, bullets started zipping all round his feet. Further right he saw a low wall, about a metre high, and behind it Taliban fighters were running off, away from the contact area. Screaming 'Enemy right – engaging,' he swung his Minimi round and fired a belt of fifty rounds, killing at least one of the fighters. Adrenalin surged through his system, this was the first person he had ever killed. He scanned the area through his gunsights. He had never concentrated so hard on anything in his life. *Are there any more out there?*

Then he heard the cry 'Man down', and rushed forward towards the firing. He expected to be hit at any moment and consciously tried to clench his skin tight, almost trying to turn it into armour. A bullet ripped through his trouser leg, tearing open the first field dressing in his map pocket. As he moved, all he thought about was whether his mates were OK.

Duffy ran into Moore, who was heading back, and, seeing the blood pouring down his arm, dragged him into a ditch beside the track. Duffy was a team medic, an infantryman who had received basic medical training – beyond immediate first aid. This was his first casualty, but he knew exactly what to do. He rapidly checked Moore's body for other wounds, then tried to carefully remove his daysack. He couldn't get it off without tearing the gunshot wound, so took out his sheath knife.

Moore said, 'Cut off my daysack and I will do you.'

Duffy ignored him and slashed through the straps. He then ripped off Moore's shirt, opened up a green first field dressing and pressed it to the bloody gash in his arm, tying it in place.

Moore said, 'Don't you dare give me any morphine, Duffy. I need to stay with it, I've got to be able to do my job.'

Duffy nodded and shoved a second dressing over the first. Then he heard someone say, 'Chris Gray's been hit. He's bad.'

Duffy felt like he had been punched in the throat. Chris Gray was his best friend. He, Croft and Gray were virtually inseparable. But he and Gray were particularly close. Duffy knew Gray's family and was hoping to start dating his sister when they got back to England. He called over an engineer who was lying on the track near by, 'Mate, you deal with Billy, he's pretty much OK. I'm going to help Chris.'

6

Second Lieutenant Rose had just radioed his report of two casualties. Major Biddick was still dealing with 1 Platoon's problem, with Holmes and his men pinned down. Now he also had to consider the implications of Rose's casualties. Their evacuation became a priority and was an extremely manpower-intensive task, with troops needed to treat the wounded, carry stretchers and provide protection. Two men down could easily use up a whole platoon's efforts. The company had anyway reached the limit of exploitation for this patrol, and Biddick made the decision to extract back to the Nowzad District Centre, or DC.

So far Biddick had not needed his reserve, 2 Platoon, who were positioned among the compounds a short distance to the rear of Holmes's 1 Platoon. He now ordered them to move back, to clear the company's route to the west, and secure an RV in the area of the 'Wedge'. This was a two-storey building with a prominent triangular doorway structure jutting up from the roof.

The whole company would pass through the RV on the way back to Nowzad DC. The platoons would carry out head-checks to make sure no one was left behind. They might have to fight all the way back to this point from their forward battle positions. It was essential that the area was protected from enemy interference.

Corporal Ryan Alexander, one of the 2 Platoon section commanders, grabbed his 2IC, Lance Corporal Oliver Penwright. 'SP, take Okotie and Hof and get up on top of the Wedge. You should be able to get good all-round observation from there. But make sure you keep low. I don't want any casualties.'

Penwright led his Minimi gunner, Private 'James' Okotie, and sharpshooter Private Neil Hassell up on to the roof while Alexander deployed the remainder of the section into fire positions on the main track, covering an area of orchards to the south. The tremendous noise of fighting to the east and north reverberated throughout the whole village, as 1 and 3 Platoons continued to exchange fire with the Taliban. The occasional bullet and RPG missile whizzed overhead.

Alexander cursed as yet again his Bowman radio refused to work. This happened all the time, and he hated it, because he was left in the dark about what was happening in the rest of the company. He needed to know as much as possible about what was going on so that he could react when necessary, to support other elements of his platoon or company. And if he ran into difficulty he had no way of summoning assistance.

The platoon sergeant, Michael Butcher, came over. 'Radio problems?'

'Yeah. What a shock.'

'Mine seems to be OK. I'll stay here with you for the moment. The Taliban are everywhere, infiltrating. From what I can hear they've been trying to flank both the other platoons. God knows how many of them there are.'

Alexander called Privates Anthony Glover and Simon Illsley to him. 'Glovebox, Illsley, set up a Claymore out there, just into the orchard, in case any of them try and get through the trees.'

Designed for exactly the purpose Alexander had in mind, anti-infiltration, as well as ambushes, the M18A1 Claymore directional mine, in its convex olive green plastic case, fires 700 one-eighth of an inch steel balls at 1,218 metres per second, shredding everything in their path.

Glover took the Claymore from his daysack. Alexander saw that Illsley, at eighteen the youngest man in the platoon, was shaking and wide-eyed. Illsley was known among the platoon as a committed Christian. Alexander pulled him away from the other men. 'Illsley. Look at me, mate. Stay calm. You know exactly what you're doing. You've done this a hundred times before, there's no difference now. We're all here with you, we'll look after you. We're all in the same boat, and we've just got to do our jobs. It's more important now than ever that we all stick together. OK?'

He clapped Illsley on the shoulder, still nervous but now a bit calmer, and sent him to help Glover position the mine. Once that was done, Alexander appointed Illsley to assist Lance Corporal Mercer's section, which was short of men for its task of securing the company's withdrawal route a couple of hundred metres further east.

Ten minutes later Illsley was lying in a fire position. His task was to cover one of the alleyways leading on to the main withdrawal route. He was holding his rifle loosely in both hands, scanning a wooded area to his front, looking over his SA80 sights. He heard a sudden rustling in the trees to his right. *What the hell's that? None of our lads are over there. Can't be Taliban. Can't be. Maybe it's an animal, a dog or something.* He braced his rifle against his shoulder and peered intently into the trees. *Nothing.* The hairs were already standing up on the back of his neck. Then he heard something move again.

Illsley was horrified to see a tall thick-set bearded man wearing a black turban and a deep-blue kurta and holding an AK47 assault rifle. He was 20 metres away and moving fast, right to left. Illsley had never shot anyone before or even seen anyone shot. This was a nightmare. His heart thumped into his chest. He knew what he had to do. But could he? Could he? No time to think.

He flicked off his safety catch and brought the tip of the bold, black arrow in his SUSAT sight on to the man's upper body. Giving a very slight lead, and tracking the fighter's movement, he squeezed the trigger. The rifle jerked in his hands, spitting out a 5.56mm bullet that hit the man square in the chest. He went straight down, and Illsley fired twenty more rounds at him in rapid succession.

Lance Corporal Mercer and two other soldiers, hearing the shots, flung themselves down beside Illsley, then raked the area, and the trees beyond, with burst after burst of automatic fire. When he was as sure as he could be that any Taliban out there were either dead or had run off, Mercer called, 'Cease fire. Watch and shoot, watch and shoot.'

This was the order to stop shooting, but be prepared to open up again at will if further enemy was sighted or heard.

Mercer called to Illsley, 'Quick reactions, mate. Good shooting.'

The others patted him on the back, 'Well done, well done.'

Every soldier wonders how he will react the first time he comes face to face with the enemy. Some serve for twenty years and never find out. Illsley, one of the youngest Royal Anglians in Afghanistan, had been scared almost witless just a few minutes before. When it really mattered, his training and his personal courage kicked in, and he killed the enemy fighter without hesitation.

A few minutes later, back in the area of the Wedge, Private Mark Stevens, lying in a fire position facing the orchard, turned to Corporal Alexander and said quietly, 'Alex, I can hear people moving in the orchard.'

'What can you hear?'

'Just rustling and walking, cracking twigs, and you can see some of the trees moving.'

Alexander gave the hand signal for enemy – thumb down – and gestured towards the orchard. The signal was passed round the troops, who pointed their rifles towards the trees, fingers on triggers, scanning intently through their sights.

Moments later they heard the sound of talking and laughter from inside the orchard. Still they couldn't see anything through the dense undergrowth and closely planted pomegranate trees. Alexander whispered to Butcher, 'Must be enemy. I am sure – I hope – none of our men would be making that sort of noise.'

Butcher had been trying to find out on the company radio net whether there were any friendlies in the area that he didn't know about, but predictably his radio was now not working either. He headed towards the platoon commander, Goodey, to find out.

Then Stevens saw them, 25 metres away, several men with long beards, wearing turbans and kurtas, carrying rifles. He pulled back the trigger of his GPMG, blasting a long, continuous stream of tracer right into the middle of the group. Alexander and the rest of the section joined in, hurling rifle and machine-gun bullets and rifle grenades through the trees.

The fighters went to ground, some killed or wounded. Despite the massive weight of fire ripping into and around them, the enemy somehow managed to shoot back at Alexander and his section.

Suddenly the enemy fire stopped, and there was no sign of movement. '*Stop!*' yelled Alexander. 'Watch and shoot, watch and shoot.'

Alexander, holding his smoking rifle in front of him and sweating on to the hot barrel, felt an immense relief. They had blasted a group of Taliban trying to get in behind the forward platoons and then move round and attack them from the rear. The fighters had clearly had no idea that he and his section were there.

Alexander had been feeling increasingly frustrated since first hearing Sergeant Larry Holmes's frantic radio messages that he was pinned down by heavy fire out in front of the company. Holmes was Alexander's best mate. They had served together in A Company since Alexander joined the battalion in Londonderry seven years before. Alexander had been beside himself with anguish, desperate to get forward to help his mate. When the shooting started he had tried to do just that, but the platoon commander had stopped him, reminding him that the situation was confused enough as it was, without someone else charging into enemy, or possibly friendly, fire. And of course Lieutenant Goodey had been right. Alexander's place was in command of his section, and if the company commander wanted him forward he would give him the appropriate orders.

There was a sudden burst of machine-gun bullets from the orchard, and again Alexander's section replied with a barrage of fire. Over the next ten to fifteen minutes, this continued. Every time Alexander shouted 'Watch and shoot' there would be a pause, then a resumption of firing.

Finally, the fire stopped for good – all enemy in the orchard were killed or had retreated.

7

Three hundred metres south-east of Alexander's position, Private Duffy, having left the wounded Corporal Billy Moore with an engineer, moved forward again. The whole place was echoing with the crash of bullets as Corporal Kisby's men continued to exchange fire with the Taliban a few metres ahead. Duffy reached the depression, sweating, out of breath and anxious. Chris Gray, his best friend, was lying pale and motionless on a field stretcher. Beside him, a stinking, open sewage ditch.

Sergeant Simon Panter, Second Lieutenant Rose's platoon sergeant, was bent over Gray. He had stripped off his body armour and shirt and was desperately giving him mouth-to-mouth. Standing beside Panter, Rose was speaking into his radio: 'Zero Alpha, this is Bronze Three Zero Alpha. Reference my two casualties, one is bad, wait out for nine liner.'

Blanking out his emotion, Duffy got straight down and grabbed Gray's wrist. *Rapid, faint pulse. Thank you. He's alive.* He put his ear against Gray's mouth, *Shallow, shallow breathing.* He thought, *He is so bad.* But he tried to reassure himself, *Chris's tough, he'll deal with it. God, I hope he will.*

Duffy examined the bullet entry wound. Left side, just missing the Osprey body armour chest plate. Not too much blood, but a sucking wound. *Asherman Chest Seal, I need to get one on quick.* From his medpack he pulled out the seal and fixed it over the bullet hole. The one-way valve allows air and blood to escape while preventing the re-entry of either.

Above Duffy, Rose was again on the radio to the company commander, confirming the helicopter landing point for the medical emergency response team, or MERT, which was already screaming towards Nowzad in a Chinook with an Apache attack helicopter as escort.

Duffy checked for the exit wound. It was in Gray's lower back, and there was a lot of blood. He put his fingers in to make sure there was no debris, then packed a field dressing against the wound and tied it off.

He put his mouth next to Gray's ear. 'Chris, Chris. Stop being weak. You're being weak. Stay with us. You can get through this. Stay alive, Chris. Please stay alive.'

Rose had given orders to the section commanders to break contact and protect the casualty evacuation party. Sergeant Panter had organized the stretcher bearers, who were waiting for Duffy's word to start moving Gray back.

Duffy turned to Panter, 'That's all I can do, Sarge, we need to get him away.'

As they moved off, under continuous hammering from Biddick's mortars and machine-guns, the Taliban fire had died down, but Corporal

Kisby's section acted as rearguard, to ensure any surviving Taliban didn't try to follow up. Carrying an unconscious man on a field stretcher across rough terrain at speed in searing heat was torture. Four men at a time carried the casualty, rotating periodically to maintain speed. They were carrying 30 kilos of their own kit as well as the stretcher. Dust filled up their mouths and throats as they ran, breathing hard. It was exhausting. But no one complained. They were desperate to get their mate to the Chinook and on to the field hospital at Camp Bastion – to give him a chance to survive.

Only Duffy stayed on the stretcher throughout, tying his wrist to one of the corners. He was determined to do everything he could to save his closest friend. All the way back he spoke to him: 'Chris, stay with us, Chris. You will make it, mate. Do not die. Please do not die. Be strong, Chris. I know you can hear me. Be strong.'

Duffy feared the worst, but there was no way he was going to give up on him, absolutely no way.

Rose, navigating towards the RV with the company sergeant major's vehicles, saw the stretcher bearers were flagging. He tapped the lead right man on the shoulder and took his place. 'Come on now, lads, pick up the pace a bit,' he shouted over his shoulder, and they speeded up. Gray was jerked and jolted on the bouncing, sagging stretcher, but the most important thing was to get him back as quickly as possible.

Finally they reached the RV, a grassed courtyard area in the middle of the village. The company medic was waiting with his Pinzgauer vehicle. Two of the company's WMIK fire support Land Rovers, which had been working in among the compounds, had arrived to provide protection, bristling with weapons.

The battle to extract Holmes was still going on less than a hundred metres away. The whole village echoed with the rattle of machine-gun fire, the whoosh and sharp detonation of RPGs and the crack of rifle bullets. The ground shook beneath their feet as mortars exploded around the Taliban positions nearby.

Private Richard Ranns, the Pinz driver, watched Panter, Duffy and the others load the casualty into the back of the vehicle. He was shocked when he saw it was Chris Gray. Earlier that morning he and Gray had joked together over a cigarette before Gray went out on patrol. Just before he deployed, Gray had said to Ranns, 'I hope we get into a fire-fight this time. I just want to make sure I can do my job.'

There wasn't much room inside the Pinzgauer, and the injured Corporal Moore said he would stay behind and get into the next vehicle that was going back to base. Ranns jumped back into the cab and gunned the Pinzgauer's engine, driving fast towards Nowzad DC, escorted by the two WMIKs. In the back, as the vehicle bounced and jolted down the rough tracks and alleyways, the medic worked at mouth-to-mouth and chest compressions, desperately trying to keep the young soldier alive.

Duffy, feeling as if his arm had almost parted from his shoulder with the constant weight of the stretcher, was utterly exhausted. Anguished, he watched the vehicle speed away with his best friend on board. *Will I ever see him again?* Then, covered in Gray's blood, he walked on his own to a compound wall, leant against it and booted it. Until now he had been totally focused on saving Chris Gray. Now his emotions took over. Tears welled up in his eyes but he fought to keep some composure. *Did I do enough for him? Is he going to live? I'm sure I could have done something else. Please – don't let him die. Please.* Duffy pounded the wall a few more times with his boot, then took hold of himself and rejoined the rest of the section, ready for the next task on this, the hardest day of his young life.

Rose told the platoon to go firm in all-round defence at the RV, watching for Taliban infiltration. He walked over to find Major Biddick, who was at a road junction with his Tac HQ a few metres forward. Rose said, 'Casualty's gone. My platoon's ready for tasking.'

Biddick said, 'How is Private Gray?'

'Not good, I'm afraid. He'll be lucky to make it.'

'Who's your other casualty?'

'Corporal Moore. He's not too bad. Bullet wound.'

Biddick looked Rose in the eye, and Rose knew he was checking him out.

'Yeah I'm fine,' he said.

'OK. Good. I'm extracting the company back to the DC. 2 Platoon will secure the RV and then provide rear guard. Your platoon will move first through them. Followed by 1 Platoon, once they have extracted Sergeant Holmes. He's still in trouble. I will use a combination of direct and indirect fire to break contact and extract. I've got Apaches coming in with the MERT, so we'll hopefully use them. I will also use F15s to strafe and drop some bombs.'

24

Rose walked back to the platoon. Moore was talking to Duffy. Moore said, 'Matt, you did a brilliant job back there. Both on me and Gray. I've never seen anything like it. Well done, mate.'

He crashed his helmeted head against Duffy's.

Rose said, 'What are you still doing here, Billy, you pussy, why haven't you gone back with the sergeant major? I thought you were supposed to be wounded.'

He punched him on the right arm, and Moore yelped in pain.

'Sorry, Billy, didn't realize that was the arm that got shot,' said Rose, feeling awful about what he'd just done.

8

A hundred metres east of the casualty RV, 1 Platoon commander, Lieutenant Nick Denning, had joined Corporal Brooks in the compound to the rear of Holmes's position, still under fire.

'Corporal B, we've got to get some fire down from here to get the guys back. The mortars and .50 cals on their own won't do it. The company commander is trying to line up an air strike, but we don't know whether we'll get it in time. We need more weight of fire here. We can use the roof of that outhouse in the corner as a fire position. The wall will act as a parapet. We're about to get another mortar fire mission. That will last four minutes and I want to use it to extract them. It's risky but there's no other option. Do you agree?'

'Yes, I can't think of anything else. Let's do it,' replied Brooks, then called out to his 2IC, Private Oliviero, 'Ollie, I want you, Redford, Hicks and Burgess over here now.'

The four men doubled over to Brooks and stood in front of him. 'I want you lot up on that roof, prepare to give fire support to the sarge so he can get out of the hole he's in. We need to cover him and his lads so they can get across the open ground back to here. Understood?'

Brooks looked into the soldiers' eyes and he knew they didn't want to do it. The building they were expected to scale was being riddled with machine-gun and rifle fire.

'You've got to do it. Just get up there, lads. We need to give cover to Larry or he'll be stuck where he is. He and the others will probably die there.'

Private Fabio Oliviero led the way up a rickety ladder they found propped against the compound wall. As he climbed, he thought he was going to die. He did not want to do this. But he knew his mates were in deep trouble and he would want them to do the same for him if he was out there. That thought drove him up the ladder, a climb that seemed to take an eternity.

As they moved up, Denning shouted, 'When I give you the word, get down as much fire as you can. We will wait till the mortars come in so we get a lull in enemy fire. When the mortars start, you need to give it everything you can.'

The soldiers crawled across the roof on their belt buckles, keeping as low as they could. Bullets were tearing apart the wall next to the building, which rocked beneath them every time an RPG exploded against the compound.

Private Dan Burgess moved to the forward edge of the roof. Trying to force his body into the hard-baked mud, he opened up the bipod legs of his Minimi light machine-gun and lined the weapon up on the muzzle flashes and dust he could just make out way across the open, where the Taliban were. Burgess, a PlayStation fanatic, had been in the battalion for six months, straight from training. Bullets were ripping just above his head, and he knew that at any moment one of them could kill him.

Sweat was stinging his eyes. He squinted down and saw Holmes and his section – his close mates – crouched behind the low wall that was still getting hammered by machine-gun fire. He blanked out his fear. At this moment he wanted only two things – to get his mates to safety and to kill the bastards that were trying to kill them.

Denning yelled up, 'Keep down, lads. Two five hundred pounders coming in. Keep down till I give you the word.'

Burgess had never felt anything like it. The first bomb dropped 200 metres away. It was like being punched hard in the chest. There was a tremendous roaring explosion, almost unbearable. The second bomb followed rapidly. He looked up and saw nothing but clouds of dust and smoke – but seemingly behind the enemy position. *They must have missed*, thought Burgess, *but if the bombs hurt me that much, I wonder what they did to the Taliban*.

The enemy fire stopped briefly and then started again – and it seemed as if the bombs had made them angrier, because the fire seemed even more intense than before.

'Get ready, lads,' shouted Denning, 'mortars coming in now. When they start landing, the sarge is going to extract, so get everything you can down.'

Before he saw the mortars exploding, Burgess heard the whizz as they passed over him, on their way into the enemy position.

In front of Burgess's outbuilding, Holmes shouted to his section, 'Go, move back to Brooksy's compound. I'll cover you when you start to move.'

He turned, and raising himself above the wall, blasted bullets down towards the enemy-held woodline. He looked round. The men were still lying on the ground, afraid to move. 'Get up, we've got to go now. Go. Go.' Still they didn't move. He had planned to be the last man away, giving the others cover. But he realized they wouldn't be going anywhere unless he showed them the example. With this much danger, orders were not enough. He jumped to his feet. 'Follow me,' he yelled, and led the soldiers back towards Brooks's compound, running for their lives.

As he ran, through sweat-blurred eyes, Holmes glanced up at the outhouse roof. Half-kneeling, Oliviero was thumping high-explosive grenades towards the enemy position from the under-slung grenade launcher on his SA80 rifle. He fired six in forty seconds. The other soldiers on the roof were also firing. But what astonished Holmes was the remarkable bravery of Private Burgess. Unable to get a proper view from his prone position, Burgess had stood up on the front of the roof and was firing burst after lethal burst from his Minimi. As Holmes watched, bullets were zipping all around the rooftop, and he could see tracer rounds screaming past, right next to Burgess's head. But Burgess didn't even flinch, he just kept firing.

Denning was standing anxiously in the compound doorway, praying his plan would work. Between him, Biddick and Brooks, everything possible had been done to get Holmes and his men back to the relative safety of the compound. But would the combination of air strikes, mortar barrage and the withering fire from Oliviero's team suppress the enemy for long enough? His soldiers could very easily be killed or seriously wounded as they raced back.

Holmes flung himself against the doorframe, drenched in sweat and exhausted. He was not entering the safety of the compound before the last of his men was inside. He shoved each man through, looked back to be certain, and then followed them in. Denning counted them all in, one to eight. *Thank God*, he thought, *I really can't believe they actually made it*.

He looked up at the outhouse roof. Oliviero, Burgess, Redford and Hicks were crawling slowly back across to the ladder, bodies pressed tightly against the mud, keeping as low as they possibly could under the rain of bullets.

Get them down, get them down in one piece, thought Denning. Everything else had come together, but he knew that these four soldiers had been decisive in keeping Holmes and his section alive as they made their dash across the open ground. Because as Holmes moved, all of the enemy fire had been directed at the soldiers on the rooftop. These men had literally been drawing enemy fire.

Holmes knew it was not over yet, not by a long way. Bullets continued to crack into the compound walls, and RPGs were exploding overhead. But he was grateful to be alive, and not quite sure how or why he was. All he wanted to do was collapse in a heap, to lie down for just a few minutes. But he was the platoon sergeant, and that was the last thing he could do, no matter what he had been through. He got a grip of himself.

He grabbed Denning. 'Never thought I'd be so glad to see you, boss,' he said, taking a lit cigarette from Denning's mouth and shoving it between his own lips.

'Hang on a minute, Sergeant H, that's not one of the local ones, that's a Marlboro, sent from home, you can't have that. Anyway I thought you gave up years ago.'

Holmes grinned, 'Yeah, yeah, boss, I reckon I'll be chain-smoking now for the rest of this tour so I hope you've got plenty more of these Marlboros.'

Holmes turned to Oliviero, Burgess and the others, now back on the ground. All of them looked as if the last harrowing few minutes had aged them by several years. 'Thanks, lads. I don't know what to say,' said Holmes, 'you saved our lives. You definitely saved our lives.'

He walked up to Burgess and put his arm round his shoulders. 'Burgess, you must've been mad standing up like that, you almost got yourself killed. I saw bullets going straight past you, I don't know how you didn't get hit. That was the bravest thing I've ever seen in my life, I promise you.'

Denning was surprised when Holmes and his men then started laughing, almost uncontrollably: 'How did we get out of that?'

But he also saw the horror in their faces.

A few minutes later, Denning said, 'Sergeant H, Corporal Brooks, I just got the word from the company commander, the company is extracting back to the DC, we need to get the guys together and start moving.'

Holmes became angry. 'We can't go back now, boss. We can regroup and start attacking this lot. We're now in a position to smash them.'

'Maybe, but the OC says we're pulling back, and that's what we're going to do.'

'No, sir,' said Holmes, 'we've got to attack them.'

Then Holmes realized he was being irrational. He had been deeply frustrated, pinned down and unable to fight back. As an infantry sergeant and a battalion boxing champion, he was only ever interested in going forward, whatever the situation. But he realized there was a bigger picture, this was not just about him or 1 Platoon. The whole company was fighting, and the company commander – whom he respected more than any other military man – had a plan. Holmes also realized that the enemy had almost certainly bugged out by now. Their immediate prey had escaped, and they had taken a battering from the air, from mortars and from the company's machine-gun and rifle fire.

Denning went on, 'Three Zero are now extracting their casualties and they will then withdraw as a platoon, through the position to our west held by Two Zero. Once Three Zero are a bound back, we will also withdraw through Two Zero. The enemy have already flanked us both to the right and left. Everyone needs to stay really on the ball as we go back, because they could pop up anywhere. There's also a good chance they'll try and keep us under pressure from behind as we pull back. The company commander has more air assets lined up to hit them if they appear any distance from us. But at close quarters, gentlemen, we're on our own.'

9

Rose and 3 Platoon led the company back towards the DC, along the route marked and secured by 2 Platoon. The enemy, decimated by A Company's ferocious fire, still tried to harass the Royal Anglian soldiers by cracking off the occasional wildly aimed shot as they moved through the deserted town, along rough alleyways flanked by 3-metre-high mud walls.

Every time the Taliban fired, 2 Platoon soldiers would reply with a withering rate of machine-gun or rifle fire to allow the other soldiers in the company to move back in safety.

Up on ANP Hill, the fire support group, or FSG, under Colour Sergeant Faupel, were supporting the company's movement by firing long bursts from their GPMGs and .50 cal heavy machine-guns at any enemy they identified, and at possible enemy fire positions. And the three barrels of Biddick's mortar section continued to slam in high-explosive 81mm bombs at every sign of the enemy.

From the air, the Apache gunship that had arrived with the MERT Chinook strafed the Taliban positions, trying to kill any surviving enemy, and make sure they were unable to interfere with the company's movement.

All of this needed to be deconflicted, or it was more than likely that a mortar shell would hit an aircraft. That was the job of Captain Charlie Harmer, the FST commander, who, as he moved, was working skilfully to make sure that air and indirect fire support was maximized against the surviving enemy.

When he reached one of the RV points, secured by the two company WMIKs, Second Lieutenant Rose realized that Moore was still with the platoon. He had lost a lot of blood, and continued to bleed, but was determined to see out this patrol with his men. Rose had other ideas. He had no intention of getting to the point where Moore collapsed with blood loss. 'Billy, get on that WMIK over there and get back to the DC, you can't stay out here with that wound.'

Moore was about to protest, but just shrugged when he saw the look on Rose's face and realized that at this stage argument was not a good idea.

Second Lieutenant Denning's 1 Platoon followed behind 3 Platoon, with Sergeant Holmes bringing up the rear. Holmes reached a small river and saw Biddick moving with Corporal Daz Bonner, his radio operator. Biddick looked at Holmes. 'Hello, Sergeant H, I see you managed to survive that little skirmish, then?'

'Skirmish, sir? That was a full-on war, sir. You should've been there.'

A burst of machine-gun fire landed a few feet away.

'That's you, Daz,' said Holmes, looking at Bonner's antenna, 'your aerial's attracting enemy fire. Why don't you put it down?'

'It's not an aerial, it's an antenna. Aerial is a type of washing powder. You should know that, Sarge,' said Bonner with a smile, automatically reciting the signallers' standard response to the ignorance of the technically uninitiated.

'I couldn't care less what it is, Daz, you might as well put a Union Jack on it if you're going to keep it up.'

'I can't put it down, the OC will kill me if I can't get comms.' With an even broader grin he added, 'Anyway, I notice you were having problems communicating earlier, Sarge. Maybe a bit of refresher training when we get back in?'

'If you weren't the OC's signaller I might just give you a bit of corrective training right now, Corporal Bonner,' laughed Holmes, realizing this was a foretaste of the kind of stick he would be getting from the company for a long time to come.

'OK, gentlemen,' said Biddick, 'we've got work to do. If your argument is complete, perhaps we should catch up the rest of the company.'

Biddick held out his arm, gesturing across the river, as though casually waving him through the door at a mess dinner. 'After you, Sergeant Holmes.'

As 1 Platoon moved along the route, Goodey collapsed the 2 Platoon security operation behind them, ordering his sections to break off and follow the company back towards the DC.

Goodey moved behind his lead section, with his signaller, Private Craig Fisher, Private Hassell, the sharpshooter, Lance Corporal van der Merwe and the interpreter, Ahmad. As Goodey's group moved along an alleyway between two compounds, the FSG on ANP Hill spotted Taliban on the other side of the compound wall. They engaged with a long burst of GPMG fire, killing the fighters.

Fisher, moving right beside the wall, felt a thump against the side of his leg. He stopped and cried out, raising his leg to look at it. He thought he had been hit by a rock kicked up by the gunfire.

Goodey said, 'Fish, stop messing about, keep moving.'

Fisher tried to walk but his leg gave way under him. It felt as if it was on fire. He turned to Goodey and said, 'Boss, I think I'm hit.'

Goodey and van der Merwe ran over and dragged him into a ditch on the other side of the alley. Crouching over Fisher, van der Merwe said, 'Where are you hit?'

'My right calf, I think.'

Van der Merwe took Fisher's knife from the sheath on his belt and cut off the right trouser leg. There was a small hole where a bullet had entered the middle of his calf. No blood, the bullet had cauterized the wound. Van der Merwe checked for an exit wound. Nothing, the bullet was still inside. He said to Goodey, crouched beside Fisher, 'Must be a ricochet from the wall. If it had hit him direct it would have torn his leg open as it came back out.'

Van der Merwe checked for any signs of broken bones. It seemed OK, but he couldn't be sure. 'Reckon the bullet must be lodged between your tibia and fibula,' he said in his South African drawl, 'pretty lucky.'

Van der Merwe took Fisher's first field dressing out of his map pocket and applied it to the wound in case it started bleeding and to keep out dirt.

'Is it painful? Need some morphine?'

'No, just burning a lot.'

Sergeant Butcher arrived and said to Goodey, 'I'll get a stretcher party, give me a couple of minutes.'

'I don't think I need a stretcher, Sarge, I reckon I can walk back, it's not too bad,' said Fisher, not wanting to force four of his mates to have to struggle back to the DC in this heat with their own equipment plus his body, weighing in at 80 kilos.

He stood up and took another step, but his leg gave way again and he cursed as he hit the dirt for the second time.

'I'll get that stretcher party,' said Butcher, jogging off to muster some men.

While he was doing that, van der Merwe pulled off Fisher's webbing and daysack, which contained his heavy Bowman HF radio and spare battery. Without being asked, Ahmad immediately picked up all of Fisher's equipment to carry back to the DC. The 'terp' was saving a considerable extra burden from the already overloaded soldiers, with whom he had struck up a close relationship even in the short time they had been in his country.

They loaded Fisher on to a field stretcher and four 2 Platoon soldiers started the nightmare journey back towards the DC. One was Private Illsley, who had fired twenty-one rounds into a Taliban fighter a short time earlier. As they sweated their way towards the DC, one of the other soldiers said to him, 'Heard about you killing that Taliban, Ills. Well done, mate. Bit ironic that the most Christian member of the battalion should get one of the first kills, though.'

All the way back, Fisher was cursing his luck. As the adrenalin began to wear off the pain was increasing. But that wasn't his real concern. He knew that getting shot meant he would be sent back to the UK. This had been the first battle he had been involved in and he had been hoping for many more. The last thing in the world he wanted to do was to leave his mates in Afghanistan at this early stage of the tour.

As the company made their way back to Nowzad DC, Gray had already arrived in the field hospital at Camp Bastion, twenty minutes flying time by Chinook. Biddick, one of the last men back into base, was informed at the gate that the battle group commander was on the phone for him, and went straight to the company ops room.

Biddick was super-fit, among the fittest men in the battalion, but even he was shattered by the physical and mental exertions of the battle they had just fought. Dripping with sweat, still wearing his helmet and equipment and carrying his SA80, he said to Company Group Operations Officer Captain Paul Steel and the ops room staff, 'Well done, all of you, and thanks for all the back-up out there. The CASEVAC worked well, really came together.'

'Here you are, sir,' said one of the signallers, handing Biddick the phone.

Biddick took off his helmet, carefully laid his rifle on the floor and put the phone to his ear, 'Hello, sir, Dominic here, how are you?'

Lieutenant Colonel Stuart Carver, the Royal Anglians' commanding officer, was speaking from his headquarters in Camp Bastion. 'Dominic, it's about Private Gray.'

10

Word went round the DC that the company was to assemble in front of the ops building for a debrief by Biddick. Nowzad DC was a shabby, dusty compound the size of five tennis courts, surrounded by 3-metre-high walls with sandbagged sentry positions on each corner. The outer walls, and many of the building walls inside, were pock-marked with bullet holes and shrapnel craters, reminders that the DC had been besieged many times by the Taliban. The ops building, like the others in the DC, was made of plaster and solid, baked mud. On the roof was a sandbagged observation and firing position as well as satellite dishes and radio masts.

Everybody was in high spirits. Many knew they were lucky to be alive. Most had been in the first battle of their military service and had finally had the chance to prove they could put into practice the combat skills perfected during long and arduous training sessions.

Private Duffy was elated. Someone had told him that Chris Gray was in a stable condition when he had been put on to the Chinook, and that meant he had a very good chance of pulling through. As they waited in the baking heat for Biddick to arrive, Duffy wondered what he would say to Chris next time he saw him – that would probably be when they got back to England. The tour would be over, and Chris would be long out of hospital by then. Or hopefully he would be able to see him when he went back to England during the tour for his R and R.

Biddick came out from the ops room and, squinting in the intense sunlight, stood in front of his men. He paused, and his face had a pained expression.

'What I am about to tell you all,' he said, 'is the hardest fact that I have ever had to relay in my life. I have just spoken to the CO and I am very sad to have to say that Chris Gray is dead. He didn't make it.'

When he heard these words, Duffy stopped listening. He was still wearing the shirt and trousers that were covered in his best mate's blood, and tears welled in his eyes. He thought about Chris's sister, Katie, whom he saw just before the tour. Then he thought about a video of Chris's little brother, Nathan, beating him up, which he kept on his phone and had showed Duffy a few days before. And Chris's other little brother, Liam, and his mum, Helen.

Duffy thought, *They don't know what's happened. They don't know any of this. But in a few hours there will be a knock on their door...*

Unheard by Duffy, Biddick continued, 'But Corporal Moore and Private Fisher are going to be OK – let's not forget about those guys. We always knew something like this was going to happen, and this was part of the deal that we signed up for. It was inevitable that we were going to face this challenge this summer. Regrettably we knew in our hearts that at some point this moment would come. It is just tough that for us it has come this early on. What we have got to do now is put this into context and what you have just achieved out there is a tactical victory. We have gone out and gone into the Taliban's backyard, where he has been unchallenged for months. We have taken them on at a time of our choosing and we have taken the initiative and we are going to build upon that momentum.

'There is no getting away from the fact that this is a real kick in the teeth to lose Chris Gray. But let's give meaning to his death and meaning to his life. The way to do that is to carry on the mission and see it through and not take a path of least resistance. As a company group this is a test of our mettle. I can tell you now we are going to retain the aggressive approach and be *the* dominant force in Nowzad. As the company commander, I am going to continue to make sure that I can justify every risk that we take. I will make sure that every risk is balanced both intellectually and tactically against a tangible outcome and legacy. I am not going to put anyone's life on the line unnecessarily.'

During the battle, A Company had fired 16,400 GPMG rounds, more than 3,000 5.56 rifle and Minimi bullets and hundreds of mortar bombs and grenades. The company had sustained a total of three casualties, including Chris Gray killed. They had killed at least twenty-two enemy fighters, all confirmed. Lieutenant Colonel Carver insisted that the Royal Anglians avoid the temptation to inflate body counts and laid down a rigid system for checking and confirming enemy dead. In reality it is likely that many more had been killed, but this could not be confirmed. Whatever the figure, it represented a major blow to the enemy – the elimination of a large proportion of the Taliban grouping that had spent many months intimidating the local population.

When Biddick finished speaking the men silently headed back to their accommodation to continue checking and cleaning equipment, replenishing ammunition and reloading magazines, preparing for the next task – which they all knew could come at any moment.

The company medical officer spoke to Duffy. 'I am so sorry about what has happened. I did my best with Chris Gray when he got back here, but we couldn't save him. You did an outstanding job treating him out there. You did everything you could to keep him alive and give him a chance. Nobody could have done more for him than you did.'

But Duffy was not listening. All he could think about was Chris Gray and his poor family.

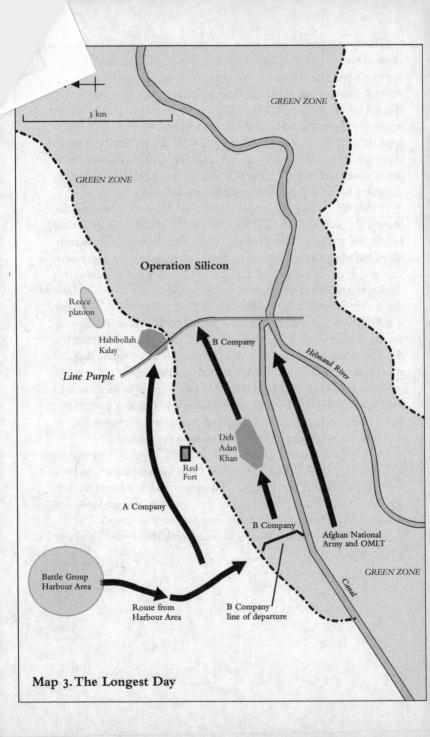

GREEN ZONE

3 km

GREEN ZONE

Operation Silicon

Recce platoon

Habibollah Kalay

Line Purple

B Company

Helmand River

Deh Adan Khan

Red Fort

A Company

B Company

Afghan National Army and OMLT

GREEN ZONE

Battle Group Harbour Area

Route from Harbour Area

B Company line of departure

Canal

Map 3. The Longest Day

The Longest Day: 21–27 April 2007

I

A Company's encounter with the enemy on 13 April was the first serious battle of the battalion's deployment to Afghanistan. Major Dominic Biddick's A Company was one of the three rifle companies of The 1st Battalion The Royal Anglian Regiment. The battalion had arrived in Helmand province, in the south of Afghanistan, in late March and early April 2007.

A Company initially deployed to the town of Nowzad, 50 kilometres north of the main British base, Camp Bastion. Bastion was a sprawling, ever-growing desert camp in the middle of Helmand. It was here that the battalion's commanding officer, Lieutenant Colonel Stuart Carver, had his headquarters.

Carver was a graduate in international relations, with twenty years' military experience and had taken command of the Royal Anglians in December 2005. He was married with two young daughters. His grandfather had fled Poland in the Second World War, and had fought the Germans with a Polish brigade on D-Day. His father, a Belfast man, had flown Lightning fighter planes in the RAF. As a service family, they had moved around a great deal, but Carver's home for much of the time before joining the Army was Saffron Walden, Essex.

Carver was a hugely experienced operational commander, having served in Northern Ireland, Bosnia, Kosovo and the Falkland Islands. He completed a tour in Afghanistan in 2003. In 2004, he had worked in Baghdad on rebuilding the Iraqi police force. In addition to other appointments in the regiment, he had a strategic planning role in the MOD's Permanent Joint Headquarters in Northwood, from where all British military operations are commanded.

Carver took command of the Royal Anglians following their return from a six-month tour in southern Iraq in 2005. He immediately recognized the intensity of the fighting his men were likely to face and the extraordinary demands of the environment and climate. He drove the battalion hard in their year-long preparation for the tour, training them thoroughly in every aspect of infantry combat and emphasizing physical fitness, battle shooting and first aid.

As the situation unfolded before the tour began, Carver and Brigadier John Lorimer, who would be his superior commander in theatre, were determined that the battalion was going to go on to the offensive against the Taliban. Carver prepared his men to take the fight to the enemy rather than defend.

Despite his aggressive stance, he also knew, and ensured his officers and men understood, that the underlying purpose behind the deployment was to protect the civilian community in northern Helmand, to work to improve their security and prosperity and to win their trust. He constantly hammered home the need for this to be a major planning factor in every activity the battalion undertook.

The full title of Major Biddick's company was A (Norfolk) Company. Each of the four fighting companies in the battalion was named after its affiliated county, and this represented links to the county regiments from which the Royal Anglian Regiment was formed in the 1960s. Not every soldier went to the company linked to his home county, although where possible the battalion tried to assign its new recruits in this way.

Like the other companies, A Company consisted of an HQ element and three thirty-man rifle platoons, usually led by a lieutenant or second lieutenant. When additional assets were allocated to a company, such as a fire support group, a Royal Artillery fire support team, a Royal Engineers detachment or a Royal Marines armoured troop, it officially became known as a company group. Each element was interdependent, together representing a potent fighting force, often totalling up to 200 troops.

At the start of the tour, B (Suffolk) Company, commanded by Australian Major Mick Aston, operated from Camp Bastion and Forward Operating Base, or FOB, Robinson, 30 kilometres to the north-east.

C (Essex) Company, under Major Phil Messenger, was a further 35 kilometres north-east of FOB Robinson, in Kajaki. Their role was strategic – protection of the hydroelectricity project that was a central component of the plan to bring security and prosperity not just to Helmand but to much of the rest of southern Afghanistan. It was in Kajaki that the first Royal Anglian soldier had been wounded during the tour, four days before Chris Gray was killed and Corporal Moore and Private

Fisher wounded. Corporal Lee Gayler, attached from the Royal Anglians' Territorial Army battalion, had been working with Fire Support Group Charlie and was shot while moving into a fire position. He was evacuated back to the UK and treated at Selly Oak Hospital near Birmingham.

D (Cambridgeshire) Company was made up of the Reconnaissance Platoon of eight Scimitar tracked recce vehicles, the Sniper Platoon equipped with .338 long-range rifles and L96 sniper rifles, the Anti-Tank Platoon equipped with Javelin imaging infra-red seeker missiles, the Mortar Platoon with its 81mm mortars and the Machine-gun Platoon, equipped with general purpose machine-guns, or GPMGs, .50 calibre heavy machine-guns and 40mm grenade machine-guns, or GMGs. Back in England, the members of the Machine-gun Platoon were double-hatted as ceremonial drummers.

Commanded by Major Charlie Calder, D Company was mostly split up between the three rifle companies, each allocated a fire support group. The FSGs were potent mobile teams equipped with snipers, 81mm mortars and Javelin missiles as well as WMIK Land Rovers armed with .50 calibre machine-guns, GPMGs and GMGs.

Echelon Company, commanded by Captain Phill Blanchfield, whose headquarters was also in Bastion, provided the glue that held the battalion together: logistics, communications, medical and administration.

The Royal Anglians were normally based at Elizabeth Barracks, Pirbright, in the Surrey countryside, but almost all of the soldiers came from the battalion's four recruiting counties of Norfolk, Suffolk, Cambridgeshire and Essex in south-east England.

Around 700 strong, the 1st Battalion was one of the two regular battalions of The Royal Anglian Regiment, which was able to trace its history back more than 300 years through the direct lineage of former regiments. Some of these regiments were heavily engaged in the nineteenth-century Afghan wars. They had won the battle honour 'Afghanistan', passed down from generation to generation and now emblazoned on The Royal Anglian Regiment's Colours, the historic rallying point of an infantry regiment in battle. The Royal Anglians' direct forebears were also deployed in Afghanistan in the 1920s and 1930s. Then, following a lengthy gap, the 1st Battalion were among the first British troops into Kabul after the 2001 invasion, doing a six-month stint there in 2002. The 2nd Battalion followed suit in 2003.

In 2007 the 1st Battalion formed the headquarters and core fighting elements of a battle group, together with 28/143 Battery (Tombs's Troop) Royal Artillery, 8 Armoured Engineer Squadron Royal Engineers and a Royal Marines Armoured Support Company equipped with Viking tracked amphibious armoured vehicles. An Estonian armoured infantry company and a Danish formation recce squadron were also normally part of the battle group. The Royal Anglian Battle Group was known officially as Battle Group North, and operated within Task Force Helmand, the British-led NATO formation responsible for security throughout the province. With all its attachments, the battle group peaked at a strength of 1,500 men and women, but fighting strength for most of the tour was around 1,000.

Just over a year before the Royal Anglians deployed to Afghanistan, the British government announced in parliament that a NATO force mostly made up of British troops would replace US ground forces in Helmand. The Royal Anglians were part of the third rotation of forces deploying under this remit, taking over from 42 Commando Royal Marines. Their operation was codenamed Herrick 6, a name generated at random by a Ministry of Defence computer.

The Royal Anglians' mission, with the rest of Task Force Helmand, was to help extend the authority of President Karzai's Kabul-based government into the lawless Helmand Province, part of an international effort to bring lasting peace and stability to the whole country.

By the time the Royal Anglians arrived, Helmand had become one of the main centres of the Taliban insurgency and a symbol of resistance to the Karzai government in Kabul. After the fall of Kandahar in 2001, the Taliban were still in control of most of Helmand. Mullah Omar took refuge here after fleeing Kandahar, and the world's most wanted man, Osama Bin Laden, spent some time in the Helmand border area in 2003.

Helmand, in the south-west of Afghanistan and roughly 500 hazardous kilometres from the capital, Kabul, shares a southern border with the unruly tribal region of north-west Pakistan. The province consists largely of furnace-like flatlands, bisected by the Helmand River, which is flanked either side by lush vegetation known as the 'Green Zone'. The Green Zone is an area of densely irrigated land, supporting almost 90 per cent of the local population. Depending on the season, crops of poppy, marijuana and maize reduce visibility to 10 metres and sometimes less. The fertility of the Green Zone makes Helmand Afghanistan's largest producer of opium.

The Green Zone, with its maze of interconnecting irrigation ditches, treelines and open fields, gives the advantage of covered movement and unlimited ambush positions. Family compounds, surrounded by almost impenetrable mud walls, delineate ancestral properties and provide considerable protection for the inhabitants and defenders. Together, the compounds form hamlets and villages, the names of which often bear no resemblance to anything on the map.

For the infantryman, the Green Zone represents one of the most complex operating environments imaginable. It presents difficulties comparable to those faced by soldiers in the primary jungles of Malaya and Vietnam, but compounded by the density of civilian dwellings. The usual advantages of modern weapons and sensors become neutralized in the Green Zone, where the ground and vegetation force engagements at brutally short range.

It is unbearably hot (55°C) in the summer and bone-chillingly cold (−20°C) in the winter, when the mountain-fringed flatlands can conjure up the most dramatic electrical thunderstorms to be heard anywhere in the world. It is a beautiful and terrifying place, where human behaviour echoes that of the landscape.

Throughout history, Helmand's inhabitants have called the place the Desert of Death.

2

While Biddick and A Company were battling the Taliban in Nowzad, Carver was planning the battalion's first major offensive operation of the tour. The commander of Task Force Helmand, Brigadier John Lorimer, visited him at battle group headquarters in Camp Bastion. The two officers knew each other well and had worked together at PJHQ, the Permanent Joint Headquarters at Northwood in England, which was responsible for controlling UK land, air and sea operations worldwide.

They now sat drinking coffee from polystyrene cups in Carver's office, a section of the white-tented Joint Operations Centre separated by a thin plywood wall from the bustling operations room with its map-covered 'bird table', lists of troop movements and the crackle of radios as news came in from bases and patrols throughout northern Helmand. Lorimer wanted to discuss the situation at Gereshk, where the rockets and mortars the Taliban were firing into the town were getting increasingly accurate and intensive.

Gereshk, on the Helmand River around 20 kilometres to the east of Bastion, is an old and isolated town, and an important agriculture and trading centre, with a population of 48,500. For months the Taliban had been hitting the town and its congested approach roads with rocket salvos that had killed and seriously wounded many members of the population. The locals were increasingly questioning the point of having NATO forces in Helmand if they allowed these attacks to go on. Gereshk was one of two towns – the other was Sangin, to the northeast – that were Lorimer's priority for reconstruction. And getting anything done there was virtually impossible without significantly improved security.

Lorimer told Carver, 'I want a Task Force operation to clear the Taliban out of their strongholds in the Green Zone to the north-east of Gereshk, to put a stop to the indirect fire. I want to secure the entire area on a permanent basis. So once the enemy is cleared out we will need to set up patrol bases as quickly as possible. I intend that the Afghan National Army supported initially by the Worcestershire and Sherwood Foresters Regiment will occupy the patrol bases when they are built.

'I want your battle group to conduct the major offensive operation to clear the enemy from the Green Zone. We need to start as soon as we can. I estimate it will take about three days to clear the area. It will send a clear message to the Taliban, and to the local population, that we mean business and we will not allow the insurgents to intimidate locals or the ANA. Other than C Company, who will stay at Kajaki, your whole battle group will deploy. We will also use the Brigade Recce Force, three ANA companies, guns, engineers and air. US Task Force 1 Fury will launch an air assault further to the north, to fix the Taliban there and prevent reinforcements coming down.'

Carver listened, characteristically displaying no emotion. But he immediately realized the significance of what Lorimer was saying. This would be the biggest offensive operation British forces had launched in Afghanistan in almost a century. Equally significant, it would be the first time that a deliberate clearance operation on this scale had been attempted within the Green Zone. The sometimes jungle-like Green Zone was infested with Taliban. It was extremely difficult country to fight in, giving the enemy infinite opportunities to infiltrate and set up ambushes. For that reason no previous British unit had entered the Green Zone in force except for short raids, and so for the Taliban it was a safe haven.

One of the targets for Carver's battle group would be the Green Zone settlement of Deh Adan Khan – known by military planners as DAK. Enjoying near-mythical status among the locals, this town was believed to be the key Taliban stronghold for their attacks against Gereshk.

As the Brigadier flew back to his headquarters at Lashkar Gah, Carver thought about what he was being asked to do. The task excited him, and he was keen to get his staff working on the detailed planning. It would be the battalion's first major battle, of that he had little doubt. It was not going to be easy either. He knew from intelligence that the Taliban could call on up to 1,000 fighters in the Gereshk valley area. Many were local insurgents, including farmers paid a few dollars at the end of the poppy harvest to have a go at the British soldiers. But even these could do real damage and would know every inch of the Green Zone like the back of their hands. Some were foreign fighters, trained and equipped in Pakistan. Most of these were from Waziristan, just across the border, but a few came from as far afield as Chechnya or the Middle East. Wherever they were from, Carver did not underestimate their fighting strengths, or their determination to keep the Green Zone out of NATO and Afghan Army hands.

Carver's other enemy was the temperature. His men would have to operate on foot for several days, over long distances, carrying up to 40 kilos of equipment: in heat that most people would find taxing if they were out for a stroll in shorts and flip flops.

But Carver did not doubt for one moment that his men were up to the task. Over the last year he had put them through week after week of tough physical training, to build them to the peak of fighting capability and battle fitness. Most of this had been done in the UK, but the training had culminated in a demanding exercise in Kenya, where many invaluable lessons had been learnt – especially about how to handle the heat.

Carver issued a warning order, giving the broad outline of the operation. This was to enable planning and preparation to begin within all elements of the battle group at the same time as the details were being worked out by operations, intelligence and logistics staff. This 'concurrent activity', a term familiar to all soldiers, allowed the frantic battle preparation before an operation to be compressed into the shortest possible time.

As soon as they received the warning order, A and B Companies put their platoons, as well as attached fire support groups, artillery and engineers, through combat rehearsals, using a mock-up village that had been built at Camp Bastion. Most of the troops taking part went through gruelling live-fire exercises, clearing dummy compounds by day and night. They practised working with the Viking vehicles they would travel in and might fight from during the coming operation.

The BvS10 Viking troop carriers consist of two box-like tracked vehicle units linked by a steering mechanism. With a ring-mount for a GPMG or .50 calibre heavy machine-gun in the forward unit, the vehicle provides armoured protection against 7.62 bullets, artillery shell fragments and anti-personnel mines. The Royal Anglians' Vikings were crewed by Royal Marines drivers and commander/gunners, who remained with the battle group for the tour in Afghanistan. As with all armoured vehicles, there was never enough room in the crew compartments, especially with the ammunition, explosives and other equipment that has to be carried with the troops.

And the almost universal experience among Royal Anglian soldiers in Afghanistan was that the air conditioning never worked. Many of the troops came to think that the stifling, cramped conditions were a way of encouraging them to jump out of the back and into the teeth of enemy fire.

3

Carver's team had just over a week to plan their part of the operation, which was codenamed Silicon. They worked round the clock for several days, putting the plan together and thinking through the intricacies of coordinating for the first time a large operation in such demanding conditions. Carver, Intelligence Officer Captain Tom Coleman and the two rifle company commanders, Majors Dominic Biddick and Mick Aston, conducted helicopter recces to familiarize themselves with the terrain. Unmanned drones were flown to provide updated photographic coverage of some of the key areas, such as compound entry points and break-in areas. Nimrod MR2 surveillance aircraft bristling with hi-tech sensors were deployed to update critical intelligence. The Royal Anglian Recce Platoon was sent on to the ground to collect detailed terrain information that would be essential to the plan.

At 1000 hours on 25 April, three days before the battle group deployed on Operation Silicon, Carver held his battle group Orders Group, or O Group, in the briefing room next to the Joint Operations Centre at Bastion. The key commanders and staff officers in the battle group, around thirty officers, warrant officers and senior NCOs, were seated in rows in front of a large array of maps and air photographs.

After a detailed briefing from the Intelligence Officer, Carver began, 'My intent is to find the enemy within Ops Box Thalatta, the area just to the north-east of Gereshk, in order to facilitate subsequent operations. At H-Hour we will demonstrate overwhelming force. This may cause the Taliban to withdraw without a fight. If not, we will clear the enemy within boundaries, then secure the area, in order to enable reconstruction and subsequent handover to the Afghan National Security Forces. Throughout I intend to screen both north and south to give early warning of enemy intentions and retain the ability to strike enemy that present themselves. Screens will be provided by the Brigade Recce Force in the south and the Danish Recce Squadron in the north. On D Minus One, the battle group will move to a harbour area in the north of Gereshk. Prior to H-Hour, A Company will move forward and secure an entry point into the Green Zone for B Company. B Company will then move through and begin an advance to contact from west to east. This advance will be paralleled in the south by an Afghan National Army company, and supported by attack helicopters. A Company will remain north of Gereshk, as a reserve, prepared to echelon through B Company, or conduct a strike against any targets that present themselves further east along the river. I aim to reach the five five easting by last light and then form a hasty defensive line. Overnight we will reconfigure to prepare for an assault by A Company on to Habibollah Kalay. This attack on D Plus One will be synchronized with strikes by the Brigade Recce Force and other Task Force Helmand elements further east.'

He looked at Biddick and Aston, seated directly in front of him. 'Once you reach the five five easting, Report Line Purple, which is the battle group limit of exploitation, you will consolidate and secure the area. This may involve advancing further east to create a stand-off, to allow the engineer group to construct patrol bases.'

Over the next hour Carver and his staff laid out the details of how all of this was to be achieved.

On the morning of Sunday 29 April, the day the battle group deployed on Operation Silicon, Major Mick Aston, B Company commander, sat on his camp bed in the large, white, half-cylinder-shaped tent that for the time being he called home. The mid-morning temperature was so great that he felt as if he was in a sauna, even though the tent, with its hard plastic floor, was air-conditioned by its own compressor unit. For days now Aston had been involved in frantic preparation for the op, and was grateful for a moment to himself before it kicked off. He was worried but excited at the same time: a feeling of nervous anticipation that permeated the whole of the Royal Anglian Battle Group before the challenges of their first major battle.

Aston was thirty-six and married with a young daughter. He had taken over command of B Company during the battalion's Iraq tour in mid-2005. His background was not that of a typical Army officer. He had joined the Australian Army as an enlisted soldier at the age of seventeen, serving initially in a reconnaissance squadron equipped with Bell 206 Kiowa helicopters. Two years later he attended the Royal Military College at Duntroon and was commissioned as an officer. Wanting to be a Blackhawk pilot, he attempted but failed pilot training and instead went to the Royal Australian Corps of Signals. After a spell instructing in leadership back at Duntroon, Aston became bored with life in the Australian Army and decided to look for a bit more action. He married Tanya, his long-term girlfriend, and straight away they both flew to Britain. A few days later in Cambridgeshire he reported for duty with The 1st Battalion The Royal Anglian Regiment as Captain Aston of the British Army. He began to develop a formidable reputation in the Royal Anglians as a straight-talking, capable and hard-driving officer.

Since B Company had arrived in Afghanistan, Aston had been impatient for action. Silicon was the chance he had been waiting for – to 'get in amongst them, and just get it done', as he was fond of telling his soldiers. And Aston was delighted that Carver had detailed his company to do the initial hard fighting – to break into and attack through the Green Zone.

From his daysack Aston pulled out his diary, a lined and hard-bound notebook. He wrote: *I am nervous about the operation and hope everything goes well. I have been thinking about it non-stop as this is the first big test of the company, going into the Green Zone and staying overnight. Nobody has done this. That is the bit that concerns me. Plus the intelligence. Enemy strengths and whereabouts are sketchy. We are pretty much going to have to do an advance to contact to find them. It is the uncertainty that is worse than anything. Not knowing what will happen. But soon we will know.*

4

That night the Royal Anglian Battle Group rolled out of Bastion in two columns each of more than fifty vehicles. They drove east down the A1 highway, which had been built during the time of the Soviet occupation of Afghanistan, and occupied a battle group harbour area in the flat desert north-west of Gereshk.

The sheer size of the convoy removed any possibility of surprise. But Carver tried to disguise their intentions by having the Afghan National Army troops conduct a large-scale patrol operation in Gereshk. He hoped this would create the impression that the Royal Anglians had arrived in the area to join a major security sweep in the town.

Any long-distance operational move in hostile country involving large numbers of combat vehicles is subject to 1,001 frictions including vehicle break-downs, navigation errors, lost communications, traffic accidents and enemy attack. The Recce Platoon was responsible for oiling the wheels of the move, policing the route, guiding vehicle packets, providing protection and keeping commanders informed of progress.

The Royal Anglians' Recce Platoon was equipped with Combat Vehicle Reconnaissance (Tracked), or CVRT. They had eight of these vehicles, also known as Scimitars. Lightly armoured, and resembling small tanks, the Scimitar had a crew of three – commander, gunner and driver – and was equipped with a 30mm Rarden cannon, a 7.62mm machine-gun and two four-barrel smoke dischargers. The machine-gun was coaxially mounted, which means its aim was slaved to that of the Rarden cannon. First brought into service in 1973, the Scimitar was an elderly vehicle, but had undergone a 'Life Extension Programme', including installation of a Cummins BTA 5.9 diesel power-pack to replace a much less reliable six-cylinder petrol engine. Although not without its problems, the Scimitar was already proving a success in Afghanistan, with its speed, all-terrain mobility and formidable firepower.

The Recce Platoon got to the harbour first. Their role was to make sure the area was clear of enemy, secure it against interference and guide the various elements of the battle group into position.

In the harbour area the battle group deployed in all-round defence, forming up into the groupings it would operate in at the start of Silicon. Final vehicle, weapons and equipment checks were carried out and last-minute briefings and orders given. Other than that, the men had only to maintain security and rest as best they could before going into battle.

The Gun Group, two troops each of three 105mm light guns from 28/143 Battery (Tombs's Troop) Royal Artillery, set up in the harbour area and would remain there, providing indirect fire support for the battle group throughout Silicon. Each gun could fire 15.1-kilogram high-explosive shells at the rate of six rounds a minute out to 17 kilometres and could also support the Royal Anglians by laying down smoke screens and illuminating the night sky.

The battle group was fully established in the harbour area shortly after last light. As a dust storm began to gather, Carver called his commanders and HQ staff together for a final confirmatory O Group, at the back of his Viking tracked command vehicle. He briefed them on an unexpected problem that would require a major change of plan for B Company, with just a few hours to go before the operation began. The company had planned to enter the Green Zone across a wide canal. A suitable crossing point for both troops on foot and Viking vehicles had been identified. But a short time earlier, Colour Sergeant Al Thurston, the Recce Platoon 2IC, had been to check the crossing point. He discovered a large earth berm blocking the route for vehicles – which had not been there a few days before. B Company would have no problem crossing on foot, but they needed the Vikings with them in the Green Zone to provide flank protection, ammunition and water resupply and casualty evacuation. The only solution was for the Vikings to drop off the company, drive west to Gereshk, cross the canal by the road bridge there, and then drive eastwards into the Green Zone to link up with the troops. It was risky. The Vikings would be driving several kilometres through the Green Zone without infantry support. That made them vulnerable to attack by Taliban with RPG anti-armour missiles in the close country. But there was no other choice.

The new plan was agreed, and watches were synchronized. The company commanders confirmed that all their men, vehicles and equipment had arrived without problems and would be ready to move in time for H-Hour.

On the far side of the harbour, Second Lieutenant Ben Howes, 5 Platoon commander in B Company, was checking his men. As with every officer and soldier on the eve of his first battle, Howes was wondering how he would perform in contact with the enemy – he had been in the battalion for only three months, straight out of training. He knew that it was one thing to show your leadership ability during controlled exercises at Sandhurst or on the Platoon Commanders' Battle Course at Brecon. It was a different matter altogether to do so with real bullets flying and perhaps with your own men getting killed around you.

As platoon commander he did not just have to worry about how he would personally perform, he also had total responsibility for the lives of the thirty men under his command. He thought how lucky he was that he had Sergeant Keith Nieves as his platoon sergeant. Nieves had guided him since he arrived in January, and he could not have wished for a better mentor. This was the eternal role of the platoon sergeant – to turn a young platoon commander from an apprentice with little more than paper leadership qualifications and no solid military experience into a commander who could earn the respect of his men, lead them to success in battle and preferably keep them alive. Nieves was doing this in the way that only the best platoon sergeants were capable of – by always supporting the platoon commander in front of the men and never doing anything to undermine his position. And by being open, frank and forthright with him in private – but only in private.

Howes also counted himself lucky to have a particularly strong group of NCOs in the platoon – his corporals and lance corporals, the section commanders and 2ICs. In his eyes there was not a weak link among them.

He walked round between the four Vikings his platoon had travelled in from Bastion. Nieves had detailed off one sentry to man each of the

49

vehicle guns, with a second sentry forward, on the ground, manning a dismounted GPMG with Viper thermal imaging night sight. Those men who were not on sentry, or 'stag', were resting beside the Vikings.

As Howes walked past one of the vehicles, Private Joseph Rix stood up. The twenty-year-old sharpshooter had been sitting on his daysack, checking his ammo. 'Sir, what time are we off?'

'H-Hour is at about 0530, so we'll be heading out of here a couple of hours before that, I should think. I'm going to an O Group with the company commander shortly, and he'll confirm the time then.'

'Why can't we just go now, sir? I can't wait till the morning.'

'Of course we can't go now, Rixy, what are you talking about?' Howes laughed.

'Yes, but I can't wait to go. This is brilliant, all of this. It's what I joined the Army for. I can't wait to have a go at the Taliban. I just want to know what a contact is really like. I've seen all the films and heard all that boring stuff from the blokes that were in Northern Ireland. But I want to do it myself, for real.'

Corporals Simon Thorne and Tom Mason had been chatting beside the vehicle and strolled over. Thorne said, 'Rixy, I'll tell you all about Northern Ireland sometime, and about Kabul too if you want. I've got so many war stories I could keep you awake till H-Hour.'

'I know, Si, I've heard them all before, every bleeding day.'

Thorne said to Howes, 'Rixy's right though, boss: every one of my lads is up for this. One or two are a bit nervous, but they all want it. I must admit I can't wait to get down there and get in among them. Tom and me were just talking about it. I just hope it happens the way we're expecting. But knowing our luck, the enemy won't even turn up. Most of Iraq was like that, nothing happening, and Kabul. It would be just our luck.'

Mason nodded in agreement.

'How about Northern Ireland, then, Si? That must've been rough,' laughed Rix.

'I'll give you Northern Ireland, Rixy. Best you get your head down before I find a four-hour gap in the stag roster for you to fill.'

Howes moved on to the next Viking. He stopped to talk to a young soldier who had just arrived in the battalion and was lying awake in his sleeping bag. 'How's it going? All set for tomorrow?'

'Yes, sir, I've got all my kit ready to go, fully bombed up.'

'OK, well done, get some doss now because it's going to be a blower in the morning.'

The soldier lowered his voice. 'Sir, I do want to do this and everything, but I feel really nervous. This is what I joined for. But I'm really worried about how I'm going to react if they start shooting at us. I just don't want to let anybody down, sir. Do you know what I mean?'

'Look, I am in the same situation as you. So are most of the platoon – and the company. Hardly anyone here has been shot at before. They're all just as nervous as you, even if they don't admit it. Even the guys who were in Iraq didn't do anything like we're going to be doing tomorrow. You've done well in pre-op training, I've seen you, and you're a good soldier. I'm totally confident in your ability, and you should be too. All you have to do is remember to stick to the bloke next to you, and he'll look after you as well. You just have to work together and you'll get through this no problem. Remember your basic skills and drills and just do what you've been trained to do.'

Howes moved on, wondering whether he'd bored the young soldier to sleep.

By now the dust storm was getting increasingly ferocious and, bizarrely for Afghanistan at this time of year, it had started to rain.

6

Howes arrived at the back of Aston's Viking. It was 2200 hours and pouring.

About fifteen people were standing around, including the company 2IC, Captain Dave Robinson, the company sergeant major, WO2 Tim Newton, the mortar fire controller, Corporal Mark Willsher, the FSG commander, Sergeant Major Ivan Snow, the air and artillery controllers, the signallers and the doctor. The other two platoon commanders were there too: Lieutenant Dave Broomfield of 6 Platoon and Lieutenant George Seal-Coon of 7 Platoon.

'Make way for the sprog,' joked Aston. This was the term for a new soldier, and he reserved it for Howes, the junior subaltern in the company. 'Glad you could join us, mate.'

Aston became brisk. 'Right, fellas, there is a change of plan with the Vikings.' He explained what the CO had told him, then continued.

'Otherwise everything else is the same. H-Hour is confirmed as 0530. Recce will clear the route from here to the Green Zone. A Company will secure the start point for us. We go in by Viking then dismount and walk the last kilometre to the line of departure, which will be marked by Sergeant Major Snow's WMIKs. After that, we follow the plan we've been over time and again. Not forgetting that a plan never survives contact with the enemy. That is true in all wars, and it will be true in this one. Any questions? No? Good. In that case, I want to wish you all good luck tomorrow. We're all ready for this. Get it done, fellas.'

As the O Group broke up, Corporal Ashley Hill, one of the Recce Platoon section commanders, who had been standing at the back of the group, remained behind to speak to Aston. He could hardly see him it was so dark. 'Sir, it's Corporal Hill, Recce Platoon.'

'Nice to meet you, Corporal H,' said Aston. 'Are all the Recce section commanders called Hill nowadays?' – a reference to Sergeant Jamie Hill, also in the Recce Platoon.

'No, sir, just two of us,' chuckled Hill.

'Well I suppose it makes it easier for you ladies, doesn't it? Now what can I do for you, Hill?'

'I believe I'm leading you down in the morning, sir, I just wanted to confirm the timings when you want to move.'

'We're rolling at 0300, assuming you fellas can be up by then. I know what the routine is in D Company.'

Hill laughed. 'It's going to be a rough ride down there, sir, I've looked at the ground, and it's really steep and broken. Visibility will be virtually nil.'

'Yeah, I know what the ground's like. You just get me there. And I don't want a rough ride, I want a nice smooth ride all the way down. You find me a good route. And I want to be right behind A Company, I mean right behind, I don't want a fag paper between us. You can do that, can't you?'

'Yes, sir,' said Hill. 'See you at 0300.'

'Yeah, that's the time I want to be *moving* by the way, not the time I'm coming round to wake you up with a nice sweet mug of tea.'

Hill smiled as he walked off, trying to appear confident. But he was petrified. This was his first Recce Platoon job, and he was responsible for leading about thirty B Company vehicles across horrendous terrain into the battalion's first battle for many years. It would be pitch black and there was a dust storm building. But, above all, he had heard just how fiery Major Aston could be if things didn't go his way.

Hill didn't get any sleep that night. Telling his men to get their heads down, he stayed on duty in the turret of his Scimitar, monitoring the radio, poring again and again over maps and air photographs showing the route into the Green Zone, setting and resetting his compass, checking his watch. He couldn't afford to doze off, with the possibility of missing the 0300 deadline. If he did, he suspected Aston would wake him up with something other than a nice sweet mug of tea.

7

A Company left the harbour at 0230, to move down and secure the start point for B Company's assault into the Green Zone. It was rough going in darkness across the broken, rocky desert terrain with its steep re-entrants, huge ruts and hidden gulleys. Even with the overnight rain, every vehicle kicked up clouds of dust, totally obscuring the view of those moving behind.

Traversing the steep, gravelly slopes, the drivers using ineffective night vision devices were unable to gauge the steep-sided wadi gradients, and two A Company Vectors rolled on to their sides. Biddick sent other vehicles to deal with them. He didn't know whether soldiers lay crushed and bleeding under the vehicle axles as he pressed the remainder of the company on. His priority was to make sure the FUP, or forming-up place, was secured on time, and nothing would divert him.

B Company's departure from the harbour area was delayed when a soldier in Second Lieutenant Howes's platoon couldn't be accounted for. He had lost his way in the dark coming back from sentry duty and ended up wandering into A Company's area. Aston was beside himself with anger. It is a crime to miss H-Hour on any operation, potentially holding up an entire battle group, and Aston made it quite clear to Howes that this was his first and last chance of the day.

Corporal Hill managed to successfully lead B Company down to their debussing point in the wadi floor, although it took what seemed like forever to cover the 3 kilometres. Hill kept having to pause, as word came up from the company behind him that their wheeled vehicles – WMIKs and Pinzgauers – were getting bogged in and had to be laboriously pulled out. The only vehicles that had no difficulty negotiating the rough terrain were Hill's Scimitars and the Vikings. Hill was concerned

53

that the company commander would blame him for not getting him the 'nice smooth ride' he had demanded, but he heard nothing and guessed that even Aston would not be able to blame him for the rugged Afghan terrain.

B Company dismounted from their Vikings in darkness. Sergeant Major Snow and his four FSG WMIKs, plus one of the Vikings, moved into the open, providing close protection for the company as they entered the FUP.

The FUP was a pre-designated area where the company would shake out ready to assault. At the forward edge of the FUP was the line of departure, a woodline that the company was to cross at H-Hour as they began their advance towards the enemy.

Howes's platoon spread out in the open ground. He pushed his men forward to a wide, fast-flowing canal. They shuffled across a narrow stick bridge and into the Green Zone. The other two platoons moved into position. It was 0500 hours – thirty minutes till H-Hour – and dawn was just beginning to break.

As they prepared to advance, Howes heard gunfire off to the left. He ran forward through the trees to observe and saw that A Company, 600 metres to the north, was in contact. A group of six Taliban had stood up to engage the B Company platoons in the Green Zone, unaware of A Company's presence. Lieutenant Nick Denning's 1 Platoon cut them down before they could get more than a couple of shots off.

As the main body of B Company moved into the FUP, Captain Will Goodman, the Royal Marines Viking Troop commander, with Company Sergeant Major Tim Newton, headed west to Gereshk with the column of Vikings. They crossed the river at the Gereshk road bridge and entered the Green Zone.

Half an hour later, trundling back east along a track beside the canal, with thick Green Zone vegetation to the left, and open country to the right, one of the Vikings threw a track, immobilizing the vehicle. Unlike some armoured vehicles, this was rare for a Viking. But you could guarantee it would always happen at the worst time. And this was a bad time. The Vikings were moving along a predictable route, in close country, without infantry protection.

The crews worked to get the track back on as quickly as they could, but it took nearly an hour to sort out. Both Carver and Aston had felt that this route in for the Vikings would be risky. The marines working on the vehicle heard the crack-crack-crack of gun fire and dived for cover as bullets ricocheted off the Vikings' armour.

Newton got some of the marines and his Company HQ soldiers together and tried to identify the enemy positions so they could shoot back or call in artillery fire. But the Taliban knew how to conceal themselves, and Newton couldn't locate them. Braving the sporadic fire, and keeping close to the ground, behind the concealment of some low vegetation, the marines eventually managed to drive the track back on, and the convoy began rumbling east again, with Newton thankful the enemy hadn't managed to bring any RPG teams into range.

Several kilometres ahead of the Vikings, the company pushed through the Green Zone on foot, heading north-east. Howes's 5 Platoon started on the left of the advance, with 7 Platoon, under Lieutenant George Seal-Coon, to their right. Both platoons did their best to keep level, to reduce the risk of being outflanked by the Taliban in such treacherous country. A short distance behind, in reserve, was 6 Platoon, commanded by Lieutenant Dave Broomfield.

The Green Zone was approximately 1,000 metres wide in most places. It was broken up by a grid of irrigation ditches, usually at least a metre deep, and some wider canal lines. Most ran with the grain of the land, following the river line, south-west to north-east, and connected up with a network of smaller lateral ditches. The irrigation system severely constrained and channelled movement, creating vulnerable choke points, which the enemy could predict and ambush. Almost all the ditches and canals were lined with trees, usually about 3 metres tall, with spindly branches and small green leaves. Between the irrigation ditches were fields of poppy, over a metre high and topped with green buds awaiting the extraction of sap for opium production.

The area B Company had to clear, approximately 12 kilometres long, was punctuated by groups of compounds, some quite small, others as big as 100 by 300 metres. They were complexes of buildings and outhouses surrounded by high mud walls. This was where the farmers and their livestock lived. As did the Taliban. Some of the compounds were their strongpoints. And they had such domination over the local population that they could move into any compound at will, to take refuge or to fight.

The battle group intelligence officer had identified all of the major complexes and numbered them as Objectives 1 to 14. The company's task was to clear each of them in turn. On reaching a compound, the sections carried out a quick recce to identify anything suspicious, then entered and searched. Only if there was confirmed enemy presence was there a need to blast down the wall, lob in explosive hand grenades and charge in shooting. This was known as attacking at 'state red'.

The platoons and sections rotated through the compounds, taking it in turn to make the entry. By 0900 hours Corporal Simon Thorne, one of Howes's section commanders, was beginning to fear that his prediction of the night before was right – 'Knowing our luck, the enemy won't even turn up.' They had been clearing through the drab, grey compounds and patrolling across the poppy fields for three and a half hours, and there was still no sign of the Taliban.

Even without the enemy, this was punishing work. The Royal Anglian soldiers were fitter than they had ever been before in their lives. But the temperature was on the rise, and most of the soldiers were burdened with between 35 and 40 kilos of kit. Knowing this was going to be a long haul, they had minimized what they were carrying. The rule was simple: take what you need to keep you and your mates alive and fighting. Weapons and ammunition first, as much ammunition as possible: you could never carry enough and you didn't know when you would get a resupply. Then water. Then food last.

Most carried eleven magazines of ammunition plus a bandolier, two L109 high-explosive hand grenades, two smoke grenades, one red phosphorous grenade and a pack of mini-flares. There were also spare belts of GPMG and Minimi ammunition to be shared around, and most soldiers carried two 51mm mortar bombs. Some had an AT4 anti-tank missile strapped to their back. Over a metre long and weighing nearly 7 kilos, it was especially awkward to carry, particularly in compounds or close country. Every man carried a personal role radio, or PRR, and commanders and signallers carried the heavier PRC-354 or 355 radios. Then there were mine-clearing tools, a bayonet, first aid kit, morphine, a knife. Osprey body armour weighed nearly 16 kilos, and every man carried 3 litres of water in a Camelbak and 2 more litres in bottles. Next it was twenty-four hours' worth of rations, biscuits and, if there was room, some kind of warm kit for the sometimes bitterly cold nights.

All of this would be stuffed into assault vests, webbing pouches, pockets and daysacks. They would carry it into battle, and run, march, climb hills, wade ditches, fight and evacuate casualties with it.

8

It was 0930 hours. The Vikings had caught up with the company an hour or so before, and were moving north-east along the track to the right of the troops on the ground. Suddenly machine-gun fire drummed the sides of the lead Vikings, followed rapidly by a salvo of RPGs airbursting overhead.

The Viking commanders swung their guns to the right and began to blast back at likely enemy fire positions. Captain Goodman shouted into his radio, 'Zero Alpha, this is Mud Two Zero Alpha, contact, wait out!'

The enemy fire continued, with the Taliban firing and moving between a network of well-concealed positions. It was virtually impossible to pinpoint exact locations, so the Vikings viciously raked hedgerows, ditches and buildings that could contain enemy.

Aston, crawling forward to the Vikings, worked out that the fire was coming from positions about 400 metres to the south. He told his JTAC, 'Get me some air – fast! I don't want to assault across nearly half a kilometre of open country. Let's try and kill them from above.'

The JTAC spoke into his radio. Aston called Seal-Coon, commander of 7 Platoon, 'Three Zero Alpha, Zero Alpha. Move your callsign forward and give close protection to the Mud callsigns. They can cover the south OK, but they'll be exposed to RPG teams coming up through the Green Zone from the east or north. Out to you.'

Then he called Howes: 'Hello One Zero Alpha, Zero Alpha. You are to attempt to identify enemy positions that are engaging the Mud callsigns and be prepared to mark with fifty-one smoke for air, over.'

Howes replied, 'One Zero Alpha, roger out.'

Sergeant Nieves and his 51mm mortar man, Fijian Private Luke Nadriva, moved, crouching, along the ditch to a position clear of overhanging trees, where they could fire and observe. With enemy fire near by, and the Vikings hosing back tracer in reply, Nieves, keeping low, scanned the open area with his binoculars. He had to keep wiping the lenses, blurred by sweat and misted up by heat from his face. He monitored the net for target identifications and descriptions from the Viking crews. Nadriva, shattered after battling his way through the undergrowth and in and out of compounds, slipped off the end cap from his mortar, and laid out four smoke bombs next to it.

The JTAC said to Aston, 'Sir, Apache on task, should be overhead in about ten minutes.'

'Brit or American?'

'British.'

Aston turned to the other members of his Tac HQ. 'OK, we're going to move over the ditch to join 7 Platoon; we need to get eyes on so we can sort out all of the offensive support for this. Follow me.'

As he ran towards the gunfire, Aston called Broomfield, 6 Platoon commander: 'Two Zero, Zero Alpha. Move your callsign north and clear Objective 7, then remain in that location until further orders. That will give us a foothold further forward and prevent the Taliban flanking from that direction, over.'

Aston led the men of his Tac HQ through the stinking irrigation ditch. Level with the rear elements of 7 Platoon, they clawed their way up on to the bank near the Vikings. As they ran, a call came for Aston on the company net from the FSG commander, Sergeant Major Ivan Snow: 'Four Zero Alpha. Contact now. My callsign under enemy mortar fire. Also receiving incoming RPG and smallarms fire. Enemy believed firing from Green Zone, north-east of your location. Enemy not identified. Am engaging likely positions. Out.'

Snow and his FSG were on the left of Aston's advance, at the Red Fort. This was the most prominent point for miles around, high up in the desert. It was literally a fortress, red-orange in colour, a large open sand area, surrounded by massive walls, 15 metres high. Because the fort was such a good vantage point, commanding the ground in every direction, it was an obvious place to go – and therefore dangerous.

As Snow was speaking, Taliban mortar shells smacked into the sand just feet away, blasting up sand and lumps of rock and hurling out jagged shards of red-hot shrapnel, several of which struck the sides of two of the WMIKs. Then there was a few minutes' pause, followed by another shell. After that, mortar fire continued, but just the odd round every now and again, and landing further away. Interspersed with the mortars was the occasional deafening RPG airburst and blasts of stuttering machine-gun fire. Snow's FSG directed burst after burst of machine-gun fire back into the Taliban positions.

The enemy fire wasn't enough to give undue worry to the calm and stoical sergeant major, although one of his WMIK commanders suggested a move might be prudent. 'That's OK, boy,' chuckled Snow, whose vehicle was the most exposed of all, 'I'll let you know when it gets dangerous. In the meantime we've got our job to do supporting B Company, and we can't do it from behind cover, now, can we?'

It was a source of amusement in the battalion that Snow had left the Army for two years to become a postman in Clacton, Essex. He was famous in the area for never delivering a bill on Fridays. Asked why he waited until Monday to post the bills, Snow, a father of three, would look nonplussed, saying, 'I didn't want to ruin their weekends.'

There wasn't in fact very much Snow's FSG could do to be of direct assistance to the dismounted elements of B Company. The rifle platoons were deep inside the Green Zone, and the enemy were using concealed positions in front of them and away to the south. The vegetation was so thick it was virtually impossible for the FSG to see where enemy or friendly forces were, and therefore they were unable to use their firepower to give effective close support. But Snow was not going to sit idle. He ordered his men to systematically scan the whole of the open area, and the fringes of the Green Zone, for any enemy movement or activity, and then to engage.

He was particularly interested in the village of Habibollah Kalay, briefed as being a likely Taliban stronghold. He considered two options. Any Taliban in the compounds there might move out into the Green Zone and attack B Company. Or by the time the battle group moved forward later in the day or the next day to strike Habibollah Kalay, the enemy might have escaped. In response to either possibility, Snow decided he would do whatever he could to keep the enemy bottled up there, and preferably kill any who showed themselves. He had assigned arcs of observation to each of his WMIK commanders, and the right-hand side of Habibollah Kalay was in Lance Corporal Oliver Ruecker's area of responsibility.

Ruecker, at present acting as a vehicle commander, was known as Teddy within the battalion on account of his tightly curled blond hair. That was as far as any resemblance to a cuddly toy went. An imposing six feet two tall, twenty-year-old Ruecker had been in the Army for just four years. He was born in America, and his father, Scott, a Bronze Star winner, had been a master sergeant in US Air Force special operations. With a combat tour in Iraq under his belt, Teddy Ruecker was a committed and focused soldier. He had only just been promoted to lance corporal and was a battalion sniper. As a sniper, he would normally have deployed on foot with the company. But Ruecker had arrived late into theatre, having just completed a course, and was temporarily assigned as an FSG WMIK commander.

It was just 1000 hours, and the sun was getting hotter. Ruecker looked intently through his permanent focus binoculars at the south-western compounds of Habibollah Kalay. After a while he saw movement. Even though he was seated in the vehicle, under the glaring heat the sweat was stinging his eyes. He rubbed them and looked again through the binos to make sure. Men scurrying between the compounds, with weapons. Taliban! He called over to Snow, 'Sir, enemy twelve o'clock of my gun barrel, 600 metres, forward of prominent compounds far right of HBK, left edge.'

Snow checked, said, 'Got that, Teddy, open fire on my command,' then shouted along the vehicle line, 'Enemy front, 600 metres, watch Teddy's tracer, all guns rapid – fire!'

As the WMIK gunners quickly swung their GPMGs, heavy machine-guns and grenade machine-guns towards the enemy Ruecker had identifed, they heard a sharp and rapid crack-crack-crack-crack of machine-gun bullets and the drawn-out rush of RPG missiles high over their heads. They had been beaten to the draw.

Ignoring the inaccurate enemy fire, Ruecker pressed the trigger of his vehicle-mounted GPMG, sending a long line of 7.62mm tracer – one tracer in four standard ball – into the compound. This was the first time he had ever fired a weapon in anger. Initially he got carried away, firing long bursts of thirty to forty rounds. Then he remembered his training and started firing controlled bursts of five to seven rounds in rapid succession. This enabled more accurate shooting, reduced ammunition wastage and didn't overheat the gun barrel so quickly.

With the combined weight of four machine-guns blasting at the compounds, the enemy fire reduced, but did not stop altogether. They couldn't go down to assault the enemy position on foot with so few infantry troops, and their job was to remain in overwatch on the high ground. But Ruecker was determined to make sure he killed as many of the enemy as possible before they could escape and kill his mates down in the Green Zone.

He shouted, 'Allie – get that GMG firing on to those positions. Watch my tracer.'

In the back of the WMIK Private Allie McKelvie had already set the range on his GMG and was lined up on the enemy. He immediately started blasting volley after volley of high-explosive grenades into the compound. The effect at the target end looked devastating as the high-velocity grenades exploded in rapid succession, tearing up the compound walls, hurling debris in every direction and kicking up clouds of smoke and dust.

The 40mm Heckler and Koch grenade machine-gun had first been fielded in Afghanistan only a few months before. It was mounted on the WMIK Land Rovers, but could also be operated from ground-based tripods. Capable of firing either single shot or automatic, up to 340 rounds per minute and out to a range of 2 kilometres, the GMG gave a huge advantage to the Royal Anglians, who could use it to engage the Taliban on foot, in vehicles or in buildings. The weapon could be fired round the clock, using its telescopic day sight, image intensifying and thermal night sights, and laser rangefinder.

With McKelvie's massive firepower adding to the rest, the enemy fire slowed further, but still didn't stop. Smoke and dust caused by the devastating FSG fire prevented Ruecker from seeing where the enemy were, but he knew they would be in carefully selected positions, moving around the compound, trying to dodge bullets while keeping the pressure on.

Ruecker's driver, Private Brian Turner, a member of the battalion's Anti-Tank Platoon, said, 'Teddy, I'm going to smash them with an AT4, OK?'

'Don't be daft, mate. They're 600 metres away, and the AT4 isn't effective that far out. I wouldn't bother wasting it.'

'Yeah, I know the range of an AT4, Teddy,' said Turner, eager for action and annoyed that he couldn't help in the FSG's efforts to destroy the enemy position.

Minutes later an RPG missile exploded directly in front of Ruecker's WMIK, flinging up debris, showering him with sand and dirt and throwing him and Turner back in the vehicle. In the rear, McKelvie was knocked off his feet by the blast.

Turner moved the vehicle into a different position, with slightly more cover. Ruecker, dust and sand clinging to his sweat-covered face and combats, fired several more bursts into the compound, then said to Turner, 'That was close. Why don't you give that AT4 a try, then, mate?'

'OK,' said Turner, jumping out of the WMIK, 'I'll aim high and see what happens.'

Turner put the American M136 AT4 anti-tank launcher on his right shoulder. The metre-long green fibreglass tube weighed nearly 7 kilos, and Turner was glad he didn't have to manpack it around Helmand in this heat. He looked back, checking there was no one behind him – when he fired it the weapon would fling out a powerful backblast, which, although suppressed by a built-in water pack, could seriously injure and possibly kill anyone in its path. Aiming well above the target compound, Turner pressed the trigger. There was a tremendous bang, and the rocket, with its shaped charge warhead, flew towards the compound at 285 metres per second. He could see the missile's tail flare as it shot upwards like a huge firework, kinked downward in the air and in just over two seconds blasted into the compound, hurling up fire and debris.

Ruecker smiled and gave Turner a thumbs-up. 'Awesome shot, mate – quality.'

9

Soon after B Company moved forward from the FUP on the edge of the Green Zone at 0530 hours that morning, Carver drove his Tac HQ out of the harbour area and on to a ridge-line in the desert. From here, Carver could see all the way across the Green Zone and the desert – a grandstand view.

Tac was made up of around fifteen vehicles, including close protection WMIKs, plus two Recce Platoon Scimitars, whose role was to provide a protective screen and to guide and escort the headquarters when it moved.

Carver's Viking and the artillery and engineer commanders' vehicles were the hub of Tac HQ. The vehicles parked close together, and this was where Carver commanded the operation. Watchkeepers and signallers monitored the various communications systems, and the ops officer kept track of the detailed movements and actions of the companies, updating the CO's map board, and making sure the CO was informed immediately of all significant developments.

Carver had expected the break-in to the Green Zone to be a tough fight, but with the exception of the small group of Taliban killed by Denning's platoon at the start, there had been no opposition. He had begun to wonder whether this, the first battle group operation, was going to be easier than expected. But that had all changed when B Company's Vikings and Snow's fire support group came under enemy fire.

At the same time problems were developing in the south. The battle group's Afghan National Army company were advancing in the open terrain beyond the Green Zone. Captain Moxey, the ops officer, told Carver he was concerned that the ANA were reporting they were about 6 kilometres forward of B Company. Like A Company in the north, the ANA were supposed to conform to B Company's movements, keeping roughly in line to prevent the enemy exploiting gaps, and getting in behind the companies. Out on a limb in front of the battle group, the ANA company ran up against a strong Taliban grouping in the town of Zumberlay. With the ANA was an operational mentoring and liaison team, or OMLT, made up of six Grenadier Guards officers and NCOs. Their role was to advise and assist the Afghan commanders and act as a link with the Royal Anglian Battle Group headquarters.

The ANA, with the OMLT, were beginning to get drawn into combat with the Taliban in Zumberlay, and reports were flying in of multiple contacts. Carver sent orders on the radio to disengage and pull back. But the contacts continued, and the ANA were apparently finding extraction difficult. Carver also realized that the ANA were aggressive and determined fighters, and the instruction to withdraw, even as a temporary manoeuvre to gain eventual advantage, would not have been received with enthusiasm.

He began to fear the worst. Then, on the battle group command net, the Grenadier Guards commander reported that the ANA company and his OMLT were cut off and completely surrounded by Taliban.

South of the ANA company, the Brigade Reconnaissance Force, or BRF, made up of two platoons mounted in WMIKs, was providing flank security for the whole battle group. Normally a Task Force Helmand asset, the BRF had been placed by Brigadier Lorimer under Carver's command for the first stages of Operation Silicon.

This was the only mobile reserve at Carver's disposal, and he sent them north-east to help the ANA. The BRF stormed up on to a ridgeline and hammered the Taliban with their WMIK machine-guns. A bloody battle between the BRF and the Taliban followed. In the face of superior firepower, the enemy eventually melted away, allowing the battered and bloodied ANA to pull back into line with B Company.

Carver knew the ANA loved going forward and attacking, always itching to get to grips with the Taliban. He admired their fighting spirit, but on this occasion there had been a near-disaster, which could have resulted in many casualties and diverted the whole battle group away from its main effort in the Green Zone.

While Carver and Moxey were dealing with the situation in the south, and monitoring B Company's battles in the Green Zone and the desert, the area around Tac HQ was also coming under attack. An 81mm mortar line from the Royal Anglians' Mortar Platoon, positioned close to Tac, began to take incoming mortar fire from the Taliban.

The two Recce Platoon Scimitars, commanded by Captain Andy Wilde and Sergeant Jamie Hill, pushed out to try to locate the Taliban mortar position. They identified a motorbike with two riders. One had an AK47 slung over his back; the other was speaking into a radio, directing the Taliban mortar fire. Hill's vehicle opened up with 30mm HE, killing the riders and destroying the bike.

10

In the Green Zone, Aston was getting increasingly frustrated. B Company was still under fire from Taliban positions to the south, and there had also been some sporadic fire from the north-east. 7 Platoon and Sergeant Nieves had identified the treeline that the fire was coming from, and the Vikings were aggressively engaging with their machineguns. But the enemy positions were well prepared, and even the heaviest ground fire was having little effect.

As Aston had asked, the JTAC secured an attack helicopter. He transmitted the grid and target description to the Army Air Corps WAH-64 Apache Longbow commander sitting overhead, but so far the pilot had not been able to identify the enemy. Nieves and Nadriva had indicated the centre of mass of the target area with smoke bombs. The helicopter had been overhead now for more than an hour, but had not engaged.

The JTAC said to Aston, 'He repeats what he told us before, he cannot fire until he has positively identified the target.'

Fuming, Aston replied, 'Well *I* have PID'd the target. *The Viking crews* have PID'd the target. *7 Platoon* has. How much more PIDing does he need?'

'Sir, he says he needs to PID it himself before he can engage.'

'Look I used to be in a helicopter recce squadron. I know how difficult it is to identify people from the air if they are well concealed, even with the kind of kit these fellas up there have nowadays. But *we're firing* at the enemy, the Apache pilot can *see* our tracer. The enemy's firing *back* at us, and the pilot can see their tracer too. *What is the problem?*'

The JTAC said nothing. He was equally frustrated and annoyed.

The helicopter circled overhead, searching for the enemy, valuable minutes ticking by. Aston, impatient to move on towards his objective, was getting increasingly angry.

'What is he bothered about? Is it civvies in the area? There aren't any. But if there had been, we'd have killed them all by now with our guns. Is it friendlies? Is he worried about a blue on blue? Tell him there are positively, *positively* no friendlies there. I can *personally* guarantee it.'

The JTAC spoke again into his radio link to the Apache pilot.

'Sir, he says he *cannot* engage until he positively IDs an armed enemy – him personally, not us on the ground.'

Aston was raging. He refused to believe the Apaches had to work under such a ridiculous constraint – in this situation. He was desperate to get moving. But he couldn't use any other aircraft while the Apache was overhead. He couldn't engage with artillery or mortars either, because of the danger to the Apache of shells flying through the air.

He said, 'Let's get rid of him now. We'll get something else on to it. Tell the pilot – repeat these words to him *exactly* from me – fire at the target now or get out. Got that? Fire at the target or get out!'

It was 1100 hours. Aston turned to Corporal Wilsher, his mortar fire controller. 'The minute the Apache clears the airspace start engaging with mortars. I want HE up and down that treeline. Can you do that, or will the mortar line commander need to drive over here and do some PIDing in person?'

He turned back to the JTAC. 'While he's doing that, get me some proper close air support.'

Within a few minutes the mortars were pounding the treeline with 81mm high-explosive shells, blasting up enormous clouds of black smoke and grey dust, splintering the trees, and shaking the ground. But they seemed to have little more effect on the enemy than the machine-guns.

Forty-five minutes later the JTAC said to Aston, 'GR7 now on task. Before I send the grid, please confirm.'

Aston checked the grid, agreed it, and a few minutes later the RAF Harrier GR7 jump jet released a 500-pound bomb.

'Splash in five seconds,' said the JTAC.

Watching the target area, Aston was amazed at what he saw. The Harrier's 500-pound bomb hurtled into the enemy-held woodline. Huge lumps of dirt flew up into the air. But there was no blast and no bang.

'What the hell's that supposed to be, delayed action?'

The JTAC spoke into his radio and replied, 'No, it was a dud.' He listened to a message coming over his radio. 'Sir, the Harrier only has a 1,000-pound bomb left. Our nearest troops are 350 metres. That is very close for a bomb that size – danger close.'

Aston and the JTAC discussed the implications. Aston concluded that there was a risk of residual blast or shrapnel, but his closest troops were under armour in the Vikings and therefore well protected at that range, and the others could get down in the ditches. Compared to the dangers of continued RPG and smallarms fire from the Taliban, he decided this was a risk worth taking.

'Tell him to drop it,' he said.

Moments later Aston was smiling for the first time in a while when the Harrier dropped a 1,000-pound Paveway II laser-guided bomb directly into the centre of the enemy position. There was a massive, deafening thunderclap explosion. The ground reverberated under the B Company soldiers' feet. A huge column of fire leapt up into the sky, followed by an enormous mushroom cloud of smoke and dust, which seemed to hang above the treeline for an age.

Aston doubted anything or anyone could have survived the hell that was created where the bomb landed. A lump of shrapnel was hurled all the way over the Green Zone and crashlanded into the dirt directly in front of the FSG, nearly 1,000 metres away to the north.

11

The airstrike ended the enemy fire from the south, and B Company started to move forward again. But almost immediately they were met with volley after volley of RPGs, coming in from the north, bursting overhead and exploding against the trees, sending showers of dirt, twigs and branches down on the forward troops, who had hurled themselves to the ground.

B Company was approaching the western outskirts of Deh Adan Khan, the mythical stronghold used by the Taliban for terrorizing the citizens of Gereshk, and they were not planning to let them in.

Aston rattled out quick battle orders to Seal-Coon, and 7 Platoon lined up behind the cover of the lead Vikings, ready to assault a compound to the north where some of the fire was coming from. Howes's 5 Platoon had closed up behind 7 Platoon, ready to push through when 7 took the compound, or to reinforce should the enemy decide to hold it in strength. As 7 Platoon prepared to move in, a torrent of machine-gun, rifle and RPG fire fell on 5 Platoon, coming from another position, further north.

It was now clear that early this morning the Taliban had been surprised by the audacity and strength of the battle group operation, something they had not experienced before. But, demonstrating their resourcefulness and fighting ability, they had now rallied forces and were doing everything they could to inflict damage on the advancing British troops.

5 Platoon section commander Corporal Si Thorne heard the rapid crack-crack-crack-crack-crack of bullets flying overhead and then several whooshes in quick succession as RPGs shot towards them from a compound 200 metres away. The men hit the ground, then immediately got on to one knee to return fire. Seconds later there was a distant rumble, followed by a series of ear-piercing crumps as Taliban mortar bombs landed 40 metres away, spewing up dirt, ripping down tree-branches and hurling jagged shards of shrapnel in every direction. Hearts in their throats, Thorne's men jumped straight into a deep water-filled irrigation ditch.

Aston, standing near by, saw an engineer fall backwards into a ditch as an RPG exploded 4 metres from him. Fearing he had been killed or wounded, Aston rushed over, but before he got there, the soldier had climbed back up and dusted himself off. He looked shocked and stunned, but unhurt.

The firing and the mortars stopped, and Thorne called to his men, 'Get back up, out of the ditch.'

They tried to scramble out, using tree roots to claw themselves up the steep, muddy bank so they could get some fire back down.

'Get that GPMG up on to the top,' shouted Thorne. 'Get some rapid fire down.'

As the GPMG gunner struggled up the side of the ditch, Thorne slipped, sliding back down into the water. A burst of fire splattered into the bank exactly where his head had been. Unable to believe his luck, he scrabbled back up the bank and deployed his men to cover the firing position to the north: 'Scan the area. Any movement, any sign of enemy – open fire.'

To the right, the Vikings opened up with their GPMGs on the compound 7 Platoon were about to assault, keeping the enemy's heads down as Seal-Coon led his troops forward.

Corporal Stuart Parker, one of Seal-Coon's section commanders, moved in with his men under the protective fire from the Vikings. To get to the compound they had to wade across a putrefying, muddy irrigation canal, 3 metres wide. As they reached the bank, automatic fire peppered the far side and splashed into the river. RPGs burst overhead and detonated in the soft ground near by, hurling up shrapnel and lumps of earth. They threw themselves to the ground, just short of the canal.

As he lay pressing himself into the dirt, Parker thought how amazing it was that he could actually see the RPGs. He always assumed they would be flying too fast. One of the senior corporals in the battalion, Parker had been in the Army for many years but never before had an RPG fired at him. In his typical unfazed and sardonic manner, he thought, *Another first to tell the grandchildren about, I suppose.*

The rocket- and gunfire was coming from a small but solid compound, 70 metres away to the left. Parker and his section stayed down as the nearest Vikings traversed their guns and began to shoot up the compound, ripping fire across the front of Parker's section. Despite the hail of magine-gun bullets blasting in from the Vikings, the enemy fire continued undiminished.

Captain Goodman, the Viking troop commander, in one of the forward vehicles, radioed to a Viking further back along the track to the west, calling for a Javelin to engage the compound. Lance Corporal Michael Auckland, a member of the Royal Anglians' Anti-Tank Platoon attached to B Company, jumped from the vehicle. He reached back in and grabbed an olive-green, 1-metre-long Javelin missile tube and his command launch unit, or CLU. Capable of engaging out to a range of 2,500 metres, the missile contained tandem shaped-charge warheads. The Javelin tube would be discarded after the missile was fired. The CLU was a portable TV-sized, cube-shaped black box with a vertically mounted black hand grip either side, with optics and numerous switches. It contained the sight unit and operator's controls, and was retained for further missile firing.

A B Company soldier followed Auckland out of the Viking, carrying the Javelin tripod. As the two exited the vehicle, bullets sliced through the air and RPGs exploded near by. Running to the side of the Viking, Auckland slammed the teeth of the CLU into the matching grooves in the missile housing, locking it in place. The other soldier had positioned the tripod on the ground, bedding it into the dirt to make a solid platform, and Auckland snapped on the CLU, securing it and the missile to the tripod. Auckland clicked the power switch to day mode, grabbed the handles and traversed the CLU until he could see the target building, 90 metres away, through the x4 magnification sight. Through loopholes in the compound walls, he could see muzzle flashes very clearly.

He squeezed the trigger on the left handgrip. Three seconds later, as the Javelin missile's seeker head activated, the picture turned green. Auckland was now viewing the target through the missile itself. Hearing a whining noise from the missile, he knew he had ten seconds before the seeker head cooled. He waited patiently for what seemed like an age, stinging sweat dripping into his eyes and blurring his vision. The amber light in his sight picture went out, and the track gates appeared – graticules making up four corners of a square. With his thumb Auckland manipulated the Xbox-style direction pad, or D-pad, on the top of the right handgrip to adjust the track gate, bringing the four corners close in around the image of the compound. He squeezed and held the left hand trigger. *Will it lock on first time?* he wondered.

It did, and the track gates disappeared, to be instantly replaced by a solid green crosshair. He left the missile on its pre-set top attack mode, hoping it would climb over the wall and explode inside the compound. Top attack was intended for targets at 150 metres and beyond, but Auckland hoped it would work at 90. He knew it would be a waste of time flying the missile directly into the compound wall, where it would explode without harming the enemy within.

He pulled the trigger on the right handgrip. Auckland had no further control over the Javelin. There was a loud whoosh as the missile screamed forward and seemed to dip towards the ground directly ahead. Immediately the second-stage propellant ignited, and the missile climbed steeply, flying towards the building, guided by its inbuilt imaging infrared seeker.

12

Still lying beside the ditch, with bullets coming in, Parker was impressed to see the Javelin missile plunge down and score a direct hit on the enemy firing position. There was a blinding flash, and a huge explosion and clouds of smoke billowed upwards and out of the loopholes. All firing stopped.

Job done, thought Parker as he led his men to the bank and down into the canal. They waded across, brown, stagnant water up to their chests.

The men, sweating and weighed down by their heavy and now water-logged equipment, dragged themselves up the steep and slippery mud bank then headed right towards the target compound, behind Corporal Steph Martin's section, stacked up along the wall waiting to break in. As they moved into position a volley of RPGs exploded near by and others zoomed overhead. On the ground again, Parker watched as two of the Vikings traversed their machine-guns and simultaneoulsy let rip at the Taliban firing positions with a loud staccato blast of bullets.

Job done again, thought Parker.

Waiting to move through, Parker and his section piled into an alley-way. Private Aaron McLure, Parker's Minimi gunner, said, 'I can hear voices.'

Parker looked at him quizzically. McLure was one of his top soldiers, not one to hear voices that weren't there. He took his point man, Private Robert Foster, and went to check the right-hand side of the compound. They rounded the corner and were greeted by a burst of automatic fire from the undergrowth to their front, cracking into the wall behind them. Foster immediately fired thirty rounds back in rapid succession. Private Josh Lee ran forward, dropped to one knee and thumped out three rifle grenades. At the same time, the whole area in front of them was ripped up by a GPMG raking to and fro from the turret of a nearby Viking.

The assaulting section blasted their way into the compound at attack state red, with bar-mines, hand grenades and automatic fire. Parker and his section raced in behind. The compound was empty. The Taliban fighters had left, using carefully reconnoitred and concealed routes through the opposite side.

Parker heard Corporal Jimmy Naylor, Aston's signaller, send a SITREP on the command net. 'All stations this is Two One Alpha. Ugly callsign reports they have engaged and killed six Taliban with heavy machine-guns and mortars moving away from callsign Three Zero.'

'Ugly' was the callsign indicator used by the British Apache attack helicopters, and 'Three Zero' was Seal-Coon's 7 Platoon. It sounded as if the Apache had cut down the enemy who were moving out of the compound to reposition themselves.

Seal-Coon moved past Parker's section, heading back the way they had come. 'Hi, Corporal P, I'm going to the OC. He has called for a face-to-face. I'll be back shortly then we should know what's happening next. All your men OK?'

As Seal-Coon walked quickly back to meet Aston, he heard ferocious gunfire a few hundred metres to the north. Second Lieutenant Howes's 5 Platoon were under attack. Howes was out in the open and exposed with Private Scott Corless. Fire poured in from what seemed like every direction at the same time. Howes and Corless flung themselves down. They crawled back towards the rest of the platoon, keeping as low and moving as fast as they could. They were both exhausted after advancing all morning in the almost unbearable heat, but adrenalin, and the torrent of bullets, made them forget that. Corless was ahead of Howes, and Howes saw bullets slicing right next to his head as he turned and called, 'Come on, boss, keep going. We've got to keep going.'

The rest of the platoon, in cover, were furiously returning fire at the enemy with every weapon they had, and some of their bullets were licking close to Howes and Corless.

Finally the two made it to a ditch occupied by one of the sections and rolled over the parapet into the muddy, waist-deep water. Corless, blowing hard and dripping with sweat after his desperate crawl, pulled himself straight back up into a fire position and began shooting back at the enemy.

Also breathing hard, pouring sweat and standing in the dirty water, Howes was on the radio, checking his sections, which were widely dispersed. They were all now under enemy fire from three sides.

Next to Howes was the surreal sight of Taff, a huge engineer and former Welsh Guardsman, who had just been CASEVACed with heat exhaustion from one of the forward sections. He was standing in the water, shirt off, and holding in his left hand an intravenous drip that had been inserted into his arm by a medic just before the firing started. With his right hand, he was firing his rifle, supported against the bank. An RPG exploded in the bank between Taff and Private Allan Sheppard. A lump of shrapnel hit Sheppard in the eye and he was CASEVACed back for medical treatment.

Bullets and RPGs continued to land horribly close to Howes and his men. A cascade of tree branches and leaves dropped on to them, cut down by enemy fire. Despite the closeness and the intensity of the fire, every man had his head up and was shooting back. Howes was impressed. For most, this was their first serious contact. All of them, even the youngsters who had only recently arrived in the battalion, were hungry for the fight, determined to give back to the Taliban more than the Taliban were giving out.

Right and left, Howes's other sections were sending blistering fire back into the enemy positions. AT4 missiles were fired at the compound walls, but they had little effect: massive blasts but no penetration of the thick, baked mud. Howes shouted, 'UGLs, try to get UGLs in through the loopholes!'

In response to Howes's order, many 40mm UGL high-explosive grenades were fired, but very few riflemen achieved the accuracy needed to send them through the tiny apertures in the compound walls. Private Thomas Cox was the exception. At twenty-six, Cox was one of the oldest privates in the company, and one of the best. With astonishing accuracy he succeeded in blasting at least six of the grenades in from 70 metres. 5 Platoon's morale was already sky high. But everyone got a boost when they heard the loud, muffled blasts inside the compounds, followed by clouds of smoke and dust forced back out through the windows, following each of Cox's crack shots. They could only imagine what became of the fighters caught inside.

Cox's accuracy was matched by his bravery. Bullets scythed through the air either side of him when he stood up, levelled his rifle and fired the under-slung grenade launcher – again and again.

The Taliban fire reduced but did not stop, and 5 Platoon's return fire continued with the same aggression and intensity as it had begun.

Company Sergeant Major Newton appeared from nowhere behind Howes's position, 7 metres away. Above the noise of gunfire, the Sergeant Major yelled urgently, at the top of his voice, 'Mr Howes, Mr Howes – on me.'

Using the military signal, he placed his hand on top of his helmet and then shook his fist, indicating, *come to me quickly*.

Responding to the Sergeant Major's call, Howes pulled himself out of the ditch, dodged the bullets and crawled on his belt buckle to the hole Newton was standing in. 'What's up, Sar'nt Major?'

'Have you got any cigarettes, sir?'

'What are you talking about, Sar'nt Major?'

'I just needed a fag, sir, thought you might have one.'

'No. I *haven't* got any fags. You've made me crawl across that *for cigarettes*?'

'Oh sorry, sir, I didn't know it'd be a big deal.'

Howes looked at him incredulously. Recently out of Sandhurst, as an officer cadet he was used to being ragged by warrant officers and senior NCOs on the staff there, but in the middle of a pitched battle . . .

Newton laughed and said, 'No, I'm only joking. The company commander wants to see you.'

Newton led Howes back to Aston, positioned near the Vikings on the towpath. Aston was standing with the men of his Tac HQ and Seal-Coon, who grinned and nodded at Howes as he arrived.

'Glad you could find the time to join us, sprog. I hope I haven't inconvenienced you,' said Aston, allowing himself a moment of humour, but knowing full well what Howes had just been through. 'Your boys OK?'

'Yeah, they're fine. Doing well.'

Aston spoke to the group. 'OK, fellas. I'll be brief. Because we haven't got a lot of time. 6 Platoon are in a compound at Objective 8 and surrounded by Taliban. They can't get out. I ordered Dave Broomfield to break out and link up with 7 Platoon. Sergeant Browning tried to lead them out but apparently he got blown off his feet by several RPGs as he came out of the compound gate. I think he's pretty much OK. Would take quite a bit to damage Ben Browning.' He smiled. 'Anyway, they're penned into the compound, but they're still trying to get out. We have to assume they won't be able to. We'll smash our way through the compounds between here and 6 Platoon and bust them out. We're at present in contact from three sides so we need to break contact first. 7 Platoon have got into that compound, and are holding there right now.' He gestured to the north, where Seal-Coon's men were waiting for orders. 'Ben. Note I am not calling you sprog. Ben, you will withdraw your platoon from where they are now and push through alongside 7 Platoon. You will then break into the compound just beyond them. Then both platoons will echelon through each other, compound by compound, until you can link up with 6 Platoon and break them out of there. I will move right behind the lead platoon and control your movement.

'I have air on task now. Fortunately the last Apache produced the goods. Unlike the one that was here before, who just held us up for an hour. But we won't get much chance to use air as this is so close, and we can't afford any friendly fire. The Taliban are doing a good enough job without us helping them.' He smiled again. 'We also have artillery and mortars if we need them. And the Vikings will give as much support as they can from the track. Just call them up if you need to use them. I will do the same if I see an opportunity. The FSG can't help us. They can't get eyes on into here let alone fire anything, but they're still pinning the enemy into HBK.

'That's it. I need momentum and I need speed. Ben, let me know as soon as you've broken contact in the north and your platoon's moving. You have ten minutes at most, do you think you can make it?'

'I'll do my best, sir,' Howes said and, without waiting for the inevitable follow-up comment from Aston, ran straight back towards the firing around his platoon.

'Just get it done, Ben,' shouted Aston after him. He grinned. He liked to see a bit of urgency.

Despite his calmness and brusque humour, Aston was only too aware of the dire situation 6 Platoon were in. They were surrounded and couldn't break out. With the resistance the Taliban were putting up throughout Deh Adan Khan, it could be a long time before the rest of B Company fought their way to them.

He wondered whether the Taliban could reinforce in 6 Platoon's area and close in to overwhelm them. They certainly knew and understood the ground well enough to be able to get very close in without being spotted, and there were probably tunnels galore all round the compounds.

On the other hand, he knew 6 Platoon was prepared and should be able to defend their compound against an enemy assault. He had Apaches up which would hopefully identify and break up any significant Taliban reinforcement.

Aston reflected, *'should be able to...'* and *'hopefully...'* Not good enough. He did indeed need speed and momentum. Before something terrible happened to the encircled 6 Platoon...

13

Pouring down a massive weight of fire, and leapfrogging back by sections, Howes and his men broke contact with the enemy to the north, then pulled back to the area of 7 Platoon's compound. It was grindingly hard work, down, fire, up, move back, down, fire. Wading streams, crawling through the dirt, struggling through thick vegetation. The men were tired and dripping sweat.

Quickly Howes briefed his section commanders, 'We are breaking into that compound. Going in red. Entry point is the left-hand side on the corner. We will use the ditch we're in to crawl up. Corporal Thorne, 2 Section will break in, I will be behind you, followed by 1 Section then 3 Section. Any questions? No. Brief the guys and let's go. Corporal T, move as soon as you're ready.'

Thorne led his section through the filthy ditch towards the compound, accompanied by two engineers, one of whom was Taff, now without his drip.

The engineers prepared a bar-mine, inserting a detonator and safety fuze into the explosive. It was actually half of an L9 plastic anti-tank mine. Just over half a metre in length and containing 4 kilograms of RDX/TNT explosive, this charge was often used by the Royal Engineers for explosive entry in Afghanistan.

With two of Thorne's riflemen providing close protection, Taff and his mate raced to the side of the building and set up the mine against the wall. They could hear voices inside the compound. Taff lit the forty-second fuze with a windproof match, then the engineers and cover men dashed into a dip in the ground and pressed their fingers into their ears. Thorne was 10 metres off, but the intense blast and pressure shocked and deafened him and sucked his breath away. He had never before experienced such an enormous explosion, intensified by the high compound walls on either side. Everything was shrouded in a massive cloud of thick dust.

Immediately, Privates Jason Tower and Ian McIlroy rushed to the hole in the wall, barely able to see through the blinding dust. McIlroy turned to look at Thorne for a thumbs-up. He couldn't see him through the dust so, rather than risk wasting time, hurled in an L109 grenade and pressed himself back against the outer wall. Three seconds later the grenade exploded, blasting out shrapnel and kicking up more dust in every direction. McIlroy swung in front of the hole and fired his SA80. After one round the rifle jammed.

Shouting 'Stoppage,' he hurled himself face-down. This was second nature. They had trained for it over and again, and now it was working. A stoppage at this critical moment must not cause any kind of pause in the momentum of the assault. Speed and shock were critical in killing the enemy and avoiding own casualties.

Tower ran straight over his back, firing twenty rapid, single shots into the room as he went. He moved right and pressed himself against the wall. Corporal Thorne, also running in across McIlroy's back, was right behind, straight in and left.

The remainder of the section poured through, each trampling over the hapless McIlroy. Once the last man was inside, McIlroy pulled himself to his feet, bruised and battered, with cuts to his face. Feeling as though he had just done five rounds with Amir Khan, he rushed into the room, knelt in a corner, cleared the stoppage and reloaded his rifle.

Thorne had already started detailing the two-man assault teams off to check each of the rabbit warren of small rooms inside the compound. As they entered, each team hurled in a grenade and followed up with rapid fire.

After half an hour the section had cleared every room and a small orchard within the compound. They found no one. The fighters who had fired at them from these buildings must have departed as soon as the bar-mine exploded.

The Taliban were employing their usual modus operandi – shoot from a compound or the area near by, try to draw the soldiers in and kill them as they approach, then escape along well-prepared rat-runs to start shooting from another position. The network of compounds, surrounded by high walls, and the dense vegetation of the Green Zone, made these tactics extremely effective. Only if the Taliban could be taken by surprise or caught out in the open was it possible to kill them.

The minute Howes reported over the company net, 'Compound clear,' Seal-Coon pushed 7 Platoon forward into the next one.

Corporal Parker's section led the assault. His engineers blasted through the wall with a half bar-mine, tearing out lumps of solid-baked mud and hurling huge clouds of dust and smoke in every direction.

Privates Foster and McLure, Parker's lead assault team, each had an L109 high-explosive grenade to shred any fighters immediately inside.

The two men were about to fling the grenades in, but the dust began to clear and they were horrified by what they saw inside.

In the same instant, both soldiers screamed '*Stop – stop – stop!*' in a desperate attempt to halt the attack.

Foster and McLure entered the courtyard, weapons in the shoulder, fingers on triggers, scanning through their sights. Nine women, several young children and an old man sat in terrified silence. Holding their hands up to stop the bullets they expected, they had the look of people who were about to die.

These were the first civilians the soldiers had seen since entering the Green Zone. Once they were sure there were no armed fighters in the courtyard or adjoining rooms, Foster and McLure each held up a hand and forced smiles, trying to reassure the locals that they were not going to kill them.

Parker moved in, followed by Seal-Coon, who told his interpreter to talk to the people, calm them down and question them on enemy activity. Foster and McLure were horrified and shaking. Both were more than willing to close with and kill the Taliban, but what they had almost done simply did not bear thinking about. McLure nodded agreement as Foster said to Parker, 'We nearly killed them. Thank God we saw them before we chucked the grenades in. I couldn't live with myself if I'd killed those old women and those kids, or that old bloke. We really scared them too. Even that makes me feel bad.'

As Foster spoke Parker heard the company signaller's voice through his earpiece. Naylor was again relaying reports from the Apaches overhead. 'All stations this is Two One Alpha. From JTAC. Ugly callsigns have identified four to five enemy moving in the open 300 metres to the north-east of callsign Three Zero's forward location. Ugly callsigns engaging now with 30mm. Out.'

14

Lieutenant Dave Broomfield's 6 Platoon had made several valiant efforts to break through the Taliban fighting positions that encircled their compound, but had not succeeded. They had other problems too. In the oppressive and debilitating 50-degree heat, the remainder of the company had received water resupplies from the Vikings shadowing their movement through the Green Zone. Despite that, two soldiers had gone down with heat exhaustion, an enemy in some cases even deadlier than the Taliban. But 6 Platoon had run out of water some time ago and could not be resupplied.

Corporal Joel Adlington noticed one of his soldiers had a glazed look in his eyes. Private Josh Hill was the youngest man in the battalion. He was eighteen, but looked more like fourteen. Having trained at the Army Apprentice College, Harrogate, and the Infantry Training Centre, Catterick, he joined the Royal Anglians just before the tour began. He had settled in quickly and was performing well in Afghanistan. Adlington was impressed by the bravery he had shown so far on Silicon, and by his determination to get the job done and never let down his mates. Now he was shaking and looking pale.

Adlington said, 'How do you feel, Hill?'

'Fine, thanks, Corporal.'

'No you don't,' said Adlington, 'you look terrible. Sit down there in the shade by the wall.'

They were outside in the compound's open courtyard. Private Jamie Muley, a half-Turkish soldier from Essex, came over to help. They stripped off Hill's assault vest and body armour. Adlington had a drop of water left and made him sip it. He said to Muley, 'Go and get some water from the well, bring it back here and start pouring it on his head and his clothes.'

He undid Hill's belt, unbuttoned his trousers and pulled up his T-shirt to let air in. Then he removed his boots and socks. Muley came back and dowsed him with well-water, soaking his hair, T-shirt and combat trousers.

Despite this Hill was deteriorating fast. His eyes started rolling, and his shaking became more severe. The platoon sergeant, Ben Browning, came across with Lieutenant Broomfield. Browning said, 'Muley, sit behind him and prop him up. He needs to be half sitting. Keep pouring water on his hair and down the back of his neck. Talk to him, keep him with us.'

He ruffled Hill's hair, 'All right, mate? How do you feel?'

Hill groaned quietly but couldn't speak. Then he started panting loudly and shaking more vigorously. Broomfield and Browning knew how serious this could get. Hill was suffering from heat exhaustion. His body temperature had risen from a normal 37 degrees to around 38 degrees or higher. If he could be stabilized he would be fine. But if heat exhaustion progressed to heat stroke he could be dead in minutes.

The two leaders walked out of earshot. Broomfield said, 'He looks quite bad. Corporal Adlington reckons he was pretty much OK ten minutes ago and now he can't even speak. I'm sure he'll be fine if they keep working on him. What worries me is if he does get worse – I mean really bad – how the hell are we going to get him CASEVACed? We can't even get out of this compound with everyone running and shooting. There's no possibility at all of carrying a casualty.'

'I agree. Absolutely no chance at all,' said Browning.

Browning looked over at Hill, propped up by Muley, eyes rolling, very, very pale. His panting seemed to be getting louder and faster. 'I think I'll radio the sergeant major and see if we can get the doc to give us some advice. See if he can tell us how to make sure Hill doesn't get any worse.'

Browning waited for a pause on the company command net then spoke into his PRC-355 radio. After a couple of minutes he got the medical officer on the radio. In a clipped message to minimize traffic on the extremely busy net that Aston was using to control the rest of the company, Browning rattled out Hill's symptoms and the treatment he was being given.

The doctor said, 'Keep giving him water. Soon he will stop shaking and he should start breathing normally. After that he will get his speech back. Let me know if this does not happen within two hours, especially if he doesn't recover his normal breathing soon. And good luck. You've been doing the right thing so far. Out.'

Everything that the doctor said would happen did happen, almost precisely in the time and sequence he had predicted. After two hours, Hill was fully dressed and equipped, back on his feet and doing his job.

15

Carver's plan had been to move A Company through the desert in the north, keeping roughly level with B Company in the Green Zone. A Company remained in their Vikings and moved forward without opposition, shadowing B Company as they fought slowly through Deh Adan Khan from compound to compound, resisted by the Taliban every step of the way.

Carver came up with a plan that he hoped might unlock the situation, allowing Aston to move through the Green Zone more rapidly. He knew the Taliban usually withdrew if they thought they were being outflanked and faced being cut off from behind. He discussed with Biddick on the battle group command net the idea that A Company would drive east, and feint into the Green Zone, well beyond B Company's forward troops. A feint is a military term for a fake move. The idea was to create the impression that they were going to strike into the Green Zone, but they would actually stop short.

Carver hoped this might panic the enemy into retreating in front of B Company. It would potentially catch them in the open where they could be destroyed from the air. He had Apache attack helicopters waiting.

Biddick suggested an even more audacious plan. A Company's objective for the next day was the Taliban stronghold of Habibollah Kalay, a village right on the edge of the Green Zone, around 1 kilometre north-east of B Company's current position. He said, 'I can attack and hold HBK today. There will be time to do it before last light if I move now. It will also create the impression that we are moving to cut off the Taliban. Two birds with one stone.'

Carver liked the idea, but there were issues to consider. HBK was assessed to be a significant Taliban stronghold. He had no doubt that A Company had the capability to clear the enemy out of the village.

But with B Company already embroiled in a tough fight, there was a risk that committing A Company to a potentially serious battle at the same time would stretch his limited resources very thin – especially air, mortars and artillery. And the day was drawing on. It would be dark in a couple of hours, and taking just part of the village then having to go firm at last light risked all sorts of nightmares as the Taliban attempted night infiltration attacks around the rat-runs of HBK. On the other hand, presenting the Taliban with a second concurrent threat could certainly unlock B Company's battle. And keeping up the momentum now might well deny the enemy the chance to concentrate resources and do damage to the battle group the following day. It was a tough decision, which could have profound consequences either way. But taking tough decisions was the battle group commander's job. Carver spoke to Biddick on the radio: 'Attack Habibollah Kalay. Attack as soon as you can, but if you don't secure the whole of the village by last light, be prepared to withdraw to the desert and go in again in the morning.'

Biddick had been keen to attack the Taliban, although his enthusiasm was tempered somewhat by A Company's experience in Nowzad a week earlier. Seated in the front of his Viking, he acknowledged Carver's orders and switched straight to the company net, 'All stations, this is Zero Alpha. We will assault HBK. H-Hour not before 1530. O Group 1500 at callsign Two Two Alpha's vehicle. Out.'

Kicking up clouds of dust, he drove forwards in the Viking to a position where he could overwatch Habibollah Kalay. He took out an air photo of the village and drew a schematic of his attack plan. The village sat in the desert, right on the edge of the Green Zone. A Company would move up from their current position to the south-west and assault from that direction. It was the best-covered approach.

Biddick motored back to the Company 2IC's Vector, positioned beside a compound to the rear of the Red Fort. Captain Paul Steel, the 2IC, had assembled the commanders.

It took Biddick less than ten minutes to give orders – 'Quick Battle Orders' according to the book – for the company group attack, involving three rifle platoons, Fire Support Group Delta under Captain Ollie Ormiston, the Recce Platoon, snipers, engineers, air and indirect fire support. As he rattled through the plan, enemy mortar shells landed near by. A Company had been harassed by mortars and rockets all day, and were now inured to them. Biddick continued his orders without even acknowledging the blasts a few metres away.

He concluded, 'H-Hour for the attack is confirmed as 1540 hours. If the fire support team can't arrange fires for that time, then H-Hour might slip, but work on 1540 unless I tell you otherwise.' He looked at his watch. 'That gives you less than fifteen minutes to brief your men and get down to the FUP. I assume there are no questions. Good luck.'

Scrambling across the desert with maps and air photos in one hand and rifles in the other, the commanders and sergeants raced to rejoin their platoons. Fifteen minutes was just – but only just – long enough to do everything they needed for the attack. But they knew time was critical. They were also used to Biddick demanding the impossible and knew better than not to deliver it.

The Vikings moved across the desert to the debussing point, shielded from Habibollah Kalay by the high walls of what looked like an old fort. They were about 400 metres from the village.

It is too dangerous to move vehicles much closer to an urban or densely vegetated area without infantry on the ground, as they are vulnerable to RPG fire. One well-aimed missile could severely damage a Viking and injure or kill the men inside.

It was a relief for the A Company soldiers to get out of their Vikings. They had been sitting in them for most of the day, waiting to move forward. They had also been listening enviously all day on the company net to reports of B Company's fighting and wanted some of the action for themselves.

Second Lieutenant Nick Denning's 1 Platoon moved rapidly on foot to a vantage point 50 metres from the Green Zone. Their mission was to act as flank guard. They would protect 2 Platoon from fire out of the Green Zone as they broke into the village. Lieutenant Bjorn Roses's 3 Platoon remained with the vehicles as company reserve, ready to react to enemy interfering with the attack, reinforce one of the other platoons or echelon through to exploit.

Lieutenant Graham Goodey led 2 Platoon into the attack. Corporal Niphit Sawasdee's section, with their engineers, blew a gap in the perimeter wall with a half bar-mine. But as the platoon assaulted into the village, a heavy weight of machine-gun fire poured out of the Green Zone.

Major Biddick was up on the high ground to the west, with the FSG. Immediately identifying the enemy firing positions he blasted fire back with his SA80. Straight away, every GPMG and .50 cal machine-gun in the FSG, as well as Biddick's Viking gunner, joined in, hosing the Taliban with bullets.

Led by Goodey's 2 Platoon, A Company blasted their way through the village, compound by compound, attacking at state red. The place was deserted. The Taliban had all left. At first the troops saw no civilians. But when they got through towards the far side of the village, they found a group of locals sheltering inside one of the buildings.

Biddick ordered the company to switch to state green, assaulting into compounds without explosives or hand grenades to avoid causing civilian casualties.

Biddick had sent Colour Sergeant Al Thurston, Recce Platoon 2IC, with his four Scimitars, off to the west. Their job was classic recce work – monitor for enemy reinforcements moving in and warn the company. If possible they would cut them down with their machine-guns or Rarden cannons before they got anywhere near Habibollah Kalay. They were also there to cut off any Taliban who tried to escape from the besieged village. But in Biddick's mind the most important part of his plan for the Recce Platoon was to draw enemy mortar and rocket fire on to their Scimitars and therefore away from the dismounted infantrymen. If handled properly the Scimitars, protected armoured vehicles capable of high mobility and fast movement, were far less vulnerable than infantry soldiers on their feet in the desert terrain. Biddick knew he was asking a lot of the Recce soldiers, but for him, emotion didn't enter the equation. It was straight, logical military judgement, and it made absolute sense.

Thurston moved east across the desert, in front of the Green Zone. He then deployed on to a high point, covering the eastern side of Habibollah Kalay, able to observe across the top of the built-up area and down into the Green Zone. His four vehicles were joined by WMIKs from Ormiston's FSG, redeployed after the initial break-in to HBK. Thurston was also joined for a time by the Recce Platoon commander, Captain Wilde, and by Sergeant Jamie Hill, in their two Scimitars. They were recceing the next position for Carver's Tac HQ.

As Thurston looked across the Green Zone, he realized that Carver's plan to induce an enemy withdrawal looked as if it was beginning to work. Expecting A Company to move south from Habibollah Kalay and drive into the rear of their fighting positions, the Taliban realized they would be caught in a trap between them and B Company's relentless advance.

They could not escape to the south, or they would be cut down in the open by Goodman's Viking machine-guns and the circling Apaches. Their route north across the desert was blocked by A Company's Vikings, the Recce Platoon and two FSGs.

In front of Thurston, almost 2 kilometres away, was a wide gap in the trees – like a massive fire-break – extending across the entire width of the Green Zone. And in ones and twos, carrying AK47 assault rifles, PKM machine-guns and RPG-7 launchers, Taliban fighters began to move as fast as they could from right to left across the gap, exposing themselves to the guns of more than a dozen Royal Anglian vehicles.

The WMIKs opened up first with their heavy machine-guns, sweeping back and forth across the fire-break. Thurston was determined that his Scimitars would not let a single fighter escape. These men had been attacking B Company all day, and those who survived would continue trying to kill Royal Anglian soldiers and Afghan troops and would carry on terrorizing the local population.

Thurston knew that his Scimitars' machine-guns, GPMGs adapted for an armoured turret and called L37s, were inaccurate at this range. An area weapon, the bullets would fall across a wide cone, known as the 'beaten zone'. Running through the beaten zone, you might well die, but you could be lucky and survive. Luck didn't come into it with the 30mm Rarden cannon, the Scimitar's main armament. Or, more precisely, the Rarden combined with one of the most effective pieces of technology available to the Royal Anglians, the BGTI, or battle group thermal imager.

Thurston gave fire control orders to his Scimitar commanders, dividing up the 'killing area' between them to avoid overkill on any particular target and make sure all were hit. In Thurston's line, commanding Iron Two Four, was Corporal Ash Hill, the NCO who had led B Company down to the FUP twelve hours earlier. Since then he had come close to death when an RPG missile fired at him from 70 metres whizzed just inches over his head. The other Scimitar in Hill's section, Iron Two Four Alpha, commanded by Lance Corporal James Ryan, had killed the three-man Taliban group with its L37.

Hill had not had any sleep at all the night before, and had been on the go non-stop for thirty-five hours. Like the rest of the Recce soldiers, he was filthy dirty, covered in dust, grime and oil, unshaven and dripping sweat in the turret of his vehicle which, for all its gunnery technology, had no air conditioning and was hotter than any sauna. He told Lance Corporal David Cadman, his gunner, 'We're firing HE.'

Cadman flicked the gunner's selector switch from coax to main armament. He peered into the BGTI's monitor, squinting in the bright sunlight that poured through the vehicle's open hatch above. The monitor resembled a small TV screen, with a green thermal picture. As soon as the first fighter entered Iron Two Four's sector, Cadman illuminated him with the BGTI's laser rangefinder. The ballistic aiming mark, a black dot, appeared over the fighter's figure. Cadman knew that, at that range, you put the dot on the target, push the button and it hits. Every time. Or virtually every time.

The 30mm high-explosive shell blasted from Iron Two Four's gun barrel towards the Taliban fighter at 1,070 metres per second. Less than two seconds after Cadman hit the firing button the shell exploded into the man's body.

Over the next forty-five minutes, the Recce Platoon and the FSG killed at least thirty Taliban fighters who were retreating in the face of B Company's advance and the feared threat from A Company.

Hill said, 'You know, Cads, I almost feel sorry for them. They've got absolutely no chance out there.'

Then he thought about his close shave a few hours earlier and said, 'Actually I don't feel sorry for them at all. Any of this lot could take a pot shot at us tomorrow, and maybe we'd get more than the extra parting we got in our hair today courtesy of that RPG.'

16

By 1730 hours A Company had secured most of Habibollah Kalay and were reorganizing, preparing to move again if Carver gave them a new task. They had not encountered any enemy in the village, but nevertheless it had been hard work in the oppressive afternoon heat. Running from position to position with their heavy battle loads, diving through doorways and holes blasted through compound walls, moving fast, keeping low. And not knowing what was round any corner, they were also using up huge reserves of nervous energy.

As were B Company down in the Green Zone. In line with Aston's plan, 5 and 7 Platoon continued their brutal clearance through the compounds of Deh Adan Khan towards 6 Platoon, leap-frogging from building to building.

Aston knew from the battle group command net, and from reports by his own platoons and the air, that many Taliban fighters started fleeing to the north-east soon after A Company entered HBK. He was determined that as many as possible would be killed as quickly as possible. He had learnt during the day that every extra second these resourceful and determined fighters were given would significantly increase their chances of survival. So he hatched a plan with his JTAC to deal with some of them up close to B Company's forward troops.

Aston called the platoon commanders on the company net. 'All stations, this is Zero Alpha. Apaches now on station overhead. I want to use them to mince as many Taliban as possible in the open. All callsigns to go firm now inside the compounds you are occupying. No further movement until ordered by me. One Zero, Two Zero and Three Zero, you are each to mark your positions with smoke, and keep that smoke coming until I order you to stop. The Apaches will hit any and all identified enemy not in locations marked by smoke.'

On Aston's command the Apaches swooped over the Green Zone directly in front of his platoons, peppering all signs of enemy movement with devastating blasts of fire from their lethal 30mm chain guns.

Once the attack helicopters had done their work, 5 and 7 Platoons continued to push forward towards 6 Platoon, without further resistance. Pouring sweat and exhausted after battling through the Green Zone all day, the platoons linked up. The 5 and 7 Platoon soldiers were jubilant that they had got through. Many of them had mates in 6 Platoon and they were all dreading the idea that the Taliban might move in and kill them.

Aston was also very relieved that his worst fears had not been realized, and as soon as the link-up had taken place and 6 Platoon resupplied with water and ammunition, he ordered the company to move forward again.

Earlier in the day Carver's Tac HQ had come under accurate fire from Taliban 107mm rockets and had moved north-east through the desert. They were now positioned near the Red Fort. As A Company were completing their task in Hababollah Kalay, Brigadier Lorimer, commander of Task Force Helmand, arrived at Tac.

Lorimer confirmed to Carver that Task Force 1 Fury, an air assault battalion from the famous US 82nd Airborne Division, would be landing to the north that night. They would aim to engage the Taliban and prevent them moving south to interfere with the construction of permanent patrol bases, scheduled to begin as soon as the Royal Anglians reached their limit of exploitation. Carver briefed the Brigadier on the day's most significant events, and his immediate intentions. Lorimer was impressed by the speed at which the Royal Anglian Battle Group had advanced through the Green Zone and the desert, which had significantly exceeded his expectations for Operation Silicon.

When Lorimer departed, Carver called Aston on the battle group command net. A Company had reached their limit of exploitation, a line on the map known as Report Line Purple, running north to south from the desert through the Green Zone and down to the battle group's southern boundary. They had entered HBK and cleared most of it. With darkness not far off, Biddick decided to move the company 800 metres north, back out into the desert, to avoid the threat of Taliban infiltration in the compounds and alleyways of the village.

The ANA company advancing in the south had also reached Purple, and had met little resistance since their earlier near-disaster in Zumberlay.

B Company, who had almost completed the clearance of the Deh Adan Khan compounds in the Green Zone, were still about 1,000 metres short of Line Purple.

Carver wanted to push B Company on to the limit of exploitation, level with the other two sub-units. He knew he would be asking a lot of Aston. B Company had taken by far the brunt of the fighting, and had been slogging it out with the Taliban in the most horrendous battle conditions virtually all day. If they couldn't achieve Line Purple, he would have to pull A Company and the ANA back a kilometre to conform with B Company, and move forward over the same ground the next day. In this terrain he couldn't risk leaving a gap at night. The Taliban would find ways to get round behind the three companies and would be in a position to wreak havoc.

Carver knew the soldiers would already be dead on their feet. He had discussed his intention with Captain Phil Moxey, the ops officer, and with the battery commander, Major Andrew Dawes. Neither had said outright that it would be a mistake, but he knew they were both thinking B Company had done enough, and the other companies should be pulled back.

This was another tough call, but Carver considered all the factors and made his decision quickly. On the radio he said to Aston, 'I want you to move forward to Report Line Purple, to the road, and get there by last light.'

Standing against a tree trunk in the middle of the Green Zone, Aston was as exhausted as his men. He looked at the soldiers near by. They were dripping with sweat, combat trousers ripped up from struggling through vegetation and hurling themselves to the ground under fire, dark rings under their eyes from lack of sleep, haggard. He was incredibly proud of what his men – many just boys – had done today. For most it had been their first day of battle. He had not seen any soldier or marine fail to do his duty. In fact, in Aston's eyes every man had done much more than his duty. Despite their exhaustion he knew their spirits were sky high, after a tough and extremely dangerous but intense and exciting day. But he also knew they wouldn't want to push on any further now, and he really didn't want to ask them to.

But the commanding officer had said what he wanted to happen, and ultimately that was good enough for Aston. As with Biddick, Aston expected the impossible from his subordinate commanders. And above everything else he believed in leading by example. If the CO wanted the impossible from Aston he had a right to get it.

Major Aston called the platoon commanders to him and told them what they were going to do, dismissing them with the usual, 'No time for questions, fellas. Just get it done.' Aston made no attempt to clear the remaining compounds on the way to Line Purple. He knew they would not contain any Taliban, as the fighters had fled en masse to the north-east.

As B Company moved rapidly in the footsteps of the withdrawing Taliban, they passed through the carnage that had been inflicted on the enemy by the Recce Platoon, the fire support groups and the Apaches. The fire-break area, just short of Line Purple, was littered with dead bodies, mostly blown to pieces by the 30mm cannons of Scimitars or Apaches. Aston saw one man lying with his stomach peeled open and his entrails spread over the surrounding area. His leg lay 5 metres away. The body of another seemed to be turned inside out. The whole area was criss-crossed with blood trails and pools of gore. The ground everywhere was pockmarked with fist-sized holes from 30mm cannon strikes.

As each platoon filed past the bodies, Aston saw that to a man the spirits of his soldiers were lifted by the sight of the Taliban dead. These were the first dead bodies many of his soldiers had ever seen. This was the physical embodiment of their success. They could see the results of their work that day; these were their enemy, men who had been trying to kill them just hours earlier.

When they reached Line Purple, Aston and his Tac HQ went firm beside an irrigation ditch. He ordered the platoons to move off to their pre-designated positions and start digging in.

He slowly surveyed the devastation near by. Something didn't quite add up. There was a large pool of blood next to the ditch...but no body. He noticed spots of blood leading right into the metre-deep irrigation ditch beside him. *A good escape route from this carnage.* He felt a tingle at the back of his neck, and that eerie feeling you get when you know you are being watched.

He turned to Naylor, his signaller, pointed to the ditch and hissed, 'Follow me.'

Aston moved, crouching beside the ditch. Naylor was across the ditch to his right, and Corporal Wilsher, the MFC, was behind. Aston suddenly realized they were on their own, moving away from the company towards an unknown threat.

He turned and called to Corporal Si Thorne, whose section was a few metres back, 'Come with us, Corporal T.' Privates Tower and Nadriva also joined the Tac group.

Aston started moving forward again, his heart now thumping with anticipation. A few metres on, he looked down into the ditch – straight at two armed Taliban, staring at him, lying just a metre away. For what seemed like an age but was just a split second, Aston locked eyes with one of them – a terrified, young, thin Taliban fighter.

As the man tried to bring his AK47 into the aim Aston fired into the heads and chests of both fighters.

Screaming, 'There's another one,' Naylor raced forward firing at a third fighter a few metres behind.

Aston moved to back Naylor up, and a burst of fire came from the right. Wilsher yelled, 'One Taliban in this hut, sir. I've killed him.'

Thorne searched the immediate area with Nadriva and Tower. He found RPG-7 warheads, AK47 rifles, belts of machine-gun ammunition. Looking at the way the weapons and ammunition were laid out, Thorne deduced that these men had been preparing an ambush, perhaps against vehicles moving along the adjacent track. He said to Tower, 'They never expected us to come up this far or this fast on foot.'

17

Back at battle group Tac HQ up in the desert, Carver was waiting for B Company to report that they had reached Line Purple and were firm in their defensive positions for the night. Instead he was shocked to hear a message from the company on the battle group command net: 'Eight men killed and three casualties, we need a medic.'

Carver felt sick. Immediately he thought, *They were totally knackered. I pushed them to the road. And now this has happened.*

There was a pause. Carver could feel everyone in his Tac HQ looking at him. They were as horrified as he was, and he knew they were thinking: That was a big call. How bad do you feel? After all the close fighting in the Green Zone through the day, he had been amazed that none of his soldiers had been killed or seriously wounded. A few minutes ago he had been thinking he couldn't believe his luck. And now the worst had happened...

But he was the commander, and he had no time to dwell on the rights and wrongs of his decision. He needed to make sure this situation was dealt with rapidly, and that the whole battle group was balanced for the night, with the defensive plan tied up. This could be a night when the enraged Taliban, decimated by the battle group's savage advances of the day, might try to use the cover of darkness to strike back.

Moments later, Carver's pain and anguish were instantly replaced by an even stronger sense of relief and elation. Moxey, who had been speaking urgently on the battle group net, trying to clarify the situation and line up the assets needed to deal with it, told him that the message had been garbled. The report had referred to Taliban dead, and B Company had captured three enemy wounded.

The following morning A Company moved back into Habibollah Kalay and completed the clearance of the village. Carver and the Royal Anglians' regimental sergeant major, Warrant Officer Class 1 Ian Robinson, visited B Company. While Carver and Aston discussed the next stage of the operation, Robinson and Company Sergeant Major Tim Newton walked round the company, talking to the troops.

Thirty-nine-year-old Robinson had been RSM of The 1st Battalion The Royal Anglian Regiment for eight months. He was from Bury St Edmunds in Suffolk, home to the Royal Anglian Regimental Headquarters. Regimental sergeant major of an infantry battalion, although junior in rank to all the officers, is second in prestige only to the commanding officer. He is the top soldier in the battalion, and has a critical, almost mythical, role in all aspects of battalion life, especially discipline, morale and the maintenance of standards. Standing only five foot six inches tall, Robinson was far from the stereotypical RSM. But most Royal Anglians – soldiers and officers – were in awe of him. He was respected even more for his strength of character, military competence and personal humanity than for the royal coat-of-arms he wore on his cuff.

Robinson went through everything with the men during the build-up to this operational deployment, and was eager to share in their hardships in Afghanistan whenever he could. Every soldier in the battalion who aspired to high rank considered Robinson to be their role model.

As they walked round the company position in the glaring morning sun, Robinson and Newton came across a group of young soldiers collecting the Taliban dead and placing them on to stretchers in preparation for handover to the ANA. The bodies had been dead for more than twelve hours and in the oppressive heat were putrefying. Most of them had been ripped apart by 30mm cannon fire or machine-gun bullets, and their insides had spilt out. Limbs and heads were detached from bodies. The corpses were blackening and covered in flies, and the smell was indescribable.

Robinson watched the soldiers, exhausted from the previous days' fighting, and looking haggard after just a few hours' much disturbed sleep lying on the rough ground. Their task was gruesome. Several of them were retching. One man moved away to throw up.

Robinson admired their stoical attitude. They were all young lads, and this was something none had done before and never expected to, even in their worst nightmares. This was not the stuff of the kind of war movies that first awaken the desire to become a soldier in most young boys who end up joining the infantry. But here they were, as ever just cracking on.

Robinson shouted out, 'Lads. Listen in. Stop what you are doing now. Go back to your platoons. You have done more than enough.'

The soldiers stopped and looked up in surprise. What was going on now? But there was never, ever, a need for the regimental sergeant major to say anything twice. And certainly no one was going to argue with this particular order.

Robinson called Sergeant Majors Mark Freeman and Jimmy Self, who had travelled with him from battle group Tac HQ, to join him and Company Sergeant Major Newton. He gathered them round and quietly briefed them on what he wanted them to do. Steeling themselves, the four Royal Anglian warrant officers completed the grim task.

Lance Corporal Ruecker, the sniper who had been commanding a WMIK in Snow's FSG the previous day, rejoined the sniper team with B Company.

The other snipers were sharing a compound with Seal-Coon's 7 Platoon. Ruecker walked through the door and looked around. The men were sorting out their kit, cleaning weapons or sleeping. And, as ever, sweating in the intense heat. They'd had a few hours' sleep but still looked worn-down and gaunt from the previous day's exertions. One or two were trying to do something about rashes they had down their backs and sides from body armour rubbing. All were scratching the flea bites they had acquired during a night on the filthy compound floor.

Corporal Parker said, 'Hello, Teddy me old mate, I didn't think you were going to grace us with your presence in Afghanistan.'

'Yeah, great to see you too, Stu. You guys been doing some fighting or something?'

Private Thrumble, Parker's GPMG gunner, said, 'It was quality, Teddy, absolute quality. What a day.'

Grinning from ear to ear, and gently caressing his machine-gun, he continued, 'I put some rounds down with this baby, mate, I can tell you. Never thought I'd do anything like that.'

'It was definitely a lot cheekier than Iraq, wasn't it?' said Ruecker. The two had been in the same platoon for the battalion's tour in southern Iraq over a year ago.

Then Ruecker looked at Thrumble's kit. He had rigged up an olive-green ammo bag, fixing it to his leg with bungees and cable ties. 'What the hell have you got on your leg, John? What is it?'

'It's great, I made it up before the op. Gives me 200 rounds link, right there, ready to use.'

'I knew I should never have left you alone without supervision. You'd better get a grip, John, mate, it looks absolutely bloody ridiculous,' said Ruecker.

'It's not what it looks like,' said Thrumble, pretending to lunge towards Ruecker, 'it's whether it can do the job. Anyway, you don't need anything like that, do you, driving round the battlefield in your WMIK. All right for some, mate.'

'Yeah, yeah, yeah,' said Ruecker. 'I'm going to find Dean Bailey – can't spend all day chatting to you pondies.'

'Pondies' or 'pond life' was the standard D Company term of abuse for rifle company soldiers. Pretty much every man in D Company had started out in one of the rifle companies, but with their elevated support weapons status, they now considered the rifle company men an inferior species, to be pitied and really only of use for carrying some of the support weapons kit like 81mm mortar bombs when there was a long foot insertion to be done.

Leaving the pond life inside, Ruecker bumped into Private Robert Foster, Parker's eighteen-year-old point man, filling sandbags in the courtyard. 'All right, mate? Do you need a hand with that?'

'No thanks, I'm OK,' said Foster.

'How was yesterday?'

'It was absolutely nectar. Best day I remember. I hope we have a lot more of them out here. How about you?'

'Yeah, quality, you sure you don't want any help?'

'No, it's fine. But I could really use a cheese sandwich if you've got one. You haven't, have you?'

Ruecker shook his head as he went in search of Bailey, his fellow sniper and close friend. Foster hadn't been in the battalion that long, but he'd already got a reputation across B Company, and even beyond, as a comedian and a real battalion character. He was what the troops called 'morale'. But to Ruecker the cheese sandwich comment was a bit random even for him.

As he walked across the yard in search of his oppo Bailey, Ruecker thought, *I don't remember seeing such high morale ever before. The blokes are really buzzing.*

During the day, Carver, the ANA battalion commander, Aston, Biddick and Major Steve Davies, the Royal Engineers squadron commander, recced locations for the three permanent patrol bases that were to be established in the area. They were to be constructed by the Royal Engineers from Hesco Bastion walling.

Hesco is made of a collapsible wire-mesh container and heavy-duty fabric liner, used as a temporary blast and smallarms barrier. Similar in concept to a sandbag, but on a gigantic scale, Hesco is assembled by unfolding its segments into open-topped cubes and filling them with sand, dirt or gravel. Originally designed for use on beaches and marshes for erosion and flood control, Hesco is used in nearly every military base in Afghanistan.

The ANA were going to occupy the bases, establishing a long-term presence in the area to prevent the Taliban from returning to threaten the town of Gereshk. Even as the recces were underway, Davies's trucks and armoured diggers moved in to start the construction work.

Biddick was called by Carver to battle group Tac HQ. He assumed he was there for a discussion on A Company's future operations, and as ever came armed with his thoughts and plans. What happened was the last thing he was expecting. Carver waved a letter at him, 'Dominic, what the hell is this all about?'

Mystified, Biddick took the letter. It was headed '10 Downing Street'. He read on. The Prime Minister was acknowledging a letter criticizing policy on Afghanistan, suggesting that the government was not morally or practically supporting British troops in theatre, or being proactive enough in its handling of media scrutiny and criticism. The acknowledgement was addressed to a private in Biddick's company headquarters who had written to Gordon Brown from Afghanistan. Carver had been sent a copy.

All Biddick could say was, 'I will look into it, Colonel.'

While the engineers were constructing the patrol bases, A Company was given the task of an aggressive forward defence, thrusting several kilometres north-east up the Green Zone to keep the Taliban at bay. Biddick scolded himself for wondering whether this task was given to him to shift the phantom letter-writer as far away from Carver's headquarters as possible. He knew it wasn't a laughing matter!

Captain Tom Coleman, the battle group intelligence officer, briefed Biddick on the suspected location of an enemy headquarters near the village of Barak zai Kalay, identified by a Nimrod MR2 surveillance aircraft. Biddick devised a plan to make an incursion into the Green Zone at Barak zai Kalay with the hope of drawing the Taliban out and identifying the precise location of the headquarters. With Ormiston's FSG Delta and four Recce Platoon Scimitars under Captain Wilde, A Company moved through the desert during the afternoon.

The FSG and Scimitars occupied vantage points on a clifftop overlooking the Green Zone.

A Company dismounted from their Vikings around 1500 hours, 500 metres back into the desert, behind the Recce vehicles. It was a bright, cloudless afternoon, and scorching hot as they sweated their way on foot with full combat loads along a zig-zag trail that led from the desert, down the 6-metre cliff face and across a canal into the Green Zone. The platoons cleared through a series of compounds on the outskirts of Barak zai Kalay.

Wilde's Scimitars, with FSG Delta, provided overwatch from the clifftops, monitoring for any Taliban activity that might reveal the location of the headquarters they were trying to identify. Biddick had expected a violent reaction from the enemy as soon as his leading troops set foot in the Green Zone. But there was nothing.

As the light began to fail, Biddick decided to move back up the cliff face to the Vikings. Before doing so, he tried one last thing. He thought that, rather than making a conscious decision not to attack, it was more likely that the Taliban had not been alert enough to see the company move into their heartland. He would give them another chance. Positioning the company for an ambush, he ordered his engineers to detonate a bar-mine to attract the enemy's attention. Still no response.

Then, moving away from the Green Zone along the track back towards the canal, 2 Platoon soldier Private Tommy Brace, covering the rear of his section, saw an armed man run between two buildings. Brace fired but missed the fast-moving fighter, and the man ran off behind one of the compounds the company had just searched.

2 Platoon followed up, racing to capture or kill him, but the man wasn't to be found.

They headed back towards the canal and the cliffs beyond and they heard a series of loud whooshes overhead followed by series of deafening explosions as a volley of eight 107mm rockets impacted in the desert several hundred metres to the rear of the overwatching Scimitars.

Colour Sergeant Faupel, with the fire support group, saw a mass of white smoke 2 kilometres away to the south-east, beyond the Green Zone – the firing point for the rockets. He called an artillery fire mission on to the position, and the 105mm gun group from Tombs's Troop Royal Artillery, positioned back near the original FUP for the start of Op Silicon, fired a barrage of high-explosive shells. Faupel heard the crump-crump-crump of the distant explosions and saw the flashes and clouds of black smoke and dust rising up into the clear sky as the artillery pounded the Taliban launch site.

As the artillery fire mission went in, Captain Wilde's gunner, Corporal Paul Kearney, spotted a group of five Taliban fighters setting up an 82mm mortar behind a line of trees in a field 1,800 metres away. Wilde's Scimitar, and two others in the line, blasted the Taliban team with round after round of the lethally accurate 30mm HE shells, killing all five and smashing the mortar to pieces.

Immediately, machine-gun, rifle and RPG fire, from a woodline 100 metres to the east, slammed in around the Scimitars. While Biddick was worrying whether or not the Taliban had identified the company's sortie into the Green Zone, they had evidently been feverishly alerting each other to the British troops' presence and fighters had been getting together their weaponry and moving fast into attack positions. In twilight, the Scimitar crews were able to use their thermal BGTI sights to track the tracer rounds back to the precise firing positions, with an accuracy that is not possible using the human eye.

On the radio, Wilde gave quick fire orders, dividing up the dispersed Taliban positions between the four Scimitars, and all engaged simultaneously with their L37 machine-guns, punching long bursts of ball and tracer into the enemy firing points. Over the next ten minutes contacts continued, as Taliban fighters moved from position to position, firing at the Scimitars. Wilde estimated that his men killed six or seven of the enemy.

It was getting dark now, but that made no difference to the Scimitar crews' ability to identify and bring fire down on the fighters. When the Taliban firing stopped, the recce vehicles maintained observation over the entire area as A Company continued to patrol back to their Vikings, several hundred metres into the desert.

Fifteen minutes later it was pitch black. A few minutes later, through their BGTI sights, the Scimitar crews identified a group of seven armed men moving out from a compound near the place where several Taliban fighters had been killed with 30mm while setting up their mortar nearly 2 kilometres away. Clearly the enemy had no comprehension of the phenomenal night surveillance and target acquisition capabilities of Wilde's CVRTs. As the fighters moved through the woods, Wilde's

Scimitars opened fire again with 30mm HE, killing them all.

While his gunners engaged the seven fighters, Wilde had been carefully tracking their movement. They had come from a compound 100 metres to the left of the mortar position. Wilde looked at his map and at the notes he had taken from Captain Coleman's intelligence briefing. It all added up. This must be the Taliban HQ they had been tasked to identify.

Wilde called Ormiston, gave him the grid reference and target description of the headquarters and asked him to attack the building with Javelin. Using the night-time capability of the Javelin CLU, FSG Delta fired two missiles in top attack mode, blasting high-explosives into the headquarters that the MR2 surveillance aircraft had identified. The Scimitars and the FSG remained in the area for a while, monitoring the building, ready to fire again, but there was no further sign of enemy movement anywhere in the area.

20

By Carver's rigorous and conservative Battle Damage Assessment, or BDA, the Royal Anglian Battle Group killed ninety-five Taliban during the first day of Op Silicon alone. These were confirmed dead – the real figure was probably much higher. B Company alone had fired more than 40,000 rounds of 7.62 mm machine-gun ammunition just on that day.

But the significance of Operation Silicon went far deeper than simply death and destruction. During a continuous twelve-hour onslaught from the ground and the air, the Taliban had been battered by infantry, artillery, engineers, attack helicopters and fixed-wing ground attack fighters. For the first time they came to realize that they could no longer operate with impunity from their Green Zone strongholds. Worse still for the Taliban, Silicon enabled the construction of three permanent patrol bases dominating the Green Zone north east of Gereshk. The bases were completed by the Royal Engineers in an amazing forty-eight hours after the end of Silicon Day 1. They were occupied straight away by the Afghan National Army with their OMLT advisers from the Grenadier Guards, and the Royal Anglians handed over reactive security in the area to The 1st Battalion The Worcestershire and Sherwood Foresters Regiment, which had just arrived in theatre to form Battle Group Centre.

Task Force Helmand intelligence reports indicated that the Taliban remnants from Deh Adan Khan and Habibollah Kalay fled north to Musa Qalah to lick their wounds. Brigadier Lorimer's primary intention – to stop mortar and rocket attacks against Gereshk – had been achieved. It was a significant step in convincing the population that NATO meant business in Helmand, and word of this spread the length of the Helmand River valley. Biddick and A Company had been blooded just over a week earlier, on Friday 13 April. But Operation Silicon was the Royal Anglian Battle Group's baptism of fire. Valuable lessons were learnt by all of the commanders and troops about themselves, the enemy and the country they were operating in.

Despite constant smallarms, machine-gun, rocket and mortar fire by a tenacious, battle-hardened and well-armed enemy, no member of the Royal Anglian Battle Group was killed during Operation Silicon. The only injury was B Company's Private Sheppard, who suffered a shrapnel wound from an RPG missile, was patched up and then just cracked on with the fighting.

The Raid: 3–4 May 2007

When the Royal Anglians arrived in Helmand, C (Essex) Company deployed straight to the Kajaki area, the most northerly British location in Helmand. Their role was to protect from the Taliban the strategically vital hydroelectric power dam. The dam had the potential to provide enough electricity to meet most of the needs of the population of both Helmand and Kandahar Provinces. It also provided irrigation for some 260,000 hectares of otherwise arid land. Ninety-eight metres high and 270 metres long, the dam was built in 1953. In the 1970s two electricity turbines were provided by the US overseas aid organization USAID. When C Company arrived they were briefed on an intention to bring in and install a third turbine, which could not happen until the security situation was sufficiently under control at Kajaki and along the route in.

In early April, just before C Company's arrival, a group of Chinese engineers was flown in to rebuild one of the turbines, but within twelve hours of being dropped off were evacuated, terrified by a salvo of Taliban rockets. C Company's main mission was to hold the Taliban back from the dam, to prevent further interference with the vital reconstruction work, and to force further back the Taliban positions, known as the 'Forward Line of Enemy Troops' or FLET.

Within weeks of arriving at Kajaki, the company had pushed back the FLET to the north of the dam by 4 kilometres, and to the south by 2 kilometres. A supplementary element of C Company's mission in Kajaki was to tie down fighters in the area, to prevent them heading south to reinforce Taliban groups intent on attacking Sangin and Gereshk.

C Company commander was Major Phil Messenger. His father had been an officer in the Royal Pioneer Corps, having risen through the ranks, and he himself had attended the Duke of York's Royal Military School in Dover. He had considerable operational experience,

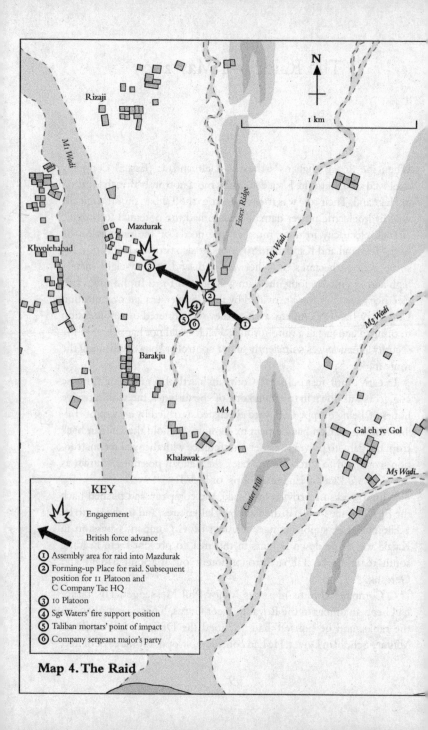

KEY

![Engagement] Engagement

![British force advance] British force advance

① Assembly area for raid into Mazdurak

② Forming-up Place for raid. Subsequent position for 11 Platoon and C Company Tac HQ

③ 10 Platoon

④ Sgt Waters' fire support position

⑤ Taliban mortars' point of impact

⑥ Company sergeant major's party

Map 4. The Raid

having completed tours in Northern Ireland, Sierra Leone and Iraq. During the battalion's previous Afghanistan tour, Messenger had been 2IC of the company he now commanded. He had an easy, relaxed leadership style when in the base, but on operations was a tough, aggressive and very determined commander with a short fuze, whose eagerness to close with the enemy earned him the nickname 'Angry Phil'.

The company was based beside the dam in Combat Outpost (COP) Zeebrugge. The base was constructed of sturdy, modern stone buildings surrounded by a barbed wire and wall perimeter. When not on patrol or guard duty, the men could swim in the icy dark-blue water of the lake which lay at the bottom of steep-sided mountains.

COP Zeebrugge had a murky history. Like many buildings in strategic outposts across Afghanistan, it had once been defended by a company of Russian conscripts. The troops avoided one particular stone building, just outside the wire. It had an eerie atmosphere. Its walls were bomb- and bullet-scarred, a reminder of a hand-to-hand fight to the death as Afghan mujahideen slaughtered Russian soldiers who had been abandoned by their officers.

A ridge-line behind Zeebrugge was permanently manned by one of C Company's platoons, dug into a network of Russian-built trench systems that overlooked the Helmand River, the base and a vast plain dotted with largely deserted villages and criss-crossed by irrigation ditches and deep wadis. Each platoon spent ten days at a time on the ridge, known as 'The Peaks', manning observation posts intended to protect the base and provide surveillance, overwatch and fire support to the company's patrols. The OPs bristled with machine-guns, Javelin missiles, radar, thermal imagers, sniper scopes and powerful binoculars.

Behind the ridge-line to the south was a vast open area of golden dunes and emptiness. Despite its beauty there was another chilling reminder of the hidden killers that lay all over Afghanistan. The dunes were a minefield, sown with anti-personnel devices by the Russians in the 1980s. Remnants of an incident during the 3rd Battalion The Parachute Regiment's tour at Kajaki still lay in the sand and could be picked out from the hill with a pair of binos. It was here in September 2006 that a paratrooper was killed and others seriously wounded in the minefield, and pieces of their equipment still lay there untouched.

Dawn was about to break on 3 May, and a few feet behind him Private Matt Woollard could make out the crouched figure of his best mate, Private Steve Walker. They had first met in Southend recruiting office aged sixteen, went through basic training together and then joined the battalion just months before the tour.

'Reckon you'll be able to hack the tab back in, mate?' hissed Woollard.

'It's you that's struggling, Matt, with your dead leg.'

On a messy night out in Southend just after his eighteenth, Woollard had jumped off a stage and broken his right ankle. Under intensive physio he missed the battalion's pre-training in Kenya. But he worked hard to get back on the road and was given the green light to deploy just before the company left for Helmand.

'Well I can still beat you on a tab, even with a broken ankle.'

'I don't think so. Anyway the birds aren't interested in who can tab fastest. It's looks that count in this game.'

'Piss off. There aren't any birds here, not even feathered ones. Anyway, if anyone's got looks it's me. Everyone knows I'm a pretty boy. I have to fight the women off.'

Despite his tender years, Woollard did have a reputation as something of a ladies' man in his home town of Westcliff-on-Sea in Essex. Or so he told everyone. He spent most of his school days chasing the girls. That and sport. He was a good sports player, excelling at tennis, badminton and squash. But football was his first love, maybe more than the ladies. He was a good player, and a fervent, almost fanatical, West Ham supporter.

And Walker knew how to wind his mate up. 'Matt, the Hammers are struggling again this season, aren't they?'

A third voice whispered through the gloom, this time with a strong Norfolk twang. 'All right, ladies, shut up both of you. Haven't you heard of battle discipline?'

This was Lance Corporal Matt Boyle, the company medic. A veteran compared to most of C Company's young soldiers, Boyle had been in the battalion for fourteen years. Regimental red and yellow blood coursed through his veins. His grandfather had been a Royal

Norfolk and his great grandfather had died of wounds he sustained serving on the Somme with the Norfolks. Boyle was as fanatical about the Army as Woollard was about West Ham. As a boy he had been both an Army Cadet and an Air Cadet at the same time, so he could go to Cadets four nights a week. As soon as he left school he did a uniformed services course in King's Lynn and entered basic training at Bassingbourn in Cambridgeshire the minute he was old enough. Since joining the battalion he had done many jobs, including rifleman, anti-tank operator, equipment repairer – even regimental tailor. For the last two years, since the battalion started preparing for its Iraq tour, he had been a medic. This was a role he had quickly grown into, enjoyed and was good at.

'If you two boys don't keep quiet I'll start telling you war stories.'

As Boyle spoke, the soldiers were suddenly lit up by a blinding flash. A split second later the ground shook from a massive explosion just behind them.

'OK, lads, that's the engineers done,' called Sergeant Matt Waters. 'Get ready to move.'

The Taliban had been using an old Russian trench system on Nipple Hill as cover to direct rocket and mortar fire against C Company's base and observation posts. Major Phil Messenger had decided to destroy the trenches to open up the ground so that his surveillance systems could get better coverage of the area. During the night the company had patrolled out, using the wadi beds as cover, and provided security while the engineers rigged the trenches with bar-mines.

Woollard's platoon had recently finished their first stint up on the peaks. Walking between the crouching soldiers, Messenger joked, 'Come on 11 Platoon, you're not up in the OPs any more, stop being idle. I hope you're enjoying your first patrol in Afghanistan. Not too much like hard work for you, is it?'

He looked around, smiling, then, walking back down the line, said, 'All right, let's head back to base. Move now.'

The soldier in front stood up, checked back to make sure Woollard could see he was moving, and began to patrol forward along the M5 wadi back towards Zeebrugge.

Woollard got to his feet, turned to Walker and said, 'Come on, then, mate, let's go. If you think you can make it.'

He turned back, took a single step and was hurled into the air by a huge blast beneath his feet. He felt his body twisting upwards in slow motion. It seemed like forever before he crashed back on to the ground. He was engulfed in thick black smoke. He felt his heart beating in his throat. His ears were ringing, really, really loud. Through the constant high-pitched screech he could hear himself breathing, also really loud. His eyes were closed and he just didn't want to open them. He dreaded what he would see.

Eyes tight shut, instinctively, he started screaming, 'Woollard, I'm hit, Woollard, I'm hit,' over and over. His cries pierced the half-light, and every soldier in the company was rocked by his terrible, blood-chilling anguish. He had unbearable pains in his head, under his helmet, and everything was stinging. He tried to move his neck and his fingers but he found he just couldn't control any part of his body. His mind went blank. Then he thought, *I've just died*.

His body was racked with terrible, piercing, stinging pain, and the pain did not leave him for a single moment.

Ten metres away, the medic Boyle watched Woollard step on the mine. He felt the flash burn into his retina. The ground shook, and a wave of heat hit him. He was immediately deafened. He saw a plume of dust and smoke, and lumps of rubble flying in every direction.

Covered in dust, Boyle dropped to one knee, shook his head and looked over. His brain told him, *That didn't happen. That didn't just happen. That wasn't a mine. It was an incoming mortar round. That missed everybody. No one's been hurt*. Desperate to wipe out what he had just seen, and convert it into something more reasonable, Boyle started shouting, 'Are there any casualties?'

The smoke cleared quickly, and Boyle saw Woollard sitting in the bottom of the mine crater. He was twisted backwards over his day sack, entwined around his LSW, which was contorting his arms back upwards. Boyle saw that he was conscious, and despite a loud ringing in his own ears, he heard his low moans.

Near by, Sergeant Waters was shouting, 'Go firm, go firm, stop moving, it's a mine, there may be more.'

He heard Messenger yelling into his radio, 'All stations – stop, stop, stop, mines, mines.'

Boyle looked at Woollard. He thought, *Sod stop, stop, stop, Woollard needs me over there – now*. A second or two after the blast he was racing to the crater, across ground that was almost certainly concealing more of the deadly high-explosive mines. He knew and he didn't care. He was a medic and his job was to deal with casualties. Simple as that.

Woollard's stump was sticking up in the air. Everything from his right knee down to the bottom of what had been his calf looked like shredded steak, with just the top of his combat boot wrapped around it. Boyle could see bare bone, and the calf muscle was hanging off, a piece of grey flesh. His foot was gone. Boyle had never seen a wound as bad as that, except in training pictures and simulated exercises. But he had been teaching first aid to the whole battalion for the month before they deployed to Helmand. Every medic had his own lesson to teach. Boyle's was the catastrophic haemorrhage. And the example he used was traumatic amputation of the lower right leg.

His training took over, and he went straight in. He didn't speak to Woollard. His one priority was to save the boy's life.

Blood was spurting out from the young soldier's ankle. He grabbed the leg with his right hand and gripped as hard as he could at the point where he was going to place the tourniquet. He could feel the bones meshing together under his grasp. He lifted the leg and at the same time with his left hand felt into Woollard's right map pocket. Every soldier carries a tourniquet in that pocket, together with two first field dressings and two morphine autojects. Except in extremis a soldier treating his comrade will never use his own first aid kit. That is reserved for himself, in case he becomes a casualty.

Propping the leg against his shoulder, as high as he could raise it, Boyle then applied Woollard's tourniquet, as close to the wound as possible. The bleeding slowed, then seemed to stop.

He looked Woollard in the eyes and tried to muster a smile that probably looked more like a grimace. 'You all right, mate?'

He knew how stupid the question was, but he needed to talk to him, to engage him. There was blood everywhere, black and mingled with dust. Woollard was bleeding from his nose and ears. The blast had burst all the small blood vessels around his face, which was covered in blood.

Because he landed on his back, buckled over his daysack, Woollard hadn't seen his wound and didn't realize his foot was gone. Boyle didn't want to be the one that told him. Instead, he took Woollard's first morphine autoject from his map pocket and banged it straight into his left thigh.

That's got that out of the way, he thought. *That's going to help him for a little while. Calmed me down a bit too. Now, what's after catastrophic bleeding? Yes, yes, breathing. Calm down. You've taught it a thousand times.*

As Boyle went over the rest of Woollard's body looking for further serious bleeding, he asked him to count to ten in less than one breath. He knew that if he could do that there was probably no penetrating wound to the chest. And he could. Woollard wasn't in too much pain to do the counting. Boyle thought, *That's good, adrenalin's got him.* He knew too that the adrenalin would constrict Woollard's veins, restricting the outflow of blood: also good.

Oblivious to whatever else was going on, Boyle worked away on him. He saw a bloody wet patch on his left thigh. The blast had come upwards and outwards, hit his thigh and both his forearms. Boyle quickly cut away his trouser leg and checked out the thigh. The sole of Woollard's right boot, bits of leather, lumps of plastic from his rifle and rock fragments were stuck into his flesh. In all his body was peppered with 160 substantial splinters of debris.

There was also a gaping hole and a lot of blood. Boyle checked to make sure the femoral artery was intact and it was. He removed the boot sole and threw it away, muttering, 'Won't be needing that again.' Then he picked out the other large objects and applied first field dressings to Woollard's thigh and forearms.

Boyle looked at the stump. *Don't want his mates picking him up with all that hanging around*, he thought, and bandaged the bloody mess up – in total he used nine first field dressings.

As he worked he chatted to Woollard – about anything that came into his head. He had to keep him focused as best he could, keep him with it. He remembered they had talked about heavy metal when they were both on the OPs. 'Matt, that band Rage Against the Machine, pretty crap, aren't they? Haven't they had to break up they're so bad?'

Woollard managed to get out through teeth clenched against the pain, 'Bollocks. They're the best. And you know that.'

'Well, you must be deaf, then, mate.'

'I am now.' He managed to force a slight grin.

'Me too, 'cos of your mine. Anyway, what's your favourite track?'

Now Boyle looked around him. Everyone else in the company had gone firm in fire positions, looking outwards, providing cover. Sergeants Waters and Armon, and several other men, were crawling forward on their bellies, prodding for further mines with their bayonets, clearing a safe path to extract the casualty.

Messenger was about 20 metres away with his radio operator. He had already sent an initial report on the company net, getting helicopters into the air, and now needed to transmit a more detailed casualty report. He shouted across, 'What have we got, Corporal Boyle?'

'One times T One, sir.'

Boyle knew that wasn't the answer the company commander wanted. But he still didn't want to be the one to tell Woollard he had lost his lower leg.

'No, Corporal Boyle. What – are – his – injuries?'

Boyle looked into Woollard's eyes and saw him staring up at him, wide-eyed. He took a deep breath, turned his head to the company commander and called out, 'Traumatic amputation lower right leg. Blast and fragmentation wounds both arms and left thigh.'

The words struck Woollard like a bullet. He forced himself up so that he could see his leg. When he saw it he just cried out, 'Oh no, no, no.'

As he lay devastated on the ground his first thoughts were: *What are my family going to be going through? Am I going to have any friends after this? Are they all going to see me as a different person and just not want to know me?*

He examined his left leg and saw how badly messed up it looked too, and his heart sank further as he wondered if he was going to lose that as well. He looked at his arms. And his hands, which were sliced open from the blast, with black blood congealed all over them. He thought he looked like he had just come down a chimney, covered in soot.

Captain Baz Alexander, a Royal Army Medical Corps nursing officer attached to C Company, managed to get to the crater, and the two medics began the next stage of the immediate first aid.

Woollard had lost a lot of blood and despite tourniquet and dressings was still bleeding from various holes in his body. His blood pressure was dropping. If it continued to fall critical organs would shut down. If it dropped below a certain level he would die. His system needed more circulating volume. They needed to get saline fluid into his body – fast.

Alexander decided there was no way they would get a line into either of his forearms. From his medical bag he took out an intraosseous kit. He pulled apart Woollard's body armour, cut away his shirt and pressed the inter-ossious patch to his sternum. He then punched the screw through his skin and began to twist, drilling into the bone. Boyle took out a 500ml saline bag. Attached to the bag was a plastic line, which Alexander fed through the screw and into Woollard's bloodstream. Boyle opened the valve, and the liquid began to flow through at a steady rate.

As the two medics packed up their kit ready to move off with Woollard, Sergeants Waters and Armon arrived. Waters grabbed Woollard's messed-up hands and held on to them. 'You're going to be OK, mate, you're doing well, you're doing well.'

Desperate to say something that might just give a fragment of hope to Woollard, he said, 'Look, mate, I've known a couple of blokes that have lost legs and had a pretty normal life. Looks bad now but you're going to get through, and we're all going to be behind you, helping.'

As his platoon sergeant chatted to him and the effects of the morphine took hold, incredibly Woollard managed to cheer up a little.

Several members of the platoon, bent and dripping sweat under their heavy battle loads, were moving up to carry the stretcher to the helicopter landing site. Others were filing past to provide protection.

As they went by, his mates called out, 'Get well, Matt, see you in England', 'Lucky bastard, you're going home,' and 'Make sure you have some West Ham tickets for me when I get back.'

The soldiers were devastated at what had happened to Woollard, but it is the hallmark of the military man to make light of every situation and not to add to the horror by appearing miserable and downcast.

The medics and the two sergeants lifted Woollard carefully on to a lightweight stretcher, and six men got round and started carrying him away. It was too dangerous to bring the CASEVAC helicopter in here so he had to be taken to Broadsword, the secure landing site outside Zeebrugge.

This was going to take some time, carrying him across rough terrain, and, with the heat beginning to build, it would be tough. Although the medics had stabilized him to some extent, he was still fighting for his life. Every soldier knew there wasn't a moment to lose. Every man dug deep, moving at speed, lungs bursting, and changing over as the weight of the stretcher felt as if it was pulling their arms out of their sockets. But there were no complaints. Saving Private Woollard, their brother, was now the most important thing in the world.

Alexander strode beside the stretcher, anxiously monitoring Woollard's condition, periodically checking his pulse. Boyle, his combat suit covered in Woollard's blood, followed behind, holding the saline, ready to adjust the flow on Alexander's command.

One of the stretcher bearers was Private McDermott, who was known in the company as 'Rooney' because of his resemblance to the footballer Wayne Rooney. With the morphine now properly kicked in, Woollard spent much of the walk back chanting 'Roo-ney, Roo-ney,' to the amusement of the troops around him.

Moving as fast as they could across the rugged terrain and with the ever-increasing heat bearing down on them, the stretcher bearers carried Woollard 2 kilometres to an RV with Company Sergeant Major Pete Ramm and his vehicle. For speed they moved across open country, out of the wadi beds, with flank protection from the rest of the company.

At the RV, they loaded the casualty into the back of the sergeant major's Pinzgauer, and Boyle and Alexander handed him over to the company medical officer.

Minutes later they arrived at Broadsword. The Chinook carrying the MERT was already on the ground, rotors turning, ready to lift off again. The MERT consisted of an infantry Immediate Response Team, or IRT, to provide ground protection, an operating department practitioner, at least one doctor, an anaesthetist and paramedics.

The medical equipment aboard the chopper was brought on by the MERT, as all helicopters were rotated through the various tasks in Helmand, including troop and cargo movement, as well as CASEVAC.

Ramm and his party carried Woollard up the ramp, where they transferred him to a stretcher fitted into the helicopter. By this time the immediate euphoric effects of the morphine had begun to wear off, and Woollard was sinking fast, close to despair, giving up. As Ramm left, he shouted calmly over the noise of the twin turboshaft engines, 'You'll be all right, mate. Keep your chin up, you've done really well since you've been in the battalion. And out here in Afghanistan. Be the person that we all know you for. The whole company's behind you and always will be. Good luck.'

Woollard whispered back, barely audible, 'Yes, sir, I will, sir.'

At this point he knew he was leaving the security of his company, his military family. It terrified him, and he didn't want to go. He wanted nothing more in life than to be back on the ground with his mates, and none of this happening. Just patrolling with both legs back to

Zeebrugge. The sergeant major's words calmed him somewhat, gave him at least a small boost, a kind of incentive to keep going.

As the Chinook climbed steeply into the sky, engines screaming, a face appeared right next to Woollard, shouting, 'You're going to be all right. You're in our hands now. You're going to be all right.'

The doctor leaned over him, jabbed something into his right arm and shouted, 'You're fine. You're going to be fine. Don't fight it. Don't fight it.'

Woollard felt his body shutting down. For the second time that day he thought he was dying. He was terrified beyond anything he had experienced before. Much more than when the mine detonated. Even more than when he heard Boyle's words, 'traumatic amputation'. He had somehow, somehow, fought through all of that. But now...he had made it to the safety of the Chinook, and now he was going to die. He fought to stay awake, to keep his eyes open. He shouted, 'You don't understand. I'm dying. I'm going. I'm about to go.'

'You're fine, you're fine.'

Woollard panicked. He thought, *I'm going. That's me.*

He kept trying to shout at the doctor, but he just heard himself moan. He needed to make the man understand that he was dying. He tried to shout again, but again just a moan came out. Then nothing. And for the first time since he stepped on the mine there was not even any pain.

Woollard had been so badly damaged that his heart stopped twice during the thirty-five-minute flight from Broadsword to Bastion. But the medical team, fighting against his rebelling body and the constant shudder and sudden jerking movements of the Chinook, managed to bring him back to life both times.

3

On the ground, the men of C Company were in a sombre mood as they patrolled back in to Combat Outpost Zeebrugge. Although one of their corporals had been shot in the groin at the start of the tour, and evacuated back to the UK, Woollard was their first really serious casualty in Afghanistan, and they knew he was in a critical condition and might not survive.

As soon as they got into the base, Major Messenger got his commanders together. 'That was terrible, terrible. But at least it looks like Matt Woollard is going to live. All the medics and everyone involved in the CASEVAC did a brilliant job. I will speak to them, but in the meantime please pass on my thanks.'

Sergeant Waters, who had been the young soldier's platoon sergeant since he joined the battalion the previous June and had worked hard with him to bring his fitness levels up since he broke his ankle, fought back his emotions.

Messenger continued, 'The job for all you lot now is to get the blokes' heads back up and crack on as normal. Or as normal as possible. We won't forget Matt Woollard, and we'll do everything we possibly can to help him get through this nightmare. But we've got a major patrol into Mazdurak early tomorrow morning. So get among the lads, get them sorted out for the next op, and then get them fed and rested. Any questions?'

Outside in the compound, several C Company soldiers walked over to Corporal Boyle. They patted him on the back, threw an arm round his shoulder and said, 'Well done. You saved his life.'

On top of the morning's events, the praise and admiration of his comrades hit Boyle hard. He thought, *I don't know how to deal with this.* He sat down on his own in the washing area. Many thoughts went through his head. *Matt was bleeding out a bit, not sure I saved his life....Anybody else would have done the same for him... Thank God I taught that lesson, that put me on to autopilot...Could I have done more? No, no, I'm pretty happy with the job I did. Poor bastard, though...*

He sat quietly for a few minutes more, hoping above all that Woollard would pull through. Then the immediate practicalities of life dawned on him, an old soldier who knew the system backwards. He had to face the nightmare of trying to get a clothing pack out of the company quartermaster sergeant to replace the combat suit that was drenched in Woollard's blood.

That afternoon at 1400 hours, the C Company command group gathered in the briefing room. Present were Captain Dave Hicks, the Company 2IC and operations officer, platoon commanders and platoon sergeants of 9, 10 and 11 Platoons, Company Sergeant Major Pete Ramm, the fire support group commander, the Royal Artillery fire support team commander, specialist fire support controllers for air and mortars, signallers and the medical officer. They had changed out of their combats, fed and showered, and even though now wearing the standard off-duty dress of flip flops, shorts and T-shirts, they were still sweltering. The briefing room was near the company ops room, within a single-storey stone building. Maps lined the walls, and there were collapsible wooden benches for twenty people.

Messenger stood in front of them. 'OK listen in, then. We get the lads straight back into it. No Coalition troops have been into Mazdurak before. We'll go in there tomorrow morning as planned. This will be a probing operation, a raid in effect. We know the Taliban consider Mazdurak as a safe haven, but we have no real idea about how many there are there, what the set-up is, or anything else much. We've done air recce and we've got a fair bit of imagery, but it doesn't tell you much. There's only one way to find out what's in there, and that's boots on the ground. We don't want to hold the place, we just want to go in and see what we can stir up. We'll test their reactions and see what we can learn. We'll kill as many of the enemy as we can and obviously it would be good if we take prisoners. One thing we can be completely confident about – they will fight to the death to defend Mazdurak. We can expect the stiffest resistance. Any questions so far?'

He looked at the faces of the men in front of him. He could see the strain in the eyes of Sergeant Matt Waters in particular. He had been very badly cut up about Woollard, one of his boys. But Messenger wasn't worried about Waters. He knew he was a strong leader who would work through it and get the job done. Tragic though the incident had been, no soldier could afford the luxury of allowing grief to dominate his life in a place like Afghanistan.

Messenger continued, 'The mission, therefore, is to determine enemy strengths and dispositions in and around the town of Mazdurak.'

According to the time-honoured military formula he repeated the mission. It was essential that everybody knew exactly what the purpose was of any operation. That way, if things got really rough, and commanders were taken out of the battle, any soldier would be able to take over and keep working to achieve the mission.

He went on: 'Concept of operations. 10 Platoon will conduct the initial assault into Mazdurak.' He looked at Lieutenant Sam Perrin, the platoon commander, who nodded. 'Once 10 Platoon has secured the first few compounds, 11 Platoon will echelon through, and we will continue to leap-frog into the town like that as far as we can get. Sam, for that initial echeloning, you will have to make the call when to start 11 Platoon moving through you. Give them the word direct on the net and make sure I am aware. I'll be right behind your platoon with Company Tac.

'9 Platoon will remain on the peaks, providing observation and fire support.' He looked at Lieutenant Clarke. 'Tom, I want systematic observation of Mazdurak and the approaches to it from now on, until the operation is complete. I want to know, on the radio, anything and everything that happens in and around the town that could possibly affect what we are doing.'

He glanced at Captain Mark Taylor. 'The FSG will deploy on to Essex Ridge and provide close support from there. You will only have about a forty-five-degree angle, but at least your positioning will allow the peaks to continue supporting us as well – without any chance of them hitting you. Mortars will provide fire support from here. We have no air support specifically allocated for this operation, but we will call it in on first contact.

'Now it may be that we don't get very far into the town. I've already said we can expect stiff resistance. We must obviously take risks to get the information we want, and to deal with the enemy we encounter, but I do not intend to get involved in a full-on battle at this stage. Remember this is a raid, not a ground-holding operation.

'Now I'll go through the detail…'

4

After a few hours' sleep the company were up at 0130 hours. They had prepared everything before they went to bed. Using kettles in their accommodation, They had a brew and a boil-in-the-bag meal from their ration packs, to sustain them through the long hours of exhausting marching and fighting, carrying 36 kilos of equipment in what would become very intense heat as the morning wore on.

At 0230 hours Perrin led 10 Platoon out of the base and through the eerily still dirt streets among the densely packed compounds of Tangy village. Barking dogs shattered the early-morning peace as the company patrolled out of the village and into the open country towards Mazdurak.

They were moving through hilly terrain, rocky under foot, and could just make out the blackness of the mountains many kilometres ahead.

They passed several small, deserted compounds as they made their way down towards the wadi in front of Mazdurak.

The company moved in a long snake. Single-file, about 3 metres between each man. It never left any soldier's thoughts that Matt Woollard had been blown up in this area only hours before. Every man was even more wary than usual that he ran precisely the same risk now. There was no moon but plenty of starlight, which allowed each soldier to see the man in front and to try as hard as he could to step in the same footprints. As always, the 10 Platoon point man, Private Kennett Facal, who had no one's footsteps to follow, needed nerves of steel.

Forty minutes after they had set out, the leading elements of 10 Platoon arrived in the section of wadi that Messenger had designated as their FUP, for entry into Mazdurak. They spread out into all-round defence, waiting for the rest of the company to close up behind them. The men were tired and sweating after their brisk march carrying so much equipment, and grateful to take the weight off their shoulders, backs, feet and knees for a few minutes.

Messenger arrived in the FUP and took up a fire position behind 10 Platoon. He was surprised that so far they had heard no chatter from the Taliban. Normally the radio would be alive from the time they left Tangy, with talk such as 'They're coming, get ready to shoot them all.'

This silence is good, thought Messenger, as he looked into the blackness, just making out the silent movement of soldiers moving into position. *Maybe we'll take the Taliban by surprise for once.*

11 Platoon, under Lieutenant Manie Olivier and Sergeant Matt Waters, now arrived in the FUP. At the rear of the platoon was the medic, Corporal Matt Boyle, whose selfless courage had saved Woollard's life the day before. Boyle had not been scheduled to come out on this patrol. But the medic who was supposed to deploy had developed severe diarrhoea and vomiting during the night, and Boyle had volunteered to take his place. Somehow he had managed to get a new pair of trousers out of the system, but all the rest of his gear was still covered in Woollard's blood, which he had been unable to remove.

As dawn began to break, Perrin whispered into his radio, 'Hello, Two Two Charlie this is Two Zero Alpha. Move now.'

'Roger out,' hissed Corporal Andrew Brown into his mike. Inevitably nicknamed 'Bomber', Brown had left the Army in 1999 but re-enlisted for this tour. A tough and aggressive boxer, he was very calm under pressure and a supremely confident leader.

'Go on then, Gibbo,' he said, and his point man, Private Gibbs, jogged across the open ground, with Brown hard on his heels – a 200-metre dash of death, hoping that Taliban fighters were not lying on top of one of the compounds, machine-gun sights set on that very piece of ground. They moved fast through the poppies, but even 200 metres seems like a mile when there is only a sliver of luck between you and a hail of bullets.

Brown's men hit compound 518 and moved straight in. No need to break down the door, the walls were crumbling in several places. Good thing. They didn't want to blast their way through, they wanted to be as silent as possible for as long as possible, retaining the element of surprise while they could. Brown waved for the next section to come forward, and then he and his men went from room to room, going through the well-practised drill of clearing the compound. No one and nothing.

Perrin came forward with Corporal Pindar, one of the other section commanders. Standing beside Brown, Perrin quickly took stock. The next compound was 15 metres ahead. The ground was overlooked by Ant Hill, 150 metres away and a firing point the Taliban often used. 'Corporal Pindar, clear the next compound. Corporal Brown will cover you.'

Pindar called his section forward and led them across the gap. Brown's men were on the walls, weapons in shoulders, fingers on triggers, peering intently through their sights, ready to fire at the slightest movement.

Brown thought, *Covering fire is all well and good, but if the enemy knows his stuff – which he does – they will take out several men in that open ground before we get the chance to give any 'cover'.* Open ground was the infantryman's worst nightmare. But Pindar made it without interference and positioned his men to provide cover as the rest of the platoon dashed across to join them. It was not yet too hot, compared to what it would be like in a short time, but they had been sprinting around with their heavy kit and were breathing hard and pouring sweat.

Behind Perrin's 10 Platoon, Messenger with his Tac HQ and 11 Platoon had now moved into the first compound, 518.

Perrin quickly pushed his third section, commanded by Corporal Tim Ferrand, through Brown's section and into the next compound. That was clear too. It was 0545 hours. The sun was coming up. Perrin was relieved. They had gained a substantial footing in this Taliban stronghold, which had never before been entered by Coalition troops. He thought, *So far so good. But this can't last much longer.*

Brown now led his section forward into Ferrand's compound. Ferrand had pushed his men up on to the roof to give all-round coverage, ready to fire on the enemy as the rest of the company moved further into the town, 10 Platoon left and 11 Platoon right. Brown sent his GPMG gunner, Private Phil Wright, on to the roof to bolster up Ferrand's fire teams.

Brown looked back and saw Perrin duck into the compound through a small door. As the platoon commander straightened up, the silence was shattered by a long, loud burst of automatic fire. Brown thought, *That must have been a full mag of AK47, thirty rounds.* Then he heard a piercing scream.

Outside, Private Craig Gordon, the platoon radio operator, following behind Perrin, had taken a wrong turn. As he moved down the alleyway, an enemy sentry, half-dozing and startled by the unexpected noise of Gordon's feet on the gravel, emptied a magazine at him from a compound door 8 metres away. Gordon was hit twice. One bullet punched into his shoulder blade, the second shattered the radio on his back. Knocked backwards by the impact, he regained his balance, instantly brought up his SA80 and fired back into the doorway. The fighter went down. But a second gunman emerged from the darkness, firing. Gordon was hit a third time. A 7.62mm AK47 bullet caught him in the stomach and spun him round. He fell into the dirt, shouting, 'Man down!' As he crawled in agony towards the shelter of a nearby wall, from behind two more fighters came out of the doorway and rushed forward to drag him away.

When they heard the shooting, Brown's gunner, Phil Wright, and one of Ferrand's gunners, Private Wayne Alden, crawled as fast as they could across to the edge of the dusty roof. Seeing the Taliban running towards Gordon, they blasted down withering bursts of fire, cutting down the fighters just feet away from their comrade. They then swung their guns over and started firing through the doorway of the compound where the men had come from.

All over Mazdurak heavily armed enemy fighters were yelling at each other as they woke, realizing that British troops had entered their village. Within seconds they had dashed to rooftops and pre-prepared machine-gun positions within the dense and ramshackle complex of high-walled compounds and narrow alleyways. RPG gunners carrying bags of missiles hurriedly slung over their shoulders ran to firing points, and Taliban commanders barked out orders. The fighters had been caught sleeping by the stealthy approach of C Company. It was just after dawn, and the Taliban were not early risers. But it was rare for them to be surprised like this.

Brown said calmly to Perrin, 'I'm going out to get Gordon.' He called his section to him and led them to the doorway.

Perrin spoke into his radio to Steve Armon, 11 Platoon sergeant, who was in a compound 20 metres back: 'Hello, Metal Two Zero Charlie this is Metal Two Zero Alpha. Enemy in compound three hundred metres north-north-west of your position. Hit them with fifty-one. Over.'

Armon took less than a minute to fire an accurate volley of ten high-explosive bombs from his hand-held 51mm mortar. He dug the metre-long metal barrel's base plate into the ground and pointed it upwards at an angle towards the target area. He adjusted the elevation, checked the spirit level and pulled the lanyard at the base of the barrel. There was a thump as the bomb shot out of the mortar. He heard a loud muffled crump, and smoke and dust rushed up from the compound. *Bang on target!* Armon reloaded immediately and fired again. The mortar was rudimentary but effective, its technology little changed in 100 years. And Armon was using it to devastating effect, dropping shells behind the towering compound walls and blasting the enemy within.

Corporal Ferrand, on the roof, saw a flash of movement in the compound next to him. He couldn't see the enemy to shoot at, but this was a threat to Corporal Brown's rescue mission. Ferrand and Private Cooper flung high-explosive hand grenades over the walls and into the building. The explosions inside were deafening, and the grenades flung up clouds of dust. At the same time Private Kennett Facal, the man who had led the company from Zeebrugge to Mazdurak, a Filipino member of Ferrand's section, punched in a volley of 40mm HE grenades with the UGL on his SA80 rifle.

Several RPG rockets swished low over their heads and exploded in a wall beyond, again hurling up clouds of dust. Private Cooper saw one of the RPG gunners in a doorway and fired a long burst of 5.56mm at him with his Minimi. The bullets splintered the door frame and dug lumps out of the hard mud, but the man ducked back into the compound. Cooper shouted to Facal, 'My gun is on that door. If he comes out again I'll shoot him. You fire your UGL.'

As Cooper spoke, the fighter was reloading his RPG inside the building. He suddenly leant out of the door and fired at them, almost in a single movement. With the missile in the air, Cooper held his finger on the trigger, sending a stream of tracer into the doorway. Kneeling up, Facal, quickly reloading after each shot, fired six UGL grenades in rapid succession. Intent on their task, neither soldier took any notice of the RPG missile that shot past, just a couple of feet above their heads.

They were being engaged from every direction, bullets and RPGs criss-crossing overhead, impacting around and below them – dangerously close. Facal saw two fighters in the distance, on a roof 800 metres away across the M1 wadi. He shouted to Private Pritchard, a sharpshooter, 'P, can you hit him?'

Pritchard levelled his L96 sniper rifle and fired. Watching eagerly through his SUSAT, Facal yelled, 'Missed!'

Pritchard fired another shot and Facal saw the man jump down from the wall, out of sight, as the bullet splashed at his feet. Pritchard switched to the second fighter and fired twice. The first round missed, but Facal saw him fall from the roof as the second tore into his body.

Looking down, Facal shouted excitedly to Corporal Ferrand, 'We're getting outflanked. Taliban moving down the side of the compound.'

Despite all the shooting, grenading and shouting, this group of enemy fighters hadn't identified Facal's rooftop position. On Ferrand's word, he, Facal and two other soldiers dropped grenades down on to them, following up with automatic fire, ripping them to shreds as they tried to get round behind the forward C Company positions.

Moments later Ferrand's gunners had a group of Taliban fighters pinned down, but protected from the bullets by a compound wall. Facal saw that they were still firing at something from behind the wall, possibly towards Corporal Brown or Gordon. 'Give me grenades,' shouted Facal breathlessly.

'You won't reach that far, mate,' said Cooper.

'I will,' said Facal.

Facal laid his rifle down beside Cooper. He ran across the roof, bullets zipping close around him, and flung a grenade towards the wall.

It fell short. He threw another and another. Both straight in behind the wall. He forgot to take the pin out of the fourth. When the sixth and seventh exploded behind the wall he heard the enemy's screams and knew he had done the job. He grabbed his rifle and jumped back into a fire position. The other soldiers were astonished he had managed to throw the grenades so far and wondered how he hadn't been shot.

'Battalion cricket team next season,' shouted Cooper, laughing.

Below, Brown led his men out of the compound and through a small orchard to a gateway leading into the alley where Gordon lay bleeding and in agony. Brown opened the door and looked out. Bullets were hitting the wall left and right of the doorframe, just inches from his face. He glimpsed Gordon, 4 metres away. He looked bad, very bad. Brown spotted a sewage ditch, a couple of feet deep, just beside where Gordon lay. He shouted out, 'Gordon, get in that ditch, get in that ditch.'

Gordon rolled in, slightly safer – but only slightly – as bullets continued to zip wildly all round the alleyway. Brown slammed the compound door shut and turned to his young soldiers, wide-eyed behind him.

'If we don't go and get him he is dead. We've got to go out there now and get him back here or he will be shot again and he will bleed to death. You can see the blood on him. Listen closely. This is how I want it to roll.' He pointed to two of the men. 'You two go out the door and left and secure that side.' He pointed to two others. 'You two out and right, go past him and secure that way. Me and Brace will go out and straight to the casualty. 2IC, you stay here in case. No time for questions, just go.'

With that Brown booted open the door, and they all rushed out, firing from the hip. Private Harris shot two shocked Taliban fighters as he moved into position.

Crouching down, Brace got hold of Gordon under the arms, ready to drag him to safety. Brown hurled a grenade 8 metres through the door of the Taliban compound. It exploded inside, shredding everything with a storm of steel fragments. He calmly winked at Gordon. 'What a shot! Are you all right?'

Without waiting for an answer, Brace and Brown, pouring sweat, dragged Gordon back up the alley and through the door into the orchard. Firing in every direction as they ran backwards, the other men followed close behind, relieved to be alive.

5

While Brown and his men were getting Gordon to safety, Armon, outside the second compound the platoon had cleared through when they entered Mazdurak, noticed movement in a smaller building to his right. Looking over, he saw a hand emerge from a loophole in the wall and slowly brush down the sill. Next an AK47 muzzle was pushed through the window.

Armon, a twenty-eight-year-old Northern Ireland, Iraq and Afghanistan veteran from Cambridge, had a reputation within the battalion for staying calm no matter what. He whispered to Lance Corporal Thomas, crouched beside him, 'I'll destroy that position. You bring your men straight out, go right and clear the compound and the one beside it.'

He thought, *Don't want the boss to think I'm attacking his compound. The last thing we need now is a blue on blue.* He hit the radio pressel switch and whispered hurriedly to the platoon commander, 'Enemy in small compound directly to the north of your position. Am attacking. Out.'

Armon crept up to the loophole, hunched down so the fighter wouldn't see him. He knelt below the opening, pulled the pins from two high-explosive L109 hand grenades, reached up and dropped both of them through the hole. As the grenades clattered to the floor he heard the fighter panicking inside, his AK47 crashing to the ground. Armon heard two muffled explosions inside the building in rapid succession as his grenades went off and smoke and dust poured out through the loophole. There was no further movement inside.

Smashing their way through the compound door, blasting bullets all round the walls inside, Lance Corporal Thomas led his section into the compound to take care of any remaining Taliban.

This whole section of Mazdurak, a compound-filled area the size of several football pitches, was now the scene of a huge battle, the air filled with gunfire and explosions. The Taliban were firing machineguns and assault weapons from dozens of firing points, and RPGs were bursting over the heads of the C Company soldiers, raining in from every direction. Then they started taking fire from Khvolehabad, another village a few hundred metres away.

As soon as the shooting began Major Messenger told his JTAC to declare a TIC on the air control net. Meaning 'Troops in Contact', this message focuses all available air and fire support on the unit involved. The JTAC called up two US Air Force A10 Thunderbolt attack planes that were loitering in the airspace above and warned them they would be needed soon. He passed the same message to two British Apache helicopters that had also come on station, ready to support the men on the ground.

Messenger called Captain Mark Taylor, commander of Fire Support Group Charlie, and ordered him to bring down fire on any enemy identified. Within seconds, Taylor's machine-guns opened up with withering fire on enemy in the northern end of Mazdurak.

Messenger told the MFC who was beside him, 'Get the mortars on to the front edge of Khvolehabad.'

'Already on it, sir.'

Almost immediately the company's 81mm mortar section back at COP Zeebrugge unleashed a torrent of high-explosive shells, hammering the Khvolehabad firing positions to stop the enemy fighters shooting at the company, who already had enough on their hands with the Taliban in Mazdurak.

Messenger assessed that at least forty Taliban fighters were now wide awake and desperately defending the otherwise deserted town. His signaller reported, 'Sir, enemy radio intercepts have been relayed over the net from Captain Hicks. He says the Taliban commander seems to be calling for reinforcements.'

Moments later Messenger got confirmation from 9 Platoon in their observation posts high up on the peaks behind Zeebrugge. 'Taliban moving forward from the back end of Mazdurak. Can see at least ten to twelve men on foot, moving fast.'

Hitting his radio pressel switch, the MFC conferred briefly with his opposite number on the peaks, and Messenger didn't need to say a word as the 81s switched targets to pound in on the enemy rushing forward through the town.

In the thick of the action, Lance Corporal Thomas's section stormed through the compounds to the right of Sergeant Armon's position. Guardsman Harrison – a Grenadier Guards soldier attached to 10 Platoon – was at the back of the team. He looked into a doorway and inside saw a tunnel entrance in the floor. As he turned to point his rifle into the black hole he was flung to the ground, a bullet fired into his right eye by a fighter in the tunnel. In agony and virtually blinded, blood pouring all over his face, Harrison somehow managed to stagger into cover behind a wall.

Racing back to help, two soldiers from Harrison's section hurled high-explosive grenades into the tunnel entrance and immediately followed up with sixty 5.56 bullets on automatic at point-blank range. Nobody in the tunnel could have survived.

Before they could get back to Harrison, the men were pinned down by another enemy machine-gun position. They couldn't move. Lance Corporal Andy Howe, a few metres away, saw Harrison writhing on the ground, holding his head. He tried to get forward, but bullets slammed between his legs and he was forced to drop down. He threw a grenade into the compound where some of the fire was coming from but was then pinned down by a rapid stream of bullets from another gun position.

The men were desperate to reach their mate, who lay seriously wounded in the dirt. He was bleeding heavily, and if they didn't get him out he was going to die. They knew that and they knew that they couldn't get to him. To have attempted to move through the immense weight of enemy fire would have been suicidal and would have done nothing to help Harrison. Their position was impossible.

6

Corporal Bomber Brown had sent the wounded Private Gordon back to Sergeant Armon's compound to be treated. Hearing reports of Guardsman Harrison over his radio, Brown led his section back out into the alleyway to try to reach the wounded soldier. But, like Lance Corporal Thomas's men, Brown and his section were driven back by the intensity of the fire.

Above the gunfire and explosions, cupping his hands around his mouth, Brown shouted to the wounded guardsman, 'Harrison. Harrison. Listen to me. When I say go, get up and run back the way you came, back to the Sarge. When I say go. We will rapid fire into the doorway. Don't worry about the shooting. We will stop when you go past...Stand by. Stand by. Now – go!'

With blood still pouring out of his eye, Harrison struggled to his feet and ran for his life down the alleyway, towards the massive blast of fire that was now pouring into the alleyway from Brown's gunners and rifle-men. He made it. Sergeant Armon grabbed him and dragged him to the safety of the building.

Armon sat him on the dirt floor and quickly checked him over. The platoon sergeant was desperate to get precise information on the enemy positions so he could help direct the platoon's fire, and if possible launch more mortar bombs into their compounds. Before handing Harrison over to the medic Armon said, 'Harrison, where exactly are the enemy? Did you see the position?'

Still oozing out blood and by now close to collapse, Harrison scrawled a map in the dust with his finger, indicating the enemy positions in the compound. He told Armon, 'I believe there is a position there, there and up there, Sergeant.' Then, in proper Grenadier Guards fashion, Harrison asked, 'Leave to pass out, Sergeant?'

As Armon was organizing the evacuation of both of his casualties, Messenger had decided to extract the company. But the extraction was not going to be straightforward. 10 Platoon were in heavy contact from multiple enemy positions and would have to withdraw under fire. Carrying the two casualties would absorb twelve men, taking away essential firepower. And most of the company would have to make it across a 200-metre stretch of open ground – which was under withering enemy fire.

Messenger discussed with the JTAC how best to use the air assets. They could be employed to engage in depth and to the flanks. But they would be really decisive attacking the enemy that were in direct contact with the company. The fighting was too close for bombing, and even strafing runs would carry a high risk of hitting his own men. 'Tell them to strafe as close as they can, but I don't want a blue on blue. Make sure they know exactly where our positions are.'

Gordon was taken back to the initial compound, on the outskirts of Mazdurak, still occupied by most of Waters's 11 Platoon. As he was brought in, the medic Corporal Boyle grabbed him and checked him over. He was bleeding, but not too hard: manageable.

Boyle was applying first field dressings to his wounds when Sergeant Armon brought Guardsman Harrison in, slung over his shoulder. As Armon was carrying him back, both men had narrowly avoided further injury. A bullet had ripped a hole in Armon's trouser leg and another cracked into his daysack, passing just beneath Harrison's head.

Boyle took one look at Harrison and realized immediately that he was the priority. He handed Gordon over to a team medic. He wound a field dressing round Harrison's head to try to stem the bleeding. As he worked, he analysed the situation in his mind. *Head injury, you're not going to mess around with this. You can stop bleeding in a limb, you can put all sorts of stuff on. Even abdominal wounds you can treat. But not head injuries. There's so much stuff that can happen there. This is not like Woollard. It's not what you can do for him, it's how fast you can evacuate him. Because there's absolutely nothing you can do for him and he needs to get back. He needs to go back straight away.*

Boyle saw that Harrison's level of consciousness was sinking. When he was carried in by Armon he was talking. Now he was slurring his speech – badly. Boyle shone a torch into the remaining eye and tried to talk to Harrison. He was going downhill – rapidly. Boyle knew there was not a moment to lose. He turned to Waters and said, 'We've got to move him now. I need a work party and a route out.'

He grabbed a field stretcher from one of the other soldiers and slid it under the wounded man. Boyle, with five of Waters's men, struggled with the typically tall Grenadier Guardsman. Gordon was going with them, but, despite his serious wounds, had said he would walk rather than tie down six stretcher bearers, and was being assisted by two men, carrying his combat equipment and weapon as well as their own, and taking some of the strain as he stumbled along.

The journey across the open ground was a nightmare. The heat was excruciating, Harrison was heavy, and the men carrying him had to keep diving for cover from enemy gunfire. Bullets, cracking in from seemingly every direction, were flying over the top of them, and blowing poppy heads off around them. Rounds were zipping in between the men as they ran. They alternated between dragging the heavy stretcher along the ground, crawling on their belt buckles and running with it, knees bent, trying desperately to lose even a couple of inches of height.

Somehow, sweating and panting, they made it across the open ground, and every man was utterly exhausted, their lungs ready to explode with the horrendous exertions in such oppressive heat. Private Liam O'Connor, front left on the stretcher, felt as if his right arm was going to drop off. He now realized why stretcher races were such a big part of the battalion's tough physical training regime before they deployed to Afghanistan.

Boyle and the work party loaded the two casualties into Company Sergeant Major Pete Ramm's Pinzgauer, waiting in the cover of the wadi, and the medical officer went straight to work on Harrison.

Already the MERT Chinook, with its surgical team, was screaming towards Zeebrugge from Bastion, tasked twenty minutes earlier by Captain Dave Hicks in the company ops room.

10 Platoon was running short of ammo, and Ramm and Waters organized a resupply. Sergeant Waters's bearer party would have to carry it back across the open into Mazdurak. While the soldiers were loading themselves up with ammunition, Waters was given new orders by the company commander on the net, 'Remain in current location and provide fire support for the company's extraction across the open ground.'

Waters acknowledged and was about to give orders to his men when the dreaded words 'Man down' again came across the radio.

Corporal Boyle heard it as well. Immediately he said to himself, *You're the medic. If someone shouts 'man down' you've got to go to him. Got to. No choice. It's part of the job. Get moving.* He knew he had to get back across the open ground, still under enemy fire. Blanking out the obvious danger, he got to his feet and began to rush back.

But Waters grabbed hold of him and dragged him down. 'Stay here. We've got to provide covering fire. They're going to bring the casualty back here. You can't treat him on the move. Stay here and help sort him out when he gets back.'

7

Messenger had ordered the mortars to increase their rate of fire. Back in Zeebrugge, the company's mortar men were furiously stoking bomb after bomb into the red-hot mortar barrels. It was hard work in normal temperatures; under the baking Afghan sun, it was utterly exhausting. But the Mortar Platoon soldiers worked on, pouring sweat, breathing hard and arms aching, achieving rates of fire they would have struggled to maintain in training back in England. They knew the lives of their mates out there among the treacherous compounds of Mazdurak depended on the bombs they were feverishly flinging into their upturned mortar barrels.

Dozens of 81mm shells crashed into Mazdurak, breaking down compound walls, exploding through roofs, hurling out great jagged lumps of shrapnel, tearing apart enemy fighters and – critically – forcing them to stay in cover as the company pulled back. At the same time the Apaches were ripping Khvolehabad apart with their 30mm guns, preventing the enemy there from interfering with the company's movements. But the heaviest fire was coming from the A10s as they viciously strafed enemy positions in Mazdurak with their 30mm Gatling guns.

Major Messenger flung himself down as a 30mm shell impacted right next to him. Turning his head, he said to the JTAC, also lying flat, 'Call the A10 pilot and ask him to adjust his fire further back into Mazdurak so we don't get killed?'

Further inside Mazdurak, Perrin was leading the extraction of 10 Platoon through the compounds they had cleared, and then out of the village. Corporal Ferrand's section was still in a toe-to-toe battle with the Taliban, and the densely packed compounds meant no one else could fire at the enemy to help them break clean.

The Taliban were very close, in the alleyway and the compound right in front of them. Hoping to buy a few seconds to get clear, Ferrand told every man to drop a grenade from the roof at the same time. On Ferrand's count, Facal and the others lobbed their grenades, and as the bombs exploded at almost the same moment, like a gigantic, lethal firecracker, they leapt down on to the compound floor and raced across to the other side, weaving and ducking as the bullets continued to pour in and the RPG missiles flew overhead.

Corporal Nick Townsend, attached to the Royal Anglians from The Rifles, was a section commander with Waters's 11 Platoon, positioned to the rear of 10. He led his GPMG and Minimi gunners forward to the corner of their compound to provide fire support for 10 Platoon's movement back. Firing out of the compound with his section, Townsend was suddenly deafened by an enormous blast 2 metres from him. The explosion sent him reeling violently sideways, but he just managed to stay on his feet. Shrapnel had torn into Townsend's neck, femoral artery, groin, leg and foot. He had eleven puncture wounds and was bleeding hard.

Townsend looked round. Behind him, Private Simon Peacock was in a real mess. He had taken the full force of the blast and was even more seriously wounded, hit in the chest. Townsend screamed out, 'Man down. Peacock's hit! Medic! Medic!'

Lance Corporal Howe, Private Ed Garner and Corporal Aaron Pinder ran to help. Peacock was face down. Howes turned him over to check his wounds, and Peacock threw up blood all over him. Howes instinctively recoiled, then he and Pinder picked up the critically wounded soldier and carried him back to the medic, Captain Baz Alexander.

Townsend staggered over to his platoon commander, Lieutenant Olivier, then collapsed. Soldiers rushed in to treat him. Private Budd tried to inject him with morphine, but Townsend shouted, 'I don't like needles – get it away from me. Get it away.'

Olivier organized the evacuation of the two casualties back to 11 Platoon's compound, braving the continuous heavy fire. Alexander and the team medics had patched them up as best they could in the midst of the battle. Sergeant Armon took control of their CASEVAC out of Mazdurak. He had to get them back across the open ground to the RV in the wadi where Waters and Ramm were waiting. The rest of the company would follow close behind.

With the casualties ready to move, Armon led the way out through the compound door. As he emerged he was met with a hail of machine-gun fire, splintering the doorframe and ripping up the wall around it. He tried again and again, but each time was driven back by a violent storm of bullets. Armon identified the enemy fire position, several hundred metres away, and radioed Messenger, 'Zero Alpha, this is Two Zero Charlie, enemy engaging my location from area of Kak e Jinan. Can you suppress with air? Over.'

Even with an air strike, Armon did not want to risk using that exit. The air might destroy the Taliban in the position he had identified, but he knew the enemy would almost certainly have this route covered by other firing points, and he could not risk being pinned down for any length of time with the two casualties. Peacock and Townsend were both in a very bad way, especially Townsend, who Armon feared might die if he wasn't given proper treatment soon. He had to get them away immediately. He looked at his air photo. There was another route out. It was not totally covered, but at least it would not mean carrying two casualties into the teeth of enemy fire. There was no other exit from the compound.

Armon called over the engineer NCO attached to his platoon. 'I intend to extract the casualties out the other side. Prepare to blow down the back wall of the compound. When the air comes in, you will blow it. I will tell you when.'

The engineer and his men went straight to work positioning and rigging bar-mines.

At Messenger's command the Apaches and the A10s launched wave after wave of ferocious strafing runs against the enemy. When he heard the firing Armon shouted across to the engineer, 'Blow it now.'

With a massive blast the wall came down. Armon and his men, showered with dust and debris from the explosion, carried their two casualties through the smoking, craggy hole and raced across the open ground, covering each other as they went. The noise of battle was deafening, with the Apaches now hurling Hellfire missiles into the Taliban positions.

Once the casualties were clear Messenger ordered the remainder of 11 Platoon, followed by 10 Platoon, back across the open ground and into the wadi, covered all the way by fire from the A10s and Apaches.

8

Under Waters's control, the work party that had evacuated Harrison and Gordon were furiously engaging with their rifles and machine-guns, giving cover for 10 and 11 Platoons' movement. Corporal Boyle was with the group, firing and helping control the other soldiers' fire. Several of the men were running low on bullets. Private Liam O'Connor, blazing away with his Minimi, had almost run out. When Boyle asked for an ammo check, several of the men called, 'Last mag.'

Boyle shouted, 'I'll go and get some more ammo from the sergeant major.' Then he thought, *Till then, it's bayonets, I suppose.* He smiled as another thought came to him, *I've always wanted to say this. It's pretty pointless but I'll never have another chance.* He got up to run across to the sergeant major, yelling along the line, 'Fix bayonets! Fix bayonets!' As he ran, he clicked his own bayonet on to the muzzle of his SA80.

Armon had just arrived with Peacock, and Ramm was moving him back into the wadi on his quad bike. Boyle quickly checked him. Shrapnel had punctured both his lungs. His arms, legs and face were bleeding from fragmentation wounds. Alexander had given him all the treatment he could back in Mazdurak, and now he just had to get to the field hospital.

'Nothing I can do for him, sir, just get him back,' said Boyle. 'Before you go, have you got any more ammo?'

Ramm could not risk Peacock's life by pulling him off the quad to get to the ammo boxes. Instead, he emptied his own pouches and passed all his magazines to Boyle.

Ramm was about to move off when there was an enormous blast, and the ground shook as a Taliban mortar impacted 30 metres away. A second explosion followed immediately, closer still. Boyle was knocked down by the third blast, which was directly in front of him. He lay on the ground, badly winded, clutching Ramm's magazines, spitting out blood and fragments of shattered teeth. Something had pierced his tongue, which began to swell. The shock wave had hit him hard. He was dazed, and his whole body was shaking.

He saw blood around his left upper leg. A large, jagged lump of shrapnel had smashed through his knee-cap and chewed up his quad muscle. It didn't feel too bad, but he thought, *That's the adrenalin pumping. That's really going to hurt in a minute*. He grabbed for his morphine autoject and, as he flicked off the cap and banged the needle straight into his leg, he gasped at Ramm, 'Not the thing I'd teach others to do, sir, it's not what we teach. Morphine comes later. But I know it's really going to hurt. And it's me. It's me this time, and that's different.' He managed a sort of grimacing smile through bloody lips.

The consummately professional medic, he took a marker pen from his Osprey and wrote a large letter 'M' on his own forehead. Realizing he couldn't write the time and date, he handed the pen to Ramm. Ramm scrawled on Boyle's head then started to apply a field dressing to his bleeding leg. Boyle stopped him. 'I'm a medic, I can do that. You need to get Peacock away. He's the priority, sir, not me. I'm OK.'

Boyle was now on his own, lying on his back, covered in Ramm's magazines. He shouted to Private Bates, in the firing line, 'Come and get these mags and get them dished out to the lads.'

He took off the bayonet he had fixed a few minutes before, thinking, *don't fancy stabbing myself on top of everything else*. He threw his magazine with the remaining few rounds to Bates, leaving one bullet in the chamber of his rifle. He thought, *Don't want to be over-dramatic, but you never know!* He recalled Kipling's advice to 'The Young British Soldier':

When you're wounded and left on Afghanistan's plains,
And the women come out to cut up what remains,
Jest roll to your rifle and blow out your brains
An' go to your gawd like a soldier.

With a long family tradition of service in the regiment, and as a keen student of regimental history, Boyle knew the poem was about the bloody retreat from Kabul in 1842, when the 44th Regiment of Foot, which had come to form part of the Royal Anglian Regiment following several amalgamations, had been brutally slaughtered.

He turned his mind back to his own treatment, wrapped his field dressing round his knee, pulled it tight and knotted it. Using his rifle, he struggled on to his feet and hopped and slid down the wadi side. The Pinzgauer containing the casualties was about to move off and as it went he managed to get himself into the back, squeezing alongside Peacock.

As the vehicle rattled and juddered across the wadi floor, the doctor started running a line through for Peacock and Townsend. Boyle held up the bag of fluids for Peacock. Peacock looked bad, very bad, and his face was white as a sheet. Townsend looked a bit better even though he had been dropped several times during the nightmare stretcher run out of Mazdurak. All the way back to Broadsword, Boyle was talking to Peacock and prodding him to keep him awake.

Waters and his men continued to give covering fire as the company broke clean from the enemy and began heading back towards Zeebrugge. Waters checked his own men before moving through the wadi, paralleling the rest of the company. He saw that Private O'Connor's daysack had been ripped open by a piece of shrapnel from one of the three mortar shells. He pulled out O'Connor's smoke grenade, which had retained the shrapnel, stopping it from taking O'Connor's head off.

While C Company moved back to Zeebrugge, the Apaches and A10s continued strafing and bombing the Taliban in Mazdurak and Khvolehabad.

Ten minutes after they got clear of the immediate area of Mazdurak, Corporal Bomber Brown called back to his men, snaking along behind him, 'Well done, lads, you all did really well back there. Now we all need to stay alert as we patrol back in. Heads up, cover your arcs, get...'

He was cut off in mid-sentence as a tremendous shock wave rocked the ground beneath his feet. It was the loudest and most deafening explosion he had ever experienced as a 2,000-pound aerial bomb landed in the centre of Mazdurak.

A Bridge Too Far: 6–16 May 2007

C Company patrolled back into Mazdurak in the weeks following the raid in early May, and by a combination of aggressive action on the ground, and the violent use of air-delivered bombs and strafing runs into the enemy fighting positions, gradually weakened the Taliban's grip on their stronghold. The fighting, often at close quarters and in the most difficult heat conditions, was very tough. Almost foot by foot, C Company were pushing the enemy back away from the dam and allowing the reconstruction work that held so much promise for prosperity among the community in Helmand and elsewhere in southern Afghanistan.

Further south, in the strategically important town of Sangin, the situation was not looking good. Sangin had suffered under a vicious Taliban siege for almost a year since June 2006, and was now almost a ghost town. The town was vital to the economy of the whole region, and its survival had much wider implications – President Hamid Karzai had said, 'Lose in Sangin and you lose in Afghanistan.'

Brigadier Lorimer, the Task Force Helmand commander, intended to focus the efforts of much of his force on Sangin in the way he had in Gereshk with Operation Silicon. The siege of the town had been broken at the time the Royal Anglians arrived in Helmand, following a helicopter-borne assault by a battalion from the US 82nd Airborne Division supported by Afghan National Army troops, and forces from Britain, Denmark, Estonia and Canada, with support from US and Dutch aircraft.

In May, the British force in Sangin, augmented by Afghan troops, was based on A Company of The 1st Battalion The Worcestershire and Sherwood Foresters, the Task Force Helmand Reserve, under the operational control of the Royal Anglian Battle Group.

On 6 May a new district governor and chief of police were installed into Sangin. The imposing and proactive Governor Isatullah Wasifi was

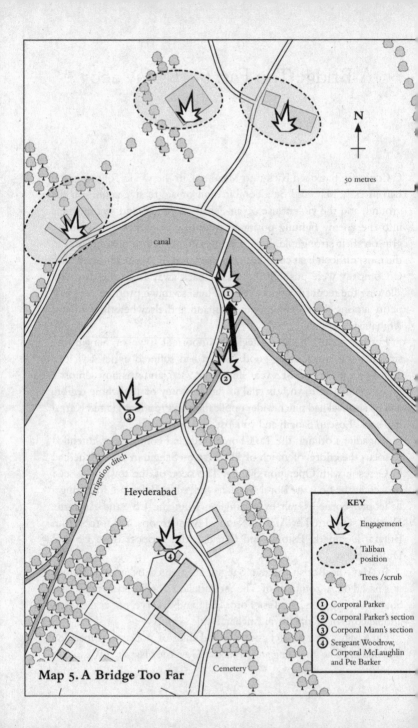

canal

50 metres

N

irrigation ditch

Heyderabad

Cemetery

KEY

Engagement

Taliban position

Trees /scrub

① Corporal Parker
② Corporal Parker's section
③ Corporal Mann's section
④ Sergeant Woodrow, Corporal McLaughlin and Pte Barker

Map 5. A Bridge Too Far

a former mujahideen commander who had fought against the Russians and was eager to work in cooperation with the British to restore normality to his town.

But since the US-led operation, known as Silver, the Taliban had continued to attack the town and intimidate its remaining residents. Understandably there was a reluctance to return on the part of those who had fled during the siege. Lorimer planned to turn the situation around, consolidating the gains of Operation Silver, improving security, encouraging people to return and boosting reconstruction efforts to help develop the local economy.

One evening in mid-May, the Royal Anglians' B Company commander, Major Mick Aston, was wandering around his troops' accommodation in Camp Bastion with Company Sergeant Major Tim Newton. Aston would often 'shoot the crap', as he put it, with the men, keeping his finger on the pulse and maintaining what he saw as the essential close relationship between company commander and soldiers. He also loved nothing more than just being with his soldiers and chatting to them.

For the brief periods that B Company spent in Bastion between operations they lived in a pod complex within Camp 501. This was the Royal Anglians' section of the base, consisting of accommodation, cookhouse, medical centre and offices. The battle group's joint operations centre, or JOC, was a short distance away.

B Company were only transient residents in their pod, which was also used by any other element of the battle group as they came and went from Bastion. The central spine of the pod was a long corridor without air conditioning, and always as hot as a sauna. Leading off one end of the corridor were launderette facilities and showers. Along the length of the spine was a series of half-cylinder-shaped tents with solid plastic floors, each housing ten men. Outside each tent was an air-conditioning unit that would pump in cold air. The men slept on American-style metal and woven nylon camp beds, and their possessions and equipment were jammed untidily into the small space between each bed.

A Battalion HQ signaller arrived in the room and told Major Aston that the CO wanted to see him in the JOC straight away.

'OK, tell him I'll be there in a minute. Hey – I'll bet that's the most sweat you've worked up on this tour, isn't it, hanging around in that air-conditioned ops room?'

Well used to this type of ragging from the rifle company troops and grinning patiently, the signaller muttered a semi-audible retort as he hurried out before Aston could start piling on the customary abuse.

A few minutes later, still dressed in shorts, flip flops and body armour, carrying helmet, rifle and notebook, and sweating heavily after his brisk march up from the accommodation, Aston entered the half-divided section of the ops centre that served as the CO's office. Carver was behind his desk. Phil Moxey, the ops officer, and Tom Coleman, the intelligence officer, were lounging on plastic chairs. Aston nodded at the two captains and said, 'Evening, sir,' to the CO.

'Thanks for coming over, Mick,' said Carver. 'I know it's a bit late, but I thought I might as well brief you now as I'm off to a meeting at Brigade first thing.'

'Are we moving out straight away, sir? Will I need to send out a warning order to the company?' said Aston.

'No, what I want you to do isn't for a few days, but I thought you might as well have plenty of time to think about it and start preparing.'

Having hoped he had been sent for to launch an immediate operation, Aston disappointedly waved away the runner he had brought with him to convey back any immediate instructions to the company.

'OK, sir, shoot.'

'We're planning an op to try to put pressure on these guys who keep carrying out attacks in Sangin. The place is really going downhill again, and I'm not sure how much longer the ANA and the police will stay. We need to do something to back them up and deal with the Taliban who keep coming in to kill them and have a go at the locals.

'Tom and I are trying to work out where best to attack, but it will be somewhere north of Sangin, because that's where they're coming down from. Maybe up in the Qalah-ye Gaz area. That's where you come in. I want you to carry out shaping ops to help create the conditions we need for success. Essentially, you will do a demonstration. Get down into the south and create a diversion. Stir up trouble down there to make the enemy think that's where we're going to attack. That way they will hope-fully reinforce themselves in the south, making our job of taking out the hard core in the north much easier. It will also get us some informa-tion about the enemy in that area. Tom?'

Coleman spoke. 'I haven't got anything specific, but I'm particularly interested in what enemy there is in Zumberlay and Heyderabad. The marines reckoned they are both a hotbed of Taliban, but we haven't seen anything much at all from down there. Maybe they've all left and gone somewhere else. It'd be good to know.'

Carver continued, 'Task Force 1 Fury are doing an op in the Heyderabad area very soon. You may want to hook up with them and take some of your commanders to look at the area before your demonstration. Phil will tie that up for you.'

'Yeah that sounds like a good idea, Colonel,' said Aston. 'What assets am I going to get for the demonstration?'

Moxey said, 'The CO wants you to leave a platoon in FOB Robinson to secure that, so you'll have two of your own platoons plus company HQ with your fire support team. And you should be keeping your own fire support group under Sergeant Major Snow. You'll have a marines armoured support troop, which will give you enough Vikings to lift the whole company. We may also give you some ANA and an OMLT. We're planning to group with you an 81mm mortar section, engineers, probably a conventional munitions disposal team, an electronic warfare team and some medics. So that you're completely self-contained we're also giving you a log detachment with an Oshkosh CST.'

'Phil, I kind of dropped off when they covered logistics crap at Staff College. What on earth's an Oshkosh? Was that what you just said? I thought it was some kind of kid's clothing!'

Moxey said, 'It's a sodding great wheeled fuel tanker. Made by the Americans. They carry 20,000 litres of diesel – should be enough to keep you going for a while. Brilliant across country.'

'OK, Mick,' said Carver, 'let Phil know if you want any more assets, and he'll get them for you if he can. Plan to start on the fourteenth and you'll have about four days to do your stuff. After that I'll probably want you to stay in FOB Robinson till the op begins, and maybe beef up the troops in Sangin during that time.'

2

Major Aston, the company 2IC, Captain Dave Robinson, and Sergeant Major Newton worked out the plan for the operation. Aston decided to leave 6 Platoon under Lieutenant Dave Broomfield, his most experienced platoon commander, to look after FOB Robinson. 5 Platoon under Second Lieutenant Ben Howes and 7 Platoon under Lieutenant George Seal-Coon would go with him on the operation. He would bounce the company in and out of the Green Zone, probing into likely enemy areas and withdrawing back out into the safety of the desert.

He intended to go in well tooled up, ready to deal with anything that was there. But the initial approach into each area would not be with all guns blazing. Instead they would aim to move in, set up a shura, or meeting, with the locals, hoping to gain intelligence and at the same time push out the key messages about what they were doing there and how they were trying to improve security and prosperity in the valley. But if they met resistance they would respond aggressively, attacking the enemy and in doing so gaining information about his strengths and intentions.

Aston thought long and hard about one really important issue. How far to push the company into battle for this diversionary mission. He was not trying to take and hold ground. He was trying to deceive the enemy and gain information. He didn't want to become decisively engaged, but if they got caught up in a fight they had to win. But how many casualties would he be prepared to take for this task? And how exactly would he measure when he had done enough? When to pull back would be a critical decision. Eventually he decided there were no answers to any of these questions. As long as he had thought it all through, as with pretty much any military operation, all he could do was call the shots as best he could on the day.

While B Company got themselves ready to head out, Aston together with Seal-Coon and Howes spent three days with Task Force 1 Fury, an air assault battalion from the US 82nd Airborne Division. They spent time in and around Heyderabad, getting to know the area. There was virtually no resistance, and Aston concluded that this would be a fairly quiet op for B Company. It seemed there wasn't much Taliban presence in the area any longer.

On 14 May Aston led the 176 men of B Company Group out of Camp Bastion, mounted in twelve Vikings and a mixture of wheeled vehicles – in all thirty prime movers. Accompanying them was a platoon of Afghan troops, ANA, mounted in their familiar Toyota pick-up trucks bristling with machine-guns. Bringing up the rear was the lumbering but articulated Oshkosh with its 20,000 litres of fuel. Aston was pleased to see it looked more like a robust combat vehicle than the sort of thing you would see on a garage forecourt in England.

In line with Aston's plan they pushed into Zumberlay later that day and then into the village of Pasab, 6 kilometres north, early in the morning of 15 May. As they entered each of the villages the company was fired on with automatic weapons and RPGs. They returned fire, killing a few enemy, and then withdrew before getting embroiled in a proper battle. The Taliban clearly had a presence here although, as Aston had anticipated, they did not seem to be in large numbers.

After Pasab, Aston moved the company back out into the desert. They spent the afternoon sorting themselves out and resting before the move late that night towards the town of Heyderabad.

In the flat, featureless and rocky desert the company formed a leaguer, two lines of vehicles, about 20 metres apart, with a few metres between each vehicle. At the front and rear of each line was a Fire Support Group Bravo WMIK to provide security. Each WMIK was permanently manned by a sentry, observing the desert, on the lookout for anyone approaching or watching their position, and ready to open fire if necessary. The FSG soldiers, as well as the men from the platoons, took it in turns to do sentry duty, or 'stag' as it was universally known.

The Viking crews went straight to work servicing their vehicles, checking oil and coolant levels and carefully inspecting running gear to make sure there was no damage that could cause the vehicle to throw a track or break down at a critical moment in combat.

Corporal Stu Parker gathered his section to the left of their Viking, where the vehicle hull afforded some protection from the relentless heat of the sun overhead. Most of the men were clacking hot water from dusty plastic bottles that had been stowed in the heat on the outside of the vehicle. Pouring sweat after leaving the sauna that was the Viking crew compartment, they would all have given a week's leave for a cold drink. Water at this temperature was horrible, but like it or not they had to get it down their necks to keep dehydration at bay.

Standing in front of his men, Parker said, 'Well done in Pasab, lads, a few close shaves there, weren't there? Especially you, Stevie, and Josh, when that bullet almost gave you an extra parting. Glad it wasn't me. I don't know how long we're going to be here, but probably till sometime just after midnight. The boss has gone to get a brief from the company commander, so we'll know when he gets back. What we're going to do now is clean weapons and sort our kit out. I expect Woody'll give us an ammo resupply later, but in the meantime top yourselves up from the stuff in the wagon if you need to.'

'The boss' was Lieutenant Seal-Coon, and 'Woody' was 7 Platoon's sergeant, Michael Woodrow, responsible for providing the men with ammunition and all the other supplies and equipment they needed to fight and to live.

Parker continued, 'Make sure you take all your rounds out of your mags and make sure they're clean and free of grit and dust. I know I don't need to tell you that, but it keeps me happy, so I will. After you've done all that get some scoff down your necks and then get your heads down if you want, although I doubt anyone'll be doing much sleeping in this heat.'

He looked at Private Paul Gillmore, temporarily attached to the section from Company HQ, 'You OK, Gillie, no problems? Don't worry, mate, you'll soon be back in HQ when Pingu gets back from R and R.'

'I'm fine, cheers, Stu. I'm enjoying it. Makes a change from what I normally do.'

'OK, well done, then, lads, now crack on and get this all sorted.'

The men unstrapped their Bergens from the outside of the Vikings and slammed them hard on to the ground. This was necessary to throw off the thick coating of dust that had got into every flap and fold of the rucksacks as the vehicles travelled through the desert.

Private John Thrumble took out a plastic pouch of corned beef hash and laid it in the sun – it would be red hot in about ten minutes. He took off his boots, laid out his sweat-drenched socks to dry and peeled off his equally soaking T-shirt. His next priority was music. He unwrapped his iPod and his prized speakers from several layers of plastic bags, balanced them on top of the Viking track and switched on the drum and bass music that he could never bear to be without. With a nod to the tactical situation, he turned the volume down well below the eardrum-bursting level that he would have preferred. Next he carefully laid out a plastic sheet on the ground. He stripped down his GPMG, dismantling it to the smallest part. He placed a second sheet over these parts to give them added shade. Then he began to lovingly dust off, wipe down, oil and chat affectionately to each and every piece.

Private Josh Lee approached, Bergen over one shoulder and fag sticking out of the corner of his mouth. Thrumble leapt up and growled at him, then cursed as his bare feet made contact with the baking-hot, stony ground. Lee sprang backwards. 'What's the matter with you, Thrumbles, I'm not going to attack you, mate, don't worry.'

'Just keep away from the gun. You know no one's allowed near the gun, especially when she's undressed. Keep away from her. If you want to touch her you'll have to ask me. And I'll definitely say no.' He spoke to the gas regulator: 'Did the nasty man scare you? I'm sorry, I won't let him near you. I'll protect you.'

'You've finally cracked, mate,' said Lee, an amused half-smile creeping across his face. 'Not surprising with all that crap music blaring out all the time.'

'Josh, Josh, don't say that,' Thrumble hissed in a stage whisper. 'Mary loves this music. I'm only playing it for her. If you say that sort of thing you'll offend her.' He added menacingly, 'Then you'll have to answer to me.'

Thrumble sat down again and picked up the body of the gun. 'I was thinking of letting Josh look after you when I go on R and R, but he's just blown that.'

Lee flicked a Pine at Thrumble. 'Smoke that and shut up, you idiot,' he laughed, shaking his head as he walked a couple of paces and dropped his Bergen next to Aaron 'Troy' McLure, who had just started cleaning his rifle.

An hour later Parker had finished sorting out his own weapon, squaring away his gear and checking the section's equipment. He was lying in the shade, boots off, head propped against his daysack. He had got through a bit more of Winston Churchill's *My Early Life*, squinting through the strong sunlight at the dusty pages. Lieutenant Seal-Coon appeared and sat in the dirt beside him. 'All right, Corporal P? I've just had a brief from the OC. I'll tell the guys what's happening when we've finished our admin. You were saying something on the net this morning about Taliban up in the trees in Pasab. I couldn't make it out, what was that about?'

'Yeah, that was just after I'd had a face-to-face with you when 3 Section were in contact. When I got back to my section I was sitting up against this wall, and Stevie Veal and Josh Lee were forward of me, and a round went just over their heads and hit the wall near where I was. Chipped a bit of mud out of the wall. Now, as you know, boss, I'm not exactly a CSI investigator.'

'Yes, Corporal P, I had worked that out for myself.'

'Well, anyway, as I say, I'm not, but I figured out it must have come from high up and there were no compounds or anything that it could've been fired from. I looked across and I wondered about the trees. I thought they couldn't be up the trees – bit too risky for them. But I had a good look and couldn't see anything so I told Thrumbles to put a burst through the trees.'

Next to Parker, Thrumble started laughing, 'That was amazing, boss. It was. Mary and me fired a couple of bursts of twenty, and bodies just started falling out everywhere.'

'It wasn't everywhere, was it, Thrumbles? Don't exaggerate to the platoon commander,' said Parker. 'But two bodies fell out of the trees. It was like some sick comedy show or something.'

'How far away were the trees?' asked Seal-Coon.

'Oh, a good couple of hundred metres. They were like green decidu-ous trees, lots of thick foliage, bit like oak trees or something. The fun-niest bit was as soon as these bodies fell out of the trees this idiot here started singing "It's Raining Men". I was cracking up.'

Thrumble said, 'Yeah, well, boss, you've got to have some morale, even in contact, especially in contact, haven't you?'

Seal-Coon said, 'I bet the guys in the trees didn't have much morale at that point, though. But with all the jokers in this section I doubt you lot will ever be short of morale.'

Private Robert Foster, at the other end of the Viking, called out, 'Hey, sir, that's not true. Thrumble isn't funny, he just thinks he is. He forces us to laugh at his stupid jokes. The only people that think he's funny are the Taliban. Oh, and Boothie, because he doesn't know any better.'

He dug his toe into his best mate, Private Booth, who was trying to get some sleep next to him. Foster had a strict rule: if he didn't want Booth to sleep, Booth wouldn't sleep.

'Shut up, Fozzie,' said Parker, 'and get on with cleaning your rifle. No one asked for your opinion. You're enough of a comedian to keep the whole brigade amused, and the Taliban as well.'

'Thanks, Parky, I'll take that as a compliment. Anyway, as I was say-ing just a couple of days ago…'

'Fozzie, I said shut up. That's the trouble with you teenagers of today, you don't know when to listen to your elders and betters. Boys like you should be seen and not heard. In fact, preferably not seen either.'

'Older is right, Parky, you're really too old to be out here...'

'Fozzie, shut it.'

Parker turned back to Seal-Coon. 'You know what, sir, I reckon that's what some of those snidey little bastards were doing on Silicon, hanging around in the tops of the trees. That's why most of the time we could never see them when they were shooting at us. I read that in some book as well about jungle fighting – might have been Vietnam. Always look up as well as left and right when you're on patrol. I'm definitely going to keep an eye on the trees out here from now on anyway.'

B Company was on the move again by 0230 hours. As so often happens with the simplest military task, it turned into a nightmare come true.

3

The journey from the company's leaguer to Heyderabad was only 6 kilometres westwards across the open desert but it took four and a half hours. In the pitch darkness, and driving through clouds of dust kicked up by the wagons in front, vehicle after vehicle got bogged in and had to be laboriously dragged out of the soft sand. With commanders and drivers trying to work their way round drainage ditches, and searching for crossing points, the column got split up several times.

As they crashed on through the desert, Corporal Parker, in the front cab of his section's Viking, was effectively blind. The windows in the vehicle were blanked out with plastic screens, velcroed into place. In front of the driver, a flat-screen monitor had been folded down and gave him the picture from the vehicle's infra-red camera. Next to Parker the communications equipment console prevented him from having even a partial view of the screen.

Above, the Viking gunner was helping to guide the vehicle and warn the driver of hazards ahead, using his image-intensifying goggles. But, as with all night visibility equipment, the driver's and gunner's sights do not give an impression of depth, so it was very difficult to avoid depressions, ruts, ditches and banks. This did not make the journey comfortable for the troops in the back and contributed to the many occasions that night when Vikings got bogged in and had to drag one another free.

Sergeant Tinkler, the 81mm Mortar Section commander, could see nothing from the cab of his Pinzgauer. Trying to get some visibility to guide his driver, he stood up with his head and shoulders out of the top. The Pinz smashed into a berm, and Tinkler was launched out of the vehicle, landing in a crumpled heap on the ground in front.

Company Sergeant Major Newton, racing round in his Viking to round up the scattered vehicles, arrived just as Tinkler was dusting himself off. 'Thank goodness you've come back for me, sir, that was getting to be a bit of a drama.'

The logistics vehicles were dropped off in the desert a few kilometres away from Heyderabad. Incredibly the huge Oshkosh tanker, carrying thousands of litres of diesel, had been almost the only vehicle in the column that did not get bogged in. It was an impressive machine, 15 metres long and consisting of a large cylindrical fuel tank towed by a 6x6 all-wheel drive MTVR tractor with an 11.9-litre diesel engine. The troops decided it would be able to make it up Everest without difficulty.

Aston set up a strong fire support base to the south of the town. Sergeant Major Snow's fire support group WMIKs, armed with GPMGs, GMGs and .50 cal heavy machine-guns, plus the Javelin missile systems with their excellent observation devices, were deployed to cover the move in of the rest of the company. This fire base would be beefed up by the Vikings, with their machine guns, once the company had been dropped off. Behind the FSG, Sergeant Tinkler set up his three 81mm mortars to provide immediate dedicated indirect fire support.

At 0600 hours, when the Vikings were 1,500 metres from the village, Aston transmitted over the company net, 'Dismount, dismount.'

It was potentially dangerous crossing this open area on foot, even with cover already in place from Snow's fire base. But it would have been even more dangerous to close up to the outskirts of Heyderabad, where the compounds provided concealment for Taliban RPG gunners, who could cause significant damage to a Viking and the men inside.

The troops dismounted beyond RPG range, in the flat, open desert, where there was nowhere for an RPG gunner to hide.

Sniper Lance Corporal Teddy Ruecker was relieved to get out of his Viking and into the air. Even though it was still early morning, the heat was building outside. But it was nothing compared to the sauna of the Viking. As usual the air conditioning wasn't working, and the seven infantrymen jammed into the armoured box, with all their weapons and equipment plus crates of spare ammo and explosives, had been sweating buckets. Not knowing what was waiting for him, as he clambered out of the vehicle, he and the other soldiers rushed straight towards the nearest piece of cover, at best a slight fold in the ground or a large rock. There was no firing. That was something at least.

As soon as they were out, the Vikings turned and ground back off across the desert to take up their fire support positions, kicking up huge clouds of dust as they went. Ruecker thought, *Glad to be out of those things, but I don't like seeing them go.* To some extent, in the middle of the desert, and with enemy potentially anywhere, the soldiers had come to think of these machines as life support, with their guns, their powerful communications, their supplies on board, their mobility and the armoured protection they provided.

Looking around, Ruecker saw dozens of Afghan civilians – men, women and children, just sitting outside the village, in the open, in whatever shade they could find. *Why have they left?* He felt immediately apprehensive again and started scanning the area in and around the village through the sniper scope on his .338 long-range rifle.

The people had seen the Vikings approach, and there were two possibilities: Taliban fighters were in the village, or they might soon be arriving. Either way they sensed a fight about to break out, and wanted to be out of the way when it did.

4

Major Aston sent interpreters to talk to the villagers, 'Are there Taliban here?'

The answer was always the same. 'No, no Taliban. They left a few hours earlier.'

You had to take it with a pinch of salt. They may not necessarily have wanted harm to come to these soldiers, but they all knew better than to talk to them truthfully about the Taliban. Self-preservation was understandably their top priority.

5 Platoon pushed out towards the left-hand side of the village first, deployed across the open ground in half attack formation, spread out ready for an immediate assault if necessary, but positioned in such a

way as to be ready to deal with enemy in any direction. Aston's Tac HQ moved close behind, followed by 7 Platoon.

Ruecker started as he heard shots ring out to his forward right. The platoon's leading section had seen two men on motorbikes a couple of hundred metres away – possibly Taliban observers, informing other fighters of the British movement towards the village. The soldiers had fired warning shots to send them on their way. The motorbikes veered off and disappeared from view. Ruecker felt tense. The bikes were another sign that they were walking into danger. They were still in the open, and as a sniper he knew more than most how vulnerable that made them to enemy snipers.

Both platoons had now reached the outskirts of the village. A few dispersed compounds interspersed with foliage and treelines criss-crossing the area. A different type of danger could reside here, but at least there was cover of sorts.

The unnerving quiet was suddenly broken by a long burst of fire from a lone machine-gun. It was immediately joined by several other automatic weapons, firing into 5 Platoon to the front.

Aston was immediately on the company net to Seal-Coon, 7 Platoon commander, 'Three Zero, this is Zero Alpha, close up right behind One Zero, ready to support.'

With the rattling, piercing sound of constant heavy gunfire ahead, Ruecker and the rest of 7 Platoon sweated their way forward along a ragged treeline. They quickly covered the 200 metres it took to get close enough to attack if 5 Platoon couldn't deal with the problem.

Seal-Coon, leading his men forward, could now see 5 Platoon, who had taken cover in a large compound. He dashed forward for a face-to-face with Howes, the commander of 5 Platoon, still under machine-gun and RPG fire. 'Ben, I'm going to put my guys into that ditch. Can you give us a shedload of covering fire while we move across the gap?'

As the troops moved forward, Aston said to the JTAC, 'See if you can get me some air.'

He turned to the FST commander: 'Get the guns ready. We'll use them if we can spot the enemy.'

Then he heard Sergeant Major Snow's measured voice: 'Zero Alpha, this is Four Zero Alpha, we're taking a fair bit of incoming up here as well. Machine-gun fire. It's coming from the west. Permission to engage with mortars.'

Aston always reserved authority to fire mortars, artillery or air for himself. Especially fighting in close country like this, where there was the ever-present risk of a blue on blue, or so-called 'friendly fire'. He felt that only he would have all the information needed to be certain they would not be firing on their own troops.

Snow sent grid references of the enemy positions he had identified, and Aston checked them with Corporal Wilsher, his MFC. They confirmed there were no friendly troops in the area of these grids, and then Aston said, 'OK, Will, tell the mortars to fire on those targets.'

Seconds after Wilsher rattled the fire mission into his radio, to Aston's horror, he saw mortar shells exploding in and around 7 Platoon's position.

As the machine-gun fire kept pouring in, Ruecker and the rest of 7 Platoon had taken cover in a dry ditch bed. Ruecker was just sorting himself out into a solid fire position so that he could scan for enemy in the distance, when the mortars started pounding in. He flattened himself into the ground, knowing that, with jagged lumps of shrapnel scything through the air, just an inch less exposure could save his life. Parker, closer to the first impact, ran down the ditch towards Ruecker, trying to get away from the lethal explosions.

In that instant, Corporal Stephan Martin, one of 7 Platoon's section commanders, looked into Seal-Coon's eyes. Without speaking, the two said: are these our own mortars? The two soldiers leapt forward into the ditch to escape the blasts. As he dived in, landing on top of Seal-Coon, Martin felt as if his arm had been ripped off his shoulder. He looked down and saw blood running down his sleeve. 'I've been hit! I've been hit!'

Seal-Coon, terrified that their own mortars would cut his platoon to ribbons, screamed into his radio handset, 'Check fire the mortars! Check fire. Check fire.'

Two hundred metres away, Aston was shouting at Wilsher, 'Stop those mortars, they're hitting our own men.'

Wilsher yelled back, 'They're not ours. We haven't started firing yet.'

7 Platoon were still under mortar fire, but Aston was momentarily relieved. *Thank Christ they're not ours,* he thought, and he said, 'Then get ours firing. On the grids I told you. And make sure of the grid. I don't want to go through that again.'

He said to his signaller, 'Get on the net and find out from 7 Platoon if they have casualties.'

He turned to the JTAC. 'Air?'

'There's a B1 bomber overhead in thirty seconds.'

Now Snow was back on the net. 'I've ID'd the mortar team. Can we have our own mortars fire on it?'

Aston replied, 'Better still, we've got a B1 up there. Send grid and we'll hit it with that.'

Snow transmitted the grid reference, Aston repeated it to the JTAC, and within seconds the B1, thousands of feet above, had identified the target.

Aston spoke into his handset, 'Charlie Charlie One, this is Zero Alpha. Two-thousand-pound bomb on the ground in figures three zero.'

As the earth shook from the devastating blast that destroyed the Taliban mortar team, Corporal Mac McLaughlan, the company medic, ran forward to the ditch. He dived in beside Martin and checked his wound. 'Steph, hold your arm out. I'll put a dressing on.'

When he had stopped the bleeding, McLaughlan said, 'OK, Steph, I'll take you back. You've lost a fair bit of blood, but I'm sure you can walk to the RV with the sergeant major.'

'Mac, get the dressing tied off then leave me alone, mate. There's no way – no way – I'm going back with that wound. No way. I'm staying here, commanding my section.'

Snow's fire support group were engaging the enemy positions with machine-gun and grenade fire. Tinkler's mortars pounded the Taliban with fire mission after fire mission. The B1 dropped several more bombs before being replaced on station by a pair of Apache gunships, which peppered the enemy positions with 30mm cannon over the next hour. Then they were called off for a mission elsewhere in Helmand.

Under this sustained assault, the enemy fire against 5 and 7 Platoons had fallen away, although 5 Platoon and the FSG continued to receive incoming enemy rifle, machine-gun and RPG fire.

∫

The platoons moved forward again, clearing from compound to compound. Many of the attacks were at state red, blasting into the mud structures with bar-mines, lobbing in hand grenades and spraying the

rooms with automatic fire. When ammunition was getting low, sometimes the assault teams would throw in a rock rather than a grenade,
hoping to fool enemy fighters into taking cover, to give that split-second
advantage that could be the difference between life and death.

The heat relentlessly increased as the day wore on. The soldiers,
struggling under their heavy battle loads of personal equipment, weapons, water and ammunition, became more and more exhausted as they
cleared compound after compound. Crawling through stinking sewage
ditches, climbing high mud walls, dashing from room to room, struggling
through hedges, racing across exposed, open courtyards – this type of
fighting, even without strong enemy resistance, can be the toughest
there is.

Virtually all the compounds were deserted – almost no civilians
remained in the town, and there was little sign of the enemy. The Taliban were rarely caught in compounds. They were highly skilled at
shooting from buildings then escaping along carefully reconnoitred,
planned and prepared routes in dead ground – invisible to the advancing soldiers.

Seal-Coon was suspicious when he found two men in one of the
compounds. The older man claimed the younger was his son. They
tried to stop the troops entering one of the rooms. Through his interpreter, Seal-Coon said, 'Open the door or we'll kick it down.'

Inside there were piles of shell cases and US grenade cartridges. The
Americans had been through the village before, and Seal-Coon figured
out this man had cleared them up for recycling – a cottage industry in
its own right in war-torn Helmand. There were no weapons, so Seal-
Coon let the men go. He didn't think they would have allowed themselves to be caught if they had been Taliban fighters.

7 Platoon continued clearing from compound to compound. They
went through two mosques. Mosques were not easy to identify until
you were up close. Rectangular blocks like all the others, normally the
only external distinction was a tannoy at the front entrance to call the
faithful to prayer. Inside there was some matting on the floor for wor-
shippers to kneel on, and the large rooms were dark with only a couple
of small windows, usually high up in the wall.

Seal-Coon and his men were well aware of the sensitivities, and they
searched mosques with greater care than most compounds, showing
proper respect to religious artefacts such as the fragments of an ancient

Koran they found in one of the buildings. But searching mosques could not be avoided. Intelligence briefings frequently reminded the men that the Taliban used mosques to conceal weapons, hoping they would be less likely to be searched than other buildings. And it wasn't unusual for the Taliban to fire at the troops from mosques.

Seal-Coon heard Aston's voice on the company net. 'All stations, this is Zero Alpha. One Zero, go firm in current location. I want Three Zero to take over the lead. You push through One Zero's position. Inform me when moving. Three Zero acknowledge, over.'

'Roger out.' Seal-Coon then called his section commanders to confirm they had heard Aston's orders, and pushed Parker's section into the lead.

As Seal-Coon's 7 Platoon moved through, 5 Platoon had gone firm around compound walls and on roofs, ready to open fire if the enemy raised their heads.

Ruecker, still moving with 7 Platoon, saw 5 Platoon's sniper team – Lance Corporal Dean Bailey and Private Scotty Fryer – on top of one of the buildings. 'All right, Dean mate, how's it going?' he called up.

It was now 1030 in the morning, and Bailey was sweating heavily on his rooftop in the full glare of the sun. He looked knackered, but had a big, broad grin on his face. 'Got my first kill: dropped a Taliban at 900 metres.'

'Static?'

'No, he was on the move, running right to left, with an AK.'

As Ruecker replied, 'Well done, mate,' Bailey could see the look of annoyance on his face. He put his thumb up to Ruecker and asked him the question to which he already guessed the answer: 'How about you? How many have you got?'

Ruecker replied to Bailey's thumb with middle finger extended and carried on walking.

The friendly rivalry that permeated every aspect of life in the battalion was just as strong between snipers as anyone else. After a tough selection, their skills had been honed to perfection in long and gruelling courses on some of the Army's most demanding training areas. The qualification 'sniper' was one of the most sought after in the infantry, and with good reason. It was extremely difficult to achieve and it tested every single one of the most important infantry skills – shooting, physical fitness, camouflage and concealment, use of the ground, navigation and communications. The sniper badge, crossed rifles with the letter 'S' above, told you its wearer was among the best soldiers in the battalion.

This was Bailey's and Ruecker's first combat tour as snipers. Along with the other battalion snipers, they had been itching for their first kill. They were not bloodthirsty men, but they were in a vicious struggle with a deadly enemy that was trying to kill them – and their mates.

Although their trade was grim, they were like any other highly skilled professional, keen to see whether the skills they had trained in did actually work, and whether they could indeed kill a fast-moving man at long range in the tough conditions of battle in Afghanistan with a single shot. A very different situation to any practice firing range, even on the arduous exercises in the hills of Brecon. Here they were unbearably hot, on the verge of exhaustion, working in filthy, dusty conditions. And something that couldn't be fully replicated in training – a skilful and ruthless enemy was trying to kill them.

Ruecker, one of the most competitive men in the battalion, realized he had just been pipped to the post by his close mate, Dean Bailey. He was not best pleased.

Over the next couple of hours 7 Platoon continued to search the compounds. Section by section, they raced across an alley, stacked up beside the compound wall, blasted a hole with a bar-mine or kicked in the door and charged in shooting, checking every room and outbuilding for Taliban. Once they heard the shout 'Compound clear,' the next section moved through and into the compound beyond. The platoon continued this gruelling movement, leap-frogging through the town section by section, compound by compound. By now the enemy fire had been reduced to the odd shot or short machine-gun burst, plus an occasional RPG.

The platoon moved through a graveyard on the slope to the right side of the main track leading through the village and down to the river. Most of the burial plots were marked by small piles of rocks supporting crooked, metre-long tree branches, planted vertically. Fluttering from each of the branches was a long, ragged pennant, mostly green or white strips of cloth.

It was only 1130 hours, but the men felt like they had been at this all day. Aston ordered the company to halt temporarily to rest, take on water and rations. Each section commander posted sentries to watch for enemy movement, while the others took advantage of the shade provided by compound walls and the odd tree as they drained water bottles and munched their way through hard and flavourless compo biscuits. Company Sergeant Major Tim Newton motored forward in his Viking to replenish the troops with ammunition and water.

Seal-Coon took the opportunity to move round his men, making sure everyone was OK. It is critical for a platoon commander in battle to keep his finger firmly on the pulse of the men's morale and well-being. He must know for himself if there are any individual problems, and he must always understand exactly what effect a particular battle is having on the men so he can judge how far to push them, and which section to use for which task. The same applies at company level, but the company commander has to rely much more on the feeling of the platoon commander as he has too many men to see individually during a battle.

Seal-Coon stopped briefly and chatted with several junior NCOs and privates. Morale was high. It had been tough going but exciting, and no one had been seriously hurt. He squatted down beside Martin, who was sitting up against a compound wall. 'How's your arm, Corporal M?'

'It's great, sir. Stings a bit, but it's fine.'

Knowing exactly what the response would be, Seal-Coon smiled as he asked, 'You sure you don't need to be CASEVACed? The sergeant major's Viking is just over there; he could take you back and get you looked at by the doc.'

'Sir, with all due respect, there's no way in the world I'm going any- where. I've never disobeyed an order before, sir, but if you order me to go back, I will disobey. Apart from anything else, there's no way I could stand the piss-taking from the troops. No way.'

Seal-Coon nodded and moved on. Private Aaron 'Ronnie' Barker was propped against a compound door, arguing with Private Luke Geater while chewing a bag of corned beef hash that had become almost liquefied in the heat.

Barker had had a tough life as a young boy, and things at home had not been good. He had been taken into foster care, and his grandmother had also played a major role in his upbringing. He joined the Army at seventeen, found the close-knit family he craved in the barrack blocks at Pirbright and never looked back. He was one of the most popular characters in the company, mainly because he was strong, loyal and utterly reliable. But also because he was one of the easiest to wind up.

And the ragging continued just as ferociously during every lull in battle as in the boredom of garrison life at Pirbright. Geater was saying, 'It's a good job your team's West Ham, isn't it, Ronnie? I bet you picked it because there's no *r* in the team name. West Ham's easy for you to pronounce, isn't it? Must have been something like that because it can't have been anything to do with the quality of football they play – if you could even call it football.'

'Well, your mob aren't exactly doing brilliantly, are they? Boring team, really boring.'

'At least I can pronounce it, Wonnie. Go on, say Arsenal. You can't can you, that's why you don't support the gweatest team in the land, because you can't pwonounce their name. While you're at it, you best change your name, Wonnie, mate. Even Awon isn't the best for you, is it?'

'Geater, I'm going to shove this UGL down your neck in a minute if you don't shut up…'

'Oh, hello, sir.'

Seal-Coon was grinning at this familiar exchange. 'All right, Ronnie? Don't waste the UGL on Geats. It's not even worth wasting a blank round on an Arsenal supporter, is it? Anyway, have you fired any yet today?'

'No, sir, just thrown a couple of grenades and a few bursts of 5.56. These UGLs aren't much good in compound clearing: just as likely to bounce back at you and blow your face off. Pity we can't get hold of more of the American ones that don't bounce so much.'

Ruecker now appeared. 'Boss, just come over the net the OC wants a face-to-face with platoon commanders. He's in that compound next to the sergeant major's Viking.'

6

When Seal-Coon arrived for the company commander's orders, Aston, Howes and the fire support coordinators and signallers were waiting. Aston said, 'Didn't get you up, did I, George? Don't worry about us here, we don't mind hanging about all day.'

He grinned, but he was only half joking – he hated being kept waiting, whether it was anyone's fault or not. 'How're your lads?'

'They're fine thanks, sir. Knackered but fine. Did you hear Corporal Martin got some shrapnel from a Taliban mortar? Thought it was ours at first. But he's OK. Doesn't need to be CASEVACed.'

'OK, well done. Yeah, those mortars had me going too, and I nearly beat the crap out of Will.' He glanced over at Wilsher, the MFC. 'I was on my way up the hill to do the same to Tinkler till I realized it was the Taliban. Should've known anyway: the Taliban are more accurate than our mortars, aren't they, Will?'

He clapped the slightly hunted-looking Wilsher across the shoulders.

'Anyway, enough of that. That was all a bit sporty at times, wasn't it? But the lads did well. Plenty of momentum getting through those compounds. Now we're going to push on down to the canal and across the bridge. I don't think I've got much of a handle on the enemy here yet, and I want to know how much this place means to them.

'Ben, I want 5 Platoon to move up on to the high ground where the graveyard is, then George, take 7 Platoon down to secure the bridge. When you've done that 5 Platoon will pass through and clear the first few compounds on the other side. Then we'll send the ANA over to talk to the locals and see what we can find out.'

'When do you want us to move?' asked Howes.

'The boys've had more than enough rest. They'll start thinking they're on R and R. So get going as soon as you get back and brief your platoon. Give me a call when you're moving, and tell George when you're in position. Then he can start dealing with the last of the compounds straight away. OK, George?'

Parker briefed his section on the new plan, 'The OC wants us to get across the bridge, and then 5 Platoon will move through.'

Lance Corporal Steve Veal, the section 2IC, said, 'You are joking? I thought we were going to head back now we've pretty much cleared the village. Across the canal? God knows what's over there. It's a bridge too far.'

'Yeah, bridge too far,' Parker laughed. 'I've seen the film too. Good film. Now get ready to go.'

As the section sorted themselves out, Parker heard the whoosh of a rocket flying over his position and then a loud explosion a few hundred metres away. Seconds later Snow was on the company net, his voice calm as always but betraying a little more concern than usual, 'One-oh-seven, one-oh-seven, impacted on my position. Can anyone see a launch point?'

The Taliban often used the Chinese-designed Type 63-2 107mm rocket. This weapon was used by armies and insurgents around the world and had been used by the Afghan mujahideen against the Soviets. It was designed as a multiple-launch system to be towed or carried on the back of a truck; the Taliban used individual launch tubes disintegrated from the multiple system. They fired them electrically from the ground, crudely propping up the launch tubes on a pile of rocks to achieve the right trajectory and direction of flight.

The 107 is far more lethal than RPGs or the 82mm mortars that had been fired at 7 Platoon earlier that day. The 18.8kg rocket contains an 8.3kg TNT fragmentation warhead. When it detonates it can produce a devastating blast of jagged metal fragments out to 12.5 metres. It was imperative that B Company identify and destroy the launch site as quickly as possible before they started taking casualties.

Capable of a maximum range of 8.5 kilometres, used singly the rocket is notoriously inaccurate, especially at longer ranges. The fact that they were now hitting close to Snow's position suggested both an experienced and capable enemy rocket team, and that they were being fired from somewhere near by.

More 107s were now impacting close to the FSG. Parker called Seal-Coon: 'Hello, Copper Three Zero Alpha, this is Three Two Charlie. I can hear the 107s getting fired. I estimate approx 200 metres forward on the other side of the canal. Can't identify the exact location from my current position.'

Before Seal-Coon could respond, Aston interrupted, 'Three Zero and Three Two Charlie, this is Zero Alpha, roger that. Get yourselves forward so you can identify the launch point and then destroy it or send me a fire mission so I can hit it with indirect. Over.'

Parker responded, 'Three Two Charlie, roger. I may need to cross the canal.'

'Roger, well get down there and get across it if you have to. Get eyes on to that launch point and give me a grid and compound number. Over.'

Several more rockets were impacting around the FSG's position as 5 Platoon moved rapidly up into the graveyard to provide overwatch for 7 Platoon's move forward.

Seal-Coon called in the three section commanders for a quick brief. 'Corporal P, get down to the bridge and see if it's clear to cross. If you

ID the fire position before you get there call the OC direct and tell him. Corporal Mann, get your section off to the left and give cover. You move now. Corporal Martin, keep your section back in the next compound to cover the rear and the right. Corporal Parker, move to the bridge as soon as Corporal Mann is in position. If the bridge is clear, push across it. Corporal Martin, you will then move down and follow him over. When they're firm, Corporal Mann, you get your guys over. We can't afford to have just one or two sections isolated on the other side of the canal. I will move directly behind Corporal P's section and we will get cover from 5 Platoon up here. Let's go.'

Parker moved to the corner of the compound in front of the graveyard. From there he had a good view of the bridge. It was about 50 metres to his front. The track next to him bent left then right and down to the bridge. He looked through his permanent-focus binos. The bridge looked a solid enough structure, constructed of mud and wattle like compound walls. It was spanned by wooden beams, and wide enough to get a single vehicle across. Running under the bridge was an irrigation ditch, a canal, about 3 metres across, deep and fast-flowing with murky brown water. Beyond the bridge was a bank. To the left there were some trees and to the right a thick green hedgerow. Beyond were some small outbuildings and compounds which marked the start of the village on the far side. Among these was a new building that appeared to be nearing completion, which looked to Parker like some kind of medical centre.

Parker thought to himself, *This is more than a canal, it's like a line in the sand. If that was my bridge I wouldn't let anyone cross. This is dangerous. Maybe it is a bridge too far like Steve said.*

He said to his section, 'I've got a bad feeling about this. It's going to kick off. Everybody take your safety catches off.'

7

Corporal Greg Mann and his section were now in place forward left, ready to cover Parker's men as they advanced to the bridge.

Corporal Parker led his section round the compound in single-file, well spread out. He pushed right from the track into a large poppy field, heading towards an irrigation ditch that ran almost parallel to the track, meeting the canal off to the right of the bridge.

When they got to the ditch Parker turned to his men, 'I'm going down to check out the bridge, make sure it's not wired up or anything. If it's OK I'll call you forward. You need to get in that ditch and go firm.'

The men looked at him questioningly, not keen to jump into the filthy trench, up to their chests in stinking irrigation water and sewage.

'Just get in,' said Parker firmly, and they knew that the look he gave them didn't allow for any discussion.

'Fozzie, you're coming with me. Let's go.'

Parker always used Foster as his point man, his lead scout. A young and inexperienced soldier, Foster nevertheless had a good feel for the ground and could read the situation well. He was a strong, brave and dependable lad, and Parker wanted him with him in what he saw as an increasingly dangerous situation.

Parker and Foster crossed the field running between the ditch where they had left the section and the track that led to the bridge. Rifles in the shoulder, scanning over SUSAT sights, looking for any sign of enemy activity. They were in the open. Exposed to an area they thought might contain Taliban – that had not yet been cleared. This was what the infantry did. And it was about as dangerous as it got for anyone, anywhere.

As they got closer to the bridge Parker was relieved to see that it looked clear. There was no sign of enemy in the compounds across the canal. Surely they would have opened up by now if they had been there, or at least Company HQ would have picked up something on the radio scanners. Perhaps if the Taliban had been there, they had moved out…

Parker spoke into his PRR. 'OK, lads, I think it's clear, we'll go across.'

As he released the PRR pressel switch his heart almost stopped as an RPG-7 rocket screamed right between him and Foster, just a couple of feet above their heads. They dropped straight down as a massive blast of machine-gun fire erupted from all over the compounds across the canal, throwing up lumps of mud and scything through poppies. Parker hugged the ground, almost trying to pull himself through the earth, and, as the hail of bullets fell round them, the two soldiers crawled rapidly forward to a low bank, desperate for the small amount of protection it would give them.

When he got to the bank, keeping his head and body low, Parker looked back. Where the rocket had landed there was a cloud of smoke and dirt. It was at the exact point he had left his section just minutes before. His heart was racing, thudding, and he had a warm taste in his mouth and a churning stomach. He felt sick. They must all be dead.

He pulled himself up the bank, wanting to keep his head down so that it didn't get knocked off his shoulders. But he needed to see where the fire was coming from so he could fire back. To the left, Corporal Mann's section were firing over the canal. He could just see the bridge through the grass in front of his eyes. No one near it, but he could see the words '82nd Airborne' spray-painted in large white letters right across its side.

Looking to the left of the bridge, he could make out what Mann's section were firing at, and then he saw smoke and flashes in and around the new building, the medical centre. This was where most of the Taliban fire seemed to be coming from. Firing rapid single shots at the corner of the building, he called to Foster, 'Watch my tracer and shoot at the same target.'

Foster fired, but after the first shot his rifle jammed. Expanded in the intense heat, the cartridge case had stuck fast in the breech. This was the worst possible time for a stoppage.

Foster shouted, 'You got any rods? I need rods. I need rods.'

Parker said, 'No. I haven't. Crawl back over to the ditch, then get back along the ditch to the section.'

Foster looked at him wide-eyed. *No*, he mouthed, *no*. Foster didn't want to go back across the open ground, through the hail of bullets. He was terrified. He didn't know what had happened to the rest of the section, and he didn't want to be the one that found out. He had seen plenty of ripped-up enemy bodies on Silicon and he didn't want to crawl back through enemy fire and find his own mates like that. If he made it back at all.

Parker said, 'Go on, Fozzie, and when you get back, I want the blokes forward, especially the guns, get the guns forward. And sort out your rifle and come back to me.'

Parker too knew that the worst had probably happened to his men, but he didn't want to admit that to Foster. And Foster had to get back to find out what had happened, and he had to get his rifle sorted. Without it he was useless to Parker where he was now.

With courage that was characteristic of the nineteen-year-old Robert Foster, the man who was always at the front of the section, the one leading the others towards the enemy, the one always in the greatest danger, he took control of his fears and crawled as fast as he could back through the fire towards that trench.

8

When the RPG flew in to Parker's section, Gillmore, the soldier attached from Company HQ, saw a little ball of light flying directly at him. There was no time to move or even dive for cover. Then there was a thunderous explosion right next to him. He felt a twist in his groin, and the next thing he knew he was looking down at his hands and shaking. His helmet had been ripped off his head and his Minimi was torn away from him, thrown 5 metres forward. He didn't know where he was. He heard massive bursts of gunfire and loud shouting. His ears were ringing, and nothing was making sense.

Behind him, a few metres back but on the side of the ditch scanning around the bridge and into the buildings beyond, Ruecker and his sniper No 2, Lance Corporal Jason Carter, dived straight into the water. Tracer bullets were bouncing in among them and ricocheting off the ground in every direction.

Ruecker called out to the men in front where the rocket had exploded, 'You OK, guys? You OK?'

He got no reply. The rocket must have hit them. It had to. But there were no screams, and he thought they must have all been killed outright. He and Carter pushed forward, keeping low, bullets still zipping over their heads.

The section were up on the lip of the ditch, where they had been in fire positions. They were all badly dazed by the shock waves from the exploding rocket but, to Ruecker's relief, they had not been killed. Bullets were smacking into the earth around them, but they did not seem to realize the danger they were in. Ruecker and Carter reached up and dragged them down into the safety of the filthy ditchwater.

Carter saw blood around Gillmore's ankle and called out, 'Gillmore's been hit.'

'No I'm OK, just twisted my hip, I'm OK.'

Carter grabbed hold of Lance Corporal Steve Veal, who had been knocked unconscious and was just beginning to come round. 'Steve,

157

Steve, Gillmore's got shrapnel in his ankle. Get on the radio for a medic.'

More RPGs were exploding overhead, impacting in the dirt above the ditch or whizzing past. A total of seventeen rockets had been fired within five minutes. A hail of bullets continued overhead. Tree branches were falling down on top of them, cut away by the devastating machine-gun fire.

Veal couldn't get through on the radio and he needed to support Parker, isolated down by the bridge. He led the men back up to the lip of the ditch and across on their bellies to a slight rise in the ground. Even Gillmore, with his ankle torn open and bleeding from the RPG shrapnel, came forward to engage. Veal identified the compounds where the fire was coming from, across the river. He gave a rapid fire control order to the section to get them concentrating fire towards the main enemy position. RPG after RPG was flying overhead, with the distinctive whoosh-bang as they tore through the air and exploded on impact.

Private Josh Lee opened up on the enemy with his UGL, sending volleys of grenades the 80 metres across to the compound.

But the enemy got their range, and they came under fire from several machine-guns.

'Crawl back, crawl back, back into the ditch,' called Veal.

The rest of the men moved back, but Private Troy McLure wouldn't budge. Rock solid and fearless, he was focused only on killing the enemy, as he emptied mag after mag across the canal. Veal had to physically drag him back to the ditch.

Seal-Coon had crawled forward and was beside Veal. 'Sir,' said Veal, 'I'm going to push my fire team forward to support Parky.'

'No,' said Seal-Coon, 'keep your men here. I don't think Corporal Martin's section are in a position to give depth support at present. We need you here to deal with any Taliban that try to infiltrate round the flanks and get behind Parky.'

Seal-Coon kept trying to send a contact report to Aston, but the radios just wouldn't work. After a relatively short military career to date he knew this was one of the unwritten but immovable laws of armed conflict – radios never work when you need them most. But that didn't help. He desperately needed to call mortar fire down on to the enemy position.

His men were pinned down here and on the canal. He needed to either extract or fight forwards. Without indirect fire support his platoon could do nothing but slog it out in a tough and unequal firefight. If they didn't even up the odds there was every chance several of his soldiers would be killed and wounded. Given the heavy weight of enemy fire it was amazing they hadn't been already.

Seal-Coon needed height to stand any chance of getting through on the radio. He clawed his way up the soft muddy bank of the ditch. Even with his antenna now above the lip of the bank, he still couldn't get any response from Aston.

Next to him, beside the ditch, was a sparse tree. Seal-Coon dared not scale the tree, but he pulled himself part-way up and – bingo, he managed to get a signal. Difficult but workable. He was through to the company main command post, and company 2IC Captain Dave Robinson, back in the desert.

'Hello, Zero and Zero Alpha, this is Copper Three Zero Alpha, contact. 1300 hours. Compound 245. Platoon minus of enemy. We are taking heavy smallarms and RPG fire. Currently trying to suppress from this side of the canal. Stand by for fire mission. Over.'

He heard the crackling response from Robinson, 'Zero, roger, send, send, over.'

Seal-Coon paused and waited for Aston's response. The company commander, located about 50 metres away, just to the rear of the platoon, needed to know what was going on and needed to confirm the fire mission. Nothing.

Seal-Coon continued, 'Zero, Copper Three Zero Alpha. Fire mission.'

He transmitted the enemy grid and the direction from him to them in mils magnetic, then finished his fire mission. 'Enemy platoon plus strength, in compounds and in the open. Neutralize now. Over.'

Several bullets whizzed straight past Seal-Coon's ears. He needed to observe the fall of shot if the fire ever came. But he couldn't stay up there a moment longer and slid back into the ditch. Maybe the MFC at Snow's position would be able to observe and adjust the fire. Maybe.

9

Behind Lieutenant Seal-Coon's rear section, Major Aston's Company Tac HQ was holed up in a small single-room building within a compound. Even here they were under blistering machine-gun and rifle fire.

Bullets were hitting and sometimes penetrating the thick mud walls. Some arced over the walls and into the compound.

Aston moved out of the building into the courtyard, trying to get through on the radio. Crouched on the ground next to the compound wall, he called up to Bailey and Fryer, the sniper pair on the roof, 'Why aren't you firing? Get some fire down. If you can't see the enemy, fire where you think they are. Get firing.'

Hugging the flat roof, Bailey's muffled call came back: 'We can't get our heads up. Too much fire.'

That wasn't the only thing that was frustrating Aston at that moment. He could just about make out Seal-Coon's broken transmission, but he couldn't manage to get his signal out to acknowledge, or to give orders. 7 Platoon were in big trouble down by the canal, and he needed to help them out. As well as his own 81mm mortars, he needed to get artillery, fast jets and attack helicopters into play. Or at least one of the above. But he couldn't communicate with anybody outside the immediate vicinity of the compound. And the fire around him was so intense he couldn't move out to find a better position to communicate from.

He had given up badgering his FST commander, Captain Pete Ridley, and his JTAC to get comms on their artillery and air nets, because they couldn't get through either. They were in the mother of all dead spots.

Aston had a sudden flash of inspiration. He took off his daysack, shuffled around and then pulled out his Iridium satellite handset. A bit like a large mobile phone, the Iridium was issued for routine administrative calls, not for operational traffic. Aston cursed when he realized the only number he had programmed in was 12 Brigade – Task Force Helmand HQ. He really wanted to speak to the JOC in Bastion or his own company 2IC, who would have direct radio communications with the fire support assets he needed. But he didn't have time to find and then dial in the number.

He hit the speed-dial for 12 Brigade, and the signal fired up to one of the sixty-six low earth-orbiting satellites in the Iridium constellation, then bounced back down to a handset in the 12 Brigade operations centre 145 kilometres away in Kandahar. In the tranquillity of the air-conditioned ops tent the watchkeeper pressed the hook button. 'Hello, Task Force Helmand operations. Duty watchkeeper speaking.'

At first the watchkeeper wondered if he was being wound up. He couldn't make out Aston very clearly, his voice was distorted, and there seemed to be a lot of loud noise in the background. 'Hello. This is Mick Aston. OC B Company One Royal Anglian. We are in contact. I need a fire mission. Take these details down.'

Providing overwatch from the area between Aston's compound and the ditch containing Parker's section were Corporal Martin, wounded a few hours earlier by shrapnel from a Taliban mortar, and his section. Visibility down to the canal was obscured by trees and foliage, but Martin had pushed two of his machine-gunners forward behind a bund-line to get better arcs of fire.

But the Taliban had picked Martin's section up, and when the firing began, bullets peppered the ground and the compound walls around them too. The two gunners, Privates James Medlock and Joel Lewis, fired back as Martin ordered the rest of the section to take cover in a small outhouse immediately behind them.

Private Ronnie Barker, UGL man and team medic, took up a position in the doorway, acting as link man with the gunners who were blasting away to the front. Corporal Mac McLaughlan, a medic attached to 7 Platoon, came running forward with Sergeant Mike Woodrow, the platoon sergeant. They had just received word that Gillmore had been hit and were racing to find and treat him.

The trees ahead of them were being riddled with gunfire, and Barker shouted out, 'Don't go down there, you're in the killing zone, get in here, quick.'

Woodrow made it through the door. As McLaughlan ran forward, Barker saw him jerk backwards then crumple to the ground, bleeding hard and screaming.

Barker knew immediately what he had to do. His heart leapt up into his mouth with the terror of it. As well as the bullets, visible tracer rounds were bouncing upwards from rocks and compound walls. It was like some horrifically lethal laser light show. Screaming, 'Man down! Man down!' the young soldier dropped his rifle and daysack and, knowing he could be dead within seconds, ran without hesitation into the storm of bullets.

When he reached McLaughlan he dropped to his knees. Attached to McLaughlan was his bulky and heavy medical Bergen and his rifle. Thinking fast, Barker knew it would be quicker to drag the medic with all his kit than to try and detach it out here, in this hell. In a superhuman feat, with bullets still zipping just inches away from him, Barker struggled back to the doorway, dragging McLaughlan, whose blood trail followed him in.

Private Richie Barke, the platoon 51mm mortar man, had been following behind Woodrow and the medic. He hit the ground as soon as the bullets started flying, and was pinned down behind a bank in the open. He just wanted to press himself into the earth. His mind raced. *One of those bullets is going to hit me if I stay here. If I move I'll also probably get hit.* He glanced left. *I've got to get to the outhouse where the others are. Could try crawling. Too slow. Better to take a chance and run.*

With bullets bouncing around his feet, Barke just made it to the outhouse as Barker dragged McLaughlan in through the door. Steph Martin shoved the door closed, but this gave them no more protection as bullets just punched hole after hole in the rusty metal sheet. Shafts of light beamed in where bullets had pierced the door, turning it into a colander. More bullets, lots of bullets, were cracking into the straw and mud roof.

Pressed against the side of the dark hut, only about 5 metres by 5 metres and crowded with the half dozen soldiers taking refuge, Barke went down on one knee and drew breath. He shook his head, wondering how he had survived out there. He also wondered how long his luck would last in here.

He looked over at McLaughlan. Ronnie Barker was on his knees, bent sweating and panting over the badly wounded medic. Barke shuffled across to help. The two soldiers pulled off McLaughlan's medical bergen and laid him flat on the filthy dirt floor. McLaughlan gasped and groaned. His eyes rolled.

Barker said, 'Mac, Mac, you're going to be OK, mate, you're going to be OK.'

He thought, *I'm not sure he is going to be OK, he looks very bad, very bad. But I've got to try and save him. Pat him down, pat him down, find out what his wounds are. Where did the bullet go?* He quickly figured out that it had entered McLaughlan through the stomach. He couldn't find the exit wound and thought the bullet could still be in him.

He tore up McLaughlan's shirt, ripped open a green first field dressing from his team medic's pack and applied pressure to the entry wound.

Barker was dripping sweat with his exertions in the oppressive heat. 'Rich, help me lift him up so we can get this round him and tie it off.'

When Barke leant over to pull the field dressing strap under McLaughlan's back, his 51mm mortar, a heavy, metre-long metal tube, swung off his shoulder towards the medic's head. *He doesn't need me to smash his face in on top of all his other problems*, thought Barke, as he just managed to stop it hitting. He reached round, unslung the mortar and placed it down on the ground.

As the two soldiers worked on McLaughlan, Sergeant Woodrow called urgently into his radio mike, trying to raise Company Sergeant Major Tim Newton, 'Three Three Alpha, Three Three Alpha, this is Three Zero Charlie, Three Zero Charlie. I have one times T One casualty at my location, compound number five three one. I need immediate CASEVAC. Immediate. Over.'

No reply, but he heard the mush of a carrier wave through his earpiece. Could this be Newton acknowledging, his voice unworkable to Woodrow. 'Hello, Three Three Alpha, Three Three Alpha, acknowledge my last. One times T One casualty, over.'

More mush. Had to be Newton.

'Now, how the hell are we going to get Mac out of here?' he said to Corporal Martin. 'There's no way out the front of this building, not with that fire coming down. We've got to get him out quickly, as soon as he's ready to be moved.' He glanced down at McLaughlan, pale-faced and writhing in agony, and said in a whisper, almost to himself, 'Otherwise he's going to die.'

It was obvious there was no other way out – just into the hail of bullets streaming up from the canal.

'Steph, get your gunners to intensify their fire, I'll try and get on to 5 Platoon to rapid fire across the canal. Maybe if we hit them hard enough we can get a lull and rush Mac out the front. It's the only thing we can do.'

As Martin called the gunners on his PRR, Woodrow hit his pressel switch again, 'One Zero Alpha, One Zero Alpha, Three Zero Charlie, Three Zero Charlie. I have to get a T One casualty out of my compound. You must rapid fire into all enemy positions, rapid fire to cover my movement. Over.'

Nothing. Nothing at all. Like Seal-Coon and Aston, he cursed the radios that never worked when you really needed them to.

Woodrow tried again and again to get through to 5 Platoon. Still nothing.

Sapper Ronald Fong, a wiry young half-Fijian, half-Chinese engineer, interrupted him. 'Sarge, I will breach this wall.' He gestured towards the back wall of the building.

'Don't be an idiot – set off a bar-mine in here and you'll kill us all,' retorted Woodrow, impatient and frustrated at his failure to get anyone on the radio. Or to have any other solution.

'No, Sarge, with this.' He held up a 1.5-metre hooligan tool. A standard item of Royal Engineer equipment, the hooligan tool is a heavy bar with a jemmy-like fork at one end, and a blade and spike at the other.

'Fong, I've seen thirty-millimetre shells hit these compound walls and just make small scabs. You'll never get through with that.'

'I can try, Sarge,' replied Fong confidently.

'Go for it, go for it. It's worth a shot. Do it,' said Woodrow, thinking, *He won't do it. Never. But anything, anything's worth a try. Or Mac will die for sure.*

The young sapper swung his hooligan tool into the mud wall. He paused to see what effect he had had. Barely a dent. With all his might, he heaved it again and again into the unyielding rock-like structure. Just standing there he had already been sweating. After three or four tremendous blows his whole body was dripping.

After several minutes, he had managed to make a small indentation. The effort was taking it out of him. He was wearing his helmet, Osprey body armour and daysack. His clothes were soaked through. He was breathing hard, his lungs hurt, and his heart was pounding. His hands were blistered and bleeding. He didn't care. He was determined to hammer his way through that wall so the medic could get out – even if his hands dropped off in the process.

After a few more minutes, one of the other engineers grabbed the tool from Fong and started swinging it against the wall. But the work was exhausting, and the soldier was flagging in a couple of minutes. Fong took over again, swinging into the rock-hard mud wall with every ounce of strength his body could muster. There didn't seem to be much hope he would ever get through – certainly not in time to save MacLaughlin, who was fading fast. But he had to try.

Barker at last stemmed the bleeding from MacLaughlin's abdomen, and he and Barke had managed to secure the field dressing round his body without causing him too much additional pain or damage. *What next?* thought Barker, then he said to Barke, 'OK, Rich, I'm going to give him morphine.'

As he reached into McLaughlan's right-hand map pocket for the morphine autoject, the medic moaned in a low voice, 'No, no morphine, not yet.'

'What? why not?'

'I need a drip. You need to put a drip in me.' He paused. 'I'm drifting off.'

Barker felt helpless. 'I don't know how, we've not been trained.'

In agony, Corporal McLaughlan groaned. 'I'll talk you through it,' he said in a weak voice, 'then you can give me morphine.'

Barke started to dig around in the medical Bergen to find the right kit.

Following McLaughlan's halting and pained instructions, Barker put an elasticated strap round his left arm, above the elbow.

'Get it tight,' said McLaughlan, 'then I need to…to move my fingers…tell me when tight.'

He managed to move his fingers then he continued, gasping with the pain, 'Start tapping…my forearm…get the veins up…then get the…needle…in. You need to…to see a flashback…a flashback…blood coming back up…up the needle.'

Barker tried twice to get the cannula into the vein but couldn't manage it. He missed altogether the first time and passed the needle straight through the vein on the second attempt.

'You've missed…again…keep trying…got to…got to get it in.'

'Here, let me have a go,' said Barke, taking the cannula.

He also missed the vein, then tried again. The fourth attempt.

'That's it…that's in…'

As time passed the adrenalin had worn off, and, without morphine, McLaughlan was in agony. With a massive effort of will and desperation, he forced out, 'Now…get the drip…on to…the cannula…and…turn on.'

As Barke held up the drip, with fluid flowing through the needle and into McLaughlan's arm, the medic, still in excruciating pain, seemed visibly relieved. Until this had been done he expected to die. Even now he knew it would be touch and go.

Martin, keeping a close eye on what was happening outside, glanced at Barker and Barke. He thought, *They are awesome, how can they stay so calm dealing with that?*

As the two soldiers worked to save the medic's life, Fong noticed the smallest crack of light glimmering through the wall. Although close to collapse, he swung the hooligan tool with even greater fury. Nothing was going to stop him now. There was still a lot of work to be done, but he was going to get through that wall.

At the other end of the village, Company Sergeant Major Newton was receiving a call from Aston, very faint, crackling, but just workable. As his radio had drifted in and out, Aston, in the compound behind Woodrow, picked up his message calling for CASEVAC. It was Aston's carrier wave, attempting to acknowledge, that Woodrow had heard. 'Hello, Three Three Alpha, this is Zero Alpha. Three Zero Charlie's got a T One casualty. Get down here and evacuate.'

'Roger, moving now, out.'

Newton raced forward in his Viking, as fast as he could, and was amazed at the skill with which the marine driver flung the careering vehicle through the narrow, twisting alleyways between Heyderabad's network of compounds.

Past the graveyard, the Viking swung round a corner and into the open, grinding to a halt as they were hit by a wall of lead and tracer streaking up from the hedgerow across the canal to their front. As Newton tried to work out what to do next, Sergeant Moxham, the marine gunner above him, immediately returned fire, sending a continuous blast of GPMG bullets back into the hedgerow.

Aston's voice crackled through his headset, 'Reverse, reverse, the casualty is behind you, reverse up twenty metres.'

Newton's driver backed the Viking up and stopped next to a soldier kneeling in a fire position. Against the odds, Fong had breached the wall and then crawled through to provide cover on the other side. Smashing through the wall had nearly killed him, and, exhausted as he was, Fong was going to protect his breach. Newton sent the company doctor, Major Andrew Tredget, head first through the jagged hole, which was only just big enough to take a man.

Inside, Tredget looked at the crumpled, white-faced figure lying on the floor and yelled at Barker, who was crouched over him, 'Where's the company medic, where's the medic, I need to know what he's done.'

Barker said, 'He is the medic. Mac the medic. I'm the team medic. I've put an FFD on him and got a drip in. I was just about to give him morphine.'

Tredget dropped to his knees, pulled out an autoject and punched it into McLaughlan's thigh.

Under Tredget's supervision they manhandled McLaughlan on to a field stretcher, and carefully fed him through Fong's hole in the wall and into the waiting Viking. The doc and Barker got in with him, and the Viking screamed back up through the village towards the emergency HLS. By now, the MERT Chinook was inbound.

From the doorway, Martin called his gunners back up. As they crawled towards him, he emptied mag after mag towards the Taliban positions.

Private Lewis had sustained a shrapnel wound to his leg while forward but had stayed in position putting down fire on the enemy. Gillmore, who had also been wounded forward with Parker's section, was carried back up the hill by Private McLure. Martin and Woodrow put the two into a second Viking that had arrived outside their compound and dispatched them to the HLS.

10

Down on the canal, with Foster crawling back to the ditch to sort out his stoppage, Parker was on his own. Just as he was thinking, *I need Thrumble up here with his GPMG*, he looked across and there was Thrumble. GPMG and 1,000 rounds of 7.62mm link on his back, he was crawling forward across the exposed field. And he was motoring, despite the tremendous weight he was carrying. Parker had never, in any circumstances, seen any soldier crawl so fast.

No one had ordered Thrumble forward in the teeth of enemy fire. But he knew that, in contact, Parker always wanted the guns with him, out in front. He could have moved along the ditch and come up further to the right. That would have been safer. But also slower, and Thrumble knew Parker would need him there fast. So he crawled forward, under fire and in line of sight to the enemy.

When Thrumble got up to him, Parker saw, as always, a big, beaming smile. Nothing fazed Thrumble, not even the breathtaking rate of enemy fire that was still pouring in all round them, throwing up dirt and fragments of rock. Parker swore that the height of the bank in front of him was reducing visibly under the weight of fire cutting into it.

The minute Thrumble got to the bank he pushed his gun up and started blazing away at the enemy firing points across the canal.

Minutes later Lee arrived with his UGL and Booth with his LMG. Parker was surprised to see Taff, an engineer corporal attached to the section. There was no specific role for engineers here, but this man knew Parker could use all the firepower he could get and came forward. And engineers, like all soldiers, have to be ready to act as infantry when the chips are down.

They had all passed by Foster, who was heading in the opposite direction screaming for rods to clear his stoppage. Before long he had found a set, forced the expanded cartridge case from the breach of his rifle and was firing again.

As soon as they had dragged Veal's men into the safety of the ditch, Lance Corporals Teddy Ruecker and J. C. Carter, the sniper team, started moving forward, along the ditch. As they went, branches, leaves and twigs were falling on them, cut down from the trees by the torrent of machine-gun fire from across the canal.

Ruecker crawled along the side of the canal towards the bank where Parker was under fire. When he got into position he called out, 'Stu, where are they? Where are the bastards?'

Parker said, 'Reference compound, left-hand corner of that compound.

Ruecker crawled along behind the bank, keeping very low, until he got to the end. Slowly, carefully, he inched forward to a point where he could just about see round the bank, towards the compound. He eased the muzzle of his sniper rifle out through the grass, desperate to avoid any sharp movement that could draw attention to his position.

Rubbish fire position, he thought. His body was bent half round the end of the bank, his rifle resting on a small lump of earth. This situation was tough for a sniper – trying to move into position in the face of an enemy that was observing and firing on to the area. And relatively close to the enemy. Far better to get in position before the enemy arrived, and to be as far away as possible, to take maximum advantage of the range and accuracy of your weapon. But you couldn't always have the situation that suited you.

Looking intently through his sniper scope, all he could see was dust and smoke where a machine-gun was firing. He couldn't actually see the weapon or the firer. He figured out the distance to the target area: 400 metres. He clicked in the correct range setting on his sight. Then he saw a face. Momentarily one of the enemy fighters had stuck his head up to observe.

This was the first Taliban Ruecker had seen. He had been near to the enemy as a WMIK commander on Silicon and had fired at them. But he hadn't actually seen any. The bristles on the back of his neck stood up as he felt a surge of adrenalin.

He carefully moved the cross hairs of his sniper scope on to the man's head. As his training had taught him, he blanked out the noise of the bullets flying all round him, and the RPG missiles exploding near by. He slowed his breathing. He took up the first pressure on the trigger, then, a split second after he hit the second pressure, he saw the top of the fighter's head peel apart, exploding in a blur of red mist.

Thrumble, to the right, shouted out, 'Well done, mate, well done.'

For a brief moment the incoming fire slowed down, with one of the Taliban machine-gunners killed. Fire from Parker's men increased as they were able to push further up the bank to engage the enemy positions. But then the Taliban opened up from further left and right. Bullets were landing much closer now, coming in behind the bank at an angle.

Steve Veal, the Section 2IC, immediately picked up on these new fire positions, splitting the men who remained back in the ditch with him, and directing them to return fire to the left and right.

Ruecker continued scanning through his scope. He identified two Taliban fighters in a dip in one of the the compound walls, both firing AK47s. Just head and shoulders. About a metre apart. Range 400 metres. He engaged the man on the right. *Hit him.* He dropped out of sight. Ruecker switched to the fighter on the left. Through the scope he saw the man looking down at his dead comrade. Shocked, the fighter failed to get down. The man looked from his comrade towards the bank where Ruecker lay. Ruecker saw on his face a flash of realization that he was about to die. He fired. The man dropped.

Ruecker was exhilarated. He had just killed three men who had been trying to kill him and his mates. He had converted theory into practice. All those long hours studying and enduring the gruelling regime of the sniper course had paid off. What he had been taught did work. For a sniper 400 metres was not a long distance, and he thought that it would have been difficult to miss at that range with the superbly accurate .338 long-range rifle. But the targets had all been small, just head and shoulders at best. Ruecker was ever critical of himself, but he thought this time he had done well enough.

Parker realized that Corporal Mann's Guards section on the left were also in an intense firefight. The amount of incoming rounds they were receiving and the rate of their own fire had increased dramatically. With fire coming at his own section from the front as well as left and right, and no end in sight, he knew it was going to be really difficult to extract both sections from this situation.

He needed mortar or artillery fire. He called Corporal Wilsher, the MFC. No answer, nothing. He called the fire support team commander. Nothing. He called Snow up in the fire support group. Again, nothing. He managed to get through to Seal-Coon, a short distance to his rear, who was also desperately trying to reach someone on the net so he could bring in fire support.

Parker kept trying to get through on the radio. He was studying his map, figuring out the coordinates just in case he managed to raise any-one who could help him and his beleaguered section. He was also try-ing to work out some way to extract.

He did not see a lone Taliban fighter rise up out of the grass 10 metres away. He did not see the man running at him, gripping an AK47 in both hands at waist height, with bayonet extended.

Then Parker looked up, suddenly aware and suddenly startled. He saw the grim-faced, heavily bearded man bearing down on him. Every-thing went into slow motion. Parker tried desperately to bring his rifle round to shoot. But the man was too close, and even as he frantically tried to point his muzzle at the charging fighter, Parker knew he would never be able to fire in time.

11

Steve Veal was scanning away from the main enemy position across the canal, back off to the right, searching through his SA80 SUSAT sight for any enemy on the home bank. He had learnt on Silicon how skilled the Taliban were at using the ground to outflank them and hit them sideways or from behind. As his sight moved on to a treeline, he heard an explosion and then saw a dense cloud of smoke on the ground. An RPG missile was streaking through the air towards Martin's section in the compound to the rear. As the smoke cleared Veal saw the firer, a tall, thick-set man, huge beard and dressed in a black turban and kurta.

He had discarded his RPG launcher and was now running straight at Corporal Parker with his AK47.

Veal brought the black arrow of his SUSAT on to the centre of the man's running body, aimed slightly ahead and then saw the fighter jerk and crash backwards into the dirt as he emptied a full mag of thirty 5.56 bullets into him, pressing the trigger for each shot in rapid succession.

That was not Parker's only narrow escape that day. Moments later, he called across to the nearest soldier in Corporal Mann's Guards section to his left, Lance Corporal Lockley, 'Lockers, Lockers, I am going to increase our rate of fire in one minute. Get your section to do the same as soon as I do.'

As he shouted he saw Lockley staring at him wide-eyed. An RPG had hurtled in from the left and skimmed off the ground right behind Parker's feet, almost scorching the souls of his Desert Seeker boots. When Parker realized what had happened, his heart went into overdrive for the second time in a few minutes.

Parker couldn't get through on the radio and therefore couldn't get the support he so desperately needed from mortars or artillery. He wanted to try a coordinated weight of fire by both sections to get the upper hand on the Taliban.

He got everyone firing rapid. Josh Lee dropped a few more rifle grenades into the compounds and then started blasting away with his rifle. Taff, the Royal Engineer, was firing single shots with his rifle so fast it sounded like automatic. Booth was firing his Minimi across the canal in short, vicious and accurate bursts, and Ruecker was trying to add to the weight of fire by using rapid bolt manipulation with his sniper rifle. Behind, Lance Corporal Veal's team continued to blast at the Taliban to the left and the right.

The heaviest fire was coming from Thrumble with Mary, his GPMG. There was no need for Parker to tell Thrumble to lay down more fire. All he had ever had to do with Thrumble was slow his rate of fire down for fear of running out of ammo or melting his gun barrel.

The enemy fire reduced a bit, but machine-gun, rifle and RPG rounds continued to land and around the platoon. Parker noticed trees to the left of the main enemy positions and remembered what had happened at Pasab just the day before. 'Thrumble,' he yelled, 'swing left, shoot at the trees.'

Thrumble didn't need telling twice. He jerked the gun's bipod round and started pouring bullets into the trees so fast that the tracer rounds looked like a laser beam arcing across the river. Parker counted seven or eight Taliban drop heavily from the bushes. He saw just the lower half of one man fall to the ground, cut in two by Thrumble's gunfire.

When the bodies stopped dropping from the trees, Parker noticed that Thrumble's GPMG barrel was glowing white hot, even in the glare of the afternoon sun. 'Thrumble – cease firing.'

Thrumble continued working his gun up and down the treeline.

'Stop firing!'

Parker had to physically pull Thrumble's hand from the trigger to stop him. 'Thrumble, get back down behind the bank and let the gun cool off, otherwise we'll get a breech explosion, and you'll be a casualty too.'

Thrumble opened the top cover of his GPMG and removed the belt, allowing air to circulate through the barrel and cool the gun. He was desperate to get it back into action as quickly as he could, and while he was waiting, he started getting the rest of his ammo sorted out.

12

Back in the village, Major Aston had called forward Captain Will Goodman, the Viking Troop commander, to give orders for the extraction of the company. Aston needed to get out of the compound he was in to have a face-to-face. As with Sergeant Woodrow's compound, the only entrance was into the teeth of the continuing storm of enemy fire. He told an engineer with Tac HQ to blow a hole in the opposite wall.

The engineer prepared his bar-mine and leant it against the mud wall. The men of Tac took cover in the courtyard. There was a huge explosion as the bar-mine blasted a gap in the wall. Aston led Tac HQ back in through the thick dust that the explosion had created and out through the wall into the alley beyond.

He needed to get across and into the next alleyway to see the Viking troop commander, but they were exposed to fire. As they crouched beside the wall, an engineer officer with Tac lobbed a red phosphorous grenade down the alley to screen their movement. It landed too close, and the men of Tac HQ were showered with burning phosphorous particles. Despite this, the red phosphorous smoke did its job, and they raced across the alleyway.

Aston ran into Lieutenant Seal-Coon. He was shattered, covered in dust and mud and soaked in sweat and ditchwater. Unable to get comms to sort out the extraction, he had run, walked and crawled back, using whatever cover he could find, but for much of the way exposing himself to intense enemy fire. For part of the way he had moved with Private Aaron McLure, helping evacuate the wounded Private Gillmore. Seal-Coon had taken a big risk, a lone figure moving in the open under the Taliban's guns, but the need to organize his platoon's extraction overrode any consideration for his own safety.

'Come with me, George,' said Aston, and they ran up the alleyway to where Royal Marines Captain Will Goodman was waiting. Ben Howes, commander of 5 Platoon, who were still in the graveyard, was also there, waiting for orders.

'OK, Will,' said Aston, 'there is only one way to get George's guys back from the bridge. You need to get some Vikings down there to bring them out under armour. Otherwise we're going to take more casualties.'

Goodman nodded.

'It's going to be extremely dangerous for your men. They will be completely exposed to enemy fire as soon as they break the compounds at the edge of the village. They'll need to really motor. Pete Ridley is trying to get some artillery and mortars on to the enemy now, and air as well. If we get it that should help you, but we can't wait for it if it doesn't come in time. So go anyway and look on it as a bonus if you get covering fire. I want your vehicles down to the edge of the village as soon as you can. Move slowly until you break cover, keep the dust and the engine noise down. Let's try and reduce the chances of the Taliban working out what we're doing. When you break cover, drive like hell.'

He turned to Seal-Coon. 'George – get back down there if you can. Call Will as soon as your guys are ready to move and then get maximum fire from your blokes to cover his movement down. Above all we've got to try to stop them getting accurate RPG fire on to the Vikings. When the vehicles are in position, I want your men mounted up as rapidly as possible. I mean quick. We can't afford to have them stationary for a second longer than necessary.'

Looking at Howes, Aston continued, 'Ben, your guys have been doing a good job smashing the Taliban from the graveyard. Keep it going and, when the Vikings start to move, you also need to really hammer the fire down. Hammer it. No time for questions, let's get on with it.'

As the three officers headed off, Aston turned to the FST commander, Captain Ridley, 'How about that fire support, Pete?'

13

Minutes later, after surviving his second dash of death, Seal-Coon appeared beside Parker. 'Parky, the Vikings are coming to get us out. When they move forward you need to put rapid fire down across the canal. Corporal Mann's section will extract back into the Vikings first, with covering fire from you and the Vikings. Once they're in, get your guys back too. If the Vikings are able to get in line abreast they should be able to put down a fair bit of fire to cover us in.'

Parker turned to Thrumble, 'Back up here with your gun and get ready to open up. How much ammo?'

'Only a couple of hundred rounds.'

'OK open up on my command only. Got it?'

He shouted fire orders to the other members of the section.

As he had been moving forward to join Parker, Seal-Coon had heard Goodman calling his vehicle commanders on the radio. He told them the plan, said he would lead the move down to the bridge, and asked for volunteers to join him in what came close to a suicide mission, with volleys of RPGs, each capable of destroying a Viking and its crew, still screaming across the river.

Every single Viking commander had answered on the radio, volunteering immediately. Goodman nominated two vehicles to go with him.

Again Goodman's voice crackled in Seal-Coon's headset. 'Hello, Copper Three Zero Alpha, this is Mud Two Zero Alpha, now on the edge of Heyderabad, ready to move. Are you ready for me? Can you talk me in? Over.'

Seal-Coon replied, 'Copper Three Zero, roger. We're ready. Move straight down the track to your front. You will not see the bridge till you break cover from the compounds. Bridge is four hundred metres forward of compounds. Enemy are all along the far side of canal. Some enemy have infiltrated on to the home side. They may have RPGs. Enemy are still putting down heavy fire. You will be exposed to fire as soon as you move forward of the compounds. Five metres short of the bridge, halt. Callsign Three Three Charlie are left on the canal line. Three Two Charlie right. Three Three Charlie will move to you first, then Three Two Charlie then my callsign. Good luck. Over.'

'Mud Two Zero Alpha, roger, moving now. Good luck to you too. Out to you.'

'All Mud callsigns, this is Mud Two Zero Alpha. Stand by. Five – four – three – two – one – *move now! Move now!*'

'*Raaapid – fire!*' yelled Seal-Coon. Parker and Mann repeated the command to their sections, and a hail of bullets crashed into the Taliban positions across the canal. At the same time a mass of fire poured in from the GPMGs, Minimis and rifles of Howes's 5 Platoon up in the cemetery. They had to do everything in their power to prevent the enemy from firing RPGs accurately at the Vikings. A single hit could easily destroy the vehicle and kill the crew.

The Viking drivers slammed down on their accelerators, metal on metal, as they left the cover of the compounds. With clouds of exhaust smoke, the roar of engines and the screaming grind of tracks biting into rock, the three Vikings surged forward and hurtled down the rough track, bouncing and lurching. The lead Viking had a .50 calibre Browning heavy machine-gun mounted on its turret. The other two had the lighter 7.62mm GPMGs. The gunners opened fire as the vehicles careered towards the bridge, machine-gun bullets flying wildly over the heads of the 7 Platoon soldiers.

The Taliban onslaught was now focused in on the Vikings. Machine-gun bullets flew towards them, bouncing off the vehicles, streams of tracer flying vertically upwards as bullets were deflected sharply by the armour. Several deadly RPGs screamed out of the enemy compounds, some missing the vehicles by what seemed to Seal-Coon like inches.

The lead Viking juddered to a sudden halt in front of the bridge, almost standing on its nose. The other two peeled off left and formed a line abreast, to bring maximum fire down over the canal.

From his turret the .50 cal marine gunner shouted at Parker's section, 'Where are they? Where are they?'

Thrumble shouted back, 'Watch my tracer,' as he poured a line of tracer bullets straight into the centre of the enemy position.

The marine held down the trigger of the .50 cal and turned the traverse handle. The heavy gun, with its distinctive loud, deliberate, thumping noise, rained its devastating stream of bullets all along the enemy position. The other two vehicles were raking the Taliban positions, and the sustained machine-gun fire almost silenced the enemy.

Corporal Mann's section were already on the move, crawling at high speed across the poppy field and into the the nearest Vikings.

'Move now, Parky,' yelled Seal-Coon as the last of Mann's soldiers got in. Parker sent Thrumble back first, almost out of ammo.

Parker and Seal-Coon were the last men into the vehicles. Lieutenant Seal-Coon threw himself into an overcrowded Viking. Sprawled on top of Thrumble, as the vehicle lurched forward his forearm touched the red-hot GPMG barrel and there was a horrible smell of burning flesh. Ignoring the searing pain, Seal-Coon pulled on the headset so he could talk to the vehicle commander. The marine asked, 'How far forward of the bridge have you cleared?'

'We haven't,' yelled back Seal-Coon, above the revving of the vehicle's engine and the thump of the .50 cal machine-gun.

'Then there's a problem,' said the marine, 'we're across the bridge.'

Seal-Coon heard him yell over the intercom to the driver, 'Turn this thing round – quick, quick. There's enemy all round. Get me out of here.'

As the Viking manoeuvred sluggishly in the cramped space on the enemy side of the bridge, the gunner traversed the .50 cal firing in every direction. Seal-Coon heard the commander calling into his mike, 'They're everywhere, they're everywhere.'

The men inside could hear bullets pinging off the vehicle's sides. They were just waiting for an RPG to blast into the vehicle's armour.

Not realizing how much danger they were still in, as the Viking moved back across the bridge, Private Pearson, in the back with Parker, said, 'That was a bit close out there, wasn't it? God knows how we didn't all get killed.'

As he said it he pressed his face close to the small window in the back door to look out. A bullet smacked into the armoured glass right between his eyes and ricocheted away.

14

As 7 Platoon extracted away from Heyderabad in the Vikings, Company Sergeant Major Newton was loading the injured McLaughlan, Gillmore and Lewis on to the Chinook for the flight back to the field hospital at Camp Bastion. The two Apache attack helicopters accompanying the Chinook had launched a devastating attack against the Taliban on the canal with their 30mm cannon as the Vikings headed back up the hill.

Aston brought the company into a leaguer in the open desert, 2 kilometres away from Heyderabad, near the helicopter landing site. The soldiers sorted out their kit, recharged magazines, found their correct vehicles and clacked down water. Having survived the toughest fighting they had been through so far, every man was in high spirits.

'I always said it was a bridge too far,' said Veal to Parker, mimicking Dirk Bogarde from the film.

'Yeah, maybe, Steve,' laughed Thrumble, 'but Arnhem was nothing to what we've just done.'

'Do you know what I was thinking all through it?' asked Foster, pouring the remnants of a bottle of water over his sweat-drenched blond hair. 'I just wanted a cheese sandwich, that's all, just a cheese sandwich.'

'Shut up about your friggin' cheese sandwiches,' said Thrumble, and added, imitating Foster's Essex twang, '"Rods, rods, I need rods." I reckon you did that stoppage on purpose, Fozzie me old mate. Got too hairy for you. Needed the pros up there really, me and Mary.'

Laughing, Foster kicked him in the leg and ran off to take cover behind Stu Parker.

Once Sergeant Major Newton had completed his head check and confirmed that everyone was present, Aston ordered the column to move back through the desert to rejoin 6 Platoon at FOB Robinson. Snow's fire support group WMIKs led the way, followed by the two platoons, the ANA and the logistics package with its go-anywhere Oshkosh tanker.

Aston travelled in the front of the Viking driven by Captain Goodman, the troop commander. As they started moving, he gave himself a moment to take stock. The mission to Heyderabad had been successful. They had identified a sizeable force of Taliban, and by a combination of ground fighting, mortar fire and air, they had killed large numbers of enemy. He was intensely proud of what his men had achieved in Heyderabad, in the face of the toughest resistance. Neither he nor any of his men had ever before seen fighting of that intensity. And he felt moved by the individual acts of bravery he had personally witnessed or had reported to him – by his own B Company soldiers, by the marines of the Viking troop and by the attached soldiers, especially the Royal Engineers.

As he ran over in his mind what had happened, he felt a sudden sense of relief. There had been numerous close shaves. Many of his men, and he himself, had been near to death over the last few hours. He was amazed that no one had been killed, and that more soldiers hadn't been injured. He started to think about the three casualties they had taken – Gillmore and Lewis, but in particular Corporal McLaughlan, his outstanding company medic. He knew Mac was in a very bad way when they got him on to the chopper. He hoped against hope that he would survive, but didn't expect to see him again until they got back to England after the tour. What happened was tragic for Mac himself, thought Aston, but he would also be a huge loss to B Company. Everyone knew and liked him. And above all they had great confidence that if wounded, he would give them the best possible chance of survival. Ironic, thought Aston, that he had effectively had to save his own life by talking the team medics through the medical procedure.

Aston wondered whether he should have done anything different. The burden of responsibility always falls heavily on the shoulders of the commander, and when you have taken casualties it is natural to wonder if there was anything you could have done to prevent it. Perhaps even more than most commanders, Aston had forged a strong bond with his men and really cared about each of them and their individual well-being.

He shook his head. It was not the time to dwell on all of this. Their task in Heyderabad complete, he needed to focus on getting these men and their vehicles safely back to FOB Robinson – without any further casualties.

He checked his map and his GPS. The vehicles were moving at a good speed along a rough track cutting through the featureless but rugged and rocky terrain. He was baking hot and pouring sweat. *Even the company commander's vehicle doesn't get working air con*, he said to himself. He noticed a pair of motorbikes across the desert to the right. Maybe 1,000 metres away. *Not uncommon*, he thought. *But what are they up to? Quite likely tracking our movements. For what? Just to find out when it was safe for the Taliban to carry on about their business in Heyderabad? Perhaps…*

They were well spread out to minimize the risk if they were attacked along the route back. Aston could just about see the Viking ahead of him, about 30 metres away, partly obscured by the clouds of dust it was kicking up. It was the rear vehicle of Howes's 5 Platoon, who were moving just behind the WMIKs. Aston knew this was Sergeant Keith Nieves's wagon.

Short in stature, but larger than life, Nieves was one of B Company's big characters. One of the great morale boosters. Aston thought, *Nieves will be just the man to have around when we get back to FOB Rob and the men start thinking about the hell they've been through*. He had known and liked Nieves for many years, ever since he had joined the battalion from the Australian Army back in 1997. Nieves was tough, hard-working and loyal, as well as a great family man. Aston counted him not just a subordinate but a friend.

Nieves's Viking was weighed down with the normal platoon sergeant's heavy ammunition loads, to resupply the men when they began to run short, plus bar-mines and boxes of explosives for breaking into – and sometimes out of – compounds.

Jammed in on top of this dangerous cargo were Private Scotty Fryer, one of the company's snipers, and Corporal Ian Peyton, the remaining company medic, as well as the five Royal Engineers who had been working with B Company since they left Bastion.

Private Luke Nadriva, the tough Fijian 51mm mortar man, was wedged into the tiny signaller's compartment directly behind Nieves in the front cab. Marine Biekes was at the wheel, and Marine Wright, thickly coated in dust kicked up by the vehicles in front, was in the cupola, manning his gun.

Three kilometres out from FOB Robinson, Aston checked his map and GPS again. The head of the column should be crossing a prominent wadi. Looking forward he could just see the lead vehicles in the distance, moving out of sight into the depression. *Another ten minutes or so and we should be in the FOB*, he thought.

He would have to get everyone together, and he hadn't yet had the time to think about what he was going to say to them. He glanced again to the right. A lone motorbike now. He had seen several off in the desert, since he spotted the first pair as they pulled away from Heyderabad. He also thought he could just about make out some kind of a 4x4 off in the far distance. *Probably nothing*.

Then he saw the vehicle in front explode.

15

The right track of Nieves's Viking had rolled over a buried anti-tank mine. The weight of the track had forced down the mine's pressure fuze, and 5.7 kg of TNT – had thrown the vehicle up from its tracks in a thunderous blast.

Nieves was knocked unconscious and didn't even hear the mine exploding. Most of the blast from the TNT went upwards through the floor on the front right side of the vehicle, searing into his right foot, ripping off his flesh and breaking the bones. A jagged shard of red-hot shrapnel ripped through his left wrist.

Seconds later he felt as if he was waking from a nightmare. The whole cab was full of a choking haze of black smoke and there was a strong, acrid smell of explosives and burning. His ears were ringing and he could hear no other sound, it was like being submerged in water. He felt a vicious heat on his left arm and slowly turned his head to see flames licking upwards from the engine block beside him. He pushed himself towards the door, forced the handle upwards and tried to shove it open. He put all his weight against it, but it wouldn't budge. It had been distorted by the explosion, jammed into its frame. He couldn't get out to the left because there was a wall of flames between the engine block and the vehicle's ceiling, getting more ferocious by the second.

He was alone in an inferno and he began to despair, *That's my lot. I'm not going to get out of here.*

He tried the door again. Nothing. Wouldn't move. He put his head right against the door and looked out through a small gap that had opened up as the blast had forced it forward. Sitting on the ground, he saw Private Nadriva, his mortar man – dazed and in shock, head in his hands.

A flicker of hope now. Nieves put his mouth to the gap in the door and screamed out, '*Help me, help me, get me out of this vehicle!*'

Nadriva didn't respond. He obviously couldn't hear him, or was too shocked to realize what was going on. Nieves's heart sank further. He now knew he was going to die in this hot steel box. He was fully conscious. He knew that it would be agony as the flames engulfed him and his body slowly burnt up – unless the engine or something else in the vehicle exploded and killed him first. That would be a mercy.

1. Corporal Billy Moore, left, and Private Clarke of A Company an hour before the battle in Nowzad on Friday 13 April in which Private Chris Gray was killed in action and Moore was shot in the arm.

Nineteen-year-old Private Chris Gray with his mini light machine-gun in Nowzad District re days before he was killed in a close-quarter e with the Taliban. Chris Gray was the first ber of the Royal Anglian Battle Group to be l in Afghanistan in 2007.

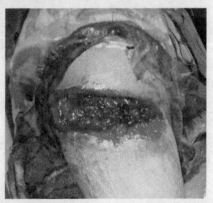

3. Corporal Moore's gunshot wound sustained on Friday 13 April in an exchange of fire with the Taliban. This photo was taken in Nowzad DC just before Moore was CASEVACed by Chinook to the British field hospital in Camp Bastion.

4. B Company prepare to deploy from Camp Bastion to the battle group assembly area north of Gereshk to commence Operation Silicon. To the right is a Vector 6x6 armoured utility vehicle. The other vehicles are Viking articulated troop-carrying vehicles, crewed by the Royal Marines Armoure Support Group.

5. Lieutenant Colonel Stuart Carver, the Royal Anglian Battle Group commander, left, and Regimental Sergeant Major Ian Robinson.

6. Scimitar tracked reconnaissance vehicle of the Royal Anglian Recce Platoon in overwatch.

7. Taliban fighter killed by B Company during Operation Silicon.

8. A WMIK from Fire Support Group Charlie moving forward with C Company at Kajaki. The vehicle is fitted with a grenade machine-gun (in the rear) and general-purpose machine-gun.

Air strike near Mazdurak, in support of C Company. With no civilian population in the area, air support could be used to devastating effect.

10. Major Phil Messenger, C Company commander, during the raid on Mazdurak, near Kajaki. Before moving south to Forward Operating Base Inkerman, C Company had many battles in the Kajaki area, and Messenger and his men were in contact with the Taliban almost every day.

11. C Company medic Lance Corporal Matt Boyle making pizza at Combat Outpost Zeebrugge shortly before he was wounded during the raid on the Taliban stronghold Mazdurak.

12. B Company desert harbou[...] area. 7 Platoon prepare equip[...] before the night move to Heyderabad.

13. 7 Platoon soldiers eating l[...] in the troop compartment of [...] Viking near Heyderabad. Seco[...] from right is Private Ronnie Barker, who later rescued the wounded Corporal McLaugh[...] under heavy enemy fire.

14. Lance Corporal Teddy Ruecker aiming his .338 long-range sniper rifle on a compound roof in Heyderabad. His Browning 9mm pistol is strapped to his right thigh.

15. Major Mick Aston briefs B[...] Company platoon commande[...] a compound during a lull in b[...] Lieutenant Ben Howes is on t[...] left, Lieutenant George Seal-C[...] right, and Aston second from right.

16. Lieutenant George Seal-Coon immediately after the battle for the bridge at Heyderabad. B Company is in a harbour area preparing to move to Forward Operating Base Robinson. Sergeant Keith Nieves would be seriously wounded in a minestrike a few hours later.

17. The burnt-out Viking in which Lance Corporal Dean Bailey was seriously wounded when an RPG7 missile struck during the ambush on the outskirts of Sangin.

18. B Company Vikings and WMIKs in Sangin DC two days after the ambush. Lance Corporal George Davey was killed in an accident at the base.

19. A Company vehicles move through the desert for Operation Lastay Kulang. British and American troops deploying for this operation sustained several minestrikes.

20. The larger-than-life Corporal Darren Bonner, seated third from left, in A Company operations room. Bonner was subsequently killed while travelling in the rear of his company commander's Viking during the deployment on to Operation Lastay Kulang.

21. Major Domini Biddick explains t purpose of Lastay Kulang to local eld during the operati The Royal Anglia made great efforts engage with the l as part of the 'batt for consent'.

Operation Ghartse Ghar. 3 Platoon A Company pause during the night insertion.

3. Major Dominic dick, centre, briefs O group in a lie-up sition just prior to our for Operation Ghartse Ghar. Left is Lieutenant Nick Denning, right, ieutenant Graham Goodey.

24. Major Mick Aston, B Company commander, on Operation Ghartse Ghar.

25. Major Dominic Biddick, left, sha[res] a joke with his signals detachment commander, Corporal Dinger Bell. Operation Ghartse Ghar.

26. Private Nickie Whaites, A Comp[any] feeding link to GPMG gunner Priva[te] Mark Stephens, in contact during Operation Ghartse Ghar.

27. B Company soldiers treating a wounded comrade during Operation Ghartse Ghar. An RPG had bounced off Private Thompson's chest plate and exploded among his section.

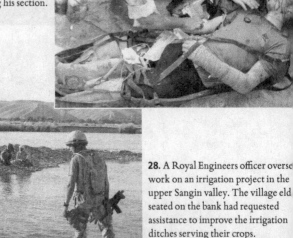

28. A Royal Engineers officer overse[es] work on an irrigation project in the upper Sangin valley. The village eld[er] seated on the bank had requested assistance to improve the irrigation ditches serving their crops.

Suddenly the horror was replaced by an intense sadness. He would never see Angie or Peter and Harry again. Never. Even worse, he thought, was the sorrow they would feel, which would be with them for the rest of their lives. Angie a widow, and the boys growing up without a father.

He took hold of himself. *That isn't going to happen.* He shouted as loud as he could, his lungs burning with the inhalation of hot smoke. '*Nadriva, Nadriva, help, help, help.*'

His whole body was stinging, his left side felt as if it was on fire, and his face was contorted against the gap behind the door. He was screaming at the top of his voice – screaming for his life.

Nadriva looked up. He was still dazed; his arms were burnt, and his body was battered by the force of the explosion. But he heard Nieves's muffled screams. In horror, he forced himself painfully on to his feet and staggered back across to the burning vehicle.

He pulled at the door. No movement. The metal of the door was burning hot against his hands. His body felt shattered by the blast that had battered it only a few moments before. But he put all of his power into trying to get the door open. Every muscle was straining, and the veins stood out on his arms, neck and forehead as he willed the door to open.

Finally it began to give. Millimetre by millimetre, the distorted steel of the door scraped against the solid frame that was locking it in place. Then it came free, and with a feeling of victory and the most intense relief, Nadriva swung it wide, groaning on its hinges. He reached in and grabbed Nieves by the shoulders. As he was dragged through the narrow opening the melting skin was torn from Nieves's left arm.

Out of the vehicle, Nieves took a couple of steps and crashed down on to the sand. He felt an excruciating pain from his foot so bad he looked down to check that it was still there. As he lay in the sand he looked up and saw the driver, Marine Biekes, staggering around, badly burnt and screaming.

When the vehicle exploded, the medic, Corporal Ian Peyton, in the back of the Viking, was deafened. He felt the whole cab being thrown up into the air, followed by a jarring crash, like an elevator dropping to the base of a lift shaft. Outside, the back cab was blazing, as the flames from the front travelled rearwards. Inside, the vehicle was heating up.

The two engineers closest to the back door were struggling to get it open, but it wouldn't budge. As in the front cab, the shock of the explosion had distorted the metal, jamming it into place.

Within the cramped space, now filling up with thick black smoke, the seven soldiers began to panic. They were trapped on piles of high-explosives and bullets as fire was rapidly taking hold of the vehicle. And they could hear blood-curdling screams from the front cab.

Corporal Peyton managed to force open the top-cover hatch in the roof of the back Viking cab. Although flames were licking around the roof of the vehicle, he clambered through and dropped down on to the sand, hoping he wouldn't land on a mine.

As he exited through the top hatch, Ben Wright, the marine gunner, dazed and in shock, realized that the troops hadn't got out of the back. Flames were licking all round the door. Wright wrestled to pull up the lever, fighting off the pain as his hands burnt up. He could hardly bear the torturous heat, but eventually he forced open the door, and the men fell out, coughing and spluttering, leaving behind everything except their rifles.

Aston arrived on the scene of devastation, running along the tracks made by the Viking. A huge column of black smoke was building up over the vehicle, and orange flames were reaching up through the gunner's hatch.

Aston shouted instructions to the soldiers: 'Get out of here! Get back along the tracks to the Vikings behind! Keep to the tracks! There may be more mines!'

He grabbed hold of Marine Biekes, dazed and groggy, and pulled him back on to the track. 'Mate, I know you're badly hurt, but stay here till the medic arrives, stay right here. If you move around you might stand on another mine.'

Goodman had followed Aston forward and he led Biekes back down the track, away from the burning vehicle.

Aston went to Nieves, lying on the ground, all his skin burnt and red raw, his left arm bleeding where the skin had peeled off, his hair singed and the top of his head badly burnt. The sight of this tough and dependable sergeant – now weak, shrunken, vulnerable, helpless and in terrible agony – horrified Aston. But there was no time to dwell on this. 'Keith, Keith, can you hear me? You're going to be OK, mate. We'll get you out of here. It's going to be OK.'

There was not a second to lose. Aston knew the vehicle, and its explosive load, could go up at any moment. He looked through the choking smoke and searing flames into every part of the vehicle, double-checking that everyone had got out. Then he and Scotty Fryer, the sniper, picked Nieves up and carried him back along the Viking track.

By now Company Sergeant Major Newton's Viking, with the doctor, Andy Tredget, had motored forward, pulling up short of Aston's vehicle. The doc, assisted by Peyton and some of the team medics, started work on the casualties.

Leaving Nieves with the doctor, Aston leant into the back of the Sergeant Major's vehicle. Captain Dave Robinson, the company 2IC, had his headsets on, map, notebook and pencil in hand, and was talking calmly into his radio mike.

As soon as he paused, Aston said, 'Dave, has CASEVAC been tasked?'

'Yes, sir, I reported the minestrike straight away and I tasked CASEVAC a couple of minutes ago, as soon as I knew we had taken casualties.'

'Good, what's the ETA?'

Dave held up his hand, then said into the mike, 'Roger, inform me when it's secure.' He turned back to Aston. 'Sorry, sir, should be about fifteen minutes.'

'What do you mean *about*? Get on to them and get me an up-to-date ETA,' said Aston impatiently.

'Yes, sir.'

'Have you sorted out an HLS to get the casualties away?'

'Yes, sir, the sergeant major's on to that right now.'

Robinson took a deep breath and said, 'Sir, can you just leave me to get on with my job? I know what I'm doing, and all this is just slowing me down. Please, sir, just let me do it.'

His voice was matter-of-fact, logical, calm. Aston looked into the young captain's piercing brown eyes. He was an excellent operator and he knew his stuff. He had been doing a great job all day, as he always did, and Aston realized he was hassling him unnecessarily. *Must calm down*, he thought, *Dave's right, I should leave him to it*.

Aston walked back to his Viking to figure out what to do next. The first priority was to move the vehicles either side of the burning Viking even further away, as it could not be long before the explosives started detonating.

A short while later he spoke to Captain Goodman, 'The Taliban were tracking our movement. Obviously those bikes we saw were doing that. They will now know their mine worked the way they wanted it to. And from here our route back to FOB Rob is totally predictable. God knows what else they've laid between here and there. I reckon we'd better look at another route. What d'you reckon?'

'I agree,' said Goodman, 'The only alternative is a hell of a long way round, it'll take us about three hours instead of fifteen minutes. But it makes sense.'

As the two officers looked at Aston's map, working out the long route home, they could hear loud explosions from the burning Viking as bar-mines, the engineers' high-explosive charges and boxes of Nadriva's 51mm mortar bombs detonated.

Sergeant Major Newton cleared an area of desert big enough for the Chinook to land. This was always done as thoroughly as possible, as the Chinook's wheels, or its rotor downwash, could set off mines buried beneath the dirt. With what had just happened, Newton took exceptional care to make sure the ground was free of mines. And he picked the least obvious place he could to bring the chopper in, just in case the Taliban had decided to position something for the inevitable CASE-VAC helicopter.

16

Propping up the badly burnt Marine Wright, Newton walked up to the Chinook's lowered ramp, struggling against the strong downdraft and the dust it was swirling in every direction. The soldiers of the IRT, infantrymen whose job was to provide close protection on the ground for the helicopter, were blocking the ramp, looking around them with concern.

Above the noise of the powerful twin turboshaft engines, Newton yelled at them, 'I've cleared the ground all round here. Get off the ramp and let me on with these casualties.'

Following behind Newton and Wright, Nadriva walked up the ramp, and Nieves and Biekes were stretchered on. Tredget gave the MERT doctors a rapid brief on each of the casualties, and the treatment they had received so far. As he was talking, the Chinook loadmaster kicked off several crates of iced water for the troops on the ground.

With a roar of its engines, and a wild blast of dust and debris, the helicopter lifted off, carrying the latest four of the seven casualties B Company had sustained so far that day.

Straight after the mine strike, Aston had pushed Snow and his WMIKs out to provide protection. While the casualty evacuation was in progress, Snow called Aston: 'Hello, Zero Alpha, this is Four Zero Alpha. Sighting. Two thousand metres north-west of your location. White pickup truck. Static. Just hanging around. Could be dickers. Over.'

Aston told his JTAC to task the two Apaches escorting the Chinook to check the vehicle out. Minutes later, the JTAC said, 'Sir, the Ugly callsigns report two men next to the vehicle, both with weapons.'

'Take them out,' said Aston.

He climbed on top of the Viking with his binos trained north-west, towards the pickup truck.

From the Apache overhead, he heard the rattle of 30mm cannon fire and watched as the explosive shells flashed around the vehicle, throwing up small clouds of dust. Next there was a long, loud whoosh followed by a thunderous blast, and Aston saw a small building near the vehicle explode.

The JTAC, next to him on the vehicle's roof, was listening intently to his radio. He said, 'Sir, the Ugly callsign says they killed one of the men with thirty mil. The other one managed to get away and take cover in a shed near the vehicle. Destroyed with a Hellfire. No sign of movement. Both enemy had AK47s.'

Aston said, 'Good. Well done. Those guys are certain to be the ones that laid the mine. They will have been checking us out to report back on how successful they had been, and probably trying to get a fix on our future movements in the hope of hitting us again. Well, they won't be doing any more of that dirty work.'

Aston gave brief orders to his commanders, and at 1600 hours the company moved off in a circuitous route that would eventually get them to FOB Robinson. He had ordered the destruction of what was left of the burnt-out Viking, to ensure nothing remained that could be of use to the enemy, and as the column drove out of the area, one of the Apaches slammed two Hellfire missiles into the wrecked vehicle.

Goodman's time estimation had not been far off the mark, and the column rolled up to the entrance to FOB Robinson four hours later, with daylight beginning to fail.

Forward Operating Base Robinson was a bleak and dusty outpost, about 600 metres by 600, surrounded by the ubiquitous Hesco Bastion walls and sandbagged sangars. Inside were a couple of basic accommodation Portakabins for permanent residents, a helicopter landing site, a compound inhabited by a detachment of US forces and a troop of artillery. In normal circumstances the men would have considered it an inhospitable dump, to be avoided at all costs. But right now it seemed like a five-star hotel.

The first four Vikings drove up the steep slope into the gates of the FOB, followed by the logistics vehicles. Now, for the first time, the Oshkosh got into trouble. The heavy tanker came off the track, careered into a steep bank and broke its axle. The entrance to FOB Rob was blocked.

Sergeant Major Newton jumped out of his Viking, at the rear of the column, and ran forward to sort out the company's latest nightmare. As he moved, a single shot rang out and a bullet smacked into the side of the Oshkosh.

Through the twilight, all eyes turned towards a lone Taliban fighter. A couple of hundred metres away, black robed, he was sitting, holding his rifle, on a moped that must have stalled at just the wrong moment. Instead of screaming across the desert on his planned getaway, he was desperately trying to coax the engine back to life, while probably at the same time sensing that his luck had just run out.

The gathering dusk erupted into a rippling carpet of red tracer. Sixteen GPMGs, two .50 cal heavy machine-guns and two grenade machine-guns opened fire from the vehicles waiting outside the FOB. They were joined by machine-guns from sentry posts all round the base.

To Newton it looked like a scene from *Star Wars*.

Ambush: 17 May 2007

When Aston got into FOB Robinson a few hours after Sergeant Nieves and the other casualties were evacuated from the desert, he spoke on the phone to Lieutenant Colonel Stuart Carver, who was at his headquarters in Camp Bastion. Aston briefed Carver on the events at Heyderabad, and on the minestrike that wounded four of his men. Carver confirmed B Company's future tasking, beginning the following day.

As a part of Operation Silver, the relief of Sangin in April, three patrol bases had been built in the town. These isolated and vulnerable outposts were manned by ANA soldiers supported by operational mentoring and liaison teams, or OMLTs, from The 1st Battalion The Grenadier Guards. The other military base in Sangin was the District Centre or DC, Governor Isatullah's office and the location of A Company, The 1st Battalion The Worcestershire and Sherwood Foresters Regiment. All four bases had been coming under daily attack by the Taliban over the previous few weeks. Carver wanted Aston to patrol the town, on foot and with his Vikings, to relieve the pressure on the beleaguered bases.

Aston issued a warning order to B Company. The company command team would reconnoitre all the patrol bases and the DC the following day, to get a feel for the ground and to consult the local commanders on the situation. This would enable Aston to draw up a detailed plan for his subsequent company group patrol operation. The command team would be accompanied by 7 Platoon and Fire Support Group Bravo for security.

The next morning, Thursday 17 May, Lieutenant George Seal-Coon, 7 Platoon commander, gave orders for the move round the patrol bases, which he had been tasked by Aston to command. At 1400 hours that afternoon, the recce group, with their security force, left FOB Robinson in six Vikings and four WMIKs. A short time later they pulled into the

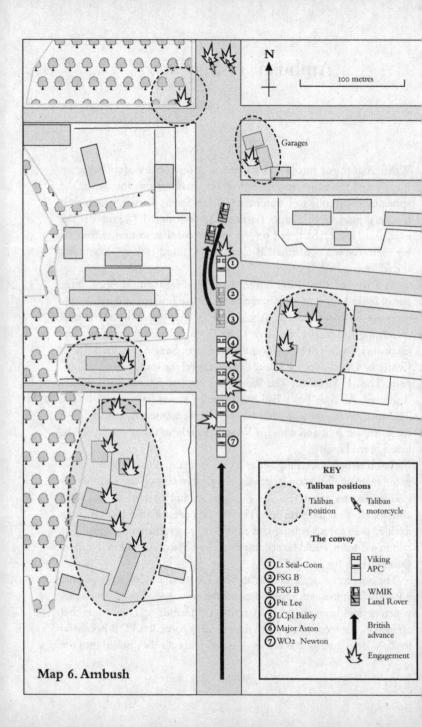

N

100 metres

Garages

KEY

Taliban positions

⬭ Taliban position

🏍 Taliban motorcycle

The convoy

① Lt Seal-Coon
② FSG B
③ FSG B
④ Pte Lee
⑤ LCpl Bailey
⑥ Major Aston
⑦ WO2 Newton

▭ Viking APC

▭ WMIK Land Rover

⬆ British advance

💥 Engagement

Map 6. Ambush

most southerly of the Sangin patrol bases, Waterloo, on the outskirts of the town, 7 kilometres north of FOB Robinson. The column remained in the base for an hour while Aston and his recce group had discussions with the ANA commander and the OMLT leader. The 7 Platoon and FSG security force waited with their vehicles inside Waterloo.

Sprawled on the roof of his BvS10 Viking troop-carrying vehicle, Private Josh Lee lit up one of the 2,000 Pine Lights his section had bought from the Afghans for twelve dollars.

Over the low, throaty rumble of the Viking's idling diesel engine, Lee heard the marine driver hammering at the vehicle's tracks. He hadn't seen this driver before. The marine had come over from another unit and was almost at the end of his tour in Afghanistan. He seemed dedicated to his vehicle like most of the marines, and was doing a 'halt parade', using the short time they were stopped to make sure the Viking was at peak performance.

Lee was chatting with Private Ronnie Barker, who was sitting on top of the next-door Viking, looking over the walls beyond the base. Lee had always liked Barker and saw him as a good and dependable mate. Having heard how Barker had risked his life to get Mac the medic to safety the day before, he looked on him with a new level of respect.

Ronnie said, 'Someone told me hippies used to come out here from the UK in the sixties for the scenery and the drugs. I wouldn't have bothered, be glad to get the hell out of here and back to the UK.'

Hacking on one of his rough cigarettes and swatting flies away with his hand, Lee said, 'Yeah, well, that's students for you. Just wasters. And the scenery, it's the same everywhere in this place. What a tip. Actually, reminds me a bit of Upton Park.'

'Don't start, Josh, or I'll chuck you off that wagon. What scumbag team do you support anyway?'

'I don't support any team. I'd rather play sport than watch it. At least I can play football, unlike your West Ham mob, Wonnie my old mate.'

Barker contemplated jumping across to Lee's vehicle and shoving him on to the ground but decided it wasn't worth the effort in this sweltering heat, so contented himself with flicking a v-sign instead.

This was the company's first time at Waterloo. *Just the same as all the others*, thought Lee, *what a tip*. A dusty compound surrounded by a

Hesco Bastion wall punctuated by four or five sandbagged sangars. The single shabby building in the middle of the base was topped by the usual CT sangar – the control tower – bristling with weapons including a .50 calibre heavy machine-gun.

Afghan soldiers were crouched cross-legged in every bit of shade, smoking, whispering to each other and eyeing the British soldiers and their vehicles. Others were sitting next to the sangars, chatting to their mates on stag. As always most of the Afghans were wearing green US-style camouflage combat suits, matching caps and flip flops.

Ronnie nodded in the direction of Sangin, a kilometre away. 'What do you reckon that's like, mate? Everyone's always on about it.'

'I heard it's been really badly smashed up, but it doesn't look like it from here. Just like any other dump in Afghan. We'll soon see, I expect.'

Waterloo was perched high on top of a jagged rocky outcrop. The heavily mined dirt track running past the base and along the valley into southern Sangin was known as Route 611. Single-storey light-brown dusty Afghan compounds lined the road into town, all surrounded by mud walls at least 3 to 5 metres high.

Lee glanced down through the hatch into the back of the vehicle. He could just about hear the slightly irritating sound of Prodigy's 'Firestarter' coming from Private John Thrumble's iPod speakers. Thrumble played it over and over, and Lee was pleased it was almost inaudible over the sound of the engines and the driver's hammering at the running gear. The iPod speakers were the only true luxury the platoon had, and Thrumble guarded them with his life, occasionally lending them out to his pals and inspecting them closely when returned.

Lee tossed his fag butt into the dust and, stepping across the metre-wide gap between the articulated Viking's troop-carrying compartment and the front cab, said, 'What's going on then, Smethwick?'

Lance Corporal Smethwick, the marine vehicle commander, was perched on top of the front cab, monitoring the radio. Smethwick and the Royal Anglians had hit it off straight away. At forty he was about the oldest man in the company group. He had an easy-going manner and was totally unflappable.

Smethwick had experience from previous operations in Afghanistan and Iraq. A marine reservist, he was nicknamed 'rubber dagger' by the rest of the Viking Troop. Lee was amused that this tough Scouser was a car salesman back home in Liverpool.

Smethwick said, 'I think we're off in a few minutes. The company commander's almost finished doing the rounds. Better get a mouthful of this down you quick.'

Another of Smethwick's nicknames was 'the brew king', and he offered Lee a filthy mug, improvised from a plastic 81mm mortar casing.

Pouring with sweat, Corporal Stu Parker, Lee's section commander, appeared at the back of the vehicle. 'Josh, chuck us a couple of bottles of water down, mate.'

Lee stepped back across to his own hatch and passed down two dust-covered bottles of warm Evian from one of the cardboard boxes strapped on top of the wagon.

'Cheers,' shouted Parker, cursing the heat, by now almost unbearable, and nudging 60 degrees.

As Parker half-drained a 1.5-litre bottle, Lance Corporal Steve Veal called from inside the vehicle, 'Just come over the net – we're moving. Mount up, lads. We're going into Sangin.'

Corporal Parker, wearing a brown T-shirt under his body armour, walked to the front cab, nudged Private Aaron 'Troy' McLure awake and handed him a bottle of Evian. McLure was sitting in the back seat, which was always allocated to the smallest man in the section as it was even more cramped than the other crew positions. And every time McLure got in it he went straight to sleep, waking only when it was time to do something. A useful skill for any soldier.

'Sorry to disturb your dreams, Troy, but even a potential SAS trooper like you needs to get a bit of hydration,' said Parker.

Lee dropped down through his hatch, balancing on the pile of brown metal ammo boxes on the vehicle floor so he had height to see and fire out. He pulled his Osprey body armour over his shoulders and strapped on his Mark 6 combat helmet. He tied his Minimi light machine-gun to the steel rail running round the hatch, using the weapon's nylon sling. This technique stopped the gun dropping over the vehicle side – and the severe embarrassment, not to mention loss of firepower that would follow – when the driver unexpectedly jammed on the brakes, swerved round a hairpin bend or dropped the tracks into a particularly deep rut.

Wedging himself into position in the hatchway, Lee gripped the Minimi with one hand and held on to the side of the vehicle with the other, braced for a nightmare ride down into Sangin. He knew that, whatever happened on the way, he would be hanging on for dear life.

Lee had volunteered to be top cover for his section's Viking. Lance Corporal Smethwick, as vehicle commander, was in the forward gun turret with his GPMG. In addition to commanding the Viking his job was to observe forward for enemy and look out for any sign of mines dug into the track or of improvised explosive devices concealed beside the road. His gun would always be cocked and ready to fire immediately in defence of the vehicle until the crew could debus and deal with the enemy on foot.

Smethwick also had to watch for civilian cars getting too close to the Viking as they moved along Helmand's dangerous roads. Many US and allied vehicles in Iraq had been destroyed, and their crews killed, by suicide car bombs detonating next to them as they drove along. The same had also occurred in Kabul and elsewhere in Afghanistan on a number of occasions. Thankfully, the British in Helmand had not yet been attacked in this way, but they were always on the alert for the possibility. They would first wave off a vehicle getting too close, then fire warning shots, and if necessary were ready to shoot directly at a car or truck to keep it away.

As top cover Lee had the same role. Smethwick would decide which side to cover at any given time, depending on the ground, the threat and the actions of other vehicles in the convoy. He would swing his gun right or left to cover the main threat area. Lee would then switch to cover the opposite side, scanning for enemy activity.

Although Smethwick was in an exposed position, he was protected by a steel armoured shield. Lee, as top cover, was even more vulnerable, with no protection at all. To observe effectively he had to expose much of his upper torso, shielded only by his helmet and body armour.

Even though top cover was the most dangerous position there were advantages to the job. You got to see out, and every infantryman wants to know what's going on around him. It was also better than being in the Viking's dark, oven-like cabins. Designed for a crew of eight, Lee's Viking had seats for only seven as the communications equipment took up so much room. And most of the rest of the space was full of ammo boxes, so the soldiers in the back were jammed in like sardines, knees virtually around their ears. The air con almost certainly wouldn't be working, or not properly anyway – that was pretty much a given. And for Lee an added bonus was knowing that he didn't have to put up with the Prodigy stuff that would be blaring out from Thrumble's speakers, just about audible above the roar of the engine and the crunching and juddering of the tracks.

With a loud groan and a bang the back door slammed shut. The Viking's 5.9-litre Cummins turbo diesel fired fully into life, and the vehicle lurched forward, following the lead wagons in the column out of the front gate. As they passed through an Afghan soldier lazily waved his AK47, complete with a bright red flower in the muzzle.

Lee caught the wistful eye of a heavily bearded OMLT corporal standing near by. He looked as if he wished he was coming with them. Lee understood why. He wouldn't want to be stuck in this vulnerable and frequently attacked outpost with only a couple of other British soldiers and a whole bunch of Afghan troops; separated from the enemy by just 2 metres of Hesco.

Moving out of the base, the convoy formed up into its planned order of march for the short journey to Sangin DC. The two FSG WMIKs, equipped with .50 cal machine-guns and GPMGs, moved out first to secure a vulnerable point at the start of the route. They would later slot back into the column. Seal-Coon's Viking led the main group of vehicles. Behind him was Lee's Wagon, followed by the platoon sergeant's vehicle, then Aston's and the company sergeant major's Vikings. In all, there were five Vikings and two WMIKs.

As the column turned left and trundled haltingly down the steep slope towards route 611, Lee glanced back. Lance Corporal Dean Bailey, top cover sentry in the vehicle behind, threw him a cheerful thumbs-up. Bailey had volunteered to be top cover in the Viking that contained Platoon Sergeant Michael Woodrow, a section of Royal Engineers and a huge quantity of explosives and demolition equipment. A determined and professional infantryman and a skilled sniper, Bailey wanted to get to know the terrain for future sniper operations that were being considered to help protect Waterloo and the other bases in and around Sangin.

Bailey went to school in South Woodham Ferrers, Essex, where he was suspended three times for fighting and an endless string of other misdemeanours. But after a few unskilled jobs he had joined the Army in 2003 when he was nineteen – and excelled. His long-suffering teachers at Sir William De Ferrers School would have been astonished to learn that Bailey had studied hard and become one of the few who passed the demanding sniper course at the first attempt. Only a few months later he attended and passed an NCOs' leadership course and was by now well on his way to what promised to be a highly successful Army career. A talented footballer and, like Barker, a dedicated West Ham supporter, Bailey described himself as 'the most handsome man in the battalion, if not the Army', while his mates called him a 'pretty boy' and, with some jealousy, 'a real ladies' man'.

Lee acknowledged Bailey's thumbs-up with a nod and a smile and turned to cover forward left as Smethwick swung his gun off to the right. Moments later, as the column of vehicles turned on to Route 611, Lee took in the rusting hulks of several Soviet armoured personnel carriers, the chilling reminder of a mujahideen ambush in the mid-1980s that had cost a Russian motor rifle platoon their lives.

The B Company column now entered the southern outskirts of Sangin, an untidy collection of light-brown single-storey flat-roofed buildings. This was the poorer section of town. One or two were shops, their façades protected by iron shutters.

The dusty streets were completely empty as the vehicles moved northwards into a stretch of larger two-storey buildings – a sign of greater prosperity. The road was lined on either side with 3-metre-high mud walls.

Lee's Viking passed an area of open ground to the left, dropping down towards a woodline in the valley. As the WMIKs in front picked their way along the heavily potholed road, two local men appeared from nowhere and pushed a rusty old black Nissan into the path of Lee's Viking, forcing the vehicle across to the right side of the road.

Lee had barely begun to wonder what was going on when the first RPG smashed into the top of Dean Bailey's Viking.

2

Lee turned and saw Bailey engulfed in flames. He just had time to catch the terrified look on his mate's face before Bailey threw himself down into the Viking's cab. Bailey tore off his burning helmet and body armour and seconds later was back up and in the fight, firing his SA80 at Taliban swarming over the compound roofs.

'Three enemy left...' In the forward turret of Lee's Viking, the marine gunner swung his GPMG to engage.

Lee dropped a gunman on the wall 40 metres away then heard a loud thumping noise from the open ground off to the left. A Soviet-designed

Degtjarev DShK 12.7mm anti-aircraft machine-gun started to hose down the column, spitting out bullets at the rate of 125 a minute. Red tracer streaked in behind his vehicle.

A GPMG gunner in one of the Vikings silenced the DShK with a long, withering blast.

By now all ten B Company vehicles were engaged with the enemy.

There was chaos inside Bailey's burning Viking. Sniper Teddy Ruecker thought they had hit a mine. Then he heard the order, 'Get out, get out, get out,' from the commander.

He shouted, 'Everyone out of the vehicle,' and booted open the heavy armoured door. He grabbed Bailey's leg and yelled up, 'Deano, get out mate – we're going – now…'

A second PG7VL 93mm high-explosive warhead spiralled from its launcher at 295 metres per second and slammed into the top of the Viking. Bailey had not made it out of the turret.

Capable of penetrating 50 centimetres of armour, the rocket exploded next to him, ripping off most of his left deltoid and triceps and almost tearing away his arm. The shock wave from the explosion punctured his lung. Shrapnel slashed through his mouth and into the back of his head, fracturing his lower jaw on the way. The blaze on top of the vehicle melted his right hand. As he dropped through the hatch into the smoke-filled crew compartment, a 7.62mm AK47 bullet tore into his chest.

Ruecker escaped with Sergeant Woodrow and eight engineers, leaving their explosive demolition charges behind. The engineers dived into cover against a 3-metre wall as Woodrow raked their attackers with his SA80.

Another Taliban heavy machine-gun opened up from the roof of a mosque, and an RPG exploded right next to them. Richie Barke, the platoon's 51mm mortar man, was hurled to the ground, bleeding from multiple shrapnel wounds. Woodrow gave him a fierce grin of encouragement as he turned his attention to Barke's attackers.

Josh Lee blazed away with his Minimi at RPG-wielding Taliban to their right. Woodrow screamed, 'Cover us while we move up to your wagon – can you see them? Are you hitting the bastards?'

Lee gave a brief thumbs-up.

Ruecker dashed into a nearby alleyway to escape the stream of automatic fire, straight into a black-bearded Taliban with a ragged turban who was celebrating one of the hits on the Viking by loosing off his

AK47 into the air. He wore an old Russian chest rig for his magazines. An RPG rocket launcher lay at his feet.

As a Sniper Number One, in addition to an Accuracy International .338 rifle, Ruecker carried a Browning pistol, which he drew and fired into the man's gut and shoulder – then eleven more times as the fighter scrabbled on the deck for his AK47.

Ruecker cursed himself for firing so many rounds, quickly reloaded and sprinted back to Woodrow and the engineers, now desperately climbing into the back of the vehicle as Lee blasted away with his Minimi to keep the enemy's heads down.

Bailey wasn't there.

Ruecker shouted, 'Where's Deano? Where is he? I'm going back to get him, I'm not leaving him.'

Inside Lee's Viking, fourteen soldiers piled into a cab designed for eight.

Lee saw another fighter down an alleyway to the rear right of the Viking, levelling an RPG launcher. He gave him a burst from the Minimi and watched him drop. He swung towards yet another group on a distant rooftop, and his gun jammed. 'Stoppage,' he yelled. 'Pass us a gat, quick.' He dropped the Minimi into the back of the wagon.

He looked down and suddenly realized he was balancing on the helmeted head of Richie Barke, covered in blood from his shrapnel wounds. Neither of them had a choice. The long-suffering Barke somehow managed a grin as Woodrow passed up his SA80 and collected full mags of ammunition from the troops inside the Viking.

At the front of the column, Seal-Coon's vehicle was getting hit by heavy smallarms fire. From within his cab, 60 metres ahead he saw a Taliban fighter armed with an RPG and another with an AK. They ducked through the large blue doors of a compound. Over the intercom he yelled a target indication to Corporal Fisher, on the GPMG above.

The RPG gunner, wearing a blue kurta, reappeared and levelled his missile launcher, pointing it directly at Seal-Coon. Seal-Coon could see his face. Everything went into slow motion as he thought, *Sixty metres, almost point blank, he can't miss.* Fisher swivelled his GPMG on to the fighter, pressed the trigger and – nothing. 'Stoppage,' he yelled, as he yanked the cocking lever back to clear it. But the fighter had seen the gun turn on him, and Seal-Coon saw the panic on his face as he fired the missile. Seal-Coon braced for the impact – perhaps his last few moments on earth, but the rocket streaked straight over the top of the Viking, just above the gunner's head.

Sitting there, Seal-Coon felt impotent. He wanted to get out and fight on his feet, to shoot the fighter who had just fired the RPG. But bullets were slamming into the vehicle, and that would have been suicidal. He watched the fighter with his RPG scrabble to try to get back through the compound doors, but Fisher, the gunner, had cleared his stoppage and ripped the man's body open with a long stream of 7.62 mm tracer.

Private Ronnie Barker was top cover in the rear cab of Seal-Coon's Viking. Taliban fighters, carrying AK47s and PKM machine-guns, were moving towards the vehicles, trying to get close. Barker cut down several with his Minimi and sent others diving for cover. He got through 100 bullets in the first few seconds and shouted down for more ammo. Seventy-five metres away, to his rear, standing next to a building, he saw another RPG gunner taking aim. The fighter just got his RPG launcher on to the shoulder when Barker fired a burst of twenty rounds, driving him into the ground.

Barker looked round and saw one of Snow's gunners firing forward, past the Viking. Snow had spotted several motorbikes, each with two armed riders, heading down the road towards them. Reinforcements. Barker watched excitedly as each of the five motorbikes was hit, crashing off the track or bursting into flames.

Behind Barker's Viking, pistol in hand, Ruecker ran the 70-metre-long killing zone, on a mission to find Dean Bailey. He was knocked off his feet by the blast of an RPG which exploded against the turret of Major Aston's Viking, wounding the top cover, Marine McNeil. The marine screamed and held his hands to his face, one eye torn from its socket, then fell from the top of his vehicle. Aston dived out and grabbed him. As he moved, a second RPG scored a direct hit, exploding on the back of the Viking.

With the marine's blood spurting all over him, Aston pressed a field dressing on to his shattered face. Sergeant Major Newton's Viking had pulled forward, beyond Aston's. Newton, seeing what had happened, ran back and dragged the wounded marine into his vehicle.

As Newton was about to get back into his cab he noticed that the rear section of Aston's Viking was ablaze, set alight by the second impact. He thought, *The whole thing's going up any second.* He grabbed the fire extinguisher he kept beside him in the vehicle and raced back to put out the flames. Bullets were flying all round the two vehicles, but Newton ignored them as he worked the extinguisher over the fire, managing to get it out in a few seconds. Somehow he got back to his own vehicle unscathed. *Talk about commander's wings*, he thought as he flung the armoured door shut behind him, wondering how on earth he had survived.

Ruecker reached Bailey's burning Viking. Thick black and green smoke filled the crew compartment and a river of fire flowed down the road from it. He felt his way to the back and glimpsed his mate inside, face down, covered in blood and oil. Around him bullets were cooking off from the heat.

Company doctor Major Andrew Tredget appeared beside Ruecker. Bailey was coughing up blood. The pair grabbed him and dragged him out. Ruecker's fist entered Bailey's exposed rib-cage. Almost out of his mind with the horror of the last few minutes, Ruecker screamed, 'He's my mate. My hands were in his chest. *Oh my God…*'

Somehow Ruecker and Tredget got Bailey back to Newton's vehicle but dropped him just short as they were caught by the shockwave of a further RPG impact. They picked up his limp body, slippery with blood, and pushed him into the jam-packed crew compartment. The doc squeezed in beside him.

There was no room for Ruecker.

He nodded in resignation as the door closed. On his own again, Ruecker ran back through the fire and the bullets.

Ruecker, utterly exhausted and covered in blood and sweat, made it to Lee's wagon. Inside, the troops started trying to treat him, but he screamed, 'It's Deano's blood – not mine. I'm not injured.'

At that point Ruecker was hit by battle-shock. He started shaking uncontrollably and crying. Thrumble held his hands and said, 'Teddy, it's OK, mate. You're OK. We're about to move out of here. We're all with you, mate.'

3

Sergeant Major Ivan Snow had ordered his WMIKs 50 metres forward, beyond the head of the column. He knew the enemy would have deployed cut-offs forward of the killing area, to mow down anybody trying to escape.

Just as Snow predicted, two fighters appeared, blasting automatic fire from AK47s at the hip. Screaming into his radio, 'Engaging two enemy forward,' he squeezed the trigger of his GPMG, killing one instantly. The other ran 40 metres into a garage. Colour Sergeant Stevie Neal sent in a volley of bombs from his grenade machine-gun, killing the fleeing man and setting the entire building alight.

Sergeant Major Newton came on the net. 'Hello, Zero Alpha, Zero Alpha, this is Copper Three Three Alpha. I've got one times T One casualty in my wagon. Must evacuate immediately.'

He was calling the company commander for instructions, but got no reply. It was the same old problem, the one that had caused so much trouble in Heyderabad the day before – radios never work when you need them most.

Snow stepped down from his WMIK and walked the 75 metres back through the killing zone to the company commander's Viking, leaving Neal and his vehicle crews to cover the front of the column.

Aston, drenched in Marine McNeil's blood, swung open the armoured door of his Viking. Ignoring the bullets scything through the air around him, Snow shouted, 'Sir, I'm holding forward OK, doesn't look like too many more enemy up there. The company sergeant major's been trying to get you on the net. He's got a T One that needs evacuating quick.'

'OK, thanks, Sergeant Major. We're going to head back the way we came, back to FOB Rob. Who knows what's ahead? Could be another ambush or roadside IEDs. We know the way back better than the way forward, and FOB Rob is more secure than Sangin DC to get the casualties out. Try to move further forward to cover us as we turn. I reckon the best place is that garage you lot have just trashed . . .'

Snow walked back to his WMIK as Newton finalized a radio head check between vehicles. It was critical that the company didn't leave anyone to the mercy of the Taliban.

Snow relayed Aston's orders to all vehicles then told his driver to push forward to the bend in the road and go firm. 'Get into the best cover you can so I can fire straight ahead and right. Stevie Neal can move up behind us and cover the left.'

4

David Broomfield, now promoted to captain, was acting as ops officer in FOB Rob, monitoring the company's operational activity and providing the communications link between B Company and Carver's battle group HQ at Camp Bastion, about 50 kilometres to the south-east. The commander of B Company's 6 Platoon had hoped for a quiet spell of duty after the nightmare of the previous day.

He was in the company ops room, a baking-hot steel freight container surrounded by Hesco blocks which gave it immediate protection against the blast of rocket or mortar attack. The ops room was positioned in the north-east corner of FOB Robinson, within a small British compound known as the 'Snake Pit'. Above the ops room was the support sangar – a high tower armed with machine-guns and surveillance equipment. He sat at a folding wooden table with a paperback and a mug of revolting coffee. His plastic chair was so hot it felt as if it might melt. Beside him one signaller monitored the company net, and another the battle group. The ops room runner and brew-boy dozed fitfully in the corner. Even though the room had been swept a few hours earlier, everything was again covered in a thin film of dust.

Broomfield's mind had wandered to the Andes, where he had spent a year climbing before joining the Army, when he heard Captain Dave Robinson's voice over the company net. 'FOB Rob, this is Copper Two Two Alpha – contact, ambush, wait out.'

The ops room switched to alert mode, the signallers poised to record every detail so Broomfield could organize the necessary support.

Seconds later one of the sentries reported on the base security net, 'This is Sangar One. I can see a huge pile of smoke over Sangin. Something big is happening down there. I can hear explosions. Many explosions…'

Broomfield hit the intercom to the support tower. 'Tower, stand to, stand to. Look in the direction of Sangin and report.'

As the tower confirmed, Dave Robinson came back on the company net. 'Fob Rob, Fob Rob, this is Copper Two Two Alpha. Reference contact, we have one times T One casualty, we are taking heavy fire from multiple firing points. We have a vehicle burning. Wait out.'

Broomfield stood the company medics to, ready to receive casualties. He told 5 Platoon to get out of their sunbathing gear, ready to storm into Sangin and help in a rescue. Sentry posts reported more smoke and continuing explosions.

Broomfield connected with Captain Phil Moxey, the battle group operations officer at Bastion, on the secure Brent phone. 'Phil, the company is being hit in Sangin. Looks like we've got at least one times T One casualty and a vehicle on fire. Can you send the MERT here right now? Let me know when they're in the air.'

The medical emergency response team consisted of an HC2 Chinook heavy-lift helicopter with a medical crew equipped for casualty evacuation and capable of surgery in mid-air. The twin-rotored chopper also had door gunners, defences against enemy missiles, radar warning systems and surveillance equipment, and two WAH-64 Apache Longbow attack helicopters – armed with sixteen Hellfire missiles and a 30mm cannon – as escorts.

Everyone in the ops room was thinking the same thing. Was it a close friend who'd been hit? They put themselves in the shoes of their mates on the ground. And it didn't feel good.

'FOB Rob, this is Copper Two Two Alpha. We have to get the casualties out. We're abandoning the burning vehicle and pulling back to your location now.'

f

In the back of the company sergeant major's Viking, Captain Dave Robinson was cradling a man's pulped head in his hands as he spoke to Broomfield on the radio. The soldier's regimental insignia had been blown off with his shirt and there was so much blood the face was completely unrecognizable. Captain Robinson had no idea who it was. He had a huge hole in the back of his head, and his wounds were so bad Robinson assumed he must already be dead. But to make certain, he put his hand into the soldier's mouth. He felt a breath. 'Doc, doc, this guy's alive.'

Perhaps hearing these words, the wounded soldier pushed himself up with one arm, let out a desperate groan and vomited blood all over Robinson.

The doc, jammed in at the other end of the wagon, yelled, 'Get some oxygen on him – *now*. Everybody get out your field dressings and find a bleeding point.'

Robinson grabbed the oxygen mask and pressed it firmly over the man's face. Some of the troops were so tightly packed together they couldn't reach their dressings, so they shoved their fists into the open wounds of the soldier now spread-eagled beneath them, desperately trying to stop him bleeding to death.

Robinson felt around the man's bloody neck and found his dog tags. He was horrified to see Bailey's name. Suddenly this was very personal. Lance Corporal Dean Bailey had been one of Robinson's boys when he led Sniper Platoon a few months earlier. They had been a particularly tight-knit team.

He shouted, 'Dean, Dean, you are going to be OK, mate. The helicopter is on the way to get you.'

To Tredget he yelled at the top of his voice, 'Doc – do something. Do something. He's one of my guys. You've got to save him.'

Tredget – now stretched all over Bailey trying to stop him from bleeding to death, shouted back, 'I'm doing all I can – we need to get this man back to FOB Rob ASAP, like now. He's losing a hell of a lot of blood.'

The column finally started trundling forward to Snow's WMIKs and turned laboriously in the narrow space beside the blazing garage. Then the drivers slammed down their accelerators and ran the Taliban gauntlet once more.

The DShK anti-aircraft machine-gun crew that had been killed when the ambush began had been replaced, and the heavy gun was firing again from the same spot in the open ground. Several rounds hit the back of Lee's Viking, but he was by now travelling too fast to have any chance of getting accurate fire back at the enemy gunners.

In Robinson's Viking, the situation worsened as the vehicle bounced at horrific speeds back through the killing area, throwing Bailey's badly broken body from floor to roof.

Gunner Hughes from the artillery fire support team was top cover in Robinson's vehicle. As they cleared the killing area, Hughes tumbled down through the hatch, screaming, 'I've been shot in the face. I've been shot in the face. Help me. Help me.' A bullet had scored across his face, but, quickly realizing it was just a graze, he went back up to his position.

One thousand metres past the killing zone the whole column arrived at a shallow wadi. Here they stopped for a further head check, to confirm they had everyone. With Newton rushing between wagons, it took two minutes, and then they were speeding off again to FOB Rob, now in sight.

The battered column screamed through the guard post, kicking up clouds of dust as it moved through the base. Newton stopped his Viking beside the company aid post, leapt straight out and ran round to the back. The medics were waiting with their stretchers. Newton pulled open the door and saw Bailey, lying face down on top of all the soldiers in the back, unconscious. He put his hands underneath Bailey's chest, neck and chin and, assisted by a medic, lifted him as carefully as he could on to a stretcher.

The medics took him into the ISO container that made up part of the aid post. Tredget followed him in, and he and a US military doctor went to work.

Corporal Parker grabbed one of the burnt engineers and helped carry him into the aid post. At the same time, the MERT Chinook came in to land on the south side of the base. Its two Apache escorts circled like vultures overhead, hunting for enemy.

Ruecker, still shaking and sobbing uncontrollably, had been helped out of the back of the vehicle by Thrumble and was shouting, 'Where's Dean? Where's Dean?'

His uniform, and his face and arms, were covered in Bailey's blood and gore. He threw his body armour to the ground and then tore off his blood-soaked clothing. Sergeant Woodrow grabbed some bottles of Evian and poured them over him. He handed a full bottle to Ruecker. 'Here clack some of that down you, Teddy.'

Ruecker gulped down 6 litres one after the other.

Lee put an arm round Ruecker, trying to calm him down. 'Teddy, how about an ash, mate? Look, have one of these Lamberts, they're gleaming. We always save them for special occasions.'

Ruecker gratefully put one of Lee's prized cigarettes between his lips and drew it down heavily into his lungs, the first time he had ever smoked.

Captain Robinson raced to the ops room. Standing up as he entered, Broomfield did a double take. Robinson was covered from head to foot in Bailey's blood, mingled with a thick coating of dust. His hair was sticking up, he was sweating heavily, and his face was deep red. He was gulping from a filthy-looking bottle of Evian.

He said loudly, 'We need an aircraft, Dave, we need one now. Get it sorted.'

Broomfield replied, 'We've got one, mate, it's just landed.'

'Good, well done. We need to get that Viking denied quickly. There's weapons and explosives inside it and all the ECM kit. We've got to deny it and fast before the enemy get into it.'

Broomfield said, 'I've asked battle group HQ for permission to deny. I've told Sergeant Dyer to get one of the Apaches to stand by to take it out with Hellfire.'

Moments later battle group ops officer Captain Phil Moxey came on the Brent phone and confirmed that authority had been given to deny the vehicle.

Over the intercom to the tower, Broomfield gave Sergeant Dyer, the JTAC, the go-ahead to destroy the smoking vehicle.

Within minutes the Apache pilot had launched a Hellfire missile, reducing the Viking to scrap. Dyer then entered the ops room and confirmed, 'We've denied the vehicle.'

As he spoke the Brent rang again. Moxey. 'Task Force has changed their mind. Do not deny the vehicle until I get back to you. Repeat – do not deny.'

Broomfield simply acknowledged the instruction, knowing it was likely to change back again. In any case it was now too late.

In the aid post, Corporal Peyton was treating the less seriously wounded casualties. Captain Keene, the MERT medical officer, had joined the other two doctors working on Bailey, and the three spent a few minutes figuring out how best to keep him breathing. Bailey was now semi-conscious. His arm was hanging off, bubbles were coming from the hole in his neck, and he was mumbling and shaking. Corporal Parker stood next to him, holding his hand and shouting at him, shouting his name, trying to keep him from drifting completely away.

After fifteen minutes the doctors decided Bailey was as stable as he was going to get for the flight back to Bastion. But, as Keene ordered him to be stretchered across to the Chinook, none of them were sure whether he would survive the ten-minute flight.

When the helicopter lifted off, sending waves of dust and debris flying over the camp, Parker rejoined his section at the back of their Viking. The lads were unusually quiet. Even Thrumble's iPod speakers were silent. They had just been told that two of the company's engineers could not be accounted for, and a radio intercept had picked up Taliban fighters in Sangin bragging that they had 'captured two cows'.

Code for British soldiers?

Fearing the worst, the OMLT team leader in FOB Robinson, Grenadier Guards Major Barnes-Taylor, instantly loaded his men up into their WMIKs ready to fight their way into Sangin to rescue the soldiers. The US Army detachment commander also mounted his men in their Humvees and started cueing up US air assets in support. And the B Company platoons were putting back on their body armour and helmets ready to face Sangin once more.

Near Parker's vehicle, Sergeant Dyer, the JTAC who had called in the air-strike to deny the Viking, was in shock, sobbing and muttering, 'I've killed a friend. I bombed a friend.'

In the confusion he thought his air-strike to deny the Viking had killed the engineers, accidentally left in the crippled vehicle.

Meanwhile Newton was tearing round the base, trying to confirm again that everyone was safely back in. It was only minutes later, but it seemed like an age, when Newton's head count confirmed no one had been left behind. The chatter about 'cows' must refer to something else. Perhaps the burning Viking with its two compartments.

Almost immediately news of an entirely different sort came from the ops room, which sent Parker, Lee and the rest of the section scrambling to the roof of their Viking. The two Apache pilots now hunting down the enemy had spotted a group of Taliban ambushers who had survived the gun battle in Sangin. About eight men were making their escape across the river in boats, trying to get back north to the safety of their stronghold in Musa Qalah.

Word spread through the camp, and British and American soldiers clambered for a high spot to watch as the Apaches blasted the escaping Taliban. They could hear cannon and missile fire as the enemy were wiped out from above. The company's mood briefly lifted as grey smoke from the burning boats rose from the water in the distance, and the two Apaches turned in a long circle to follow the Chinook back to Camp Bastion.

The men jumped from their vantage points. For the first time in hours things were beginning to calm down. But there was no time now for them to dwell on the critically wounded Bailey or their other wounded mates in the Chinook, or even to think about the nightmare they had just been through. The message from Aston, as always, was to crack on. The priority was to sort out weapons, ammunition, vehicles, equipment and get everything ready for the next task. Whatever that might be. Or whenever – it could be in five minutes or it could be tomorrow.

6

B Company had taken thirteen casualties in two days. The company was very close knit, and many of the men came from the same towns. To lose so many soldiers in such a short period was a real blow. The mood was sombre, but the junior NCOs got in among the troops and started doing their job – giving orders, encouraging, cajoling, checking, leading.

In the 'Arm Pit', an inhospitable dust bowl in the middle of the FOB that was the temporary home to soldiers and vehicles, Parker closed in his section. He began to organize the after-action routine of ammo checks and kit checks, and he detailed people off to help the Viking crew get their vehicle sorted out. There was a lot of blood in some of the wagons that had to be sluiced out, and the crews set about the urgent tasks of running repairs and refuelling to make sure the vehicles stayed on the road and were ready for further combat.

Parker said, 'I know we're all upset about Deano and the others. But whatever happened today, priority from the sergeant major is get everything ready so we can go back out and smash them if they start anything else. And we don't know whether the CO's got any more tasks for us. We've got to be ready anyway. Get your heads back up and get on with it. And Thrumble – get that horrible bloody music of yours back on, mate. I feel incomplete without it.'

Ruecker drifted across, wearing a clean T-shirt and combat trousers he had scrounged from one of the other lads to replace the uniform that had been covered in Bailey's blood. 'Josh, mate, give us another one of them Lamberts, I could get used to them.'

'Not a hope, Teddy, I told you we keep them for special occasions, and that's finished now. Officially. Here, have a Pine.'

Ruecker, who had been through even more horror in Sangin that day than most, already seemed to be back on track, though he was still a bit edgy and subdued. As he headed to the fire support group area, puffing on his Pine, Sergeant Woodrow appeared and spoke to Parker. 'Everyone OK, Stu? Send Steve Veal across to me in ten minutes with your ammo states and we'll sort out ammunition and water replens...Oh, and Lee, here's my rifle. Get it cleaned. You fired all those bullets through it, lad, it's filthy.'

'Come on, Sarge, I've got my Minimi to clean. It's totally minging; I fired even more through that.'

Woodrow grinned and walked off, shaking his head, SA80 in hand. He turned and called back, 'Oh, and Stu, the OC's having a debrief for the whole company in an hour. Get your section over to the Snake Pit at eighteen hundred.'

Outside the 'Snake Pit', the area of the ops block and aid post, Lee and Ruecker, and seemingly most of the company, sat smoking Pine Lights and gulping down water. A few moments later Aston arrived with Newton. Aston had not had a moment to spare since getting back into the base, and hadn't had time to give any thought to what he was going to say. He looked around at his men, seated on the ground in a semi-circle. It was evident from the look in the eyes of all those who had been with him in Sangin that they had been through the mill.

He said, 'I'll be brief, boys, then go and get yourselves some scoff. What we had out there, that was a well-planned ambush. You can't take it away from the Taliban, they set that up really well. But the idea of an ambush is you destroy all the enemy in it, or at least you cause them real damage. The initiative was with the Taliban today. Shouldn't have been but it was. And they should have come out on top. But they didn't. Yeah, we took a battering, we all know that, and we're all hoping Dean Bailey will pull through, and the others will be OK too. But I reckon all the ambushers are dead now. The ones we didn't get were killed by the Apaches. We'll go through the BDA assessment when we've got time, but, talking to people so far, I reckon we took out at least ten to fifteen – probably a lot more too. And the JTAC reckons the Apaches confirmed another eight going across the river. The enemy came off worse because of the full-on aggression and the professionalism of every man out there today. Several of you did some really, really brave things – and that won't be forgotten.

'I can see some of you look pretty low. Like you're at the bottom. I can understand that. But don't forget what I always say. We are a team.

A company team. You always hear that people like working with B Company. Why? Because we include them in the team. And we're all in it together. No one's on their own. So you take the good days with the bad. And we've had a couple of bad days. But let's not lose sight of what I said a minute ago. We killed a lot of enemy today. And we killed eighteen yesterday in Heyderabad. And remember back in Silicon, our first big contact. That was the day for B Company. We killed lots of Taliban, and you all saw them dead on the battlefield. Think back to that. These last couple of days, particularly today, is just one of the bad days. That's the business we're in. You take the good and the bad and you just get on with it.

'I'm not wrapping you in cotton wool. I'm not going to ask the CO for a break and I'm not going to give you a break. We're going back into Sangin tomorrow, or maybe the next day. But soon. And we will just get on with it and get it done.

'OK, diggers, that's it. I'm incredibly proud of you all. Keep your heads up, get yourselves some scoff and some rest, and get ready to go out again.'

Josh Lee headed back to the Arm Pit with the rest of the section. He sat in the dust and fixed up his food – twenty-four-hour ration pack Menu B. The only one the CQMS ever seemed to issue. Beef stew and dumplings plus chocolate pudding. He thought, *That must be it. We can't get anything worse than that for the rest of the tour now. That must be as bad as it gets. And I really don't want to go through anything like that again. I just don't.*

7

Two days later, on 19 May, B Company went back into Sangin – up the same road. Carver wanted them in the town to provide reassurance to the local population and the Afghan Army and police. And he did not want to wait too long before his troops used that road again. It was the only way in, and they simply could not afford to see it as too dangerous to travel.

There was understandable apprehension among the B Company soldiers. But Carver deployed some ANA troops around the buildings at the most critical points, to reduce the risk of ambush. And the commander of the US troops based in Robinson sent one of his vehicles along with the B Company column. Aston was grateful. The American, whom he had barely met, didn't need to do this, to endanger his own men. But he knew that having the US presence would enable Aston to call on the full might of American air and artillery support, which would not be available unless US troops were directly involved in the battle.

In the event, they arrived at Sangin DC without incident. The company conducted foot patrols around the town and into the Green Zone and were able to relax a little in the base and swim in the river that flowed through it.

The following day, Sunday 20 May, at 1220 hours, tragedy again struck B Company. Lance Corporal George Davey, a section 2IC in 5 Platoon, accidentally shot himself in the chest while cleaning his rifle. He was evacuated by Chinook to Bastion but died after four and a half hours on the operating table. The bullet had hit his lung, spleen and stomach.

The men of B Company were utterly devastated. When Aston heard the news of Davey's death, he thought, *After all that we've been through. God knows how we survived the fighting without anyone getting killed. And now this...*

In Lieutenant Colonel Carver's eulogy, he wrote: 'Lance Corporal Davey was a popular NCO who, in true Royal Anglian style, always put his men's interests before his own. His death is a tragic loss felt throughout the Battalion.'

The next evening in Sangin DC, B Company held a company memorial service for their comrade, the first of their soldiers to die in Afghanistan.

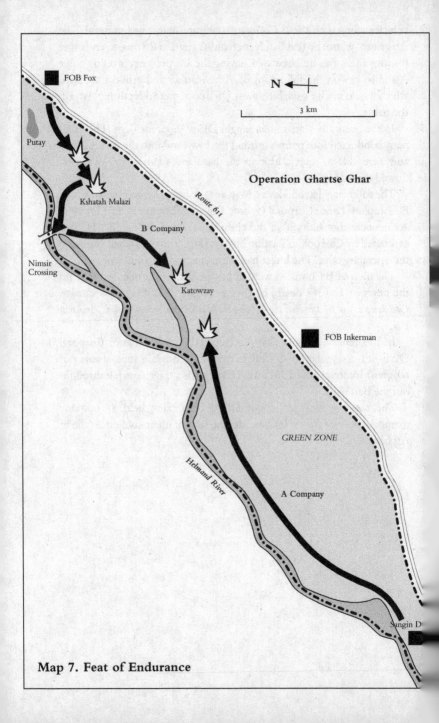

Operation Ghartse Ghar

FOB Fox

Putay

Kshatah Malazi

B Company

Nimsir
Crossing

Route 611

Katowzay

FOB Inkerman

GREEN ZONE

Helmand River

A Company

Sangin D

N

3 km

Map 7. Feat of Endurance

Feat of Endurance: 29 May–5 July 2007

I

Brigadier Lorimer's first priority in Helmand had been to prevent Taliban attacks on Gereshk in order to enable better security, reconstruction and improved prosperity for the local community. Operation Silicon, in late April and early May, had succeeded in creating the conditions to enable the brigadier's objectives to be achieved.

His next focus was Sangin, 30 kilometres north-east of Gereshk, along the River Helmand. With a population of 14,000, Sangin had traditionally supported the Taliban and was notorious as one of the central locations of the opium trade in southern Afghanistan. Since the first British deployment into Helmand in 2006, Sangin had been the scene of many bloody battles, and by the time the Royal Anglians arrived in theatre, thirteen British soldiers had been killed there. Like Gereshk, Sangin was critically important to Task Force Helmand's overall goal of achieving security, prosperity and the rule of law in the province. It was the district's principal town and main trading centre.

The Taliban recognized the importance of the town just as much as Brigadier Lorimer, and they worked hard to keep its population under their ruthless domination, desperate to avoid any hint of progress that could be attributed to the Kabul government, NATO forces or other international organizations. As well as attacking British, American and Afghan troops in and around Sangin, the Taliban threatened, attacked and killed locals and fired rockets and mortars into the town. Their assaults and threats had been so effective that the once thriving bazaar, or market, that was the cornerstone of daily life in and around Sangin no longer existed.

Lieutenant Colonel Carver and his staff planned an operation to achieve the same effect in Sangin as had been achieved in Gereshk. The idea was to clear the Green Zone either side of the Helmand River north-east of Sangin, to dislodge the Taliban and begin the process of loosening their stranglehold on the town and surrounding area. The major difference from Silicon, and one that made a similar operation north-east of Sangin much more difficult, was the Helmand River. In this area, it was virtually impossible for the Royal Anglians to cross, yet the Taliban had the ability to get over using improvised crossing methods such as small boats and rubber tyres leashed to wires strung across from bank to bank. They could easily escape or reinforce across the river.

Carver learnt that Task Force 1 Fury, the airmobile battalion from the US 82nd Airborne Division that had taken part in Operation Silicon, might also be available. The operation that he planned included the troops from the 82nd. He envisaged the Royal Anglians operating on one side of the river with the Americans on the other.

Carver proposed an operation to Lorimer, who liked the idea and ordered his staff to draw up a detailed plan – Operation Lastay Kulang.

The preliminary stage of Operation Lastay Kulang began on 27 May, when Carver deployed his Danish Recce Squadron to the north, in the vicinity of Musa Qalah, to deceive the Taliban into thinking the battle group would strike there rather than in the Sangin area. Once the operation began the Danes also had the role of screening the area between Sangin and Musa Qalah to give early warning of Taliban reinforcement southwards.

The following day, as A Company deployed from Bastion to take part in Lastay Kulang, the company commander's Viking struck a mine. Corporal Darren Bonner, A Company's Signals Detachment commander, who was travelling in the back, was killed outright. A committed Christian, only weeks before Daz Bonner had conducted a memorial service for Private Chris Gray, killed in action on Friday 13 April. As well as being a highly competent and respected soldier, Bonner was one of the best-liked characters in the battalion and the whole of the Royal Anglian Regiment. He was a fanatical Spurs fan and never let any of his fellow soldiers forget the fact. Physically impressive and covered in tattoos, he was a weightlifter and night-club bouncer in his spare time, but also a man of great compassion and ever willing to help and advise others.

Bonner's death had a huge impact on the company and the battalion. The mine that killed him had been planted by the Taliban, and the power of the blast indicated that two or three anti-tank mines may have been buried one on top of the other. There were three further mine-strikes during Operation Lastay Kulang, resulting in injuries to soldiers travelling in vehicles. The Taliban fighters had monitored the battle group's movements, sending IED teams ahead to plant and camouflage mines.

Operation Lastay Kulang proper began on 30 May. In addition to A Company, all of the Royal Anglian Battle Group elements were involved, and there were numerous sorties by attack helicopters and strike aircraft. The planned Task Force 1 Fury assault across the river was delayed for twenty-four hours, and during the insertion into the Green Zone a Chinook was shot down with the loss of five American troops, one British and one Dutch soldier.

Lastay Kulang lasted for eleven days, during which an estimated 200 Taliban were killed. Although the enemy fired smallarms, RPGs, rockets and mortars at the battle group from a distance, the Taliban did not stand and fight. When the Royal Anglians arrived in an area, they simply melted away. Most of the enemy were killed from the air and by long-range or indirect fire.

That didn't make the job any easier for the Royal Anglian infantry-men with their attached engineers, artillery and medics. They still had to sweat their way through dense Green Zone undergrowth, laboriously clear through compound after compound and patrol for kilometre after kilometre across exposed, rugged and angular desert. All in searing heat and carrying 30-odd kilos of combat equipment.

Despite efforts to try to stop them, many of the Taliban who had been fighting the battle group managed to escape across the river north to Musa Qalah.

To maintain long-term dominance in the area north-east of Sangin, on 2 June the Royal Engineers constructed Forward Operating Base Fox at Putay, and this was initially occupied by the Estonian armoured infantry company that formed a part of the Royal Anglian Battle Group.

After Operation Silicon, the patrol bases that had been constructed north-east of Gereshk came under frequent attack by the Taliban, whose aggression was focused against the Afghan National Army and NATO forces there rather than the civilian community in the town. The same happened at FOB Fox, which from 16 June was hit frequently by Taliban 107mm rockets.

2

At the end of Operation Lastay Kulang, A Company's 1 Platoon, under Lieutenant Nick Denning, moved into Sangin District Centre. They were joined four days later, on 11 June, by the remainder of the company group, which was based there for the rest of the battalion's tour in Helmand. Their mission was to provide security for the town, build the fragile confidence of the local population and encourage and support reconstruction in the area.

The base at Sangin was about the size of one and a half football pitches, surrounded by the usual Hesco Bastion rubble- and sand-filled wire and fabric cases, arranged in 5-metre walls whose corners were guarded by permanently manned sangars.

Two main buildings overlooked the town from within the base, referred to by everyone as the 'DC', which was split in two by a fast-flowing canal leading off the Helmand River. About 5 metres wide, during the hot summer months the canal was used by off-duty troops for bathing. A rope was tied from bank to bank, to stop soldiers being carried downstream into the town of Sangin itself. A light alloy infantry assault bridge provided a link across the canal, joining up the two main buildings, the three-storey FSG tower and the ops room, whose roof had two heavily armed, sandbagged sangars reached by an ominous thirteen steps.

The troops lived jammed tight on camp beds in two stone buildings within the DC. Every wall in the base was pock-marked with bullet holes and splash marks left by RPGs slamming into the outside. Throughout its occupancy by the Parachute Regiment and then the Royal Marines, until April 2007 Sangin DC had been under almost permanent siege by the Taliban and the scene of some of the fiercest fighting to date in Helmand's recent history.

One wall, close to the ANA accommodation, was covered in religious graffiti and childish cartoon character faces marking an Afghan soldier's increasing unhappiness with his stay there. Day one's face was smiling, and then progressively the faces grew longer and more miserable.

Although Lastay Kulang had succeeded in killing and driving out large numbers of Taliban, it was clear that they weren't going to give up Sangin that easily. But with their stranglehold on the town and the surrounding areas loosened, many people who had left to avoid the constant battling and intimidation flocked back. During the latter stages of Lastay Kulang, soldiers had seen children swarming into areas as they were cleared of Taliban.

As soon as A Company moved into Sangin, Major Biddick started driving forward reconstruction tasks, with the same vigour as he fought the Taliban in battle. Although substantial progress was hard to achieve, and for the long term, Biddick's determination to help the community back on to its feet was received with gratitude by the locals.

The Taliban didn't like anything that might lead towards normality and began to strike back, conducting a series of bloody attacks. Realizing things were quickly beginning to slip backwards again, with significant Taliban reinfiltration, Carver knew that Lastay Kulang had not achieved the decisive effect he had hoped for. The attacks against FOB Fox continued, and the Taliban were gradually restoring their reign of terror in and around the town, including the kidnap and murder of the son of Sangin's police chief. Battle group intelligence officer Captain Tom Coleman confirmed that his intelligence sources as well as events on the ground were telling him what Carver was thinking. Significant numbers of Taliban had come back down to the Sangin area from Musa Qalah.

In an update briefing to Carver, Coleman told him there was intelligence that Tor Jan, one of the main Taliban commanders in the area, was putting pressure on his people to increase the killings and to get concrete results against the government in Sangin. He said, 'There are signs that he's trying to get more experienced people in to bolster up the locals – possibly foreign fighters. It looks like the valley now has some very serious players in it, and they want to do some real damage in Sangin.'

Sitting at a dusty, battered, collapsible wooden table outside the operations centre at Camp Bastion, Carver briefed his planning team. 'I want to get a clear message to the Taliban that he's not welcome in this area, and if he comes in he's going to be killed. It's also critical that the locals understand we're here to stay and protect them. We've got to demonstrate to the Taliban that we are not a transient force. We are here for the long term. That means another battle group operation into the Green Zone between Sangin and Kajaki. A clearing operation. To give us breathing space to get reconstruction projects underway so we can demonstrate tangible benefits of our presence. B Company will patrol south from FOB Fox, driving the enemy into the teeth of a steady forward advance from A Company, who will patrol north towards them from Sangin.'

Carver knew that a conventional assault into this area would end in the Taliban escaping westward over the Helmand River, either as they saw the Royal Anglians moving in or after a fight – as they had done during Operation Lastay Kulang. The battle group would then be back to square one – facing the same reinfiltration problem.

The whole question of preventing a Taliban escape across the river, which they had not been able to properly deal with in Lastay Kulang, applied just as much to the proposed new operation. Carver wanted to position his forces on the western side as well as the east, to cut off escaping enemy. But that was easier said than done. There were just two bridges that they could cross – at Gereshk, and further north at Kajaki – and both were too far away. He considered helicopters, but there weren't enough airframes available. The Royal Anglians had no boats, and the risk of using their amphibious Vikings was too great – just one toppling over in mid-stream could drown eleven soldiers and wreck the operation. The river was 200 metres across and at this time of year it divided into channels, with fast-flowing and dangerous undercurrents in the middle, making wading impossible.

Carver's only option was to cut off the Taliban on the eastern side, before they could cross the river. His troops would have to infiltrate on foot over many kilometres, and at night, to achieve surprise. He and his staff agonized over whether such a challenging plan could work. Carver knew his men were at peak fitness and had trained long and hard – he had personally supervised the battalion's physical training. But it would still be extremely tough. They would have to carry everything they needed, as they could not depend on a resupply by vehicle or from the air.

Casualty evacuation was another major concern. The RAF wouldn't land in the Green Zone, even for CASEVAC: flying over the area was too high-risk. Intelligence reports suggested the Taliban had brought Stinger surface-to-air missiles into the very area they were going to attack. And Carver was mindful that the 82nd Airborne Chinook had been shot down as it came in to land, in just about the same area. One of his main worries was that even a relatively minor wound to one of the troops, even an accidental injury, could ruin the operation, with the wounded soldier having to be stretchered out. Without helicopters, a casualty would have to be carried back to base over many kilometres through enemy-infested country. It took at least six men to carry a stretcher and more would be needed for security.

Above all everyone was worried about the heat. Long periods of patrolling and fighting in 50 degrees and more, without any guaranteed water resupply, could prove deadly.

Some of Carver's planning team believed the operation – codenamed Ghartse Ghar – would be too hazardous, and they said as much. Carver understood the huge risks involved, and he knew that if the operation went wrong a lot of soldiers could be killed or wounded. He also knew that, as ever, all responsibility would fall on his shoulders.

He balanced these concerns against the pressing need to protect the townspeople of Sangin, critical to the successful completion of the battalion's mission in Afghanistan. To achieve this he knew that he had to show the Taliban they could not come back into the Green Zone with impunity. The price for them had to be higher than a long-range shoot-out then withdraw to fight another day. And to win the support of the local community, it was important to demonstrate to them the physical dominance of the battle group over the Taliban. This war was as much about psychology as it was about fighting.

It was a tough decision.

3

Carver called battle group operations officer Captain Phil Moxey into the hardboard-walled box next to the Joint Operations Centre in Bastion that served as his office. Maps and air photos covered all available surfaces, and the fan did little to tackle the stifling heat. Carver said, 'I've decided we're going to do Ghartse Ghar. I want you to push out a warning order tonight. You know pretty much what I've got in mind. A Company will start at Sangin in the south and patrol north. B Company will start at FOB Fox in the north, enter the Green Zone on foot, cut off the escape routes across the river, and drive the Taliban south into the open jaws of A Company. We'll need to fly B Company to FOB Fox as soon as possible.'

Three days later, on 23 June, FOB Fox was hit by a devastatingly accurate volley of 107mm rockets, which killed two members of the battle group's Estonian armoured infantry company and seriously wounded a female nurse. The following day, the Estonians, reinforced by Captain Ollie Ormiston's FSG Delta and the Royal Anglian's Recce Platoon under Captain Andy Wilde, attacked the Taliban in the village of Lwar Malazi, believed to be the mounting base for the rocket attack.

The combined force killed seventeen Taliban fighters, with Wilde's Scimitars and Ormiston's Javelin team accounting for many of the enemy dead. During the fighting, a bullet hit the chest plate of Ormiston's body armour, and Private Peter Howell, one of the FSG soldiers, was shot in the stomach. His body armour saved him, and he sustained only minor injuries.

On the same day B Company arrived at FOB Fox to prepare for Ghartse Ghar. They were flown in by Chinook from Nowzad, where they had been based since Operation Lastay Kulang.

FOB Fox was positioned on high ground next to the Green Zone, overlooking the village of Putay, 10 kilometres north-east of Sangin. It consisted of two run-down Afghan compounds, with security provided by Recce Platoon Scimitars and Viking vehicles. There was no space in the compounds for B Company, so they harboured up in the open outside the compound walls.

Corporal James Murphy, a section commander in Captain Dave Broomfield's 6 Platoon, lay soaked to the skin under his makeshift shelter fashioned from camouflaged nylon ground sheets, stretched and attached with bungees to a pile of ammo boxes at one end and two large rocks at the other. He wasn't sure whether the rain was a bonus or not. Whatever – there was no way of keeping dry anyway. He looked out of the shelter and saw several of the lads just standing out in the downpour, stripping off.

'Come on, lads,' Murphy said to Privates Jason Thompson and Jamie Muley, who were under the shelter with him, 'I haven't had a shower for ages. Lend us some soap. It'll be a laugh – pass the time away.'

It was a bizarre scene; one of those moments between battles when a group of infantrymen will snatch any diversion from the boredom of just waiting. For about fifteen minutes they stood around naked in the open, showering in the downpour as if they were in the bathroom at home. Pointing to a female medic who had emerged from a shelter a few metres away, one of the lads shouted, 'Look, it's a bird.'

With uncharacteristic modesty, the group of naked soldiers scattered more rapidly than they ever had in the face of Taliban fire. They took cover behind the Vikings until the woman had gone, then raced back to their shelters for towels.

There was constant ribbing between these troops during the quieter times. Most of the lads were from London's East End, Essex, Suffolk, Norfolk and Cambridgeshire. Often it was about football. Murphy, from East Bergholt near Colchester, Essex, supported Arsenal; Muley was a Spurs fan; and Thompson followed Manchester United. The guarantee of a long series of heated discussions in the pouring rain under their shelter. Thompson, Murphy's fearless point man, was a karate fanatic and looking forward to getting started on the sport at Army level after the tour.

Even stronger than sporting rivalry was the bickering about which was the best platoon. 6 Platoon called themselves 'Mighty 6', and 5 Platoon were the self-named 'Fighting 5'. The two groups were close, but fiercely competitive. Most of them were tattooed with their platoon number. The soldiers of 7 Platoon – 'Lucky 7' – who remained at Nowzad for Operation Ghartse Ghar, had tattoos of a dice somewhere on their bodies.

That afternoon they continued as usual, bickering away, sniping at each other, arguing over football, movies and, on one occasion, who was the biggest 'prat' in *Wind in the Willows*. Some members of the platoon asserted that it was Ratty. Others went for the more obvious Toad, although vilifying the fast-driving and flashily dressed amphibian went slightly against the grain. Essex was home of the boy-racer, and Toad's behaviour and sense of social worth appealed to many of these men who were dreaming of their post-Afghanistan 'millionaire weekend' – the British soldier's way of blowing his hard-earned cash saved while on operations.

They talked endlessly about going on boozy trips to the clubs of Ibiza or, for the more ambitious, a few weeks in California. Several planned the America trip, dreaming of being feted by girls throughout the US because of their Army status and British accents. For a few privates their first flashy car beckoned, a proper 'bird puller'. It wasn't exactly the done thing to talk openly about putting a down payment on a house: anyone who did would be shouted down, and the rest would yawn loudly and walk off.

Eventually the arguing died down and the talk turned to who wanted to eat what at the end of the tour. It was a source of non-stop discussion. Someone wanted a bag of crisps. For most the meal of choice would be fish and chips.

For whatever reason one of the men's mother had sent out plastic toy soldiers. They sat about in the mud, setting up opposing armies and discussing ambush and counter-attack strategies, until a couple of Royal Marines sauntered over, wondering what all the laughing and arguing was about.

'What're you lot doing?'

'Fighting a war – it's a laugh,' came the reply.

'What about an air-strike on those little fellas?'

'What you got? A 1,000-pound laser-guided bomb? You a B1 bomber? Or an Apache? Let's have a laser-guided and a couple of Hellfire missiles dropped on them, mate.'

Another soldier produced a plastic aeroplane from a parcel he had been sent.

The two marines, Viking drivers, laughed, knowing the lads were off on a serious operation soon. They picked up sticks and stones for Hellfires and bombs, then launched their air-strike on the little plastic infantrymen on the ground.

And so it went on for the rest of the afternoon, mucking about in the dirt, killing time, having a laugh, still finding time to bicker about football teams and platoon rivalries.

Thoughts of the ensuing operation were never far away. As they sat around the troops were 'bombing up' magazines, checking their machine-gun link, painstakingly cleaning their rifles and packing as much as 5 litres of water into daysacks.

By now many of them had shed more than a stone in weight and were leaner than ever before, most of the fat gone on countless slogging foot patrols and the battles that invariably came as a result of them.

4

B Company spent four days in the austere and wet FOB Fox. It was largely uneventful, although the odd 107mm rocket was fired at the base, and one day the men watched a US Air Force AC-130 Spectre gunship mowing down a Taliban fighter 800 metres away. The Spectre used its 20mm cannon, and the men were disappointed not to have witnessed the legendary ground-attack aircraft firing its 105mm howitzer.

The company commander, Major Mick Aston, held the final briefing for his commanders at 1400 hours on Thursday 28 June. Lieutenant Ben Howes was commander of 5 Platoon, and Captain Dave Broomfield led 6. Aston told the two platoon commanders that A Company would be the main effort for Operation Ghartse Ghar, and B Company would initially be doing a feint. There was a wry smile on his face as he looked at them and said, 'Well, as you know, fellas – B Company doesn't do feints. I would quite like us to be the main effort to be honest, and that's the way it's going to happen. We're going to go in there looking for a fight.'

Broomfield thought, *I would have expected nothing else. There's no way he's going to allow A Company to steal a fight from under him.*

Aston looked straight into their eyes and concluded with his pre-deployment mantra, 'Account for every one of our soldiers at all times – that is the number one priority. I do not want anyone going missing. So down to the section commanders and the private soldiers, tell everyone to keep an eye on each other and stay in as tight formation as you can. One of our lads going missing on this operation is not an option. They are your responsibility out there, and the Taliban would dearly love to kidnap a British soldier. That, gentlemen, is my worst nightmare and yours, and it is not going to happen. At every point you stop, and the platoon sergeants check everyone is accounted for.'

This exact, chilling message had come straight down from the commanding officer ever since pre-deployment training back in Pirbright, and it was banged into them before every major operation.

After their final briefing, the troops downed as much water as they could, ate from their ration packs and then set off at 1500 hours.

With FSG Delta under Captain Ollie Ormiston providing overwatch from his WMIKs on the high ground, the company walked out of FOB Fox in a long snake down into the Green Zone. Lieutenant Ben Howes looked around at his platoon as they patrolled deeper and deeper into the ditches and treelines. He knew this was going to be tough and relentless. They would be patrolling longer and further on foot than any British unit in Afghanistan to date.

The men who had been larking around like boys in the mud and the rain just hours ago were silently pacing across the soggy ground, stooping slightly, and shifting the weight of their daysacks, webbing and weapons. Squinting in the blazing mid-afternoon sun, heads up, alert, looking beyond the poppy fields and the maize, sweat dripping off them. Howes noted with satisfaction that every man was painstakingly covering his allocated arcs, weapon at the ready, poised to open fire at the first sniff of the enemy, knowing that his mates to the left and the right depended for their lives on his alertness and quick response. Some hardened NCOs had called the young private soldiers the PlayStation Generation, but in Helmand they had proved themselves time and time again. Howes was intensely proud of his men and he knew they would be more than equal even to this operation, which promised to be the most physically demanding of all.

The company continued patrolling for another hour across the cultivated ground, left waterlogged and boggy from the downpour of the previous two nights, troops caked in mud and swearing about how it reminded them of Brecon. They waded and jumped across irrigation channels filled to the brim with brown water.

A hundred metres ahead there was a group of compounds.

Always a danger sign, thought Howes.

Then there was a long, loud blast of fire.

Automatic tracer arced through the air and straight over the heads of Howes's point section, leading the way across the open field. Corporal Tom Mason and his men hit the dirt immediately.

Private Scotty Corless, just behind Mason's section, fell to the deck and remembered that soldiers' phrase 'digging in with your eyelids' as an RPG whizzed a metre over his head. Corless's section, under Corporal Paul Kennedy, began hurling a massive weight of machine-gun fire at the treeline ahead of them, where muzzle blasts from the enemy guns were now flashing at an increasing rate.

Howes yelled into his radio mike, 'Zero Alpha One Zero Alpha, contact wait out.'

He saw bullets cutting up the ground all round Corporal Tom Mason and Private Dan Smith, who were well forward, caught in the open.

The whole platoon went instinctively into their contact drills, on their belt buckles and working their way forward into a baseline to return fire.

Fearing he was about to start taking serious casualties with so much fire pouring into the lead section, Howes had to suppress the enemy so

Corporal Mason could pull his men back into cover. He yelled at his 51mm mortar man, 'Haldenby – see that tree line, fifty metres? Get some HE down right in the middle of it. *Now*. Get as many bombs down as you can. Quickly.'

Under the sustained blaze of fire from both of Howes's sections, and with Haldenby's high-explosive mortar bombs blasting into the heart of the enemy, the incoming fire slackened and then stopped altogether. 5 Platoon continued to rake the Taliban positions as Mason and his section crawled back to the gully.

Howes called Mick Aston on the net. 'Zero Alpha, this is One Zero Alpha. Reference contact. Engaged from woodline south of my location, fifty metres. Estimate five to six enemy. Am engaging. Over.'

Aston came straight back, 'Roger. Get your callsign up on the left flank, get through the compounds, assault and clear the enemy position. Two Zero will provide fire support from current location. They will give you fifty-one smoke cover as you move round. Get it done. Out.'

There was not a moment to lose. Howes knew Aston intended to shock the Taliban with a lightning assault, to destroy any surviving enemy. He shouted the briefest orders to the section commanders and led the platoon round in cover to a compound on their left. As they moved, Howes heard the continuous hammering of fire into Taliban positions and saw the build-up of smoke as the mortars arced down in front of the enemy, obscuring their view of his platoon.

Howes and his men cleared through the Taliban position, blasting away with their rifles and Minimis. There were only Taliban dead. The survivors had escaped along carefully planned, concealed getaway routes.

The platoon found RPG warheads, AK47 assault rifles and full magazines. Howes told his men to pile the weapons up, then called forward an engineer who was attached to the platoon. 'Destroy them with a bar-mine.'

At the same moment 5 Platoon came into contact, 6 Platoon were also hit. Captain Broomfield was moving along a street flanked by two high walls, immediately behind Corporal Joel Adlington's section. Adlington's point man saw an RPG lying in the street, raised his hand and called, 'Stop.'

That second a long burst of PKM machine-gun fire zipped along the wall, and Broomfield and his men dived for cover.

Howes grabbed Private Oliver Hare and dragged him forward, shouting, 'Get the GPMG firing down the street – at that compound.'

Kneeling behind him, Broomfield fired five rounds over his head as Hare opened up with burst after burst.

Corporal Murphy and Corporal Adlington pushed round the corner and saw eight armed Taliban withdrawing fast along the wall of a compound beyond. Murphy opened up, killing two. The remainder escaped.

The platoon rapidly cleared the position they had been engaged from. They attacked at red, blasting their way in with a bar-mine, following up with grenades and automatic fire. It was empty: the enemy had got away.

Private Ross Green had been firing his GPMG in the direction the Taliban had escaped. RPG rockets were being launched from that area towards the platoon, and one exploded close to Green, dazing him.

Above Broomfield, a tree disintegrated in a rapid series of explosions. It could only be a GMG. Immediately realizing that FSG Delta, still up on the high ground, must have mistaken his position for an enemy firing point, Broomfield called them on the net, yelling into his mike, '*Check fire! Check fire! You are engaging my callsign!*'

Broomfield led the platoon forward, and they cleared through the area where Murphy had killed two Taliban. They discovered 82mm mortar bombs, plastic explosives and piles of expended PKM ammunition links and spent cases. The two bodies were a middle-aged man and a boy aged about sixteen. Broomfield and Murphy searched them but found nothing of intelligence value.

Adlington and his section moved forward to another group of compounds. Broomfield followed with his signaller, Private Andrew Archer. On the radio, Broomfield heard Adlington's voice calling urgently, 'Boss, drop now!'

Broomfield and Archer dropped straight to the ground, and immediately Adlington's section opened up with rifles and Minimis, killing two Taliban they had seen in an alleyway. Had the platoon commander and his signaller remained on their feet they would have been shot by the fighters.

Adlington and Corporal Jay Owen pushed forward with their sections, through the alleyway, looking for further enemy. They killed two more in a ditch. Searching them, they found weapons and a Taliban propaganda tape.

The platoon pushed forward, and Broomfield heard his point section firing again. He looked through his binoculars to see what they were firing at. Standing frozen in the middle of a field 200 metres away was a man in a black and grey kurta with a traditional flat Afghan hat and a grey beard. He couldn't see a weapon.

Broomfield raced down to his men shouting, 'STOP – STOP FIRING!'

The men stopped straight away. A soldier, kneeling in the grass, looked up. 'What's the problem, sir? Why have we stopped?'

'He's not armed.'

'But he's Taliban.'

'He's not armed. You can't shoot him. You don't know he is Taliban.'

When the firing finished the man slowly walked away towards a compound.

Maybe he was Taliban, maybe he wasn't. Broomfield wondered why someone would be around here in the middle of this battle if they weren't involved. But he didn't know and, like all the Royal Anglian officers, he rigidly enforced the rules of engagement.

'Only if they are armed!' he shouted.

'If you see a weapon then open fire – if not, then remember the rules of engagement.'

It reminded Broomfield just how tough the soldiers' job was out here, often fighting in among the population. They had crashed straight into a Taliban position, taking the enemy by surprise. Had any of his men hesitated for a moment, they could have been killed or allowed the enemy to escape. But they hadn't hesitated. They had all automatically followed the infantryman's code – *hard, fast and aggressive*. Because of that they had hunted down six enemy and killed them as they tried to get away. But even as this pursuit unfolded, with the men still pumped up on adrenalin, they had then encountered an unarmed man, and in this environment, restraint had to be as much second nature as aggression. The red mist had to clear instantly.

Suddenly it had gone quiet. There was no noise except the heavy breathing of exertion and the click of metal on metal as the soldiers reloaded their magazines and checked their weapons. Some clacked their bottles of water or sucked through a tube attached to their Camelbak water bag.

Others checked for injuries. Often in the thick of battle the adrenalin and noise would be so intense that a soldier might not realize he was bleeding, and infections set in quickly in this filth and heat – especially as much of the Green Zone became swamp as they advanced nearer the river.

It had been fifteen minutes of intense fighting. None of the Taliban had survived, and bodies lay in the open. The men from Aston's Tac HQ searched them. They found cigarettes, a few personal items, some wrappers containing dubious-looking powder and mobile phones. Sometimes mobiles found on Taliban fighters contained stored videos or pictures of beheadings recorded elsewhere in Afghanistan or in north-west Pakistan, where many fighters were trained before coming into Helmand.

Another 200 metres south of the first battle they found two more Taliban bodies, shattered by heavy fire from the FSG on the hill as they had fled the B Company counter-attack. AK47s lay beside them.

ſ

It was now early evening and the men were shattered. They had only been on the go for two hours, but the heat was searing and the destruction of the Taliban positions had been utterly exhausting. The adrenalin rush that sharpened an infantryman's senses in combat also drained away huge amounts of his energy.

Checking his map, Aston worked out that the enemy that escaped from his platoons must have fled to the nearby village of Kshatah Malazi. He pushed the company towards the sparse collection of shabby, decrepit compounds and sent Howes's 5 Platoon to skirt round the village and cut off any further retreat, while 6 Platoon under Broomfield cleared through the compounds.

Corporal Owen led his 6 Platoon section along a narrow alleyway between two of the compound walls, rifle in the shoulder, scanning over sights, ready to fire. One hundred metres ahead, a man in dark local dress leant round the corner of the wall, aiming his AK47. Owen levelled his rifle and killed him with three rapid shots. With his section following, he dashed up to the enemy fighter, lying in a pool of his own blood. A second fighter, also armed with an AK47, was running down the alleyway, and they cut him down with a hail of bullets.

Aston was straight on the radio to Broomfield. 'Two Zero Alpha, this is Zero Alpha. There may be more. Push your complete callsign right through the village and find them or flush them out. Move now. Out.'

Following close behind with his Afghan interpreter, Aston questioned three local men, all aged around forty, all friendly. They said there had been twelve Taliban fighters in Kshatah Malazi, and they had now gone to Katowzay, a nearby village. His immediate thought was to take the company straight to Katowzay to deal with them, but he had other orders from the battle group commander. The company was to move to the Helmand River and create a screen. Focusing on likely enemy crossing points, the objective was to identify and kill enemy trying to escape across the river as A Company advanced through the Green Zone from the south.

Reluctantly Aston got on the company net and gave orders to his platoons, 'Hello, Charlie Charlie One this is Zero Alpha. Move now to task locations on the river line. You all know where you're going. Order of march One Zero, my callsign, Two Zero. Report when in position. Out.'

B Company arrived at the Helmand River in darkness, and the platoons moved into their pre-planned positions, silently setting up their observation posts.

Aston collocated his Tac HQ with Broomfield's platoon. Their home for the night was the sand, low in the bushes right beside the river.

Once they were set up the men gulped water and squeezed their cold boil-in-the-bag rations into their mouths. They took it in turns to keep watch and get some rest. They slept on the open ground within the compounds. Despite the exhaustion of hours spent marching and fighting, few got much sleep in the fetid heat, and they were constantly attacked by midges, fleas and other insects.

The only noise in the compounds was the whispering as sentries shook their replacements awake, and the occasional snore. Outside the wild dogs howled like wolves in the distance, and there was the constant creaking of crickets, almost deafening in the Green Zone as soon as darkness fell.

Carver called Aston on his Iridium satellite phone during the night.

'Move your company towards Jusulay to try and push the Taliban south into A Company. So far there hasn't been much enemy down there.'

As Carver spoke, Aston was checking the map under the glow of his red head-torch. A slight dog-leg would take them through Katowzay.

'Do you mind which route I take to Jusulay, Colonel?'

'No problem. Whichever way you want. Just get down there.'

'Roger, sir, in that case I'll swing by Katowzay and have a little look round. I've heard some of the enemy we ran into yesterday may have gone there.'

6

At 0300 hours Howes and 5 Platoon led the company away from the river, towards Katowzay. It was very dark, with a low moon. As soon as he set off, Howes began to pour sweat. Even in the small hours, without any sun, they were drenched within minutes.

Approaching from the north, Howes halted his men 1,000 metres short of the village. It was 0500 hours, and the rising sun was sending long shadows across the Green Zone.

The company moved into a well-concealed defensive formation in a network of irrigation ditches. The men stowed their night observation kit and – glad of a brief respite – slumped down to chew on the hard biscuits from their twenty-four-hour ration packs.

Half an hour later they were on the move again. Aston had pushed Howes's platoon to the right and Broomfield's to the left as they approached the village across open ground. His Tac HQ was in the centre, just to their rear. Aston was thinking how much he would have given for some cover.

Also sensing the danger presented by the open ground, Howes pushed 5 Platoon even more rapidly than normal into the compounds on the edge of the village. Aston's Tac was close behind.

6 Platoon were still 400 metres out, in the open, when a long blast of automatic fire opened up around waist height.

There was a scream. 'I'm hit.'

That was the last thing Broomfield wanted to hear while they were still out in the open.

A bullet had ripped between Private Luke Watson's arm and upper ribs, slicing into his bicep and chest. Watson was on the ground, writhing in agony. A medic crawled forward and pressed a field dressing on to the wound.

As soon as the firing started, the men of 6 Platoon hit the ground then blasted fire back into the enemy-held compounds. Lance Corporal

228

Ashby fired an AT4 anti-tank missile into a compound, and fire from there stopped but continued to pour in from at least two other directions.

Looking forward to the outskirts of the village, Broomfield saw Howes's men appear on compound walls and roofs, firing down into the enemy positions.

Aston turned to his MFC, Lance Corporal Tony Warwick. 'I want a fire mission on those buildings over there. Figure out the grid and check with me before you engage. Quick as you can.'

The JTAC, in an observation position 1,000 metres away on the high ground at the edge of the desert, made an immediate call for air support.

The FST commander, Captain Ridley, was figuring out deconfliction between the mortars and air.

Seconds later the Taliban positions were being hammered by high-explosive bombs fired by the Royal Anglians' 81mm mortars. Aston was impressed at the speed with which Warwick had managed to get the fire mission on to the ground, but he wasn't surprised. Warwick was an outstanding MFC.

The ground shook, and mud, dust and bits of compound wall flew into the air. With the enemy heads down, Broomfield was able to pull Watson and the rest of the platoon back into cover.

The mortars continued to pound the enemy positions, and there was a loud blast near by. A Taliban 107mm rocket streaked over their heads and exploded 200 metres in front of Aston's position. It was followed by three more.

'Harriers on station,' the JTAC reported.

Aston agreed the target grids. The JTAC radioed his instructions to the pilots, and in moments every member of the company felt the massive shock waves of two 500-pound bombs, destroying everything in and around the rocket launch points.

Crouching down, Broomfield moved along the ditch to where Watson was lying. He said to the medic, 'What's the score?'

'Not too much bleeding. Looks like the bullet missed any bones, so he's lucky. But we need to get him CASEVACed.'

'Are you certain about that?'

'Yes, he needs to go back.'

Watson said, 'It's OK, sir, I can keep going, I'm not too bad.'

Broomfield thought, *It's good that he doesn't want to take the easy way out. Not surprising because Watson's a tough lad. But there's no way I'm going to be influenced by the bravery of a nineteen-year-old soldier pumped full of adrenalin. He may not be too bad now, but he's taken a high-velocity bullet to the arm. He is very likely to go into shock. And how do I know he won't get much worse in two hours' time. We can evacuate him now – it might be a lot tougher then.*

On the radio Broomfield informed Aston that Watson would have to be evacuated.

'Zero Alpha, that is not going to happen,' said Aston angrily. 'Can he walk? Over.'

'Two Zero, yes. But he does need to be CASEVACed.'

The conversation went back and forth on the radio with Aston getting increasingly impatient.

Broomfield waded 150 metres in filthy water, waist deep, along an irrigation ditch for a face-to-face with the company commander. He found Aston sitting against a wall, thunderous.

'Does he need to go?'

'Yes, sir.'

'Does the medic agree?'

'Yes, sir, the medic agrees.'

Aston stared straight into Broomfield's eyes, shaking his head.

'OK, so he goes,' said Aston resignedly.

He was single-mindedly focused on pursuing the enemy and clearing them from the area in line with the battle group commander's intent. There was nothing personal or emotional about it. This was, quite simply, his job. In the extraordinarily difficult circumstances of infantry operations in Helmand, it was very easy to allow 1,001 things to divert you from the task in hand. Dogged determination was the only way to succeed.

Aston knew what evacuating a casualty from here would mean. They could not get a helicopter in, so there was no choice but to get Watson out on foot. They couldn't split up the force, so the whole company would have to patrol back out of the Green Zone to RV with the Vikings. It would divert all of the company's efforts and resources for several valuable hours.

He cared more about the lives of his soldiers than anything else – including his own life. But he had wanted to be absolutely certain this evacuation was necessary before he agreed to it. It still didn't please him. With undisguised annoyance he rattled out his orders on the net. The company would extract from Katowzay, patrol back across the Green Zone for 1,500 metres and secure an area close to the desert near Route 611 for the Vikings to come in and evacuate the casualty. The company would then turn straight round and make best speed to get back into the fight.

6 Platoon led B Company north, away from Katowzay, alongside a canal.

They had been moving for fifteen minutes when there was a sudden whoosh-whoosh. Two RPG missiles landed in front of them, flinging up lumps of earth and shards of red-hot shrapnel. Aston identified the firing point – compounds 400 metres away to their left – and told War-wick to pound them with mortar fire.

Warwick hit the pressel switch and urgently started calling in the fire mission.

Then Aston yelled, '*Incoming! Take cover!*'

Almost as one, the men of B Company Tac dived into the canal as burst after burst of automatic fire pinged into the ground where they had been standing. Bullets cracked into the trees, showering leaves and branches on to their heads. Moments later four more RPGs exploded in the bank above, covering them with dirt and more branches.

The whole company was now in the ditch, and Aston drove them forward, wading at snail's pace through the thick, sucking mud in the bottom of the canal. After 500 metres they were hit again by RPG and gunfire from the north.

Aston decided that the Taliban must think the tables had turned, and the British patrol was running back the way it had come. He was concerned they might start summoning reinforcements up from the south. This wasn't the way it was supposed to go – Aston's men were meant to be driving the enemy south into the fire of A Company.

The JTAC had called in all available air. Overhead, two Apaches and six American jets were stacked up, and above them a U2 spy plane was listening out for enemy communications. As the company advanced steadily along the canal, the aircraft provided cover, sending cannon fire and missiles into the compounds ahead.

With his point section leading the company through the waist-deep water, Broomfield identified a Taliban firing position. The JTAC couldn't see to talk the Apaches on, so Broomfield switched his radio to the Clear Air Ground frequency, or CAG, enabling him to speak direct to the pilot. 'Hello, Ugly Five One, this is Copper Two Zero Alpha. I am the forward Copper callsign. Target indication over.'

After hours of sweating across the Green Zone, scrambling in the mud and the ditches, shooting at the Taliban and being continuously fired at, the icy cool response, from an air-conditioned cockpit sitting 700 metres above the battlefield, sounded surreal. Broomfield was amused that the Apache commander had the calm, measured voice of a Boeing 747 pilot on a routine flight from Heathrow addressing the passengers. 'Ugly Five One, roger, Copper Two Zero Alpha, can you mark the target please.'

It was a point of pride to the Royal Anglian commanders that, when they were talking to each other during battles, they should sound as laid-back as possible. The worst possible insult would be to say, 'Roger – I understand. Now try and stay calm.' They joked after contacts about how they had enjoyed a 'calm-off' competition between themselves. Afterwards they would bicker at each other with insults about who had remained calmest throughout life-and-death situations and who had, indeed, won the 'calm-off'.

'He's trying to win the calm-off with me,' said Broomfield, to the amusement of Archer, his signaller.

Broomfield's platoon sergeant, Ben Browning, and his 51mm mortar man, flung up their last remaining smoke bomb. In the calmest, most measured voice he could manage, Broomfield came back on the net: 'Ugly Five One, this is Copper Two Zero Alpha. Reference smoke, come 300 metres west of smoke. Haystack. North of haystack. Treeline. Enemy in treeline.'

'Ugly Five One, no, target not identified, can you provide a further indication please, over.'

6 Platoon had run out of smoke bombs, so Broomfield told Private Scott Bramman to fire an AT4 missile towards the target. He would talk the pilot on from the impact of the missile. But – click – the AT4 misfired and Bramman slung it off to the side of the ditch.

Broomfield tried to talk the helicopter on by referring to the hay-stack, but the pilot advised him that he could not see the haystack. *How can you not see that, it's absolutely massive*, thought Broomfield. Then he thought, *Yes but I'm seeing it from a worm's eye view, and he's so far up, I suppose it's not surprising it's difficult to identify*.

Broomfield gave up with the Apache; he couldn't spend any more time static and needed to move on. He switched off the CAG and back on to B Company net. The JTAC took over further attempts to direct the helicopters, but although they continued firing at depth targets – well ahead of the company – they were not able to engage the closer-up enemy positions, which presented a greater threat to B Company.

Broomfield continued along the ditch. A short time later two Amer-ican Apaches arrived on station, replacing the British aircraft that had now departed to refuel. The American presence was a huge morale boost for the troops. They flew so low that Broomfield could read the letters on their underside – about 20 metres off the ground. He fully understood why British Apaches never came down to this height, espe-cially in the Green Zone, but the close presence of the American heli-copters made everyone feel a lot safer.

The feeling of safety was an illusion. As they reached the end of the ditch, an RPG missile whizzed straight into 6 Platoon, passing between two soldiers, just 3 metres from their heads. It splashed into the water and exploded in the mud behind Corporal Murphy. Fortunately it sunk in so deep that nobody was hurt.

Broomfield had to move out of the ditch and he decided to head into a compound 150 metres away. Sporadic enemy fire was still cutting into the bank. He had no expectation that they could move across the open area without being shot at. But they couldn't stay here. They had to keep moving, to get Watson back and then to resume the offensive.

Broomfield formed the platoon into a rough baseline, firing at likely positions. But they couldn't identify the enemy, so it did little good. Corporal Murphy's section led the way across the field. Running as fast as they could, well spaced out, the men moved across the open, bullets zinging overhead and smacking into the dirt at their feet.

When Murphy's section hit the compound, relieved and amazed they were all still alive, they formed a base of fire and sent rifle and machine-gun bullets towards the enemy in an attempt to provide some cover for their mates as they in turn did the 'dash of death'.

As the rest of the platoon followed Murphy's section, the US Apache pilots, seeing the danger the British infantrymen faced, brought their gunships in even lower, hoping to deter the enemy from shooting at the ground troops. The pilots were putting themselves and their aircraft in much greater danger. As Broomfield ran, he looked upwards. Directly overhead, so low he thought he could almost touch it, an Apache was blasting 30mm cannon shells in the direction they were running.

Dripping sweat and panting hard, Broomfield leant against the compound wall. Miraculously every one of his men, including the wounded Private Watson, had survived the dash through Taliban bullets. Broomfield took stock. This compound was too exposed to enemy fire to form the rallying point Aston would need for the company before moving on to RV with the Vikings. The next compound into the complex would be safer, but it necessitated crossing another open area.

He called Aston, who was back in the ditch with Tac. 'Zero Alpha, Two Zero Alpha. Moving my callsign into Compound 127. Recommend company consolidates there prior to moving to RV, over.'

After a brief pause Aston said, 'Roger. JTAC is reporting enemy movement in Compound 129, identified by air. Apaches will fire flechette into that compound just before you move to 127. I will confirm on this means when flechette attack is complete. You will then move. Out.'

Broomfield led his men round the compound ready to run another 200 metres to Compound 127. Everybody was exhausted, and Broomfield, Browning and the section commanders had to get around the troops, encouraging them, telling them to stay alert and switched on, getting them ready for a further huge effort.

As the Apaches carried out their devastating flechette attack, Broomfield heard a sound like an incredibly loud pneumatic drill, blasting out from above. Each warhead contains eighty tungsten flechettes, each dart weighing 18 grams. When fired they separate and form a disk-like mass which breaks up with each flechette assuming an independent trajectory, using kinetic energy to penetrate the target. They work on the same principal as grapeshot: their purpose to kill people over an area as big as a tennis court.

6 Platoon repeated the dash they had made from the ditch, using fire and manoeuvre to get to the compound. Broomfield's men searched the buildings. It was occupied only by four women and an old man, all

of whom regarded the soldiers with expressionless resignation. Broomfield gestured them into a room and indicated they must stay there.

He reported to Aston, 'Compound clear. Now firm.'

Aston led Tac from the ditch to join them. As he ran across the open field, bullets splattering around his feet and zipping overhead, he thought, *This is going to end in disaster. I am going to watch somebody getting shot here.*

He thought he was running super fast but, looking at the ground, realized it was almost slow motion, carrying his 36 kilos of kit, weighed down even further by the canal water. 6 Platoon covered them across, and the Apaches continued to circle low overhead, blasting 30mm shells.

From the compound, Broomfield and his signaller, Private Archer, saw 5 Platoon moving towards them along a different route. They were crawling up a ditch, 150 metres away. Broomfield saw heads bobbing up and down. As he watched, Taliban machine-gun fire raked the top of the ditch, bullets ripping into the dirt all the way along the line of 5 Platoon soldiers.

Howes had led his platoon along a ditch branching off from the main canal, towards Broomfield's compound. The ditch led into a 100-metre-long concrete pipe, with gravel and water in the bottom. This would take them closer to the compound, and Howes hoped to avoid the 6 Platoon dash of death. He led them into the dark and airless pipe. As they crawled through, bullets were thudding into the concrete from both sides. This was the heaviest fire they had experienced so far. Howes wondered when the first bullet would drill through the pipe into him or one of his men.

It was stifling hot inside the pipe, even hotter than under the baking late-morning sun outside. It was a terrifying experience, but as he crawled Howes managed to amuse himself with the thought: *Now I know why I've spent so much of my Army career to date crawling through concrete pipes like this on assault courses and live firing exercises. I'll never call them pointless again.*

5 Platoon's problems didn't end when they got through the pipe. They still had to cross almost 100 metres of open ground. 6 Platoon laid down as much fire as they could to try to help their mates survive the race across the open through a gauntlet of gunfire.

Broomfield watched the men of 5 Platoon throw themselves into the compound entrance next to him, almost collapsing as they came through. Then there was a tremendous roar overhead, the loudest sound he had ever heard. A shadow passed by. The ground and the compound shook. He looked up and saw, flying very low, the enormous, sleek black shape of an American B1B Lancer strategic bomber, which had been called in to provide a show of strength against the Taliban. When the bomber had passed over, there was silence. There was no more firing. Everything seemed suddenly and eerily calm.

Aston looked around at his men. Sentries had been posted, and the rest of the company had collapsed to the ground, grateful to be off their feet for the first time in ages. Everybody looked totally exhausted. It was 1100 hours, and B Company had been in contact for nearly six hours without a break.

Aston was keen to move on, hand Watson over, and return to the fight. But he could see the men needed a rest and reluctantly told his commanders they would stay here for an hour to sort themselves out.

Most of the men were low on water or completely out. They found the well and filled up water bottles and Camelbaks. The water, from 20 metres underground, was ice cold and refreshing, and the soldiers tipped it over their heads to cool down. Some of the troops poured lemon powder into the water to kill the taste of the puritabs they had added. The powder, called 'screech' because it is so sharp it makes you wince when you drink it, came in ration packs and contained vital salts to replace those lost through sweat. Most grabbed something to eat – a biscuit or a liquefied helping of boil-in-the-bag corned beef.

The men removed their webbing and body armour and opened their clothing. Some treated sores and rashes from webbing and equipment. Others, still pumped up by the adrenalin of their close encounters with enemy fire, moved around chatting to mates they had not spoken to for what seemed ages.

Despite the state they were in, morale was high. They had been through a lot together, and they were happy and relieved just to have a pause, even though they knew there was much more to come.

Now the company was settled Aston allowed the Afghans out of the room they had been kept in. Some of the soldiers gave them sweets and food from their ration packs. One of the women walked round the compound tending her chickens.

The man told Aston's interpreter, 'We don't mind you being in our home. You are welcome. But I have my family here, and please respect them.'

Overhead, the Apaches had spotted more enemy movement just beyond the compound and were engaging again with 30mm cannons and flechette. Aston was now getting worried about the possibility of a friendly fire incident. He noticed a huge carpet hanging up, airing, in the middle of the compound. It had a large red square in the middle of it and he told the JTAC to lay it out as a panel marker so the aircraft could clearly identify their position.

Gunner Hughes, Aston's signaller, called him across to listen to a call from the watch keeper in the Joint Operations Centre at battle group headquarters in Bastion.

'Copper Three Zero Alpha, this is Copper Zero. Be aware we have received an enemy communications intercept stating that the Taliban commander Tor Jan with eighty fighters has surrounded a British force near Katowzay and is preparing to assassinate them.'

The U2 spy plane flying 20,000 metres above had picked up radio chatter from the Taliban near by. They were talking about B Company.

Aston called out to his men, 'Tor Jan can piss off. I will be the judge of who assasinates who.'

8

The company patrolled off in the midday heat, led by Howes and 5 Platoon. Within half an hour 5 Platoon were in contact again as the Taliban opened fire from a compound to their left. It was a hit and run attack, the enemy escaping as 5 Platoon poured fire back into their positions.

6 Platoon had gone firm briefly in a village. It was 1300 hours, and the sun was at its hottest. Broomfield saw that Corporal Adlington looked wobbly on his legs, and he seemed very pale.

'You OK, Corporal A?'

'Yes, boss. No problem.'

Adlington's eyes rolled back and he keeled over sideways, his kit clattering on the ground.

B Company now had two casualties, and the situation was bad – six of them had to carry a stretcher, and the casualty's kit was spread between several other soldiers, effectively tying down most of the platoon – and further exhausting those with the extra burden, adding to the risk that they too might go down with heat exhaustion.

As the company moved forward again, Aston and his Tac moved out of a ditch and were met by a loud explosion 200 metres away. There was a whoosh and another blast and a blinding flash as an RPG warhead detonated 5 metres in front of them, kicking up lumps of earth. Tac dived for cover, and 5 Platoon, off to the flank, dashed forward and began hammering fire towards the area the rocket had come from.

Above the intense rattle of 5 Platoon's machine-gun fire, Aston heard Lance Corporal Tony Warwick shouting, 'I've been hit! I've been hit!'

Aston crawled over to his MFC, who was writhing and grimacing on the ground. His trousers were torn up, and his leg, ripped open by shrapnel, was oozing blood. His ankle was shattered, and he was in agony.

'All right, mate,' said Aston. 'We'll sort you out. You'll be OK.' He took out Warwick's field dressing and started to patch him up. A medic crawled across and took over.

When they had done their best to stem the bleeding, assisted by members of 5 Platoon, they got Warwick on to a stretcher. Pouring sweat, low again on water, and taking it in turns to carry the stretchers and kit, the exhausted company moved their three casualties back as fast as they could – running most of the way in the scorching heat. Warwick in particular needed to get to the field hospital at Bastion as quickly as possible.

Most of the soldiers were now really feeling the heat. Hearts beating like mad, dizzy, almost fainting and on the edge of throwing up, they were being stretched to the absolute limit. Many were moaning, as soldiers do no matter what the circumstances, but as always they were just getting on with it.

Somehow, the shattered company emerged from the Green Zone and staggered into their desert RV with the casualties at 1400 hours. It was 50 degrees. The casualties were loaded on to a Viking and driven immediately back to FOB Fox for evacuation by Chinook.

Aston was busy planning the next move. Howes and Broomfield and their platoon sergeants moved among the troops, chatting to them and checking they were OK. Morale was still at a peak. The men were ragging each other about everything from expected football results and girlfriends back home to narrow misses and mishaps during the incessant contacts of the last few hours. After everything they had just been through, the bond between them was even more solid than ever.

Broomfield flopped down beside Private Jamie 'Pez' Perry and Jason 'Jiz' Thompson. The two were best mates and never stopped ragging each other. 'Boss,' said Perry, 'don't sit there. Jiz's breath'll make you feel ill. It's really rank. I'd have moved myself if he didn't need me to supervise him all the time. I almost had to carry him down that ditch today he was so scared. Did you see him flinch when that RPG came past. Weak, sir, wasn't it?'

Broomfield opened his mouth to attempt a witty comment, and Thompson made a retching noise, turning his head away.

'You're complaining about me, Pez. Have you smelt the boss's breath? That's disgusting, sir. Has something died in your mouth? I wouldn't have expected something like that from a member of the officers' mess. I thought you lot were supposed to have standards, boss. You want to get something done about it. If you hurry, boss, you could get on that CASEVAC chopper that's coming in for Watson. I reckon your wound must be worse than his going by that smell.'

One of the other lads called across, 'Shut up, you two, it's all we ever hear from you, complaining about people's breath. Give it a rest. Just ignore these clowns, boss. How is Watson? Has he gone yet?'

The men needed a lot of water and were low on ammo. Every soldier had fired mag after mag in the countless firefights of the last two days. Some of the soldiers' clothing was falling off them – torn up by fighting across the rough ground and over jagged compound walls and disintegrating with the sweat that kept them constantly soaked day and night. A few of them managed to get replacement combat trousers with the sergeant major's ammo and water resupply.

Seeing the state of the Royal Anglians' rotten and soaking socks, two Royal Marines Viking Crewmen who were helping the sergeant major took off their own boots, removed their socks and threw them to the nearest soldiers.

Company medics checked over some of the men. Most were suffering from infections in their face, legs, genitals, ears and eyes – in fact anywhere that had come into contact with the filthy, germ-ridden canals they had been wading through. Ointments and cures were dished out and dozens of packets of zinc oxide for their feet. Every man in the company was now suffering from blisters, and the treatment helped get rid of the pain and stop the wounds from infecting. Rolls of bandage were distributed as the medics saw the soldiers were suffering deep, bleeding lacerations from carrying so much weight on top of rough and wet webbing.

As the men sorted out their kit and their bodies, they saw Apaches overhead and heard in the distance the sound of a Chinook landing with the MERT to extract the three casualties, who had by now arrived back at FOB Fox.

With the casualty evacuation and resupply complete, and wounds licked, at 1600 hours Aston marched the company back into the Green Zone to set up overwatch positions to interdict enemy trying to cross the river. He bolstered the company's firepower with FSG snipers and a Javelin missile team he had ordered to join them at the RV.

The platoons moved into their overwatch positions, set up observation posts, and the men took it in turns to rest. The moment they arrived, Aston was on the satellite phone to Carver. He was itching to get back in and deal with the Taliban at Katowzay. Carver agreed his attack plan and, with just two to three hours' sleep under their belts, Aston led the company out again just after midnight.

9

Aston deployed 6 Platoon into a compound covering the eastern edge of Katowzay outside the village and sent 5 Platoon to assault from the north.

Exactly at first light, Corporal Mo Morris and Lance Corporal John King, two snipers positioned on 6 Platoon's compound roof, saw a fighter emerge from one of the buildings 600 metres away on the outskirts of the village. An AK47 was slung over his shoulder and he was speaking into a mobile phone. Corporal Morris called down to Broomfield, who was sitting on the stairs leading up to the roof, asking permission to open fire. Broomfield gave them the thumbs-up. The two snipers did a countdown and fired at precisely the same moment, dropping the fighter where he stood.

A second fighter rushed out of the building, carrying an RPG, and Morris and King shot him as he emerged. A third man, brandishing an AK47, followed the other two out and was also shot.

5 Platoon attacked into Katowzay and cleared through the village. It was completely quiet, there was no sign of life, and they didn't encounter any enemy. The platoon went firm on the far side of the village, and 6 Platoon moved across from their compound, closing into Katowzay with Aston's Tac HQ.

Lieutenant Howes sent his lead section across a poppy field on the edge of the village. They got half-way across the open area when there was a burst of machine-gun fire from a woodline just 70 metres away.

As Howes yelled, 'Pull back! Pull back!' several soldiers from the other sections dashed to the compound roof and started firing at the enemy positions, shooting over their mates' heads as they ran back. The soldiers managed to get back to the compound as bullets tore up the ground behind them.

Howes called Aston: 'Zero Alpha, One Zero Alpha. Contact now. Six enemy with automatic weapons in treeline seventy metres south of my location. Engaged my forward section. No casualties. My callsign now moving to assault.'

Leaving a section on the roof for fire support, Howes led the rest of the platoon round to a nearby compound from where he could attack the enemy position using a covered approach. But several enemy fighters had crept round to the flank, and as soon as Howes's men tried to get out of the compound they came under fire. Using the section on the roof to blast at the enemy, Howes tried three times to leave the compound, but each time was driven back by enemy bullets. The men on the roof saw other fighters moving stealthily through the undergrowth and shot at them, but were not sure they had hit.

Howes called Aston, 'My callsign is pinned down in this location. Cannot move out of the compound. Looks like the enemy are trying to move round the flanks and get in behind us.'

Aston was concerned that 5 Platoon could become cut off from the rest of the company. He needed to act urgently. And they were too close to the enemy for mortar fire or air attack. On the radio he gave detailed orders to the two platoons. Broomfield was to move 6 Platoon into a compound near by then attack and destroy the enemy under covering fire from 5 Platoon to their left.

It was 0830 hours. Broomfield took a few minutes to brief his section commanders. 5 Platoon were still under fire. Broomfield and his commanders crouched behind a wall, the best cover they could find. 'Corporal Murphy's and Corporal Ashby's section will assault the enemy position. You will move down the ditch line dead ahead. Corporal Murphy's section will lead, followed by Corporal Ashby. I will move behind Corporal Ashby. 5 Platoon will provide covering fire from their compound to the left. Corporal Owen's section is to move down the ditch to the right and provide flank protection from there. You will move first.'

Corporal Owen led his section off to the right, followed by Sergeant Browning with the 51mm mortar. As they moved Broomfield got on the radio to Howes. 'One Zero Alpha, Two Zero Alpha. My callsign moving now. Increase fire from your callsign.'

Howes had pushed every man that could fit up on to the compound roof, and now their fire became devastatingly intense, hosing long bursts of tracer into the Taliban positions.

Broomfield gave Owen five minutes to get into position then signalled thumbs-up to Corporal Murphy. Murphy, his back seeping blood from the equipment rubbing against his sodden shirt, feet taped up and unable to walk properly, led his section into the ditch. He was unable to fight his way through the mass of entangled, thick brambles that blocked the ditch. In a low voice he called back to his men, 'We'll have to get up on the bank, but keep down as low as you possibly can. Try to use the trees for cover.'

Bullets were cracking close overhead. Lance Corporal Ashby and his men were right behind Murphy. When the last soldier had moved past, Broomfield and his signaller, Archer, started to follow. On the radio Broomfield heard a call from 5 Platoon: 'AT4 firing – now!'

There was a loud explosion from 5 Platoon's compound as the AT4 launched. Broomfield then heard an enormous explosion in the ditch ahead, at exactly the spot Corporal Murphy would be.

He felt sick. *Blue on blue. I don't believe it.*

10

But the AT4 did not cause the explosion in the ditch. At the same moment as the AT4 was fired by 5 Platoon, Private Thompson looked into the eyes of a Taliban fighter with an RPG launcher on his shoulder. Private Perry, just behind him, started to swing his weapon towards the fighter.

When Thompson locked eyes with the Taliban fighter everything slowed right down. Before either Thompson or Perry could react, there was a loud bang. Thompson saw a jet of flame flash from the back of the launcher and a cloud of blue-grey smoke, and the missile in the air, spinning straight at him. The rocket glanced off his Osprey chest plate and flung him violently into the bank, knocking the wind out of him. It exploded against the side of the ditch between him and Perry.

Thompson was engulfed in the enormous blast, and he felt as if he was on fire. He saw a blinding flash and the air was filled with smoke. Everything went silent, and then he heard screaming.

Straight away he tried to get up, but his legs buckled under him. He looked down. He was covered in blood, and he immediately felt utterly terrified. He was disorientated, his whole body was stinging, he was in agony and he thought he was going to die. His right femur and left patella were shattered, his wrist and jaw were broken. His whole body was cut up by RPG shrapnel, with fifty holes in his legs alone.

Beside him Perry lay bleeding and moaning, 157 separate shrapnel wounds in his arms, legs and nose. Corporal Murphy, who was close by, was hurled to the ground by the blast. He felt his legs, peppered by shrapnel, compressing and burning. He looked down and saw his trousers had been torn away and his legs were covered in blood.

Private Ross Green, Murphy's GPMG gunner, towards the rear, and an engineer behind him, were also badly wounded.

The fighter ran off down the ditch, and automatic fire started to pour in from Taliban positions further out.

Behind Murphy's section, Corporal Ashby felt the shock wave, shook himself and immediately crawled forward along the bank, avoiding enemy fire. Ashby saw the bleeding bodies in the ditch below and started to move forward to help them. Then he saw muzzle flashes in the undergrowth 50 metres away. He feared the enemy would rush forward to finish off Murphy's men. His priority was to protect them; others would crawl up the ditch to deal with the casualties.

He grabbed the wounded Green's GPMG and crawled further along the ditch. He was moving closer to the torrent of bullets scything into the bank, but needed to get forward to fire at the enemy position, and to cover the distance between them and the wounded soldiers. He started blasting fire towards the Taliban muzzle flashes, conscious of his own muzzle flashes and the puffs of smoke shooting out of his gun barrel every time he hit the trigger. He felt exposed and vulnerable, but he would do anything to protect his mates lying bleeding beside the ditch.

An engineer had crawled up after him and started firing his rifle. The Taliban quickly picked up Ashby's position and started to focus their fire at him. Their shooting was accurate and close, bullets ripping into the ground right next to him. But Ashby and the engineer remained exposed and firing, desperate to keep the enemy back until Murphy and his men could be got to safety.

Broomfield heard the explosion and the screaming, but could not see what was happening further along the ditch. He called Browning on the radio, 'Move to my location. Casualties.'

He then called Murphy, 'Send SITREP.'

After a pause Murphy came on the radio, sounding remarkably calm, 'I can't see what's going on. I am in the ditch with shrapnel in my legs, over.'

He saw Ashby on the bank firing his GPMG.

At that moment Private Green staggered back round the corner of the ditch. He had multiple shrapnel wounds in his leg, he was covered in blood, his clothes were shredded, and he looked dazed. Green had also been hit by an RPG just the day before, but this one had done real damage. Broomfield grabbed him by the shoulders, 'Greeny. Greeny. Look at me. Go over there. Sit down over there. We'll sort you out in a second.'

Ashby and the engineer kept firing. The engineer's rifle jammed, and Broomfield crawled over and swapped weapons so he could keep firing.

Sergeant Browning and Corporal Owen moved back down the ditch to the right, under enemy fire all the way. Owen and his men went forward to bring back the casualties. Browning started to organize their first aid.

Owen directed his men to each casualty. 'Get them out quick. Drag them back up the ditch.'

He went to Thompson, took out his knife and cut through the straps of his daysack. He and Private Tony Purcell carried Thompson back through the slush and the mud, twigs and branches falling on to them as bullets ripped into the trees above.

Broomfield saw two men dragging another wounded soldier back down the ditch. The man's body armour had ridden up round his face, and Broomfield couldn't see who it was. He grabbed the soldier's bleeding legs and helped carry him back to the casualty area, in an alleyway between two compound walls.

Broomfield ran back to make sure all the casualties had been brought out and positioned soldiers to protect the area where the wounded were being treated.

When he was satisfied, Broomfield returned to the casualties. Browning had lined them up along the wall. They were bleeding and moaning, and their clothes had been blown off them or were hanging in shredded rags. There were four Royal Anglians and a Royal Engineer, whose helmet had been split right down the centre by a splinter from the rocket.

Broomfield looked down at Thompson, who had been ragging him for bad breath the previous afternoon. Private Hare had tied tourniquets round both of his legs, trying to stop the blood oozing out of the puncture wounds. Another soldier was trying to get a drip into him. He was writhing in agony, and Hare was about to give him morphine when Broomfield snatched the syrette from his grasp. He wanted do it himself. He was devastated to see his soldiers lying bleeding and in agony. He needed to do something to help them. He took the morphine syrette. He had done it many times before in training but now couldn't remember which end to punch into Thompson's leg. He looked at the instructions on the tube, then pulled off the red end cap, pushed the yellow end on to Thompson's thigh and pressed down on the black plunger, now understanding why an 'idiot's guide' is needed.

Pulling the long needle out, he thought, *What the hell am I doing? I can't get sucked in to treating individual soldiers. I can't let emotion get hold of me, I've got my job to do.*

He looked at the soldiers treating the casualties. Agonized emotion was all over their faces. They weren't just treating casualties, they were treating the horrific wounds of mates with whom they had been through so much in the last few months, who had become closer than brothers.

Aston was there now, and Broomfield briefed him. 'We have five casualties, all being treated. Security is deployed to protect the area. There is a lot of kit that we won't be able to carry out of here. Personal kit, four bar-mines and a Javelin missile. I've told the engineers to deny it.'

Aston looked as upset as Broomfield to see the men like this, but he remained calm. He had already ordered CASEVAC from battle group HQ. Because of the seriousness of the situation the RAF commander decided to take the risk of bringing a British Chinook into the Green Zone.

Aston sent 6 Platoon to secure a landing site 1,500 metres away, beyond the danger from enemy fire, and Tac HQ and the snipers secured the casualty evacuation route out of the village. 5 Platoon carried the casualties to the helicopter, leaving a section to cover the enemy positions in the woodline in case Taliban survivors tried to get forward.

Within half an hour the Chinook swept into view with two more Apaches overhead for protection. The pilot sent the helicopter into a dramatic low dive, rotor blades seeming almost to touch the ground as it landed heavily. The poppies had recently been harvested, and the air was full of cut stalks hurled in every direction by the powerful rotor downwash.

The stretcher bearers were shattered after a forced march of one and a half sweltering kilometres across rough terrain. Five of them were close to heat exhaustion. Broomfield helped carry Thompson on to the Chinook, while an interpreter held his drip.

As the injured were loaded on board the helicopter, the roar of a Harrier almost deafened them. Two 500-pound air-burst bombs detonated just above ground on the Taliban position in the woodline. Apache attack helicopters dived down to strafe the surviving enemy. The Apache pilots reported twelve dead Taliban, killed by a combination of the air attack and B Company's fire.

The company had begun Operation Ghartse Ghar with just two under-strength platoons. Having accumulated eight casualties over the last two days, their fighting ability was now limited. Aston put his men into a defensive perimeter in an irrigation ditch and contacted Carver by Tac Sat. The two officers agreed that B Company needed reinforcements, and an hour later the Helmand Reaction Force, a platoon from No. 3 Company of the Grenadier Guards, landed in a Chinook.

II

For the next five days B Company continued to march through the Green Zone, covering a total of 70 kilometres on foot. This period of almost continuous patrolling and fighting was the hardest test B Company faced during the tour. They had sustained eight casualties in three days. But the Taliban were put on the back foot by Aston's relentless thrusts into the area they had previously considered their own.

A Company also achieved a remarkable feat of endurance during Operation Ghartse Ghar. On the first day of the operation alone they conducted a gruelling 10-kilometre night insertion. For the company there followed a day of constant advance to contact, in which they had numerous short-range firefights with the Taliban, killing many enemy fighters. Even more were killed as A Company flushed out the enemy and brought in air strikes to hit them in the open. At the end of a hard day of fighting, Private Michael Charlesworth was shot in the wrist, and several ANA soldiers more seriously wounded in a lengthy firefight on the river line.

Later that night A Company snipers identified a large group of Taliban trying to exfiltrate across the river, 3 kilometres to the north. Out of range of direct fire systems, Major Biddick, the company commander, tasked Apaches to attack, killing twelve enemy as they were about to escape.

Carver's plan for Operation Ghartse Ghar had succeeded. The battle group had cut off escape routes over the Helmand River and accounted for at least 100 enemy dead. The Taliban perception that the area was a safe haven had been shattered, at least for the time being, and word of their vanquishing quickly spread among the local population.

Immediately after Ghartse Ghar the battle group occupied Forward Operating Base Inkerman, a large compound beside the Green Zone, to enable continued domination of the area to the north-east of Sangin. Almost straight away, Inkerman became B Company's bleak new home.

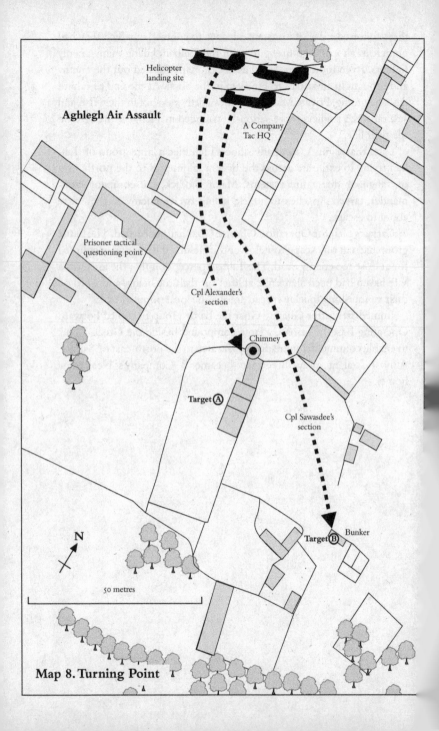

Helicopter landing site

Aghlegh Air Assault

A Company Tac HQ

Prisoner tactical questioning point

Cpl Alexander's section

Chimney

Target (A)

Cpl Sawasdee's section

Target (B) Bunker

N

50 metres

Map 8. Turning Point

Turning Point: 7–12 July 2007

Before Operation Ghartse Ghar began, Major Dominic Biddick, A Company commander, planned an operation to enable the repair of the ruined Jusulay irrigation ditch. Having consulted with the locals to identify their priorities for reconstruction in the Sangin area, he had identified this as top of the list. Nine kilometres north-east of Sangin, the Jusulay ditch was the single most important irrigation channel between Sangin and Kajaki, servicing vast areas of crops. Its repair promised to bring renewed prosperity to several thousand people.

On the last day of Ghartse Ghar, 5 July, Biddick put his plan into action. He deployed A Company to provide protection against Taliban interference, organized local labour and plant and supplied Hesco Bastion walling to build a dam to divert water from the Helmand River into the ditch.

The Jusulay irrigation project took two weeks to complete. With Biddick's security and organization, and a workforce from the local people, the project helped demonstrate to the community the readiness of the Royal Anglians to listen to and act on their needs and showed what could be achieved by cooperation between the locals and the British troops.

The increasing security brought by a permanent British presence after Operation Silver, reinforced by the major blows against the Taliban in Operation Lastay Kulang and Ghartse Ghar, was beginning to bring normal life back to Sangin. Or at least what passed for normal life in this poverty-stricken, desolate and much-fought-over town. Steadily people were returning to their houses, more and more shops were opening, and street life was getting busier. For the first time since the Taliban's violent reaction to the arrival of the British forces in 2006, Sangin had a functioning market. Some said the market was more vibrant than they had known for years. And the market was the real key to Sangin's present and its future.

In helping to bring about this change, A Company had built on the success of Operation Silver, the relief of Sangin, which had been conducted as the Royal Anglians arrived in Afghanistan at the start of their tour. Silver had been carried out by US forces, including elements of the 82nd Airborne Division, supported by troops from the Royal Marines and Afghan National Army.

People came here to trade from all along the upper Sangin valley, almost as far away as Kajaki, 40 kilometres to the north. For over a year, people in the town and surrounding villages had had nowhere to purchase basic commodities like bread. Even before that, they would have to buy at exorbitant rates from gangsters and drug dealers. Now they had the market. They could travel into the town to trade produce freely, without fear of extortion, intimidation or attack. It is difficult to overstate how important the market was to the people of Sangin.

For the Taliban, and for the leaders of the narcotics trade, this return of confidence and normal life was too much to bear. It signified encroachment into their territory by the reviled Karzai regime in Kabul, backed by the British occupiers, who were denying them freedom of action, influence and revenue. At every opportunity they struck back at the foreigners, as well as the hated Afghan National Army and police, who operated under the authority of Isatullah, the ally of Karzai who had been installed as Governor of Sangin two months earlier, in May.

Shortly before nine on the morning of Saturday 7 July, a twelve-year-old boy stood in the main street of Sangin, watching the activities of the market traders. Just over five feet tall and skeleton thin, he was dressed in a clean grey kurta with matching round cap. He had only recently travelled down from Kabul to stay with relatives in the town, and the market life of Sangin was strange and intriguing to him.

The boy was startled by the approach of two young men, one in a white and the other a green kurta, both wearing turbans and the familiar black beards.

'Do you want to earn a hundred Afghanis, boy?'

'For myself?'

'Yes, for you.'

'What do I have to do?' asked the boy in disbelief. This was a lot of money, and he had never seen these men before.

'Just push my trolley up the street and park it over there, outside the baker's. Then you can leave it.'

He looked at the trolley, a rusty old push cart with phone top-up cards hanging all over it, a familiar sight in the streets of Kabul as well.

'That's all?'

'That's all. Here's the money.' One of the men thrust the grimy Afghani notes into the boy's hand.

He pushed the cart along the road. It was heavier than he expected with its cargo of phone cards. But he was a strong lad and he put his back into it. He turned to look at the men. They stood where he had left them, watching. The man in the green kurta had what looked like a mobile phone in his hand.

The boy stopped outside the baker's. He looked again at the two men to see if they were satisfied where he'd left it. They were still watching him but had now moved further back along the street.

The boy was about to move away from the cart when a police pick-up drove towards him. He stopped to look at the vehicle, fascinated. He hoped to be a policeman himself one day, when he was old enough.

There was an earth-shattering explosion as the bomb in the cart detonated.

2

At twenty-nine, Captain Tom Coleman, the Royal Anglian Battle Group intelligence officer, or IO, had been in the Army for seven years. He had done a six-month tour in Iraq in 2005 and had spent six months with ISAF in Kabul in 2002. He had only been IO for about eight months before the start of the tour, but in that time had submerged himself as best he could in Afghan culture and had spent a lot of time talking to people who had previously worked in intelligence in the country and had some understanding of the Taliban. He had inherited the analytical thinking essential for an IO from his parents, both of whom were circuit judges. An Arabic speaker and a competent linguist, with a basic working grasp of Pashtu, Coleman felt that some knowledge of the local language helped in his efforts to understand how the people thought and behaved.

Coleman had been in Sangin District Centre for several days. He was normally based with Carver in Camp Bastion, but he had come here to increase his understanding of the enemy groupings and activities in the area to help the CO develop the operational plan for the upper Sangin valley.

Governor Isatullah, with his intricate knowledge of local connections and relationships, was happy to work closely with the British, exchanging information and imparting his understanding of the people, their leaders and the workings of the local area, all of which was normally impenetrable to outsiders. Isatullah's insight was vital to Coleman.

As Captain Coleman was walking into the governor's compound within the DC for his normal morning meeting, he heard the blast in the street outside, nearly 2 kilometres away.

Minutes later the casualties started arriving. As well as the boy from Kabul, the cart bomb had killed an Afghan police officer and seriously wounded another. Several injured locals, including children, were also carried or staggered through the gates, and A Company's doctor and medics set about the familiar work of patching up shrapnel and blast wounds. Sangin had suffered many bomb attacks in recent weeks.

Although A Company had immediately dispatched a quick reaction force to help the police deal with the situation on the ground, Coleman knew that the first person to have a handle on what was going on would be the governor.

Despite the carnage outside, in his office Isatullah retained his customary air of calm and authority. Coleman entered with Ahmad, his interpreter. He first exchanged the traditional greetings in Pashtu and then reverted to the interpreter. Isatullah sent for some tea.

'Tell him how sorry I am that his people have been killed and wounded, especially his police officers. Tell him the company is already helping outside, and the doctor is treating the injured, but if there is anything more he needs from us he knows he only has to ask.'

The interpreter relayed Coleman's sentiments, and Isatullah placed his right hand across his heart and bowed his head in a gesture of appreciation. As Coleman knew he would, the governor explained to Ahmad what had happened just minutes earlier.

The interpreter translated, 'The governor says every bomb in Sangin is a terrible tragedy, and they seem to be getting more and more frequent. He is very worried by it. But this one is a hundred times worse than all of the others. Not because it is bigger. Not because it has killed more or injured more than others. It is none of these things. The terrible thing about this bomb is that the Taliban used a young child to place it, and they detonated the bomb as the boy pushed it into position. God will never forgive these evil men. Never. He says we must do all we can to stop these agents of Pakistan and Iran. He knows he can count on the assistance of Mr Carver and the whole of his regiment. Only this morning the governor was on the telephone to President Karzai and he told the president what excellent support Mr Carver gives to us here in Sangin. Without him and his officers everything would be much, much worse. The governor says he already knows who carried out this terrible atrocity, and his people and your people must work together to rid the country of him.'

Coleman leaned forward. 'Ask him who it was.'

After Isatullah had spoken Ahmad said, 'The governor says you know this man. A very bad man. He is working for Pakistan and for the Iranians and he has attacked your own people before. The governor says it is Shir Agha.'

Coleman knew exactly who Shir Agha was. A local criminal, up to his elbows in every kind of illegal activity in Sangin and beyond. He had ambushed a foot patrol of The 1st Battalion The Worcestershire and Sherwood Foresters, who had been based at Sangin before A Company had arrived. And although he was not believed to have personally led the ambush against B Company's vehicles on the outskirts of the town on the 17th of May, intelligence confirmed that he had identified the position and led the ambushers into place.

'Ahmad, thank the governor. Tell him I am sure he has many things to do at this time and I will leave him. But tell him again, if there is anything more he needs from me now, he should call.'

Outside Coleman saw Sergeant Stewart 'Tiger' Gardner, a Royal Anglian intelligence NCO who had been on the ground with the Afghan police helping deal with the aftermath of the bomb attack – and doing his best to collect information about what had happened. Gardner confirmed what Isatullah had told Coleman about how the attack took place. He had taken digital photos of the scene, including the cart and the remains of the hapless twelve-year-old boy who had been blown up with it. In the bright sunlight, Coleman squinted at the images in the small screen on the back of Gardner's camera.

'Sir,' said Gardner, 'I spoke to a bloke that saw everything that happened. Got his details if you want to talk to him. He was pretty disgusted and he said he'd be willing to talk to anyone about it.'

'Thanks, Sergeant G,' said Coleman, 'that could be useful.'

Lieutenant Colonel Carver was back at the battle group main HQ in Camp Bastion. That evening Coleman called him on the secure phone link to brief him on the events in Sangin.

'That's really bad,' said Carver. 'Shocking. But we know how low these people will stoop. It doesn't really surprise me. It may also be an opportunity for us to beat the Taliban at their own propaganda game for a change. Here's what I want you to do. Get those pictures of the attack on to Powerpoint. We'll show them at the Sangin shura along with our presentation on the reconstruction projects. And get hold of that eye witness of Gardner's and see if he'll stand up at the shura and say what he saw. I'll call Isatullah and clear it with him and try to get him on message. He's normally pretty good at this sort of thing anyway.

'Happy? Right, get on with it, and I'll see you down there in a couple of days. By the way, did Colour Sergeant Neal get those clean socks to you? I gather your other ones were walking on their own.'

Coleman had originally been sent to Sangin for just one day, but the CO had then told him to remain there indefinitely, and bits and pieces of his kit had been sent out from Bastion to keep him going.

3

'The Fighting Ninth have been selected for the first air assault mission that has been launched by Task Force Helmand since this tour began. It will be a precision strike operation against a Taliban bomb-making factory 25 kilometres east of Sangin. L Hour is planned for tomorrow morning, between 0650 and 0800 hours.'

It was midday on 10 July, and Biddick was speaking to his command team. He referred to A Company as 'The Fighting Ninth', a nickname given to the 9th Regiment of Foot, which later became the Royal Norfolks, subsequently amalgamated with other regiments to form The 1st Battalion The Royal Anglian Regiment. Biddick's A (Norfolk) Company considered themselves to be the direct descendants of the 9th of Foot.

The command team were gathered in the operations room at Sangin DC. Although there was no air conditioning, the room was below ground level and usually quite cool. But with twenty-five bodies packed into a room big enough for no more than ten comfortably, and the temperature in the high forties, the place was stifling.

Whenever possible Biddick liked to include all his leaders down to section commander in an O Group. This was unconventional. Normally a company commander would brief his platoon commanders, who would disseminate down to their NCOs and privates. But to Biddick it was vital that as many of his commanders as possible could hear his intentions and plans first hand, ensuring that the whole command team were brought into the mission in the shortest amount of time and giving a better chance to junior leaders who might have to take command if their superiors were wounded or killed in battle. The sergeants and corporals appreciated this technique, feeling more included in the command team, and better informed.

Better informed, but right now extremely uncomfortable. Mostly dressed in T-shirts, desert shorts and flip flops, they were sweating heavily, jammed in, standing round the bird table. This was a large table, covered with air photographs and maps overlaid with critical information for the forthcoming operation: attack targets, flight paths, drop-off points, cordon locations, cut-off positions, possible enemy exfiltration routes.

'Before I talk you through my plan, I'm going to hand over to the IO, who will brief you on the enemy picture.'

Captain Tom Coleman stood up, pointing a green radio antenna at one of the air photos. 'This is the target area,' he said, 'the village of Aghlegh, 25 kilometres east of here. We have precise intelligence indicating that these compounds, here in the west side of the village, are the centre of the Taliban IED operation in this whole area.'

Coleman had seized their interest. The commanders were looking intently at the air photos, heat and lack of air forgotten.

He held up a picture and handed it to Lieutenant Graham Goodey, commander of 2 Platoon, seated in the front row. 'Pass this round. It shows two men digging in what is almost certainly a mine. The image was taken two days ago in the Eastern Desert by Surveillance assets.'

He handed across two other photos. 'The second photo shows the men leaving the area on a motorbike. The third shows the compound they went to. In Aghlegh. Needless to say, these guys had no idea they were on camera.'

The grainy photos looked like they were still captures from a video camera. While they studied them and passed them on, Coleman continued, 'From this and other intelligence which we have, I assess that the Aghlegh compound is either a bomb-making factory or at least a storage and distribution centre for IEDs. We estimate there are about four or five people operating in and around that compound.'

He pointed again at the bird-table image of the compound. 'That is Objective A. There is what seems to be a bunker of some sort next to it – here. Thirty-five metres away. People seem to move frequently between Objective A and that bunker. The two are therefore presumably linked in some way. Perhaps the bunker is a storage location. That bunker is Objective B.'

Biddick said. 'We'll deal with all questions at the end. Thank you, Tom, that was very clear.'

Coleman squeezed back a bit to allow more space for the company commander.

'Gentlemen, I think we're all pretty clear on the Taliban tactics that led to the death of Daz Bonner and the other casualties the battle group has sustained in minestrikes.'

At the mention of Bonner, everyone sat up, even more interested. Bonner had been killed in the back of Biddick's Viking when it ran over a mine six weeks earlier. He had been one of the best-known and most popular figures in the regiment.

Biddick continued, 'And on top of that, as we all know there have been huge numbers of IED attacks on the ANA and the civilian community in and around Sangin itself. That is why this operation is so important. We must do everything we can to disrupt these attacks – and save lives. And as you have just heard, for once we have some very precise intelligence to enable us to do just that. The mission is to strike, cordon and search the suspected Taliban compound at Aghlegh in order to disrupt Taliban operations and increase security in Sangin district. My intent is to conduct a detailed search of the objective, once secured and cordoned, employing aviation assets to achieve tactical surprise and deploy fighting troops rapidly and simultaneously to deny enemy escape. Concurrent to the search, local nationals will be engaged and reassured. Any additional intelligence gained will be exploited immediately.

'This action will disrupt and deter Taliban IED and mine operations in Sangin district and demonstrate UK Forces' ability to achieve a precision strike at a time and place of our choosing – thereby increasing the security of friendly forces' operations.'

'Finally, I do not want to alienate the community in Aghlegh any more than we have to. Preferably not at all. It is imperative we explain to the locals what we are doing and why, and also that we compensate the innocent members of the community for any harm or damage done. You all know the importance I attach to winning and keeping hold of hearts and minds.'

Biddick surveyed his audience, as though looking to see that his message was clearly understood.

'Concept of ops. We will fly in by Chinook, landing on the western edge of the village. 2 Platoon, you are strike platoon. OK, Graham?'

He looked at Lieutenant Goodey. 'You will simultaneously enter and secure Objective A and Objective B, as described by the IO. Main effort is Objective A. When you have secured the two objectives, you will call forward the Royal Engineers Search Adviser and his Search Team who will do a detailed search first of Objective A then B.'

'Insertion and extraction will be by three Chinook. Because of available air windows we will be on the ground for exactly four hours.'

Thirty minutes later the O Group broke up, the commanders thankfully piling out into what was still the unbearable heat of the early afternoon but at least there was a bit of air. Within a few minutes the whole base was alive with activity as the company began its detailed preparations to translate Biddick's concept of operations into reality on the ground in Aghlegh.

4

The following morning, in the dark, Corporal Ryan Alexander of 2 Platoon led his section out of the accommodation on to their predesignated position beside the HLS. They lined up in their embarkation stick then sat silently, ready to go. Alexander had a feeling of expectation and excitement. This was an important mission. He and his men knew that if they succeeded they could be saving their mates' and their own lives, stopping the deadly anti-tank mines that could kill any of them any time they crossed the desert and setting back the Taliban's terrorist campaign against the local population.

Alexander couldn't help thinking about Darren Bonner. This operation was to some extent about him. The people they were flying across the desert to capture or kill could just possibly be the very men responsible for his death. Even if they didn't succeed in getting them, they would hopefully seriously disrupt the network. He had never before in his life been more determined to do anything properly.

Biddick, the IO, the three platoon commanders and the JTAC were in the ops room, next to the HLS, waiting for updated intelligence from the British surveillance assets. This was a tense time. Outwardly, Biddick was calm, but prior to a complex operation a thousand thoughts go through every commander's mind. An air assault had so many moving parts that could go wrong, even without interferace from the enemy. Waiting was always the worst part.

Half an hour later, Goodey sent a runner from the ops room to brief 2 Platoon that intelligence reports indicated people entering the compound, Objective A. Three males, wearing green kurtas and dark turbans. *Excellent*, thought Alexander, *coming together. Almost too good to be true.*

As the word was passed round the men, he heard excited murmurings from the dark shapes behind him. The men all felt the same. They were about to seize the initiative. And they were all thinking of Bonner.

A few minutes later the soldiers' elation slumped a little when Goodey came across from the ops room and spoke to them. As every soldier does automatically in the dark, he spoke in hushed tones, though there was no need to. 'Lads, there is a problem with the Chinooks. Not sure what has gone wrong. They're still coming but they're going to be delayed.'

'Shock,' said someone at the back of the line.

Gradually the sun came up, deep red, and the heat began to build as the troops sat in the open beside the HLS. Messages came out of the ops room that the helicopters were on their way. Then that they weren't. No one seemed to know what was happening or why.

Alexander knew that, in the ops room, Biddick would be sitting calmly and coolly, but that inside he would be getting increasingly annoyed.

'They get *EastEnders* on BFBS at this time of the morning back in Bastion,' said Private Luke Chumbley, a young Essex lad who was Alexander's Minimi gunner. 'The crabs wouldn't want to fly out here before that's finished. Even if they thought Ross Kemp was out here instead of on the TV.'

Private Mark Stevens, Alexander's GPMG gunner, said, 'Yeah, and maybe the chef didn't get up in time to do their breakfasts. The crabs can't leave in the morning without a full fry, it's against their regulations. I expect it's breakfast in bed this morning. Actually, thinking about it, I'm surprised you didn't join the RAF for the breakfasts, Chumber Wumber.'

With as little effort as possible Chumbley booted him in the back in token retaliation.

'If the Yanks were flying us we'd be well on the ground by now,' piped up Private Anthony Glover, the section's point man, jumping to his feet, suddenly animated. 'If they think there's the chance of a fight they're all over it. Sarge, can't we ring up the US Air Force and see if they want to play? Isn't Teddy Ruecker's dad in the Yank Air Force? Why don't we get hold of him and ask his old man to call in a favour?'

'All right, sit down, Glovebox,' said Alexander, 'you lot all take a chill pill, there's nothing we can do about it, we just have to wait for the crabs to get here. Take some of your kit off and cool down a bit. Illsley, Whaitesy, nip over to the ops room and bring some water here so we can have a drink.'

A few minutes later they were at it again. You can never stop the troops moaning and ragging each other. The old saying that soldiers are never happy unless they're complaining is absolutely true, and in situations like this it helped pass the time. 'The Taliban will be gone by the time we get there. We were supposed to take off an hour and a half ago,' said Chumbley.

'They'll still be there,' said Stevens, 'and Chumber, if we do ever get there, no shooting at birds, got it? I know you're the section anti-aircraft gunner, but remember, these guys are inside the compounds, not flying around the trees.'

Chumbley, who in one contact on Operation Ghartse Ghar had kept firing high, had never been allowed to forget it by the rest of the section, especially by Stevens, one of the platoon characters and a tough and determined soldier. Chumbley now leapt on top of him.

Two hours later than planned, for reasons they never learnt, the increasingly irritated men of A Company finally began to hear the all-pervading thudding as the three Chinooks approached Sangin.

5

Minutes later they were filing up the tail ramps. There were only three helicopters to transport the 120 men of A Company Group, swollen beyond their normal strength by the ANA platoon and engineer search team. The red plastic webbing and silver tubular metal bench seats running down either side were folded up, and the men crammed in sardine-like, standing as if it was rush hour on the London Underground.

The Chinooks flew in towards the western outskirts of Aghlegh very fast and very low. The men were grinning at each other, some were slapping each other on the back. They were going in. To what? Anything could happen on the ground. The Taliban could be waiting for them, an ambush. They all knew an American Chinook had been shot down in the Green Zone during Op Lastay Kulang at the end of May. Or maybe it would all go to plan? Maybe...

The Chinook dropped like a stone and crunched on to the dirt. It was the hardest landing Alexander had ever experienced, and if the men hadn't been packed in so tight and holding on to the sides and to each other, it would have knocked them off their feet.

The ramp was already down, and the second the wheels hit the ground Goodey, followed closely by Alexander, led the men off the back of the chopper, running blind through thick clouds of brown dust, kicked up by the Chinooks that had landed next to each other. The noise of the three sets of powerful engines was intense and deafening. Alexander was running as fast as he could. He was desperate to get into clear air to see where things were. They had trained for this, and during their rehearsals they learnt the direction from the back of the Chinook to the target compound. But now they had no idea. They had been told the Chinooks were going to land in a different position, probably facing a different direction to the plan. Alexander also ran fast to lead his men away as quickly as possible away from the bullet magnet that was the helicopter.

Alexander looked left. There was Objective A, their target. Easily identified by a 5.5-metre-tall chimney within the compound. Shouting, 'Boss, over here, it's over here, follow me,' he wheeled left without looking to see if Goodey was following. The platoon were behind him.

A young soldier, recently arrived, for some reason was running in the opposite direction. Without pausing, Alexander reached out and dragged him back on course.

As he ran towards his target, Alexander looked around. Quite a sparse village, small compounds, well spread out, just as the photography showed. The whole place was deserted, no one in the streets.

Alexander hit the compound. It was 25 by 15 metres. The walls were lower than normal, less than 2 metres tall. He looked over and quickly took in the layout. Open courtyard, no vegetation, no one inside that he could see. Three small shed-sized buildings on the left. Inside the wall nearest him, the chimney. The whole place looked more like some kind of industrial set-up than a dwelling. Probably a brick kiln.

The plan had been to go in red, kick the door in or blast through the wall and then grenade the compound. There was no need to bar-mine their way in. There were no doors on the compound, and the low wall was broken down in places. They could see into the courtyard, and no one was there, so there was no point grenading. It would only slow them down. Speed was critical if anyone was in the rooms within the compound. 'We're going in green,' he shouted. 'Go in green. Green.'

Without orders, Chumbley and Okoti had taken up positions outside the compound, covering over the walls with their Minimis.

Glover and Smith, Assault Team 1, charged through the doorway and into the compound. They moved straight to the chimney and checked inside the large brick-built kiln at its base. 'Clear, clear,' shouted Glover.

Alexander was in next, then Assault Team 2, Waites and Illsley. They cleared the first two buildings, weapons in shoulders, ready to shoot. 'Rooms clear, no one inside,' yelled Illsley.

The two engineers, also acting as an assault team, raced in and cleared the last building. 'Room clear.'

Finally the two Minimi gunners moved into position inside the compound, covering the whole area around it. Less than three minutes after landing Objective A was secured. But empty of Taliban bombers.

Alexander moved from person to person, issuing and confirming their arcs of fire. Whaites, on the eastern side of the compound, called out, 'Alex, Alex, there's a bloke over here acting suspicious.'

'Grab him, search him. I'll get a terp.'

6

The RESA and his search team, or REST, were waiting on the outskirts of the village to be notified the compound was clear. Alexander couldn't call them. He and his men had all switched off their radios before entering the compound. They had been instructed to do so during the O Group, as radio emissions could potentially trigger a remote-controlled IED.

Alexander sent his 2IC, South African Lance Corporal Werner van der Merwe, to get the search team in. Meanwhile he took the interpreter together with the Afghan that Whaites had got hold of to the RSM for questioning.

A few minutes later the RSM told Goodey that the man had informed him that Taliban had been in the Objective A compound and the same people had also used a different compound, which he had identified. Goodey sent Corporal Sawasdee's section to clear and search it.

Led forward by van der Merwe, the RESA and his eight-man search team filed into the compound carrying their specialist equipment. Some of the engineers commenced searching the three small buildings and the kiln.

Meanwhile two engineers were systematically combing through the outside part of the compound. 'Can you shift a bit, mate, so we can check under here,' said one of them to Glover, who was in a fire position in the corner of the compound. Moments later the engineer told Glover he had been balancing on two anti-tank mines concealed in the undergrowth.

'Alex,' said Glover, calling Alexander over and pointing at the mines, 'I've just been standing on them.' His face was white. Alexander always used Glover as his point man. He was an excellent soldier, who had a lot of common sense and could read and react to the ground well. That was why Alexander identified him as point man during the pre-training in Kenya. But as the tour wore on Glover grew more and more to fear mines. Hardly surprising. Always out in front of the section, and often the platoon and the whole company, if anyone was going to trigger a mine or an IED it was the point man.

A few minutes later the engineers found a 100cc motor bike with a mobile phone lying on the seat. Almost certainly the bike that had been photographed. And Alexander thought the phone just lying there was an indication that the bomb-makers had left in a hurry, probably minutes before his section crashed into the compound.

Leaving the engineers to continue searching, Alexander led his section into the compound immediately south, from where he could provide better all-round protection to the search. Inside was a family. They were scared and compliant, and Alexander and his interpreter centralized them all in one room where they would be monitored more easily while the search proceeded.

Goodey called Alexander on the radio, now switched back on. 'Bronze Two One Charlie, this is Bronze Two Zero Alpha. Callsign Two Two Charlie has found some interesting stuff in the compound that bloke identified as associated with Objective A. Roger so far.'

'Two One Charlie Roger.'

'Roger. Two AK47s and two IED remote control systems. Pass on a well done to the soldier that picked the bloke up.'

At that time an IED was being set off about every two or three days in Sangin, wounding and killing large numbers of civilians and Afghan soldiers and police. They were all initiated by remote control. Alexander knew first hand the deadly effects of these IEDs. The first day A Company arrived in Sangin a bomb had killed three Afghan soldiers in the centre of the town. Alexander, Sergeant Butcher and another NCO had the grizzly task of picking up the bloody remains, legs and arms hanging off, and putting them into body bags.

A few minutes later Goodey called again, this time letting Alexander know that the engineer search team had found several more anti-tank and anti-personnel mines at Objective A.

Now the RSM came into the compound. 'Corporal Alexander, I need you to question some prisoners. Hand your section over to your 2IC and come and deal with this lot that the ANA have rounded up.'

Alexander was the only qualified interrogator in the company. He moved out of the compound with the RSM. There was a group of about thirty Afghan men, mostly in green kurtas. Alexander said, 'Why were these men arrested?'

'As far as I can make out it was just random,' said the RSM. 'The ANA picked up whoever they saw of fighting age. I think they concentrated mainly on the ones in green kurtas because of the int.'

Alexander walked along the row, looking to see any sign of more than usual nervousness or stress. 'It's a pretty vague way of doing it,' he said to the RSM, 'but there's nothing else to go on and we've got to have some kind of priority. I'd like to do them in groups of three, sir. Can we get them blindfolded and then get a guard to take one man into each of the three rooms in the compound? I'll question them individually. But we haven't got any leverage over them if they've been arrested at random. Unless they volunteer information or they trip up because they're scared we probably won't get anything out of them.'

The men were fitted with pre-prepared goggles blacked out with masking tape that the troops had got ready for prisoners. Alexander went from room to room questioning them, with his interpreter, Muhammad, and a Military Police NCO taking notes. He took their names and asked each man where he lived. If they weren't from the village, why they were there? He asked about their background and whether they knew the people that lived in the compound with the chimney. And whether they knew of any Taliban in the area.

Intending to spread alarm and uncertainty, and foster distrust within their own ranks if any had been Taliban, he told them that spies in their midst had provided information that led the troops to the compound.

The whole process took an hour and a half, and, as Alexander had predicted, no one said anything that was of any use. *Maybe I questioned the bomb-makers*, he thought, *but without any leverage, how would you know? Perhaps I've even spoken to the men that killed Daz Bonner!*

Once the interrogation was complete, in the village centre Biddick assembled the elders together with everyone who had been stopped and searched or questioned. Speaking through his interpreter, he explained what they had been doing. 'We came here because there have been many mines laid to kill and injure British and Afghan soldiers who are working for your government and working to help your security and to improve quality of life here by trying to provide irrigation and electricity. There have also been many bomb attacks against innocent civilians and police in Sangin. We have information that the bombs were manufactured here, and we have found several items of bomb-making equipment and mines that have confirmed that our information was correct. But I know that those involved are a very small number of people. I have no doubt that most of your people do not support this murderous activity, and I know that even some from this village have lost limbs from these mines, and been blown up in bomb attacks. These attacks have been disrupting trade in this whole area, making people poorer and denying them the opportunity to buy and sell goods in Sangin. I hope you can understand why we have come here and done what we have done. I know we have inconvenienced some of you and we will now pay money to you for the time that we have taken. What I ask is that if you do hear of or see any insurgent activity, any bomb-making, laying of mines, or anything else of that sort, please contact us. You can inform the police or the Army, or you can tell us directly. We will distribute cards that show how to get in touch with us.'

The engineer search teams bagged up the technical items that might help them counter future IED attacks.

As Alexander's section headed back to the drop-off point, with the Chinooks inbound, there was a massive explosion outside Objective A. The mines, the motorbike and anything else that would be of use to the bomb-makers had been rigged for demolition by the engineers, on a delayed safety fuze. The charge might have been on the large side, or the delay too short. Either way, debris landed all round them, and the motorbike engine narrowly missed van der Merwe.

Four hours after they had landed, A Company lifted off in the three Chinooks, heading back to Sangin DC escorted by a pair of Apaches.

Alexander walked off the HLS. Biddick spoke to him: 'Well done, Corporal Alexander, your men did a good job there.'

'Thanks, sir, pity we didn't get those bastards that killed Daz.'

'It is, that would have been the icing on the cake. But even so I see it as a success. We have probably disrupted their physical operation for a while, but as we all know there is no shortage of mines, shells and other bomb-making stuff around this country. Much more significantly I think we may have instilled fear and uncertainty into that group. We landed at a time and place of our choosing. We had accurate intelligence and we went straight in to where they were putting the devices together. That must worry them. How did we know? Who's been talking to the enemy? Who can no longer be trusted in the team? Just dealing with those uncertainties may well reduce the effectiveness of their operation. Even if that only mitigates the threat from them to a small extent, I consider that to be a success.'

Biddick was right. The company air assault disrupted the Taliban bomb-making operation, at least for a time. Up until the raid into Aghlegh, there had been an IED attack in Sangin every other day. After the raid there was not another IED for four weeks.

7

The Sangin shura was held on 12 July in the governor's compound. Forty elders from the town and across the upper Sangin valley crowded into the long room. Several of them had walked many miles or travelled by motorbike to get there. The rows of chairs were reserved for the more important men, the others sat cross-legged on the floor. These were all people of influence hand-picked by the governor because he thought each of them was capable of making things happen in their communities – rather than just the normal well-intentioned but unproductive talk that was prevalent in Afghan local affairs.

Among the gathering were two or three younger men, looking slightly shifty. The Taliban normally managed to get their plants into the shura to relay back what the governor and the British were discussing.

Seated behind a table at the front was Governor Isatullah, flanked by Carver, Coleman, Biddick, the Sangin chief of police and Colonel Rasool, the local ANA commander.

Isatullah spoke first. He was a gripping and expansive speaker. He spoke in Pashtu, and all the while the interpreter whispered a translation for the benefit of Carver and his officers. After an elaborate welcome, Isatullah spent some time telling those present how they should be grateful to the British and Americans for the help they had provided Afghanistan in fighting off foreign invaders. First the Russians, and now the terrorists sent into the country by Pakistan and Iran. This theme met with the visible approval of the elders, most of whom nodded vigorously and muttered their agreement. Pakistan in particular was considered by all present to be the greatest enemy.

Isatullah handed over to the chief of police, who continued the governor's theme. Then the ANA commander spoke. He had lost many of his men to Taliban attacks in the north of Sangin, and his speech had a much harder edge. A huge man with the largest beard in the room, he berated the elders for allowing IEDs to be laid. He told them they had to stop this happening. He looked threateningly around the room as he concluded that, if the attacks continued, those present would all be held responsible.

266

The elders shook their heads in concern, but many shrugged as if to say, 'We can do nothing.'

Carver took the floor. He spoke in English, pausing frequently for the interpreter to translate his words to the gathering. Carver had wanted to demonstrate to the shura the work that his men had been doing to improve life for the people of Sangin and the surrounding area. The elders had often been briefed on the various reconstruction projects, but most hadn't seen them. And they were frequently told by the Taliban propaganda machinery that no progress was being made and the British were doing nothing to help them. In a town without newspapers, and with such low literacy levels, the people understandably didn't know what to believe.

Carver had managed to get a projector into Sangin. In normal circumstances an unremarkable achievement, but this had taken considerable effort against the vagaries of the military supply chain. His words were accompanied by Powerpoint pictures thrown up on the wall behind him, showing the Jusulay irrigation project, electricity pylons being repaired and work on schools. The audience was enthralled. Most hadn't seen any of this before, and few had ever seen projected images of any kind. As Carver went through the presentation the excitement grew, especially when the pictures showed people and places they recognized.

Then Carver flashed up a photograph showing the devastation in the market place a few days earlier. 'And this is what the Taliban are doing. They are attacking you. They don't want you to have a market. They don't want you to have the prosperity that the market brings you. They want to destroy your market.'

He threw up more gruesome photographs, of the wrecked phone-card cart, the destroyed police vehicle, of wounded and panicking locals, and finally, the remains of the dead twelve-year-old boy.

'You have seen everything that we are doing. It is all taking you forward, to greater security and prosperity. But this is where the Taliban want to take you. They want to take you back. Back to the time before May when there was no market. They have even stooped to using a child to destroy your market, killing this young twelve-year-old boy in the process.'

The elders were shocked. They were muttering and tutting loudly and shaking their heads vigorously at the visual evidence of what the Taliban had done in their town.

Carver continued, 'If my words and these pictures are not enough to convince you, then listen to one of your own people. He was there. He saw the whole thing happening.'

The eyewitness that Gardner had found after the attack stood up and told his story. He was clearly nervous, both at speaking to such a distinguished audience and because he knew the dangers of a simple man like himself speaking publicly against the Taliban. The elders were visibly shocked and impressed by the grisly description he gave.

When the man had finished Carver concluded. 'So what can you do to help stop these atrocities and to prevent the Taliban taking away your market? He paused, then continued, 'You can spread the word about what happened last Saturday morning, what you have now seen with your own eyes, and what you have heard from this brave man who witnessed the terrible bombing. Tell your families and your friends and neighbours and your colleagues and your communities the truth. Because, as you know, the Taliban are spreading the word in the town that it was our soldiers who killed the boy. You can see that it was not and you have heard from our friend here that it was not. And please tell your people to tell us if they see or hear anything about attacks being planned. If we know about them in advance, we can try to stop them and prevent more of your people dying unnecessarily. This is most important. If we are to protect you and your people, we must have this information, we must know who is plotting to kill you, and how, when and where they are trying to do it. It is only by your people and my soldiers standing together, shoulder to shoulder, that we can prevail over the Taliban.'

8

The Sangin DC hotline number, used for passing information on Taliban and other criminal activity, was publicized at every opportunity and had become well known to the locals. Before the 12 July shura, however, the battalion received only about one call a week on the line. After the shura, with Carver's powerful message to the elders, the number of calls went up dramatically, to an average of four or five a day. And the number of people prepared to come to the base in person to pass on what they knew also increased significantly.

While much was just gossip, misunderstanding or even mischief-making, some turned out to be useful information that helped Coleman and the A Company intelligence staff build up a clearer picture of what the enemy was doing and planning. Carver's well-timed message had hit the target.

One evening Coleman took a call from an unknown number on the Sangin DC hotline. In his rudimentary Pashtu, Coleman said hello and asked the caller to wait. He handed the phone to Ahmad, the interpreter. 'Captain Coleman, this person is called Salaam. He is a taxi driver in Sangin and he wants to come and tell you some important things tonight. He would like to meet you at the back gate at eleven o'clock.'

Two hours' time. Coleman agreed. A night-time meeting at the south gate to the DC would be risky. Obviously Salaam knew enough about the base to realize that it was unlikely anyone would see him coming in that way, especially under cover of darkness. But a set-up was also a possibility.

Just before eleven, Coleman strapped on his Browning pistol, went and found Shah, then spoke to Biddick. 'Dom, I'm going to meet someone at the south gate. Could you let the guard know a lone man will be approaching shortly from the town – don't shoot him. But let me know if there is more than one person or they see anyone following or shadowing him. And can I borrow one of your guys to come out there with me?'

As he approached the darkness of the south gate, Coleman looked up and waved at the sangar sentry whose job was to scan the area for approaching enemy. With Ahmad and the A Company escort, Coleman walked through the gate and out on to the dirt track that ran along the side of the canal beyond. Visibility was virtually nil, with hardly any ambient light from the base or the town.

Coleman couldn't help feeling slightly apprehensive. He pulled back the slide on his Browning pistol, chambering a round, and then returned the weapon to its holster. Fifty metres away was a line of razor wire that ran across the canal, and 100 metres beyond that the woodline where Corporal Bryan Budd VC from the 3rd Battalion The Parachute Regiment had been killed a year earlier in a firefight with the Taliban while on a routine patrol around the base. Coleman fingered his pistol, while at the same time realizing that it wouldn't be much use to him if he was about to be the victim of a pre-planned set-up. He hoped Biddick's escort was on the ball and at least a half-decent shot by night.

From the south, Coleman heard footsteps, moving slowly towards him. He could see nothing. He pulled out his weapon and pointed it towards the noise, finger on the trigger, thumb on the safety. Seconds later a figure emerged from the darkness, just a few feet away. 'I am Salaam,' he said, using faltering English.

With the escort close by, Coleman walked over to him, switched his pistol into his left hand, and shook the man's hand. He may be Salaam, he thought, but is he really here just to talk? Coleman searched the man, with the escort covering. It would not have been the first time someone had attempted to bring a bomb into a British base in Afghanistan.

He was clean, and without delay Coleman led him through the gate and into a small shed just inside the perimeter fence. He thanked the escort and sent him back to his duties. They sat down at a small wooden table. Salaam was tall and very thin, with a dark-coloured kurta and the standard black beard. He was a shy man and was clearly trying desperately to hide his nervousness at coming to the base. There was no question that in coming here he was taking a big personal risk. He could easily be killed for his trouble.

Salaam accepted a can of Coke and then, through the interpreter, Coleman asked him what he had to say.

Using Coleman's interpreter, the man rambled for about five minutes, saying there were some very bad people in Sangin who wanted to kill all the British and the Americans and were trying to turn the locals against them.

Tell me something I don't know, thought Coleman, as Salaam went on and on. *Well this is obviously going to be another waste of time, but at least he's prepared to come in and talk, so I suppose that's something.*

Salaam mentioned two local Taliban leaders, and Coleman's ears pricked up. He knew about them from other intelligence. He knew how deeply involved the two were – this wouldn't be common knowledge; at least the man must know something. Salaam continued on with more generalizations for several minutes, with Coleman making a few notes. But nothing new, nothing earth-shattering, nothing of real value. As he had expected.

Then Salaam said, 'And Haji Bowadin is going to attack you with rockets tomorrow.'

Coleman sat up sharply in his chair. He had heard of Haji Bowadin. A known Taliban leader, his name had come up in reports about mortaring

FOB Robinson, to the south of Sangin. He asked Salaam, 'Do you know when and where he's going to attack from?'

'I know these things, yes.'

Coleman had brought in some air photos and maps of the Sangin area in case he needed them. He spread a large-scale air photo on the table, showing most of the upper Sangin valley.

Salaam turned the map round on the table and started moving his hand across it, pointing at various features, apparently trying to pin-point exactly where the attack was coming from. This went on for some time before Coleman realized the man had no idea what he was looking for, or even what the map represented. He said, 'Salaam, do you know whether the attack will come from the north or the south?'

The response confirmed that the man had no concept of the points of the compass any more than he had about reading a map. *And why should he?* Coleman reflected. *He's a taxi driver, not a soldier or policeman.*

He got the man to describe the area Bowadin would attack from, and by deduction pinned it down to a place 6 to 8 kilometres north of Sangin in the Musa Qalah wadi. This was slightly odd, as Bowadin was normally thought to operate in the south, and this would be out of area for him. But still possible, and Salaam seemed pretty certain.

Coleman hadn't been to the Musa Qalah wadi. It was still very much bandit country, and the battalion hadn't yet attempted to clear it of enemy. The Taliban effectively had free run, so it would make sense for them to launch an attack from there.

But Coleman had studied the northern section closely and knew a lot about it. After a good half hour of painstaking questioning and check-ing his maps and air photos, he managed to pin down the attack posi-tion to a single compound, near a village, next to a river. His confidence increased when Salaam told him that just across the river was a large clearing in a wooded area. The air photo showed the feature Salaam was describing, in just the right place.

Now the question was: when? Salaam had said tomorrow, and he was now saying tomorrow afternoon. *What does that mean?* Coleman won-dered. *The Afghans usually go to sleep in what we call the afternoon, and when they get up it's the evening.* Coleman asked whether it was going to be before or after lunch. Salaam said it would be about lunchtime.

That means about 1300 or 1400 hours. Not precise enough.

Coleman was already thinking of trying to launch an air strike against Bowadin and his rocket team, and to get that he would need an exact time. He decided to go for 1330 hours. Pretty much a guess, but he couldn't do any better.

Then Salaam remembered that Bowadin's plan was to mortar the base while the shura was running, to kill those in the base, including people attending the shura, and also to scare the elders and discourage them from coming to future meetings at the DC. Well, 1330 would certainly fit the shura timings. He hoped.

So now he knew where, or he thought he knew where. And he knew when, or at least he had an idea of roughly when. So what was actually going to happen? Salaam had said a rocket attack. What did he mean by that?

'Do these rockets go along through the air, or do they go up and then down?'

'They go up and down.'

Coleman figured out it must be mortars. Mortars would fit with what Bowadin had been involved in before. Good. Looking at the range, at least 8 kilometres, it had to be a heavy 120mm mortar – an 82mm would never travel that far.

Salaam told him that with Bowadin there would be four other fighters to carry the mortar barrel and the bombs and to fire them at the base. The target was definitely Sangin DC.

Now Coleman had the full picture – when, where, how, who, what. At least he hoped he had. Much of this was speculation and deduction. And it was all based on uncorroborated information from a man about whom he knew virtually nothing.

Coleman escorted Salaam back to the place they had met a couple of hours earlier, outside the south gate. Then he went to find the CO. Although it was well after midnight, Carver was sitting in the smoking area next to the ops room, puffing on a Pine Light and working on a tedious-looking document. Several soldiers were sitting around smoking, so Coleman took Carver out of earshot. It was essential that as few people as possible knew about this, first to protect Salaam, and second because it was a military practice never to discuss future operations with anyone who doesn't need to know – and Coleman definitely had a future operation in mind to deal with Bowadin and his mortar team.

As he led the CO to a quiet spot, Coleman felt the pressure building on him. In reality he had only the sketchiest information, and absolutely nothing solid. He was going to ask the CO to authorize the use of scarce air assets that might be urgently needed on some life-or-death task elsewhere. And if his calculations were wrong, or if he failed to convince Carver to back him, there was always the very real risk that the mortar attack would go ahead, perhaps killing several Royal Anglian soldiers, and perhaps Afghan military, police and civilians in and around the base.

With all the confidence he could muster, Coleman took Carver through the picture he had pieced together. Carver said, 'Tom, we've had loads of this sort of stuff before, and how often has it come to anything? Why should we put our money on this one?'

'Of course we can't be certain, sir. But this guy did tell me some stuff about the local Taliban that I already know to be true. He's obviously in the know, to some extent at least. And we have virtually never before had time, place and type of attack all together. We can't pass up this opportunity. We have a complete target picture.'

Carver said, 'Yes, but maybe he's misheard something, overheard the wrong thing, or maybe someone was just bragging about something that's not going to happen.'

Coleman paused and thought for a moment. Then he said, 'All true, Colonel, but I just have a gut feeling that this guy is right. A lot of it adds up, it makes sense. Trust me.'

Carver thought for a moment, then said, 'OK. Go for it. See if Jamie can get you some air.'

Coleman woke up Captain Jamie Lindsell, the CO's JTAC. Within fifteen minutes Lindsell confirmed that a pair of American F15 Eagles would be allocated to the task. He had booked them to be on station for initial reconnaissance by midday. About ten hours away.

Coleman went to bed, but had difficulty sleeping as he pondered all the holes in his intelligence. He had been open with the CO, but had he given the impression of being too certain about his facts? The timings in particular could be way off. Had Salaam misunderstood something he had overheard? He could well have done. Had he made the worst error that an IO could make and exaggerated the strength of the information he had gained to suit his own mindset or false expectation? He hoped he had not. He had effectively staked his reputation on this intelligence.

9

Coleman's plan was to use the F15s to strike the mortar team the minute it could be identified. He first wanted the aircraft to look into the area, using camera pods, to confirm that the terrain was as he thought, and that it was at least feasible that the mortar position could be as shown on his map. Then he wanted the aircraft to scan the general area to try to identify the Taliban as they were moving into position. All the while the planes would be standing off at a height and a distance so as not to spook the Taliban – they would not be able to either see or hear the F15s.

Lindsell, the JTAC, set up the camera downlink terminal in the Sangin DC courtyard, near the monument to British troops killed in the town. Coleman looked at the brass cross, made of 30mm cartridge cases, and hoped there would be no more names to add to its roll of honour as a result of today's activities.

The terminal needed line of sight to the aircraft so had to be positioned outside. The cylindrical pod that received the signal from the camera sat on top of the courtyard wall. This was connected to a rectangular decoder box, also on the wall but covered with a plastic sheet to protect it from the sun. In turn the decoder was linked by a wire connector to a laptop, which was on the ground in the shade of a cam-net.

Coleman and Carver squinted into the laptop monitor as the sometimes fuzzy, sometimes sharp colour picture came and went. Coleman followed the movements of the camera, marking off areas on his map. Lindsell was talking on his radio handset to the pilot, getting him to check into likely sectors the enemy might move through, and receiving information for Coleman about the picture on the ground.

Everybody in the base had been warned about a possible mortar attack. Those who could be were behind hard cover, and the remainder were wearing helmets and body armour as they went about their duties.

1330 hours came and went. The aircraft had not identified any suspicious activity in the area. Absolutely no sign of any Taliban in an attack position or moving towards one. Nothing. Ten minutes later Carver

274

looked at his watch again and then at Coleman. Coleman pretended not to notice his glances and just kept staring at the screen.

Oh well, it was worth a shot, he thought. *I'll just have to put up with the ragging I will definitely get from the officers who know about this – and one thing is certain in this battalion – every officer will know all about it within a day or so. And I won't ask the CO to trust me again.*

Seconds later the ground in and around the DC shook with the tremors of a massive explosion. A 120mm mortar round had impacted in the shingle bank of the river 400 metres north of the DC.

At that moment the downlink monitor crashed and the screen went blank. *Inevitable,* thought Coleman, *absolutely inevitable.*

Out in the desert the Taliban fighter sat on his motorbike, looking across the north side of Sangin. He spoke calmly into his radio, in Pashtu. 'Direction is good, direction is good. Distance increase two hundred metres. Increase two hundred metres.'

He watched the next round explode seconds later, closer to the base but still falling short. 'Distance increase another two hundred metres, two hundred.'

The third round landed short too. 'Increase one hundred, one hundred increase. Now it should hit.'

Eight thousand metres away, Bowadin relayed the instructions to the fighter just in front of the mortar tube, his hand on the sight. The second the fighter made his final adjustment there was a loud whoosh, and they were all hurled off their feet by a massive, violent, deafening blast, followed immediately by a second.

Bowadin struggled to his feet, dazed. He could barely stand, blood trickled down from his ears, and there was a gaping wound in his arm. He looked around. All but one of his men were dead, cut to ribbons. As he made his way towards the dislodged mortar barrel, the survivor stood up. Bowadin shouted, 'Brother, we are finished, we are dead. Let us try to fire, let us try to kill some of them before we die.'

They picked up the heavy mortar barrel and set it back on its baseplate and tripod, pointing it again in the direction of Sangin. Bowadin grasped a shell and dropped it into the barrel. It was the last thing he ever did. The bomb exploded inside the damaged mortar, killing both of the surviving fighters.

Moments later their remains, and the 120mm mortar, were obliterated as two further massive explosions engulfed them.

Coleman was staring at the blank computer screen. Despite the three mortar bombs creeping closer and closer to the base, he, Carver and Lindsell had not moved from their position beside the downlink monitor. Movement in the DC had frozen. Everyone else had taken cover.

Lindsell was speaking urgently but calmly into his handset. Then he held it away from his ear. Turning to Coleman and Carver he said, 'One times Taliban one hundred and twenty millimetre mortar and five times enemy fighters identified by the Dude callsign. The Dude has dropped four five-hundred-pound bombs. He reports all targets destroyed.'

The locals in Sangin continued to provide valuable intelligence to the Royal Anglians, right through to the end of the tour, symbolizing a changed attitude towards the troops. The Taliban's plan to use a twelve-year-old boy to attack the police and the market had backfired, and this represented a significant turning point in the level of consent for the activities of British troops in the town.

29. Lieutenat Colonel Stuart Carver, Royal Anglian Battle Group commander, in Sangin bazaar

30. A Company Group HQ in the Sangin DC. On the roof is a sangar covered by a camouflage net. The sangar was used for observation and also had machine-guns and other weapon systems.

31. Lance Corporal Kisby, left and Private Symonds of A Company treat a wounded local in Sangin DC.

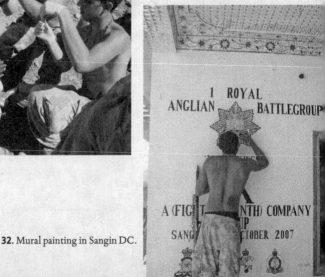

32. Mural painting in Sangin DC.

33. Remains of phonecard cart used by the Taliban to kill Afghan police in Sangin. The explosion also killed a ten-year-old boy who had been told to push the cart into position. Sergeant Tiger Gardner deployed on to the ground as part of the immediate response.

34. A Company air assault. A CH47 Chinook, used in Afghanistan for troop a cargo lift and CASEVA

35. A Company air assault.

36. C Company troops' accommodation at FOB Inkerman. Corporal Bomber Brown seated second from left, Sergeant Spud Armon standing with a brew.

37. Fire Support Group Delta in FOB Inkerman, one of their WMIKS in the background. On the right is Lance Corporal Alex Hawkins, who was later killed in a mine attack on his Vector. Second from left is Private Harry McCabe, who dragged Hawkins from the wrecked vehicle and gave immediate first aid. On the left is Private Peter Howell, who was in the Inkerman FSG tower during the attack which Captain Hicks was killed.

38. A section from 11 Platoon C Company prepare to move during a patrol near FOB Inkerman. Second man Minimi gunner Private Ray Rawson, who was killed in a vicious firefight with the Taliban shortly after this photograph was taken.

39. Private Rawson, centre, with his fire team, taking five minutes out during a long patrol near FOB Inkerman. On the left is platoon sharpshooter Private Vaughan with his L96 sniper rifle.

40. Captain David Hicks MC, acting company commander of C Company at Inkerman. Hicks was subsequently killed during a violent attack against the FOB on 11 August.

41. Royal Anglian 81mm mortar team fire mission. The mortars provided the only guaranteed, immediate indirect support to the battle group wherever they went.

42. Royal Artillery 105mm Light Gun firing in support of the Royal Anglian Battle Group.

43. 105mm Light Gun detachment firing from FOB Robinson. The guns were based in Robinson but also frequently deployed into the desert to support battle group operations.

44. Lance Corporal Tom Mann observes through his sniper scope. To his right, an Afghan interpreter monitors a radio scanner to intercept Taliban communications.

45. Troops sort out their kit in a break during a Mastiff patrol.

46. Lance Corporal Tom Mann and Private Dan Gent, battalion snipers, prepare to engage a Taliban command team near FOB Inkerman. The irrigation ditch allowed them to move undetected close to the Taliban fighters.

47. Private Robert Foster, B Company, taking time out in a compound during an operation. Foster would later be tragically killed in an airstrike at Mazdurak.

48. Private Booth and Private Foster, right, at the back of a Viking.

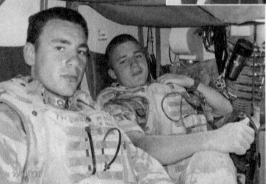

49. Privates Aaron McLure, left, and Lee in the back of a Viking. McLure killed and Lee wounded in an airstrike Mazdurak.

50. Private John Thrumble and his beloved machine-gun, 'Mary'. Thrumble was also killed at Mazdurak.

51. Privates Josh Lee, left, and John Thrumble, centre, and Corporal Stuart Parker. Parker and his section saw some of the battle group's most intensive fighting, and he was later seriously wounded.

19/05/2007

2. Private Josh Lee, left, and Private Rich Barke at the field hospital in Camp Bastion following the airstrike at Mazdurak. Lee was later CASEVACed to Selly Oak Hospital with his section commander, Corporal Stuart Parker.

53. B Company section in contact with the Taliban at Kajaki. The red and yellow 'Minden Flash', worn by members of the Royal Anglian 1st talion, dates back to a recognition badge used in World War II

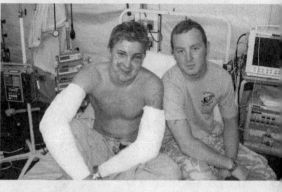

54. Personal equipment laid out on a camp bed ready for packing prior to Operation Palk Ghar. Note the yellow hand-held GPS navigation system, five dark-green high-explosive 51mm mortar bombs and one light-green smoke bomb, and the Bowman secure radio at the far end of the bed.

55. A Company night foot insertion from Sangin to the line of departure for Operation Palk Ghar.

56. Firing UGL rifle 40mm grenade

57. C Company Viking resupply at the end of Operation Palk Ghar day one.

58. Royal Anglian Sniper Platoon, Operation Palk La Back row, third fro right is Private Oli Bailey, fourth fron right Private Clay Donnachie. Front second from left is Lance Corporal T Mann and second right Lance Corpe Teddy Ruecker.

The Battle of Inkerman: 17 July–16 August 2007

Towards the end of July, Lieutenant Colonel Carver decided to move B Company out of Inkerman to replace C Company at COP Zeebrugge in Kajaki. B Company's tour so far had been very tough. While it would be just as busy for them in Kajaki, and the fighting would be hard, Carver felt that they would benefit from the more settled routine that was possible there. C Company were to move south. 9 Platoon, under Lieutenant Tom Clarke, would occupy the base at Nowzad together with the company's fire support group, FSG Charlie. Company Headquarters along with 10 Platoon, under Lieutenant Sam Perrin, and 11 Platoon, under Lieutenant Hermanus Olivier, would replace B Company at Inkerman. Meanwhile A Company were to remain based at Sangin DC, where they were establishing effective relationships with the local people and community leaders.

Carver briefed Major Messenger, C Company commander, on the situation at Inkerman. He told him that there had been a total lack of any Taliban activity in the area since Operation Ghartse Ghar had ended and that he was surprised there hadn't been an attack on Inkerman yet.

FOB Inkerman had been occupied by the ANA up until the later stages of Operation Ghartse Ghar, the epic march of A and B Companies through the Green Zone. B Company had moved into the FOB straight after Ghartse Ghar, two weeks earlier, and had set about patrolling the surrounding area to maintain long-term dominance north-east of Sangin in an effort to reduce the Taliban's ability to attack the town's community and security forces.

The bases constructed by the Royal Engineers at the end of the Royal Anglian Battle Group's first major battle, Operation Silicon, had become a massive thorn in the Taliban's flesh, disrupting their attempts to continue an attack campaign against the town of Gereshk. The Taliban had commenced a series of attacks against the bases, which suited

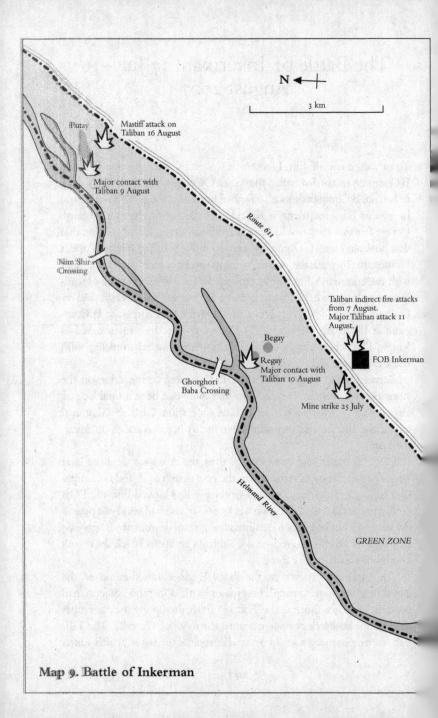

N

3 km

Putay

Mastiff attack on
Taliban 16 August

Major contact with
Taliban 9 August

Route 611

Nim Shir
Crossing

Taliban indirect fire attacks
from 7 August.
Major Taliban attack 11
August.

FOB Inkerman

Begay

Regay
Major contact with
Taliban 10 August

Ghorghori
Baba Crossing

Mine strike 25 July

Helmand River

GREEN ZONE

Map 9. Battle of Inkerman

Brigadier Lorimer, the commander of Task Force Helmand, whose objective was to keep the enemy away from Gereshk to allow reconstruction and increasing prosperity.

There had been a similar experience after Operation Lastay Kulang, which ended with the establishment of FOB Fox. Angered at the effect Fox had on their freedom of manoeuvre, the Taliban had launched attack after attack against the base, one of which killed two soldiers from the Estonian armoured infantry company that was grouped with the Royal Anglians. Carver had expected a similar reaction at Inkerman, but the FOB had received no attention at all from the Taliban. He knew they would not simply accept this permanent challenge to their own heartland.

Carver reckoned the Taliban were reeling after Kulang and Ghartse Ghar. The survivors would be up at Musa Qalah, licking their wounds. They would obviously need to get hold of some weapons and ammo to replace what they had lost, but that wouldn't be a problem or take very long. Their biggest challenge would be replacing the men who had been killed or wounded. They would have to bring in fighters from Pakistan, especially to replace the leaders who had been taken out. Carver did not know how long that might take, but he told Messenger they must assume that the Taliban could be poised to attack Inkerman, or C Company's patrols in the area, at any time.

The B and C Company moves between Kajaki, Nowzad and Inkerman were completed between 17 and 20 July.

C Company had been fighting the Taliban almost every day in Kajaki, in their efforts to keep the insurgents away from the vital hydroelectricity installation which was destined to supply power to the whole of Helmand and much of Kandahar province. They had inflicted heavy losses on the Taliban and pushed them further and further back, denying them their goal of disrupting the development of the energy project.

C Company had seized the initiative as soon as they arrived at Kajaki on 3 April and they had held on to it, dictating the terms of engagement to the Taliban and using overwhelming air power to back up their constant offensive against the enemy strongholds. None of their men had been killed during the fighting, although Corporal Lee Gayler had been shot soon after they arrived, Private Matt Woollard had lost his leg on a landmine and five soldiers had been wounded during a ferocious raid against the Taliban stronghold of Mazdurak.

Despite their almost daily battles fought over rugged terrain and in unbearable heat, C Company had always considered themselves fortunate in being based at COP Zeebrugge. Every soldier compared it favourably with the run-down accommodation they occupied back at their base in Elizabeth Barracks, Pirbright. It was far from luxurious, but Zeebrugge was a purpose-built camp, with stone accommodation blocks, air conditioning, a cook-house and showers. There was also the welcome opportunity to cool off in the reservoir after sweating their way back from a battle. It was therefore with horror that the men of C Company eyed up their new home at Inkerman when the dust cleared after they ran off the tail-gate of the Royal Air Force CH47 Chinook that had brought them the 25 kilometres from Kajaki.

2

Inkerman was a large Afghan farming compound, built on a desert hillside beside Route 611, which runs through Sangin and up to Kajaki. A resident ANA platoon occupied the section of Inkerman that fronted on to the 611 and they manned a permanent vehicle checkpoint on the road. To the west, beyond the highway, was a poppy field, now harvested. Across the 200-metre stretch of baked earth and dried-out poppy stalks was the jungle-like Green Zone. To the east the desert rose up, overlooking Inkerman, and in the far distance there was a mountain range, about 10 kilometres away.

The FOB was surrounded by high walls of baked mud, broken down in places by shelling. Inkerman was 150 metres by 150 metres, a bleak, open dust-bowl, and the troops' living quarters consisted of a camp-bed under camouflaged nylon sheets stretched across to stakes in the ground by elastic bungees or string. Known as a 'basha', this was a familiar arrangement for the infantry and was used to provide patrol shelters in woods, forests and jungles the world over.

An extra layer of protection from the sun was provided by large camouflage nets suspended from the compound walls, about 3 metres off the ground. These also provided a shaded area to sit about preparing equipment, cooking, eating or just chewing the fat. In the rare moments they had any time off some soldiers sat under the cam-nets playing battle games on their hand-held Nintendos and PlayStations; others read war books or novels sent out from home.

There were only improvised showers and there was no cook-house. Everybody had to prepare their own food from compo ration packs, either cold or heated by half an hour of exposure to the sun or a burner. What there was, though, was dust, and plenty of it. The fine grains of dust and sand got everywhere – into clothing, boots, weapons, sleeping bags, hair, food, everything. That was when there wasn't any wind. When there was it got into everything and a lot more besides. And of course there was the heat, the almost undendurable 50 degrees by day that barely seemed to diminish at night, when the troops would lie sweating on their camp-beds, often unable to sleep for long despite their almost constant state of exhaustion.

Of course, C Company, like all Royal Anglians, were used to working, living, training and fighting in such harsh conditions. It was part of the deal of being an infantry soldier, and they would very soon get used to their new home. They had been fighting hard at Kajaki, and so far had experienced more frequent and intensive contacts than the other companies. But the one advantage they had was the austere yet comparatively comfortable conditions of COP Zeebrugge, with its purpose-built barracks. The change in C Company's domestic circumstances was an inevitable source of amusement for the men of Fire Support Group Delta, commanded by Captain Ollie Ormiston, who had now been at Inkerman for two weeks. With C Company's own FSG based at Nowzad alongside 9 Platoon, FSG Delta would initially be supporting Messenger's troops at Inkerman.

The fact that many of the FSG soldiers were good friends with the lads in C Company increased the warmth of C Company's welcome as they were greeted with endless comments like, 'Hope this won't be too rough for you after your vacation at Club Zeebrugge,' and 'Just keep walking that way, mate, the outdoor pool is up on the left, just the other side of that cam-net.'

The worst ragging was reserved for Corporal Matthew Willan, one of the section commanders in 11 Platoon. Willan had joined C Company after they deployed to Afghanistan, and had previously been in the Royal Anglians' Drums Platoon. The Drums Platoon, dual-roled as machine-gunners, is a part of D Company, which is the parent company of the FSG members, so most of Willan's close mates in the battalion were in the FSGs – including FSG Delta.

'All right, Matty, shall I carry your Bergen up to your apartment, the bed's already made for you,' shouted one wit.

'See you in the bar for a pina colada – that's what you lads drink up at Kajaki, isn't it?' said another.

After he had dumped his gear, set up his basha and checked on his men, Willan went to see who he could find from the FSG. The first person he bumped into was one of his best mates, Lance Corporal Alex Hawkins, 'Stephen, mate, how are you? Haven't seen you for months.' Willan always called Hawkins 'Stephen', after Professor Stephen Hawking.

Even though they hadn't seen each other in ages, there was little outward emotion in their greeting. Both were quiet, deliberately spoken men from rural Norfolk: easy going and understated in their day-to-day lives; but when they needed to flick the switch, they would turn instantly into fiery, hard and aggressive fighters. Both had demonstrated these attributes back home when their mates were in trouble in the pubs and clubs of Woking, Guildford or Norwich; and they had done so on a rather more serious level during numerous firefights in Helmand.

The two men had joined the Army and the battalion at about the same time. As boys they were even Army Cadets together, and attended the same training camps, but had not known each other well. The two were very keen on maintaining the highest standards of physical fitness and back in Pirbright had often worked out together in the gym. They had also been students on the same Potential NCOs' Cadre in Pirbright. The NCOs' Cadre is a critical step for a soldier with aspirations to climb the promotion ladder in the battalion. It is an old adage that the rank of Lance Corporal is the most difficult to gain and the easiest to lose. They were both in agreement on the first part of this saying. The NCOs' Cadre had been a testing six weeks, and the two had helped each other not only to pass, but to excel, by giving mutual encouragement during the arduous endurance battle tests, and helping each other revise before the important practical and written examinations.

'How was Kajaki then, Matty?'

'Good. We had our moments. Attacking the Taliban most days. We pushed their FLET back a fair way. I got quite a few rounds down myself. Blokes did brilliantly. All of them. And before you say anything, Steve, yes. Zeebrugge was like a five-star hotel.'

'Bollocks, I was up there myself for a bit. The camp wasn't that great. A lot better than this, though, I must admit. But you lot were always on the go, never stopped from what I could see. I reckon the time I spent up in Kajaki was about the busiest of the tour. That was my first kill, up at Kajaki.'

Hawkins was a battalion sniper. After returning from the Iraq tour in 2005, he had volunteered for the sniper course. It was a tough course to pass, but Hawkins succeeded and in 2006 was awarded the coveted sniper badge.

The two continued to chat under the red-hot sun, both pouring sweat even though Hawkins was clad only in running shorts and trainers – plus a thick layer of the ubiquitous Inkerman dust, broken up by rivulets of sweat. The conversation, as always, turned to home and to love life. Willan's girlfriend was looking forward to qualifying at the end of her midwifery training at Barts Hospital in London. Hawkins updated Willan on his plans to marry his girlfriend, Louise, after the tour. He told Willan how he was trying to figure out whether marriage and his aspirations to undergo selection for the SAS would be compatible. As devoted as Hawkins was to the idea of joining the SAS, Willan knew him well enough to realize that, if both could not be achieved, it was going to be Louise who came out on top.

3

C Company's first week at Inkerman was uneventful. The platoons patrolled each day, getting to know the area and learning the pattern of life. One major difference from Kajaki was that there was actually a civilian population here – the whole area around Kajaki was empty of civilians, with all the villages and compounds deserted except for Taliban.

The troops were surprised at the lack of enemy activity after all the stories that had filtered through to them in Kajaki. They had heard about the vicious and high-tempo fighting in this area with A and B Companies. But they welcomed a bit of a break – it was an opportunity to draw breath after the frenetic time they had spent at Kajaki. Some of them joked that the enemy had pursued B Company up to Zeebrugge.

Early on 24 July, Messenger received a secure email from Captain Phil Moxey, the battle group operations officer, based at Bastion. The message told him that, according to intelligence, Taliban fighters were going to be moving down the river on the west side from the north, crossing, and then heading south to Sangin.

Carver and his staff in battle group HQ had been watching for signs of a counter-attack by the Taliban after they were driven out by Operation Ghartse Ghar. They had been surprised nothing had happened yet and were wondering whether this intelligence indicated the start of a reinfiltration, which could signal renewed attacks against Sangin and perhaps against Inkerman. Was this the start of the Taliban fightback, which was as certain to come as night was to follow day?

Moxey requested that Messenger get eyes on to the crossing point, attempt to confirm whether the enemy were trying to move across the river, and if so to interdict them.

The crossing area could not be observed from Inkerman, and Messenger needed troops close by in any case. He could call in air strikes, but at night he preferred to have direct, close-up visibility, and a capability to react immediately. As the intelligence contained no detail on likely timings, he decided to move a force to the crossing area as quickly as possible to get the best chance of intercepting the enemy fighters.

Messenger quickly made a plan. Leaving the ANA platoon to guard the FOB and the FSG in reserve, 10 and 11 Platoons and Company Tac would deploy, establish observation on to the crossing point and be prepared to react if enemy were identified.

The company patrolled out of Inkerman in the late-morning heat. After patrolling for two and a half hours through the grass and the maize fields, using irrigation ditches and treelines for cover, the troops arrived, sweating, tired and covered in dust, in the area of northern Jusulay, 500 metres from the crossing. Deep in the Green Zone, they took up overwatch positions in two compounds at a bend in the river. From rooftop positions, 10 and 11 Platoons watched a kilometre length of the river and saw nothing suspicious during the afternoon. This looked like another uneventful patrol.

Around dusk, Sergeant Major Taylor arrived in a column of Vikings with a resupply of water and rations. Ormiston had accompanied the sergeant major in two FSG WMIKs and a Vector. They had brought a two-man surveillance team with Javelin command launch units.

The CLU was the most powerful piece of observation equipment Messenger had available. The size of a portable TV and weighing 6.4 kilograms, the CLU was held with two handles and contained a thermal imager capable of turning night into day. Its optics had x4 and x9 magnification. Normally used for guiding a Javelin missile, for this task Messenger required the CLUs only for surveillance.

The CLU teams were deployed to the platoon observation posts. The company sergeant major and his Vikings headed back to Inkerman, and Ormiston's FSG vehicles moved out of the compounds to provide rear protection for the company.

Later that night, Corporal Willan moved back to the FSG position to collect some new batteries for the CLU that was deployed with his platoon. In the dark he could make out the figure of Lance Corporal Hawkins sitting on the ground beside his Vector, eating from a ration bag. Willan squatted beside him. 'How's it going, Steve?'

'Pretty boring. Anything happening up front?'

'No, not a thing. I reckon this is another wild goose chase. Doubt we'll be seeing anyone tonight. But you never know.'

Wishing his friend a good night, he moved round to the back of the vehicle, collected the batteries and returned to his rooftop observation post, sweating from the exertions of his 200-metre round trip in the night-time heat.

Later, Willan's CLU operator showed him four black dots in his eyepiece. Four figures, heading down the hill towards the river. He roused the platoon commander and told him, but no weapons could be identified, so it was impossible to know whether these were Taliban or local farmers. Willan continued to monitor their movement until they disappeared from sight.

No other activity was identified during the night, and at first light the men packed their equipment into daysacks. The CLU teams returned to Ormiston's vehicles, and the FSG headed back along the Jusulay track, which weaved its way across fragile mud bridges over the network of irrigation canals and ditches up to Inkerman.

Messenger led the company in the opposite direction, intending to patrol down the river and beyond the crossing before eventually working their way back during the morning to Inkerman.

The men had been walking for ten minutes when a huge, echoing boom rang through the valley, making them hurl themselves to the ground to get cover from what they thought must be a mortar or rocket attack.

There were no further blasts. Messenger looked back in the direction of the explosion. A huge black smoke plume was rising above the eerie quiet of the Green Zone. He knew instantly that the smoke was coming from the area of the Jusulay track – at just about the spot the FSG vehicles would by now have reached.

Messenger leapt to his feet. He took a deep breath and yelled into his radio, 'Two Zero Alpha and Three Zero Alpha, this is Zero Alpha. Move towards the explosion.

'All callsigns, move as fast as you can.'

He shouted to the men of his Tac HQ, still lying on the ground, 'On your feet and follow me! Let's go!'

As he ran he yelled into his radio mike, telling Captain Dave Hicks, the company 2IC back at Inkerman, to be aware of possible casualties and to start to stand up assets back at Bastion.

4

Fifteen hundred metres away, Private Harrison McCabe had been battered against the sides of the Vector as it was forced upwards by the explosion. Shocked, disoriented and deafened, he didn't know what was happening. The Vector's top hatch had been forced open by the blast. McCabe managed to stand up and shove his head out of the hatch to see what was going on. But the vehicle was engulfed in black smoke, which was now filling up the rear compartment where McCabe stood.

He could see nothing, but he could hear Private Patrick Henning's screams. He pushed open the back door, jumped out and ran round to the front, through the thick smoke and the acrid smell of burning. With him was Private Michael Smith, clutching his cracked ribs. Henning was still sitting in the driver's seat, hands bleeding, engulfed in smoke, screaming, 'Where's Alex? Where's Alex?'

McCabe looked into the commander's seat, where Lance Corporal Alex Hawkins had been sitting. He was not there. They dragged Henning out of the vehicle and then ran round to the other side to look for Hawkins.

He was lying splayed out through the door, feet still in the foot well and his head under the chassis. McCabe and Smith pulled him clear and carried him away from the immediate danger of the smoking vehicle. Shaking and dazed himself, McCabe started to check Hawkins over. He looked bad. Blood was coming out of his mouth and nose, there was a bad wound to his neck, and his legs were bleeding. His jaw was swollen and looked broken. He was unconscious.

McCabe and Smith put him into the three-quarters prone position. Drummer Jonathan Cucciniello and Lance Corporal John King, from the WMIK in front, raced back to help. McCabe put his fingers into Hawkins's mouth to make sure his airway was clear then put his ear to his mouth. Hawkins was breathing – but very slowly. McCabe wanted to check for a response and started screaming at him, 'Alex, Alex, can you hear me? Alex! Alex!'

Hawkins seemed to murmur something, and his hand jolted.

McCabe applied a field dressing to his bleeding neck, and then checked for his pulse. His own hands were shaking so much from adrenalin that he couldn't find it.

Messenger, an extremely fit soldier and natural runner, struck out fast in the direction of the smoke column. He called back at his Tac to keep up, but the gap between him and them was opening, with Messenger focused totally on getting himself to the FSG. As he ran, he heard the urgent voice of Captain Ormiston on the company net, 'Contact. Explosion. Wait out.'

It was 0530 hours. The sun was still coming up. Ahead of him the column of thick, black smoke was building and rising higher and higher. He ran between two racks of maize, head height. Tac was following, but they were way behind. He was isolated and hoped he wouldn't encounter any Taliban. He didn't know the ground well. He had no time to look at a map. He oriented himself on the hills to his left and the smoke plume ahead and just kept running – and wondering what he would find when he got to the track. *Was it a mine? An IED? A mortar? Were there any casualties?*

His last question was answered seconds later when Ormiston again came on the radio: 'Casualties. I have casualties. One times T One.'

Messenger stopped. He was halfway to the explosion. He was soaked with sweat and breathless, but he didn't care about that. He had got his platoons moving to the explosion but he hadn't given them any direction beyond that. He needed to.

What's happening at the FSG? Ollie will be dealing with the casualties. He has team medics but no fully qualified medics. He will need security. We need CASEVAC.

He rapidly fired out instructions on the radio: 'All stations, this is Zero Alpha. Two Zero, you are to continue moving towards the explosion and you are to go north and provide security from there. Three Zero, you are also to continue moving to the explosion. You are to go south and secure. Both callsigns are to move your medics forward. Get them to the site of the explosion as quickly as you possibly can. All callsigns to be aware of the risk of secondary devices. Ensure you carry out full checks when you arrive. Two Zero and Three Zero, roger so far over.'

One after the other, panting hard into their radios, the two platoon commanders answered, 'Roger over.'

Messenger continued, 'Zero, this is Zero Alpha. Confirm MERT has been tasked and is on the way.'

From the makeshift ops room back in Inkerman, Captain Hicks spoke calmly into the radio: 'Correct. MERT tasked figures three ago. I will confirm when they are in the air.'

Messenger was already on the run again, Tac closed in behind him, as he impatiently yelled back, 'They better be in the air now if you tasked them figures three ago. Get a grip of them!'

Hicks, a consummately professional and totally dependable operations officer, was fully in control of the CASEVAC efforts and didn't need additional pressure from Messenger. But he was used to bearing the brunt of his company commander's short fuze and knew how much pressure Messenger was now under. He replied, 'Roger, will deal with it now. Out.'

To Messenger's flanks, 10 and 11 Platoon were going through an ordeal they would never forget. There was not a cloud in the sky, and even this early in the morning the heat was becoming intense. Underfoot the ground was uneven, broken up and often boggy, and chunks of thick, heavy mud clung to their boots. They had to leap or wade through ditches that were waist- and chest-high, and fight through maize fields and scrubby undergrowth. As always, they were weighed down by weapons, radios, helmets and body armour.

Every man was carrying a heavier load of ammunition than usual, as the company had deployed ready to ambush Taliban fighters crossing the Helmand River. GPMG gunners were each carrying at least 1,500 rounds of 7.62 link and platoon sergeants had daysacks stuffed with twenty 51mm mortar bombs, alone weighing almost 18 kilos. They had just taken on more water, and each man carried 5 to 6 litres, weighing another 6 kilos. They had 1,500 metres of unrelenting Green

Zone to cross, and they had to do it fast. The men did not know what lay ahead of them. But they knew there were casualties, and they knew that it was a life-and-death situation in which every second would count.

At one point Willan thought he was running through a vacuum as the air was so thin, and he could hardly breathe. As he ran on and on, clambering over or crawling under felled trees, battling through boggy grassland and oozing mud, wading ditches, it reminded him of nothing more than the 'steeplechase', a gruelling physical test that every infantryman goes through during his basic training at the Infantry Training Centre, Catterick, in the moorlands of North Yorkshire. But he knew this steeplechase had an outcome even more serious than a possible bollocking from the platoon sergeant for not making his cut-off time and 'letting down the whole platoon'. Willan knew that whoever was lying bleeding around the FSG vehicles, it would be one of his mates, because he had been in D Company for three years and he knew all of them. They were all his mates. But he didn't dare to think about who the casualties might be.

Messenger waded through a deep canal and dragged himself up the bank on the other side. He moved through the treeline and broke into open country. He had reached the Jusulay track and was astonished at the scene that confronted him.

Beside the track were two compounds, one destroyed, rubbleized by an air strike. The other damaged but largely intact. In front of him was a WMIK, abandoned on the open track. Fifty metres ahead of it, just where the track began a steep rise, was the FSG Vector. It was buckled and smashed up. The smoke had dispersed, but fumes still rose from the vehicle, and there was a strong smell of burning. The front left-side wheel had clearly struck a mine and had been driven straight up into the passenger compartment. There was no one in sight and Messenger couldn't hear a sound apart from his heavy breathing. *Where the hell are they?*

Then soldiers were running everywhere, as the platoons started arriving and the medics moved forward to deal with casualties. Messenger walked past the vehicles and up the rise in the ground. The track turned ninety degrees, and there, behind a high bank, were Ormiston and the men of the FSG.

Hawkins, covered in blood, was lying face up on the track, the ground around him strewn with medical wrappers. Kneeling astride him, dripping with sweat from the exertion, Corporal Andrew 'Bomber' Brown was thrusting his hands up and down on Hawkins's chest. On his knees next to Hawkins's head, rifle discarded beside him in the dust, Sergeant Steve 'Spud' Armon was breathing into his bloody mouth. They were giving him CPR – cardiopulmonary resuscitation. Brown pushed down on his chest thirty times, Armon breathed twice into his mouth. Again and again and again and again.

Brown had run like a madman through the Green Zone, and he had been the first to arrive. Armon was right behind him. When they got there, Hawkins's heart was racing – a last-ditch effort to survive. It wasn't looking good, but they weren't about to give up on him. Messenger saw the grim determination in the eyes of these two tough and experienced commanders. Both shattered from the race through the Green Zone. Both intent on saving Lance Corporal Hawkins.

Beside the track sat Private Henning, bleeding, grey, shocked and covered in dirt, being treated by a medic. The other members of the FSG stood around, covered in dust and some with blood on them from the wounded. All shocked.

Messenger could see the casualties were being well looked after, and he didn't need to interfere. The platoon commanders had deployed their men into position, and the whole area was secure. He now had to focus on getting the casualties out. He identified a suitable HLS, a poppy field right beside the track, and radioed the grid to Hicks at Inkerman, just 600 metres away.

Willan was tasked to secure the HLS. He sent his section 2IC to physically clear the ground where the helicopter would land, and then went with Private Tony Rawson to check the two compounds and make sure they were clear. It wasn't likely any Taliban would still be in the area after planting the mine, but you could never be sure. And the last thing they needed was for an enemy to spring up from nowhere and fire an RPG missile or a burst of machine-gun bullets into the landing Chinook.

Sergeant Major Taylor arrived with a group of four Vikings from Inkerman and took over the casualty evacuation.

Corporal Ian Peyton, the company's senior medic, was with him. Tall, dark-haired and thin and with a huge medical Bergen over one shoulder, he raced across to Hawkins. Peyton's arrival at any scene of devastation gave everybody a lift. If the casualties themselves were conscious they knew their chances of survival were increased by Peyton being there. And the men around them – desperate to see their mates stay alive – were reassured by the knowledge of just how good this experienced and dedicated medic was.

Peyton was always utterly unflappable when treating the wounded, even if enemy fire was landing close by. Watching his steady hands, intense concentration and total confidence in what he was doing, the troops were full of awe, particularly when they recalled that, back home in Pirbright, Peyton spent more than his fair share of time in front of the Military Police or the RSM explaining the outcome of his activities the previous night in the pubs and clubs of Woking.

Brown and Armon were still hard at work. While they continued, Peyton knelt beside Hawkins. He looked at his chest and saw there was no rise and fall. Most of Armon's breath was escaping through the hole in Hawkins' neck. Not enough was getting into his lungs. Peyton checked his breathing. Nothing. He checked his pulse. Again, nothing. He looked at Brown and Armon and thought, *There isn't much hope. But I'm not giving up on him any more than these two are. Let's see if we can get him back.*

Peyton opened up his medical bergen and took out a BVM – 'bag valve mask' – a hand-held device used to provide positive pressure ventilation. He attached a small oxygen bottle and put the mask over Hawkins's face and handed it over to Armon. It would be more effective than mouth-to-mouth. Peyton then punched an intraosseous screw into Hawkins's left leg, drilling into the femur . He plugged in a saline drip, trying to boost his fast-falling blood pressure. Over the next fifteen minutes, Peyton, Brown and Armon fought to bring Alex Hawkins back.

The Chinook swooped down in a storm of dust, right next to the track where Hawkins lay. Dirt, stones and dried-out poppy stalks swirled violently through the air, and Peyton, Brown and Armon lay across Hawkins's body to shield him as best they could. A hornets' nest was blown on to Armon, but he swiped it away, and with the other two and Sergeant Major Taylor carried Hawkins straight up the helicopter's tail-ramp. Two soldiers assisted Henning into the chopper. Peyton shouted a briefing to the doctor on board, and they laid Hawkins on a stretcher on the vibrating floor of the helicopter.

Armon ran back down the ramp, with his hands stained with Hawkins's blood, picking twelve hornets out of his arm, which was already beginning to balloon.

The chopper rose rapidly into the sky, then dipped its nose and banked southward, heading towards Camp Bastion and the field hospital.

Back on the ground, one of the FSG soldiers grabbed Peyton's arm and said, 'He's going to be all right. He *is* going to be all right, isn't he?'

Peyton looked into the soldier's tear-filled eyes. 'Don't worry. He's on board now. He's got surgeons, he's got the anaesthetist, doctors. He's got the best available care.'

Messenger ordered the removal of all equipment from the blown-up Vector and then sent the sergeant major's Vikings and the FSG WMIKs back to Inkerman. He moved the company clear of the danger area and then ordered the Apache that had accompanied the MERT Chinook up from Bastion to deny the Vector. He watched as the Apache unleashed two Hellfire missiles, and a new column of smoke and flames rose up from the stricken vehicle.

∫

Before heading back into Inkerman, Messenger reflected on what had happened. It had been a textbook attack. It was only 600 metres from Inkerman. The compounds provided perfect concealment for the fighters positioning their lethal device. The damage that had been done to the compounds, the surrounding area and the track itself, meant that any signs of digging would be hard to detect. The device was positioned at a narrow point on the track, just where it began to rise. And once the FSG vehicles had deployed out of Inkerman along the Jusulay track, there was only one way for them to come back. A well-reconnoitred, carefully planned and perfectly executed operation. There was no doubt in Messenger's mind – this was a professional piece of work, carried out not by locals but highly trained and experienced Taliban fighters.

Carver had been telling Messenger ever since he arrived at Inkerman that it was just a matter of time before the Taliban returned to the Green Zone north of Sangin. And they would want to demonstrate to the local community, as well as their leaders in Musa Qalah and in Pakistan, that they were far from beaten. They would do this by striking back at the British, on the ground and in their bases. Although it had not materialized last night, the intelligence that the Taliban were reinfiltrating fitted with this well-executed ambush.

The battle group intelligence officer, Captain Tom Coleman, had mentioned the callsign 'Farouk' to Messenger on several occasions. They knew virtually nothing about the man that used this radio callsign, but there was intelligence that he was a seasoned commander and might be the leader of a renewed Taliban offensive in the area, bringing in battle-hardened jihadists from across the Pakistan border. Messenger wondered whether the shadowy Farouk was behind this morning's attack.

If that is the case, he thought, *this is just the beginning...*

Soon after he got back into Inkerman, Messenger was informed on the telephone by Lieutenant Colonel Carver that Lance Corporal Alex Hawkins had been declared dead on arrival at the field hospital in Camp Bastion. It was a devastating blow for C Company, their first fatality of the tour. It was even more devastating for the men of FSG Delta, who made up a tight-knit team and together had seen a great deal of action in Helmand. The loss of one of their number was no less a blow than would have been the death of the closest family member.

After Messenger had given them the news, the FSG soldiers sat on their camp beds under cam-nets in tearful silence. Private Harry McCabe spoke to Private Michael Smith about the comrade they had worked so hard to save. 'One thing I'll always remember about Alex. You know how if you ask someone a silly question you get the piss taken? Even if you ask rank about something, they still rip you apart, don't they? Well, the one person in the whole company that I always used to be able to ask a silly question, you know if I was worrying or wondering about something? It was Alex Hawkins. You always knew he wouldn't take the piss, no matter how bone the question was.'

Sergeant Major Taylor spoke to Corporal Matt Willan. 'Matty, I'm sorry about what happened. Must have hit you really hard.'

'What do you mean?' said Willan. 'I didn't know the bloke.'

Earlier, when he had asked one of the FSG soldiers about who had been wounded, they had said 'Alex'. Willan assumed it must be a new soldier in the FSG, as he didn't know anyone called Alex. Despite their closeness, he only ever knew him as Steve or Stephen, the nickname he had given him. When the sergeant major told him that it was Alex Hawkins, his long-time mate almost since school days, Willan felt sick.

6

A few days later, Messenger temporarily handed over C Company to Captain Hicks. Messenger was heading back to Camp Bastion and then to the UK for his R and R. Every soldier in the battalion took a period of fourteen days' R and R during their six months' tour in Afghanistan. Although two days were taken up flying to Brize Norton in Oxfordshire, it allowed around twelve days to see the family and recharge batteries.

Many soldiers found it hard to relax on R and R. They were so tightly wound by the intensity of operations in Helmand, coming back so quickly into normal day-to-day life in Romford, Chelmsford, Ipswich or the villages of rural Norfolk or Cambridgeshire was a surreal experience. It was often frustrating and bewildering. The age-old story of the soldier returning from the front. No one they met, chatted to or drank with had the slightest idea what they were doing in Afghanistan or what it was like. And very few cared.

The wife might want to let off steam about the trouble she had been having with the kids. Trying to hold down a job and look after them single-handed. And there wasn't enough money to pay the bills every month, never mind actually get out of the house and away from the depressing and gossip-ridden married quarters area.

Mates from civvie street were absorbed with the day-to-day politics at work, who was nicking who's girlfriend, why West Ham were being so crap this season, how little the dole paid out, and how much a pint cost.

Of course the iniquities of the latest in a fast-moving string of West Ham managers was of critical importance. But apart from that the Royal Anglian on R and R was not interested in the banality of day-to-day civvie life, and their mates and families were not much interested in what they had been doing either.

And the soldier on R and R was poor company. Peering wistfully into his pint, remembering that insane dash across the Green Zone, pouring sweat, legs almost giving out, heart almost bursting through rib cage .... And always distracted, thinking about Sangin, Inkerman, Kajaki, FOB Rob. Looking at the watch. Nine p.m. here, getting on for 0200 hours there. What will the lads be doing now? My platoon will still be up on the peaks overlooking Kajaki, some on stag others in their doss bags. The rest of the company will probably be getting ready to go out on patrol, or maybe they're moving out now ... Wonder if they're OK? Didn't hear anything on the news today, not about Afghanistan, although two of our lads were killed in Iraq.

In the same way as civilians have found it impossible to understand in other wars, many of the Royal Anglian soldiers just wanted to get back to the front line, back with their mates, back where – for the time being – they belonged.

Before Messenger left for his R and R, he and Hicks ran through the plan for the next couple of weeks. Hicks had been in the Army for five and a half years. An experienced infantry officer, before coming to Afghanistan, he had served on operations in Iraq and Bosnia, and had done a stint as an instructor at the Infantry Training Centre, Catterick.

Hicks had spent most of the tour so far tied to the company ops room, first in Zeebrugge, then at Inkerman. It wasn't through choice. He had been desperate to get on the ground, but Messenger needed him in the base. With a range of powerful communications systems to keep the battle group headquarters in Bastion informed about the company's activities and intentions, and crucially to cue up combat support, resupply and CASEVAC, the ops officer's role was crucial.

But it was deeply frustrating for most infantry captains, like Hicks, who just wanted to be on the ground, commanding soldiers and fighting the enemy. Hicks was eager to take over the reins of the company in Messenger's absence. It would get him out on the ground every day, and it was a great opportunity to prove – to himself and everybody else – that he could command a company in combat. And much as he liked and worked well with Messenger, it would give him a welcome break from the hour-by-hour demands that this hardest of taskmasters made on him, plus the chance to bring his own, very different, leadership style to the company, if only for a short time. But as well as being enthusiastic about the prospect of command, Hicks was apprehensive. Stepping up from second in command to company commander was always tough. Somehow it was much more difficult, and in this sort of situation, just as you are getting used to running the show it is time to hand it back. And Hicks didn't know the ground very well. The company had only been at Inkerman for a couple of weeks, although Messenger had made sure he had got out into the Green Zone a few times, standing in for one of the platoon commanders during his R and R.

Above all, Hicks hoped that the decisions he would have to make as a commander would keep the men of C Company safe. Like his company commander, he cared about his men more than anything else. He knew what his responsibilities were for keeping them alive and making sure they did their job effectively. He liked and respected them, and the feeling was mutual. Again, like Messenger, Hicks was one of the most popular officers in the battalion – among all ranks. He had earned their trust, affection and admiration not by letting them take the easy option or by being 'one of the lads', but by doing his job diligently and effectively, and by his actions making it absolutely clear that he cared for them and was as loyal to them as he was to his brother officers and his superiors.

Squinting out of the window of the Chinook as it flew south towards Bastion, Messenger worried about what lay ahead for his men while he was away. He had no qualms about leaving the company in Hicks's hands. He trusted him utterly and knew that he was more than capable of doing the job. But ever since the attack that killed Alex Hawkins, he had speculated on what the Taliban were up to. It had gone quiet again since that devastating blow, and, most worrying, there was an almost total intelligence vacuum.

Messenger had driven the company harder than ever since Hawkins's death, knowing that he had to continue to dominate the Green Zone north-east of Sangin. He had to find out as much as he could about Taliban activity, by talking to locals and by observing what was going on – getting ever-greater insight into the normal pattern of life so that he could spot the abnormal. He had to have troops on the ground as much as possible to try to deny freedom of movement to the enemy. And he needed to maintain a presence in order to reassure the locals that the British would be staying and would defend them when the Taliban came back.

He had told Hicks to maintain this momentum, to patrol in strength in the Green Zone as often as possible, and preferably every day.

7

On the morning of Tuesday 7 August, the Taliban launched a series of 107mm rockets at FOB Inkerman. They landed harmlessly outside the base, but this was the beginning of the campaign of attacks against

Inkerman that Carver had predicted. There were further attacks the following day and the day after that.

On Thursday 9 August, Captain Hicks, acting company commander, led 10 and 11 Platoons and the FSG on a patrol to the village of Putay, 7 kilometres from Inkerman. The company group moved out of Inkerman mounted in a column of Vikings, WMIKs and Vectors heading north across the desert. A thousand metres from Jusulay, in the desert, the men dismounted and patrolled towards Putay, in the Green Zone.

The Vikings, with their turret-mounted machine-guns, and the FSG with their guns, GMGs and Javelin missiles, remained on the high ground in overwatch. But their utility to the company was limited. Once the men on foot passed through the first row of trees on the edge of the Green Zone, the Vikings and FSG could not get a clear enough picture of them, the enemy or the civilian population to be able to provide any effective fire support.

It was early morning, but the sun was already beating down hard, and after only a few hundred metres on foot, the men of C Company were dripping sweat as they crossed the 611. Entering the Green Zone, with its multitude of well-concealed ambush sites, jungle-like undergrowth and deep, muddy irrigation ditches, was never a great experience, but at least the heat was mitigated to a small extent by the Green Zone's intermittent shade.

Corporal Andrew 'Bomber' Brown, normally a section commander, was today commanding 10 Platoon. Lieutenant Perrin, the platoon commander, was still on R and R, and Sergeant Armon had an injury and was under treatment in Bastion. Brown, a tough and energetic NCO, whose courage and leadership under fire had saved the lives of Private Gordon and Guardsman Harrison during a heavy contact in Mazdurak in May, was relishing the opportunity to command at a higher level.

As 10 Platoon approached Putay, leading the company in, Brown saw a scene he had never witnessed before. If the Taliban were preparing for a fight, the local farmers and villagers would often up sticks and head out of the area, returning when the shooting ended. But this was different. A vast mass of people, mainly elderly men, women and children, were running towards them out of the area dense with compounds. It was an exodus, and the women, covered by black robes and head scarfs, were bent double under piles of their possessions, some carrying babies, others dragging goats and cows.

Brown got on the net to Hicks, who had also seen the amazing spectacle. 'Zero Alpha, this is Two Zero Alpha. There are at least five hundred. We're definitely in for a hard fight any time now. That is the most obvious combat indicator I've ever seen in my life, over.'

Captain Ormiston with the FSG was also on the radio, reporting that the leading elements of the refugees had reached the high ground in the desert and were now just sitting on their boxes, cases and bags, settling down to watch the fight unfold. He confirmed Brown's estimate of at least 500 people.

Hicks spoke to all the commanders on the radio: 'All stations, this is Zero Alpha. I agree this looks like a fight ahead. We will continue pushing into the Green Zone. I want to probe to try to find out the scale of the enemy presence in this area. But I want to avoid becoming decisively engaged. All commanders are to do their best to remain balanced and not get drawn in. If we come into contact, we will cause as much attrition as we can and then extract.'

Brown stopped an old man with a long grey beard. His interpreter showed the man a map and asked, 'Where are the Taliban?'

The man couldn't make head or tail of the map, but pointed a long, crooked, leathery finger at a compound 200 metres away, through a field of maize. He whispered in Pashtu, 'Allah protect you. Be careful,' and hurried on his way, following the others into the desert.

Well into the Green Zone now, Brown pushed his men forward across an open ploughed field, with a crop of high, golden maize to their left. Burdened down by the usual massive weight of ammunition, water and equipment, daysack straps cutting into their shoulders, boots already sodden from wading irrigation channels, the men were alert and poised for action, carefully scanning their arcs, fingers ready to flick off safety catches and blast back fire at the enemy.

Brown and his radio operator were moving with the second fire team of his point section. The lead fire team, under Lance Corporal Michael Robinson, a sniper now acting as section commander, had just reached a wide irrigation ditch and were starting to wade across.

No matter how many contacts you have been in, the opening shots always come as a shock, and Brown flinched as he heard the whoosh-whoosh-whoosh-whoosh-whoosh as five RPG-7 missiles zipped above their heads, then exploded loudly just beyond, throwing up clods of dirt.

As the men dived for cover a torrent of bullets fell all around them. The weight of fire was breathtaking and very, very frightening. Brown had never before, in Kajaki or here in the Green Zone, experienced anything as fierce. Pressing himself into a furrow, his first thought was, *How are we not all dead?*

The rest of the platoon, 50 metres back across the field on a compound wall, under Corporal Tim Ferrand, opened fire across the maize field. They couldn't see the enemy positions from where they were, but fired their machine-guns into the area to suppress. It wasn't working, and if anything the enemy fire pouring in around Brown and the other five men in the ploughed field intensified.

There was a sudden lull in the firing. *Mag change*, thought Brown and, yelling at his men to follow, ran faster than he had ever run before in his life. They dived into the canal and found themselves among Robinson's fire team, chest deep in water.

The enemy fire started up again, bullets cutting up the banks on both sides, and spattering into the water among them. Somehow, seeing the criss-crossing lines as bullets torpedoed through the water, passing right by their legs, made this even more terrifying than all the other contacts.

Brown could hear Ferrand's men, on the compound behind, rattling down fire. Again and again he called Ferrand on the radio, trying to find out where the enemy were. As always, at the crtitical moment, his radio wasn't working, and neither was Robinson's. This time, though, Brown didn't curse the system that had supplied such unreliable comms equipment – they were deep in an irrigation ditch, and the radios were submerged.

Brown and Robinson worked out roughly where they thought the enemy fire must be coming from, and ordered the UGL men to start hammering grenades up from the ditch.

Brown tried to move down to where the ditch bent round, hoping to find a position where he could get eyes on the enemy. The channel was about 5 metres across and very fast-flowing. He moved towards the corner, but the current took him. He was being dragged straight towards the enemy position. Thinking he was almost finished, and would be shot or drowned – or both – Brown just managed to grab hold of a tree root sticking out of the bank and hauled himself to safety.

Fifty metres back, Corporal Ferrand had pushed a GPMG gunner, Fijian Guardsman Jope Matai, together with Private Ed Garner, up on to the compound roof. The two men saw a group of fighters moving down the treeline towards them and opened fire, cutting them down with burst after burst of automatic fire. As soon as they opened up, enemy from another position began engaging them, and bullets started cracking into the solid earth roof. The soldiers pushed up against a 60-centimetre-high lip running round the roof, trying to get protection. It helped, but they had to raise themselves back up into the teeth of the enemy fire in order to continue engaging.

Ferrand thought Brown and his men were all dead. He had seen them move into the irrigation canal, but then a mass of enemy fire had poured in on them. There had been no movement from the water, and not a word on the radio.

Hicks arrived at the back of the compound, and Ferrand briefed him. Straight away Hicks spoke to Lieutenant Manie Olivier, 11 Platoon commander, and told him to move round from his position on the right, to support the extraction of Brown's men – if they were still alive. He had called in air, which was now screaming towards them, but would not be able to use it or indirect fire immediately, as his troops were so close to the enemy. He needed Olivier to help them pull back and create a gap so that he could pound the enemy from above.

By now Brown and Robinson had pushed their men up on to the canal bank and were hammering fire down across the maize field in the direction of the enemy. They managed to find covered positions just below the bank and behind a high earth berm next to it. The old infantry cry *win the firefight* reverberated in Brown's mind. His men were doing their best to outgun the Taliban, but they were outnumbered, and the enemy were firing from well-concealed, carefully prepared and covered positions. Brown and his men had to move up to fire, get off a few bursts and then change position quickly to avoid getting hit by the torrent of lead that was raining down on them.

About half an hour after he moved out of the ditch and behind the earth berm Brown's radio crackled back to life. He called Hicks, who told him that Olivier's men were on their way to help.

Ten minutes later, Brown slid back into the canal and met Olivier, who was leading his men through the ditch. The two commanders had a brief discussion, then Olivier led 11 Platoon through Brown's section and into a position where they could bring the maximum weight of fire to bear on the enemy.

As 11 Platoon blasted fire into the Taliban positions, supported by Ferrand's men firing from their compound, Brown and his section extracted, racing back across the ploughed field, keeping close into the maize to give cover from view. They ran as fast as they could, and Taliban fire crunched into the ground all around them.

8

Back at Ferrand's compound, Brown's men, shattered, soaked by filthy ditchwater and their own sweat, and amazed they were still alive, didn't have time to draw breath. They clambered up on to the compound wall with Ferrand's firing line and started to engage the enemy with their rifles and machine-guns to cover 11 Platoon in their extraction under fire.

Hicks called Brown and Olivier together in the compound. 'Well done, both of you. God knows how we didn't get any casualties. There are a lot of Taliban out there. I now want to extract back to the desert. I don't want to get committed here. The Taliban are still in the treeline leading up to the main canal. We've got to deal with them or we won't get out of here. Manie, I want you to take 11 Platoon and clear through the treeline. Corporal Brown, leave some fire support here, and move down with the rest of your men and secure a line of departure for 11 Platoon's clearance. Let's go.'

Robinson's section had just managed to clack a few mouthfuls of water, and then Brown led them back out of the compound, beside a wall and into the irrigation ditch leading towards the Taliban-infested treeline.

They waded through the knee-deep water, struggling with the oozing mud which was trying to suck their boots deeper and deeper in. With the whole section in the ditch, the Taliban opened up on them from both sides. Brown and his men dived down into the water and hugged the banks, bullets smacking in close to them, closer than ever.

Guardsman Jones, half-submerged beside Brown, looked at him and shook his head. The expression on his face said, *We are going to die.*

Brown agreed, *There's no way out of this one.*

But he was not about to give up. He raised his eyes up to the lip of the ditch. There was maize either side and through the maize, about 7 metres away, he could see the enemy. All he could make out were the legs and flip flops of three or four men on either side. He crouched back down into the water and over the noise of gunfire pouring into the ditch, yelled out to the men. 'They are just inside the maize, about twenty foot. They've got to have a mag change soon. When they do, front four up and fire to the right, the rest of us, fire left. Get ready. Any minute. Give it everything. Just blast them.'

Just as Brown predicted, a few seconds later the firing stopped, and his men stood up and fired burst after burst of machine-gun and automatic rifle fire straight into the maize on both sides of the ditch.

The enemy dropped where they stood, and Brown led the section splashing through the water, back to the compound. As he ran, Brown again wondered how anyone could have survived that onslaught – the fire had been even heavier than they had experienced a short time ago in the ploughed field. *Not our time, just not our time. No other answer.*

That day was Robinson's birthday, and as they ran back into the compound, Brown shouted, 'Robbo, your luck can't hold, mate. You're going to die on your birthday.'

'Oh my word,' laughed Robinson, breathing hard, 'not my death day as well as my birthday!'

'Well, I suppose it's tidier like that.'

While Brown had been in contact in the ditch, Olivier had led his platoon along a different route to clear the treeline, but when they got there the enemy had withdrawn.

Ferrand's men had seen signs of the enemy moving further into the maize field near the compound. They would need to suppress or kill them as they left.

The Vikings and FSG, back up on the high ground, had started to fire machine-guns and GMGs into the maize, but Ferrand was horrified when their gunfire started splintering the compound door near his men. Their view into the area was badly obscured by foliage, and Sergeant Major Taylor got on the radio and ordered, 'Check fire.'

Hicks said to Brown, '11 Platoon are heading back direct out to the desert from where they are now, and we will move out from here. My Tac will go with your platoon.'

'Roger that, sir. We need to suppress that field as we go, I will take care of it.'

He turned to Ferrand, 'Tim, make sure you're ready to move, you take the platoon out, followed by Tac. I will be last to go and I'll cover your back.'

As the company got ready to break out of the compound, Brown ordered Guardsman Matai to come down from his position up on the roof with his GPMG. He said, 'Matai, in a moment the company's moving out. You and me will be last to go. We're going to give them cover as they clear the open ground. When I say go, I will boot the door open in front of that field, and I want you to spray the whole field. Just spray everything. There's definitely Taliban in there and we need to kill them all.'

The big Fijian shook his head. 'Bomber, I can't do it.'

Brown was incredulous. There wasn't time for this. But he controlled himself. 'What's the matter, mate? Why can't you do it?'

'I cannot. I have killed too many today. I cannot do it.'

Brown walked across the room and said to Lance Corporal Thomas, Matai's section commander, 'What's he playing at?'

Thomas said, 'Bomber, he's been up there killing Taliban all day. He's had incoming all round him. He's been really brave. He's very religious and he thinks he has killed too many.'

'OK, OK,' said Brown, trying to keep calm.

He turned back to Matai. 'Here, mate, give me that gun, you take my rifle. You go with Tommo and the others.'

Private Ed Garner, who had been on the roof with Matai, said, 'Bomber, I'll do it with you.'

Ferrand led 10 Platoon and Tac out of the compound. At the precise moment they started to move, Brown booted open the compound door adjacent to the maize field, and he and Garner jumped out into the field, spraying their machine-guns into the maize. Standing in front of the doorway, each man fired a belt of 200 rounds and then turned and followed the platoon across the open ground and into the wadi that would lead them back to the desert.

When they were almost clear of the Green Zone, the Taliban opened fire again, from a group of compounds to the right. 10 Platoon and Hicks's Tac turned in an extended line and started firing back. The FSG and the Vikings also identified the enemy positions and rained machine-gun and GMG fire into the compounds.

Hicks called in the air he had overhead, and a pair of A10s swooped towards the enemy, peppering them with 30mm cannonfire.

Within minutes, all enemy fire had ended. The troops continued their movement back to marry up with the Vikings on the high ground.

Brown again wondered how he and his men had got away with it. It had been without doubt the heaviest and most vicious series of contacts he had ever been in. He thought about Matai. The Guardsman had performed superbly all day, firing belt after belt from his GPMG. And he had worked like that since they arrived in Afghanistan – fearless and strong as an ox – one of the best, most effective GPMG gunners in the company.

Brown thought, *Well, Matai's human. He did a little bit too much. He just needs a cup of tea and I'm sure he'll be back in it again tomorrow.*

9

By the time C Company had got back to Inkerman, Sergeant Matt Waters was there, having just returned from R and R. Waters was platoon sergeant of 11 Platoon, and he had flown back to the UK just as the company moved down from Kajaki. On his arrival back in Inkerman he was told he would be acting platoon commander of 10 Platoon until Lieutenant Sam Perrin finished his R and R.

Waters wandered across to chat to his 11 Platoon soldiers. Under their cam-net, several of the lads, having shed their soaking uniforms, were dressed in shorts and flip flops, sitting on their camp beds cleaning weapons. As Waters walked under the cam-net, Private Tony Rawson, his arms covered in tattoos, jumped up with a huge grin on his face and shook his hand.

Rawson was known by everybody in the battalion as 'Nicey'. He had been given the nickname soon after he arrived in the battalion over three years previously, because he was so friendly, helpful and willing to go out of his way for everybody. Unlike most infantrymen, he would never play tricks on new recruits, but instead did everything he could to help them settle into their new life. He was a man who would do anything for anyone. At twenty-seven he was older than most privates, and he was well respected by all of the other privates as well as the officers and NCOs. A dedicated and professional soldier, he also had the nickname 'the Colonel', as after platoon 'O' Groups back in Pirbright he would keep all the privates back to give them his own semi-serious briefing. He had a superb sense of humour and was always good for morale, whatever the circumstances.

After vigorously pumping the bemused Waters's hand, he said, 'Sarge, you war dodger, didn't think we'd be seeing you out here again. Thought you'd find some reason to stay back on the rear party or something. 'Specially now we're down here at Inkerman, where the proper war's going on. I thought that was why you conveniently went on R and R just when we moved here. Thought it was all a bit too stressful for you, what with you being a Poacher and everything.'

Waters, who had started his Army career with the Royal Anglian Regiment's 2nd Battalion, nicknamed 'The Poachers', just stood there shaking his head. Then he said, 'Finished have you, Nicey?'

'Actually, Sarge, no I haven't. We were all wondering…'

'Nicey, give it a rest, you twat. If I've got to put up with your verbal for the rest of the tour I might just try and get myself back on to the Rear Party. Never been on one in my life, but it would even be better suffering Major Stefanetti's wrath than putting up with your verbal diarrhoea.'

Major Dean 'Stef' Stefanetti was OC of the Rear Party back in Pirbright. A huge bear of a man, and a tough and professional soldier, he had risen from the rank of private in the battalion and was much feared by all ranks – including sergeants.

'Any old excuse for dodging the war, eh, Sarge?'

'Nicey – I don't know how you can talk like that, mate. You spend all your time on patrol taking cover when you don't need to. I've never known anyone to spend so much time on the ground in fire positions when there's no Taliban anywhere near.'

Rawson had a knack on patrol of always tripping over tree-branches, logs, rocks and anything else that appeared in his path. When attempting to leap even the narrowest irrigation ditch, he almost invariably fell in.

'That's professionalism, Sarge. At least I get into fire positions. I'm not afraid of getting into the mud or the water. Trouble with you rank is you all think you're bullet-proof. You're lucky you've got lads like me out here to look after you, eh, Sarge?'

Waters grinned. 'How about that time up in Kajaki, then, Nicey, when that A10 strafed right next to us instead of the enemy? The look on your face. I've never seen anything like it. Horror. Horror is the only way to describe it. Sheer horror, Nicey. Don't know why you were worried anyway. Look at the size of you. There's no way anyone's ever going to hit you, Nicey.'

'Yeah, yeah, Sarge. Actually, looking at you, did you eat quite a lot on R and R? Few too many pies. Looking a bit podgy now?'

'That's enough, Nicey, I'm going to see the sergeant major. I'm putting in for a posting back to the Rear Party. I'm more scared of you than Major Stef.'

10

Late that night Captain Hicks gave orders for a patrol the next morning through the Taliban-dominated village of Regay and on to the Jusulay irrigation project, to provide security to the locals working in the surrounding fields. After a few short hours of sleep, the company deployed out of Inkerman in darkness at 0430 hours, Friday 10 August. Wearing helmets and Osprey body armour over their T-shirts, sweating under the weight of weapons, ammunition and water, the men entered the Green Zone, moving fast to reach Regay by first light.

Lieutenant Manie Olivier's 11 Platoon led the company. The combination of R and R and casualties of various types left the platoon short of troops, and each of Olivier's three sections was down to four or five men instead of the usual eight.

Corporal Matty Willan had four soldiers in his section – Privates Tony Rawson, Matthew Cain, Curtis Cumberbatch and Scott Garrett. As they moved fast through the ploughed fields and dense foliage, they heard bursts of fire in the distance. All around the Green Zone, Taliban sentries were alerting their men to the imminent arrival of the British troops. Interpreters monitoring the Taliban radio frequencies reported the net had come alive with messages as the enemy tracked the British movement and ordered fighters into their pre-planned positions.

Willan had been to Regay many times before and was confident they would have a battle with the Taliban. Next to a large re-entrant leading down to a shallow crossing point over the river, Regay was an easy place for the Taliban to infiltrate. But the extent of the fire and the intensity of the radio chat was different. He thought, *That is a combat indicator of a scrap if ever there was one. I reckon this is going to be big.*

Snaking down the Green Zone in a single long line, tramping across the baked mud, stumbling over unseen obstacles in the dark, jumping streams and wading through irrigation ditches, every man in C

Company had his own thoughts about what was signified by the volleys of fire echoing around the valley. The mood of most soldiers as they advanced towards the inevitable firefight was, as ever, one of apprehension. The initial contact would almost always be on the Taliban's terms: at the time and the place of their choosing. It was impossible not to be unsettled by the thought that the first bullet could come at any time and from any direction, and it could have your name on it. Once battle had been joined apprehension disappeared in an adrenalin-fuelled burst of intense activity as the soldiers raced to take cover, identify enemy positions and return fire all at the same time. Then things were more level, and the race was on to tip the balance one way or the other. After the battle, the mood generally switched to elation. Happy to have got some fire down, even happier still to be alive. If anyone had been killed or wounded the feeling of elation was tempered by sadness and perhaps loss. But that would take hold later on, after the patrol, back in base. For now, the men were apprehensive, alert, switched on, covering arcs, ready to react.

The company entered Regay at 0515 hours. As they approached, the sun was rising into the cloudless sky, with every promise of a hotter than usual day ahead.

In the middle of the typical lush Green Zone foliage, densely planted fields and deep irrigation ditches, Regay was a devil's lair of near-impenetrable compound systems, high channelling walls, rat-run alleyways, ambush ditches criss-crossed by narrow foot bridges and streams with oozing beds to slow you down just at the moment you were in trouble. The village was controlled by hard-core Taliban, many brought in fresh from Pakistan, well trained, determined and unwilling to give a single inch of what they regarded as their territory. It was in Regay and places like it that the Taliban were consolidating, building back up, intent on re-establishing themselves in the Green Zone, intimidating the local people, attacking the foreign forces and striking back into Sangin.

It was C Company's job to prevent this from happening, to unsettle the Taliban, deny them any safe haven in the area, kill as many as they could and drive the others away. And behind these actions, the intent was always to reassure the local population and demonstrate to them that they would not be abandoned to their fate, under the heel of the Taliban, who wanted to control them, prevent any prosperity that could be attributed to foreign governments or the Kabul regime and extort from them their property, produce and money.

With 10 Platoon behind, 11 Platoon patrolled through the back-alleys of Regay and arrived between two high mud compound walls. So far all quiet. No sign of the enemy. The platoon went firm, stacked up behind the cover of the compound walls. They had been moving virtually non-stop for the best part of an hour, mostly at speed. Olivier ordered them to pause briefly to draw breath, adjust kit and gulp down half a litre of water.

Olivier had a quick look around the men to make sure they were OK, then a few minutes later said, 'Let's go. Corporal Watson, lead off.'

Lance Corporal Dale Watson led his five-man section away from the cover of the wall, out across a wide, open dirt area between the compounds, the size of a football pitch. Olivier followed him out, and Corporal Darren Farrugia's section was close behind. This was an incredibly dangerous place for any infantryman to be – in the open. They had almost got through the village, and nothing had happened. After all the firing earlier, it just didn't add up. The men were spread out, weapons in the shoulder, hands tightening on pistol grips and trigger guards, alert, covering their arcs – expecting trouble at any moment.

Willan's section followed. They were now 30 metres from the wall, and Willan saw that Watson's men had almost reached the other side. Willan was tense, poised to react. His eye caught a sudden movement and in the same instant he heard a shot. Ahead, Watson jerked up his rifle and fired across the high, green flag-leaves of maize to the left, towards a compound 70 metres away.

Immediately Watson's and Farrugia's sections were engulfed in a storm of machine-gun and rifle fire. RPGs whooshed overhead, air-bursting in the distance. Watson's men threw themselves into the tree-lined ditch to their left, with gunfire following on their heels, kicking up clouds of dust and and hurling stones and dirt in every direction. Farrugia's men, further from the ditch, threw themselves to the ground and crawled fast through the dirt.

Taking in the maelstrom ahead, Willan rushed to the earth bank running beside the ditch to the left. He was desperate to take the heat off the two forward sections and yelled out, 'Rapid – fire!'

It was an unnecessary command. As each man hit the bank he started firing through the corn towards the compound beyond. Rawson, an outstanding Minimi gunner, was first into position, firing as he landed on the bund-line, his gun spitting out 5.56mm ball and tracer at a devastating rate.

Private Matthew Cain was on the left of the section. He headed for a tree and lodged himself against the trunk, getting some protection. He began firing, then unclipped his daysack and dragged out more belts of ammo. Scanning through his sight, he could make out three enemy beside a white compound in the treeline, about 100 metres away through the cornfield. They were moving fast up and down the treeline, changing positions.

Willan glanced over to the area where Watson's section had taken cover and saw a large tree virtually disintegrate under his eyes, enemy fire tearing off branches and splintering open the trunk, sending a shower of shredded bark all over the troops below.

Rapidly identifying his position, the enemy switched fire away from the other two sections and began blasting Willan's section. Cain heard the crunch of bullets smacking into the tree-trunk above his head. Willan realized there must be at least eight enemy firing at his section, and they were beating him. As bullets scythed in around them, he yelled to his men, 'Into cover! Into cover! Get back down the bank!'

II

Sergeant Matt Waters, acting commander of 10 Platoon, raced along the alleyway that 11 Platoon had come from before breaking out into the open ground. Captain Hicks was standing on the corner with his Tac HQ, rifle in one hand, studying an air photo and talking to his JTAC, who was back at Inkerman, on the radio.

Waters looked at him. Hicks had just run forward to this point himself and was pouring sweat. But he looked calm, and was giving measured instructions over the net to coordinate fire support. When he had finished he looked up and, raising his voice above the crescendo of two-way fire behind him, said, 'Sergeant Waters, 11 Platoon is pinned down out in the open. There must be at least ten Taliban in prepared positions over there, in the treeline beyond the maize field. I've got mortars coming in now.'

As he spoke, Waters heard the whizz of 81mm mortars arcing above in their high trajectory, fired from Inkerman. Moments later there came the crump-crump-crump as three rounds impacted in the distance. Kneeling on the other side of the alley, where he could observe the fall of shot, the MFC immediately started calling adjustments into the net, bringing the mortars closer to their target.

Hicks continued, 'I need you to get at least one of your sections into that compound, just to the left of 11 Platoon.' He indicated towards a large brown compound surrounded by a high wall, slightly left, just behind the ditch, beside Willan's section. 'Blast your way into it, get some guns up on the roof and try to suppress the enemy that are engaging 11 Platoon. My plan is to use your fire, and the mortars, to get the enemy's heads down so we can manoeuvre 11 Platoon back across the open ground, then smash the enemy from the air. F15s will be on the way shortly, I've just briefed the JTAC.'

'Roger, sir, will do. I'll go back now and brief my lead section. I'll get my platoon sergeant to get some fifty-ones down as well.'

'Let's do it. I'll call 11 Platoon and let them know what you're doing.'

He clapped Waters on the shoulder and, as the sergeant tore back down the alleyway to brief his men, Hicks hit the pressel switch to radio Olivier.

When Willan pulled his men back down the bank under a horrible weight of enemy fire, Cain, protected to some extent by his tree, stayed in position, blasting away with his Minimi. The enemy fire shifted again on to Farrugia's men, and Willan called to his section, 'Lads. Get back up the bank. The minute you've got muzzle clearance get firing as rapid as you can. We will only beat them if we can get their heads down before they switch back on to us.'

Willan crawled back up and started firing rapid shots with his rifle. The enemy again started blasting into his section. He heard the impact of a bullet and out of the corner of his eye saw Rawson's head spin. He looked at Rawson, a metre away to his right, and yelled, 'That was close, Tony, you lucky...'

He stopped mid-sentence. There was blood everywhere. A bullet had ripped through Rawson's helmet and into his head.

Privates Garrett and Cain continued pouring fire back at the enemy as Willan crawled over to Rawson. He was not moving and not making a sound. His eyes were open. No pulse, no breathing. Tony Rawson was dead.

Willan shouted, '*Man down! Man down!*'

He called into his mike, 'Three Three Alpha this is Three Two Charlie, I have a T Four casualty. T Four casualty.'

Sergeant Major Taylor cut straight in with a shocked voice, 'Three Three Alpha. You know T Four means dead? Confirm over.'

'Three Two Charlie. I know it means dead. T Four, over.'

Hicks was on the net. As always, calm. Efficient. But beneath it he was devastated to hear that one of his men had just been killed. 'This is Zero Alpha. Air will be on station very soon. When they attack, Three Zero callsigns are to extract. As I said previously, Two Zero Alpha will also give covering fire when he is in position.'

C Company's JTAC had called for air as soon as the ambush began, and as Hicks spoke into the radio, NATO jets were screaming towards the position.

Willan weighed up exactly what that meant. It would be a 30mm strafing run along the enemy position. With any luck it would take them out, and it would also throw up so much dust that any surviving enemy would be blinded for at least a couple of minutes. Vital time for him to extract his section.

Olivier, further along the ditch with the other two sections, called into the radio, 'All stations Metal Three Zero, this is Metal Three Zero Alpha. When the air comes in callsign Metal Three One Charlie is to move to compound immediately to our right, clear and secure it and give covering fire from there.'

Three One Charlie was Watson's section. Olivier ordered Willan's section, with the casualty, to move in to join them in the compound. Farrugia's section would remain in position until the other two were firm, giving covering fire. He was then to move in himself, covered by fire from Watson in the compound.

Willan acknowledged Olivier's orders then started removing Rawson's daysack, webbing and body armour. However slight Rawson was, getting the dead weight of his body across the open ground, perhaps under fire, was going to be a struggle, and every bit of unnecessary gear had to be ditched.

Protected though he had been by his tree, Cain had decided a few minutes earlier that he had been firing from that position for too long and was tempting fate by staying there. He had crawled further down the bank to the left and was now firing from just beside the compound Waters and his men were heading for. He glimpsed movement over his shoulder and looked back. 10 Platoon soldiers were near the compound and seemed to be waving and shouting to him. He couldn't hear them over the din of the gunfire, so shrugged and carried on firing. Seconds later there was a huge explosion as 10 platoon's bar-mine detonated. Lumps of compound wall and rubble cannoned into Cain's back, and he was covered in dust and debris.

Corporal Farrugia heard the call, 'Air in thirty seconds,' and passed it along his section, who were up on the edge of the ditch firing across the cornfield. *With the enemy so close*, he thought, *I hope the air doesn't get us instead of them.*

There was the roar of an F15 overhead, then Farrugia was shocked to hear a rapid-fire succession of loud explosions as 20mm shells splattered the ground directly behind his section. *They have got us – or very nearly.*

To his right Olivier was yelling into the radio, 'Stop the air, they're strafing us. They're 70 metres out.'

Farrugia's blood ran cold when he heard, from his left, 'Man down! Man down!' the second time in just a few short minutes.

Lance Corporal Ben Lake, Farrugia's 2IC, called out, 'It's Snowy, he's been hit in the face.'

Private Johnathon Snow from Scunthorpe had been firing his Minimi when the shells impacted behind him. He was hurled sideways and thought he had been punched. Then he felt warm blood fill his mouth and drip down his chin. A shard of red-hot shrapnel had torn into his cheek and out through his lip, ripping away two teeth.

Private James Budd, firing next to him, rolled across and looked at his bleeding face. He reached into the map pocket of Snow's combat trousers and pulled out a first field dressing. 'Hold still, Snowy, I'm going to put this on you.'

10 Platoon had not been able to get on to the roof of their compound, but Waters's gunners had positioned themselves on top of the compound wall and were blasting into the Taliban positions. The combined vicious rate of fire from the two platoons had not beaten the Taliban, but their fire had slowed, and was now divided, firing at both 10 and 11 Platoons.

Olivier decided it was worth taking the chance and trying the extraction, even though the air had not found its target. With Snow wounded, he changed the order of extraction, telling Farrugia to move first with his casualty. Olivier spoke into his radio to Waters: 'Two Zero Alpha, Three Zero Alpha, my callsigns extracting now. Increase to maximum rate of fire, over.' Not waiting for the response, he yelled, 'Corporal Watson, keep the fire going down. Corporal Farrugia, get your men into the compound. Move now!'

As Watson's rate of fire intensified, Farrugia led his men racing under heavy enemy fire across the open ground and into the compound. Dripping blood from his face, and aided by Budd, Snow managed to run into the compound behind the section. As he slumped down on a step, Farrugia came across. In his invariably quiet, calm and reassuring way, he said, 'You all right, Snowy mate? Don't worry, we'll get you out of here, you'll be fine.'

Snow nodded and attempted a grin that didn't work through a bleeding and ripped-up face. Farrugia patted him on the shoulder and, leaving him to Budd, hurried back to the doorway to find a way of getting fire down to help the others get across the open ground.

Olivier was on the radio and ordered Willan to extract. He was further away from the compound and would have more ground to cover – dragging Rawson with him.

'Lads,' shouted Willan, 'we're extracting right, to that compound over there. Garrett, you give me a hand with Nicey. Cain, you give us whatever covering fire you can with your Minimi. Keep as low as you can – we don't want anyone else getting it.'

Willan and Garrett began to drag Rawson towards the compound, each with a hand hooked under his armpit. As they left the cover of the bank, bullets started pinging near by. They kept as low as they could, trying to crawl as they dragged him. It was impossible; they were making virtually no progress.

'We're going to have to get up,' said Willan. They crouched as low as they could, sometimes throwing themselves to the ground as the bullets got too close. Watson's men were keeping up a furious rate of fire at the enemy and getting incoming themselves.

Keeping pace with the other two, and determined to give as much cover fire as he could, Cain was standing up, exposed, as he rattled down belt after belt. He could no longer see the enemy, but he knew where they were and was firing in their direction, hoping to keep their heads down.

It was getting towards 0900 hours, and the temperature was climbing rapidly. Willan and Garrett were struggling with Rawson. They were moving as fast as they could, dripping sweat and panting hard. 'Well done, Garrett, mate. Keep it going, you're doing great,' said Willan, who could feel for himself how tough it was and was really impressed by Garrett's determination.

Garrett was a brand new soldier. He had joined only a couple of months earlier, since the battalion had arrived in Helmand. He had come straight from basic training, where his instructor had been a mate of Private Rawson from their own time in training.

The three soldiers continued their terrible ordeal. Every minute it took them to cross the open ground, Willan, Cain and Garrett wondered how they had not been hit and expected it at any moment. They were brothers, welded together in the crucible of Afghan combat. They were prepared to die for each other, and on that morning they very nearly did. And Rawson was their brother too. And they were risking their lives to get his body back home. It never occurred to any one of them for a single moment that they could do anything else. It made absolutely no difference whether he was dead or alive: they were going to get him back.

Farrugia saw Willan, Garrett, Cain and Rawson nearing the compound. Corporal Thomson, a sharpshooter attached from the Royal Regiment of Scotland, and Farrugia raced out into the gunfire and helped drag Rawson the last 30 metres into safety.

12

As Willan was moving Rawson across the open ground, Sergeant Major Taylor and Corporal Ian Peyton, the medic, had made their way, under fire, through a filthy irrigation ditch, into the compound. When he heard there were casualties, without any regard for his own safety, Peyton started to dash across the open, towards the compound. Taylor grabbed him. 'Hang on a minute, Norm, you're going to get shot yourself doing that. We need you to treat casualties, not become one. Just wait for a couple of minutes while I get some fifty-one down, then we'll go round through that ditch under cover of the smoke.'

Peyton crossed to the wounded Snow and removed his field dressing. He cleaned the blood away, then dropped his medical Bergen and took out the kit he needed. The troops were horrified to see Snow stick his tongue through the hole in his cheek.

'Put it away,' laughed Peyton and slapped a HemCon pad against Snow's face. An American product, HemCon was designed specifically to prevent the main cause of death on the battlefield, bleeding. It controls bleeding by becoming extremely sticky when in contact with blood, and its adhesive-like action seals the wound and forms a barrier between an open lesion and dangerous bacteria.

As Peyton finished bandaging Snow, Rawson was brought in. Farrugia stood silently looking at Rawsan, grief all over his face. They were the closest of friends and had been through basic training at Catterick together. Peyton removed Rawson's helmet. He looked at the horrific wound. *There's obviously nothing I can do for the poor bloke*, he thought, *but I can give him a bit of dignity*, and he carefully put a field dressing over the hole in the back of his head.

While Peyton bandaged Rawson's head, Taylor started organizing the CASEVAC. Covered by Waters's 10 Platoon gunners, Watson's section now came crashing through the compound door, Taliban bullets cracking into the dirt at their feet as they ran across the open ground.

Watson was on fire, smoke pouring from him. He tore off his daysack and webbing and dropped them smouldering on to the ground.

'What happened to you?' asked Willan.

Still pouring sweat and breathing hard from his run into the compound, Watson replied, 'I threw some red phos to cover our extraction, and the grenade bounced off a tree and got me, just as I was about to run! Never was much good at cricket anyway,' he grinned.

The compound itself was now coming under heavy fire from the Taliban. Farrugia had managed to find only one firing position to shoot back, and his men were taking it in turns going up the steps to fire.

They got Snow on to a stretcher and, dodging bullets, rushed him out of the compound to the irrigation ditch they were going to use for extraction. Realizing how much of a burden he would be to those carrying him, despite his loss of blood and the agony of his face wound, Snow climbed off the stretcher and insisted on walking.

Corporal Nick Townsend, who had himself been wounded by a UGL at Mazdurak in May and had recently returned from hospital in the UK, flung Rawson's body over his shoulder and carried him down into the ditch. It was tough going. The ditch provided protection from enemy fire through most of its length, but the height of the banks was uneven, and the men had to duck down as they crossed the exposed areas. They were wading through thick, oozing mud, with the stinking ditchwater waist high, and constantly stumbling over tree stumps, branches and roots.

Olivier took Rawson from Townsend and carried his body on for a few hundred metres. Then Watson took over. But as they progressed they realized it was too hard going, so, with one man at each corner, they floated him along the ditch.

As the men of 11 Platoon struggled through the irrigation ditch with Rawson and Snow, Hicks was coordinating the arrival of the MERT team to evacuate the two soldiers. The Chinook couldn't land at Regay because the risk of getting shot down on landing or take-off was too great.

From his map, Hicks identified a suitable landing site west of the neighbouring village of Begay, a small cluster of compounds near the edge of the Green Zone, 500 metres away. He gave orders for the company to break contact. 'All stations, this is Zero Alpha, callsign Two Zero is to secure a covered route west out of Regay, exiting at the same point we broke in. Two Zero is also to secure an HLS to the west of Begay for the evacuation of casualties. Three Zero is to provide rear security and break contact with the enemy, if possible no further west than the edge of Regay.'

Sergeant Waters, commanding Two Zero, 10 Platoon, with Corporal Tim Ferrand, his acting platoon sergeant, blasted their way through compound after compound to get a clear and covered route through the village and out the other side, with their sections under fire from the flank most of the way.

Exhausted, soaking wet, bedraggled and gasping for breath, the men of 11 Platoon, carrying Private Rawson, emerged from the irrigation ditch into a compound secured by Corporal Ferrand. Ferrand placed Rawson's body on to a lightweight stretcher and covered it with another. Corporal Willan, Corporal Farrugia, Lance Corporal Ben Lake and Private Suly Saumi carried the stretcher along the secured route and out of Regay. They left Regay and entered a deep and muddy irrigation ditch, with water waist high, that gave a covered route all the way to Begay.

By the time they reached the open, ploughed field the other side of Begay, the stretcher bearers' arms felt as if they would drop off. To the rear, there was sporadic gunfire as Corporal Townsend attempted to break contact with the enemy. Looking up, Farrugia saw Waters's men on a compound roof, in all-round defence, protecting their movement and the landing sight.

Beside one of the compounds, Sergeant Major Taylor said, 'OK, Corporal Willan, Corporal Farrugia, you guys can leave the stretcher here, go back and rejoin your sections.'

Farrugia knew he would never see Rawson again. His body would be flown to Bastion, then back to England for his funeral. He wanted to see him off the battlefield and on to the safety of the Chinook. The last thing he would ever be able to do for the friend whom he had known since basic training. But he didn't argue with the sergeant major. He knew he had to get back and sort out his section. He looked down at the stretcher and saw the lifeless shape of Rawson's body underneath its cover. He crouched down, touched Rawson's head and whispered, 'Bye, Nicey mate.'

A few minutes later the air was screaming with the sound of Apaches, prowling overhead, hunting for any sign of the enemy, before the Chinook arrived. Then, in a cloud of dust, the big twin-rotored helicopter swooped to the ground. The IRT soldiers raced off and took up fire positions, and Sergeant Major Taylor, assisted by the wounded Private Snow, carried Rawson up the ramp.

After the helicopter left, the platoon sergeants moved around their platoons, carrying out head-checks and making sure everyone was OK, getting ready for a swift patrol back into Inkerman.

Sergeant Waters sat on the bank of a narrow irrigation ditch, and Captain Hicks slumped down on the opposite bank. Waters knew Hicks well. The two had served as instructors together at the Infantry Training Centre, Catterick. Hicks was composed, but Waters could see he was upset.

Hicks pulled a pack of Marlboros from his pocket and held it out to Waters. Waters had given up smoking in Kajaki, but he needed one now. As the two men puffed on their cigarettes, Waters said, 'I really can't believe what happened. I can't believe Nicey's gone. The platoon – even the company – they're not going to be the same. He was such a big character.'

'Yeah,' said Hicks, shaking his head, 'a brilliant bloke.'

He stared back at Regay for a moment, then flicked his fag butt into the ditch, stood up and said, 'Let's head back to Inkerman.'

13

That night, tired after a physically and emotionally draining day, Hicks sat in the dust-coated Inkerman ops room and wrote about Private Tony Rawson for publication on the MOD website. He sifted through the eulogies he had asked for from Rawson's mates, to be emailed back to Bastion and then transmitted onwards for publication with his own.

Among them was a characteristically brief message from Corporal Farrugia, 'I've known Rawson since day one of training; what a good bloke. You don't get the name "Nicey" for no reason. You will be missed, mate.'

And jointly by Private Curtis Cumberbatch and Private Scott Garrett, who had struggled across the open ground in Regay with Rawson's body: 'Mr Nice Guy: Never let any one of us down even at the hardest of times, a great friend and just a brilliant soldier. Thanks for showing us the ropes when I first got to the Battalion. We felt privileged to be in the same section as you. Missed but never forgotten.'

Hicks, who personally knew Rawson well, then wrote his own piece. 'Private Rawson epitomized not only the core values of the British Army, but also embodied the spirit of the British Infantry. Selfless, good-natured even in the face of adversity and courageous under fire, he will be sorely missed by all his comrades within C (Essex) Company. His loss will be felt deeply by all those who knew him. All our thoughts are with his family and friends at this time.'

Private Harry McCabe was on night stag in the FSG tower on the roof of the ops room where Hicks continued to work on reports from the day's battle. McCabe was the Javelin operator who had dragged Lance Corporal Hawkins from his blown-up Pinzgauer a week earlier.

The FSG tower was made up of an outer layer of green sandbags, double thickness and four high. In the middle was a sandbagged sangar, about 10 metres long, topped with a roof of corrugated iron to keep the sun off. In one corner was the FSG command post, with maps and radios. The tower was bristling with weapons: GPMGs, Javelins and a grenade machine-gun. The whole was draped with sand-coloured cam-nets to break up the glare of the sun and provide some concealment against sniper fire.

When he came on duty, McCabe had been briefed to be on the lookout for movement in the area of the Four Archways, a distant two-storey compound. He was told that intelligence showed Farouk, the man believed to be responsible for organizing the Taliban's return to the area north of Sangin, may have been in and around that building. McCabe had also been reminded of the change to the Rules of Engagement that had just come into force. Until this time, British forces in Helmand had been able to shoot identified Taliban fighters. That did not mean they had to be carrying or using weapons at the time. Now they were only allowed to fire an enemy that were positively identified carrying weapons.

It was 0030 hours and McCabe had been on stag for two hours. There was no movement at all across the vast expanses outside the compound and very little inside. The minutes ticked by slowly. It was stifling hot, and the only sounds were the wild dogs down by the river howling at the bright, eerie moon, whose glare was unbroken by clouds. Sometimes all of the dogs in the valley would start up at once, with their blood-curdling yelping, howling and screeching.

McCabe moved the CLU steadily from left to right, scanning through the whole of his arc, viewing the dim green image that clearly showed the detail of the ground all round the FOB. He tracked slowly past the Four Archways and then jerked back on to the buildings, hundreds of metres away. *Was that movement?*

Fixed on the compound, he peered intently through the sight. *It was!* He counted: *Two, three, four.* He could make out four shadowy figures moving. *Is Farouk among them? Is one of them the man who led the ambush that killed Nicey Rawson a few hours ago? Maybe all four were there, firing machine-gun bullets and rockets at the C Company patrol. And maybe one of them dug in the mine that blew me up and killed Hawks.*

'Come over here and look at this,' he hissed to Drummer Jonathan Cucciniello. McCabe handed the sight to Cucciniello. 'What do you reckon mate?'

'Definitely people down there. I can see four people.

'Any weapons?'

'Can't make it out, yeah, one of them has ... no, not sure. Can't really see. What do you reckon, Harry, shall we whack them.'

'We can't, can we? The ROE change, remember. I'm going to call Captain Hicks and let him have a look.'

When Hicks got the call he had just finished his reports and emailed them to Bastion and was chatting to Captain Ollie Ormiston, the FSG commander. They were discussing girlfriends back home. Hicks asked Ormiston about Rachel and told him about how he and Nicola were planning to buy a house after the tour ended. Hicks said, 'I'll be back in a minute, Ollie,' then scaled the makeshift ladder cobbled together from steel pickets, and appeared next to McCabe in the tower.

Some commanders might have been irritated to be called out at this time of night, especially after such a hard day's fighting. But not Hicks. He was always even-tempered, and he knew and understood what men like McCabe and Cucciniello had to go through for hour after hour of mind-numbing, tedious, uneventful sentry duty. He often deprived himself of hours of valuable sleep at night, going round the sangars, chatting to the troops, taking brews round, encouraging them, breaking up the tedium.

Hicks was on the same wavelength as the men, and while they scanned their arcs he could happily chat about football, nightclubs, women and beer – although most found it hard to understand how he could prefer some weird-sounding concoction he called 'Old Speckled Hen' over an honest pint of good British Stella.

For the soldier in combat the most important quality in an officer is that he knows how to do his job, and can think and act quickly enough to keep them alive. But a very close second is to care. Officers who look down on their men, treat them as numbers or are just not interested are despised by all. Those who look at them as individuals, who speak to them like human beings and have a genuine care for their welfare, their interests and their concerns are respected and sometimes liked. Hicks was the personification of that type of officer. He revered his soldiers, genuinely enjoyed their company and would do anything for them. In return they loved him and would follow him anywhere.

'What's up, lads?' he said.

'Have a look through there, sir,' said McCabe. 'We've PID'd four possible Taliban at the Four Archways.'

Hicks squinted into the CLU. 'Yeah, seen. Well done for spotting them, McCabe. I would have said fire at them, but because of the ROE change I can't. No weapons. If you hear any shots from over there, go for it – splat them.'

Twenty minutes later McCabe was relieved in the tower and went down to get some sleep. He was back up again at 0500 hours, and it was all quiet. Even the dogs had packed up their howling for a bit. And there didn't seem to be any movement at all now at the Four Archways.

14

McCabe's last stag of the night finished at 0700 hours, and he went back to his camp bed, as Inkerman was rapidly coming alive with soldiers washing and shaving, organizing brews, checking kit and getting themselves sorted out for the day's operations.

Although he was knackered after having spent the whole of the previous day and most of the night on duty, it was too hot to get straight to sleep, so he read a bit more of his sun-bleached, grit-encrusted and dog-eared paperback, *Sharpe's Tiger*, a novel centred on the Battle of Seringapatam, in which the 12th of Foot, one of the Royal Anglians' former regiments, played a major role. Although the tale was set over 200 years ago in Mysore, 2,500 kilometres south-east across the Indian subcontinent, McCabe couldn't help chuckling about how little life in the Army had changed over the centuries. Sentry duty, get no sleep, fight for hours, eat rubbish food, get everything squared away at the double then wait for hours before you get to go anywhere. Moan about waiting to go in then moan when you're in. Too hot to sleep, too knackered to do anything else.

Wouldn't have it any other way, he thought. He chuckled again and nodded off.

After a few hours' fitful sleep, McCabe was almost thrown off his camp bed by the ground shock and deafened by the ear-piercingly loud explosion as an 82mm mortar bomb slammed into the base. He was showered in dust and the wall next to him shook as a bomb landed on the other side.

It was 1330 hours, and baking hot. All round Inkerman, C Company and FSG soldiers, dressed in T-shirts, shorts and trainers, who seconds earlier had been drinking brews, cleaning weapons, smoking, reading and ragging each other, were hastily throwing on helmets and body armour, grabbing weapons and ammo and dashing to their stand-to positions on the walls.

McCabe pulled on his body armour and helmet, put on his boots without wasting time with the laces, grabbed his rifle and ran out of the cam-net. He looked at the WMIK-mounted .50 cal machine-gun point-ing over the wall near by and thought, *No, I'll get up the tower. Probably be more useful on a Javelin. I want to fire one anyway. Maybe this'll be my chance. More exposed up there, but what the hell. When it's your turn…*

He ran to the tower as volley after volley of mortar shells and SPG-9 anti-tank missiles were striking the compound, the area outside and the walls. In the tower he positioned himself behind a Javelin and CLU and immediately began scanning for targets. Lance Corporal Ian Goodship and Private Nicholas Stevens were on the tripod-mounted GPMG (SF) guns, blasting fire down into the Green Zone. Lance Cor-poral Alistair Procter, a broad grin on his face, was blazing away with his GMG.

Captain Ollie Ormiston, pouring sweat in the midday heat, was directing the fire, scanning through binoculars, checking air photo-graphs, and with him was the FSG 2IC, Sergeant Nathan Love. Ser-geant Alex Potter, the JTAC, was demanding air. He reported to Ormiston, 'B1 bomber has been allocated, but they reckon it can't be here for thirty minutes.'

Just after McCabe arrived in the tower, Dave Hicks scaled the ladder, wearing running shorts and trainers with his helmet, body armour, rifle and radio. Just before the attack, Corporal Ian Peyton, the company medic, had finished talking to his fiancée, Donna, and handed Hicks the satellite phone. Hicks managed a brief conversation with Nicola, his girlfriend, then, when the first shell crumped into the base, said a hasty goodbye, grabbed his kit and came up to get eyes on so he could plan and direct the company's response.

Hicks could have stayed in the comparative safety of the company ops room, receiving radio reports from his commanders in the FSG tower and the sangars and stand-to positions. But he understood only too well the iron rule that the commander must position him-self where he can see the battle as best he can and where he can make a difference. He could do little from the ops room, and not much more from the tower. But at least from here he could get a first-hand feel for what was happening and work out for himself what to do about it. Of course it was much more risky, and he was exposed to enemy fire. But that was of secondary importance to Hicks. His pri-ority was to direct the battle and to lead from the front, whatever the dangers.

Above the din, Sergeant Booth, an MFC attached from the 2nd Battalion, yelled to McCabe, 'What can you see? Any targets? Any targets?'

McCabe replied, 'Can't see anything. There's rounds coming in everywhere, can't see...Hang on a minute, Sarge, hang on. I think I can make out something, something at the X-Ray Two Three compounds. Maybe a mortar, can't really make it out, there's too much dust and stuff. I can't engage. It's out of Javelin range.'

Before McCabe had finished speaking, Booth was on the radio to Sergeant Adrian Evans, whose 81mm mortar section was set up ready to fire from inside the base.

'Hello, Iron One Three, this is Iron One Three Alfa. Fire mission. Three mortars. X-Ray Two Three. Enemy mortars in the open. Ten rounds fire for effect.'

Evans brought his mortars into action, and Booth squinted intently through his binos to see where the rounds landed.

X-Ray Two Three was a pre-arranged mortar target, and less than a minute after Booth gave his fire orders, the mortars were spitting out the first three of thirty rounds that would pound the enemy mortar position. In normal circumstances, mortar fire had to be authorized by the company commander, but in this situation every second could save lives if Booth was able to take out the enemy mortars and stop the bombs falling into the base.

McCabe scanned across the desert into the Green Zone, searching, searching desperately for any further signs of enemy. Mortars, RPGs and SPG-9s continued to blast all round the base, non-stop. They had never seen anything remotely like this before. Machine-gun and rifle fire was slapping into the mud building below, pinging overhead and thudding into the sandbags all round them.

McCabe flinched and ducked, 'That was close, Stevo.'

Next to him, Stevens was blasting away with his GPMG (SF), firing so fast it seemed his tracer formed almost continuous arcs of fire into the X-Ray Two Three compound. The two soldiers were laughing. Although he had learnt over recent months about this nervous reaction to coming so close to death, to getting shot at continuously, even as he laughed, McCabe was incredulous that he could do so at this, the most terrifying moment of his life.

Stevens had been firing so many rounds, and so fast, that he was running low on ammo. 'Going down to get some more rounds,' he yelled, ducking bullets as he weaved across the roof and slid rapidly down the ladder.

Stevens ran to grab the ammo boxes from one of the WMIKs. There was a large explosion and the sound of tearing steel as an SPG-9 missile blasted into the Oshkosh close support tanker truck parked at the rear of the compound. There was a blinding flash and a fireball flew into the air where the missile had hit. Immediately the truck caught fire and a huge, billowing column of black smoke headed skywards. Quickly the fire died out. The 5,000 gallons of diesel inside the tanker did not ignite, but noxious black smoke continued to pour from the vehicle.

All hell was breaking loose in Inkerman. The FSG tower was hammering fire back at the Taliban, and the C Company and ANA soldiers in their sangars and stand-to positions around the wall were searching for targets and engaging enemy movement.

As Stevens headed back to the tower, an RPG missile landed in the middle of a group of ANA soldiers near the compound wall. Above the gunfire and explosions, cries of 'Medic, medic!' resounded round the compound. Corporal Peyton grabbed a stretcher, and Stevens saw him race across to the far side of the compound, towards the ANA.

Peyton came upon a scene of smoke and gore. An ANA soldier was lying in the rubble, pouring blood. He had taken a direct hit from the RPG. Two of his mates dragged him towards Peyton, who grabbed the top half of his body and put him on the stretcher. His legs were almost severed, dragging limply behind him, held on by threads. The soldier was conscious, but he wasn't screaming. Peyton thought, *How can he be so calm?*

He took out several packets of QuikClot, an American haemostatic powder designed to arrest high-volume blood loss in large wounds, stopping the haemorrhage before the casualty goes into shock. Peyton poured the powder into the seething bloody cavities where the soldier's legs had been. The blood flow slowed, but Peyton was frustrated to see that it didn't stop altogether. He slapped on some HemCon pads, which had similar effects to QuikClot, and then dressed the soldier with stump bandages before punching a morphine autoject into him.

Helped by the other ANA soldiers, Peyton carried the half-dead man back to the medical centre, put fluid lines into his arms, and continued working on his legs.

15

The radios were alive with traffic, and Sergeant Waters, acting commander of 10 Platoon, scaled the tower to give Hicks an update on what was happening on the ground. Hicks was standing up, scanning the area, trying to get an understanding of exactly what they were faced with. How many enemy were out there? This ferocity of attack and its accuracy were something completely different to anything they had seen before. The enemy were firing several different weapon systems from multiple, well-concealed firing points. Carver's assessment that the Taliban had sent in their hard-core, properly trained fighters, perhaps from across the border, had come horribly true.

Did they plan to try to storm into the base? Looking around, he knew the enemy wouldn't stand a chance if they did. He had too much firepower, and they would have to get across the open. What other options did they have?

After Waters had briefed him, Hicks shouted above the noise, 'OK, thanks, Segeant Waters. Well done. Keep your lads on the wall. Make sure they stay totally vigilant. I'll keep you informed by radio.'

Waters departed. Hicks called to McCabe: 'Where are they? Can you see them?'

McCabe turned and shouted, 'No, sir, nothing, can't see anything.'

McCabe turned his head back and saw a black rugby-ball-shaped object, flying towards the tower from the left, hurtling straight towards him. Everything went into slow motion. He felt sick, his mouth went completely dry, his stomach cramped, and he thought, *I'm dead. Can't outrun that. That's me gone.* The Soviet-designed rocket-assisted fin-stabilized 73mm SPG-9 Spear anti-tank missile slammed into the FSG tower at 700 metres per second. There was a blinding flash and a massive, deafening blast, which shook the whole building and threw up thick clouds of dust and debris. Heavy jagged shards of red-hot shrapnel scythed viciously through the air, ripping apart everything in their path.

The tower was a scene of almost total devastation. All of the soldiers had been hurled into the roof by the blast. Smoke poured from Lance Corporal Goodship's body armour. He was concussed and had twenty shrapnel wounds on the back of his head, his shoulders, arms, back and legs. The blast sucked the breath out of Ormiston, deafened him, threw him across the sangar; the wall collapsed on top of him, crushing his ribs. He lay in a crumpled heap under the sandbags, struggling to breathe. Blood dripped from Love's ears, covering his body armour. He was knocked off his feet, dazed and battered. Stevens was flung across the roof; he was stunned and disorientated, and a large chunk of shrapnel tore into his leg. McCabe was also thrown across the roof; he was bleeding from multiple shrapnel wounds in his hip, arms and calf, his eardrum was perforated, and he was knocked unconscious.

Captain Hicks took most of the SPG-9's force. There had been only sandbags in front of him when the missile screamed in and exploded. The blast picked him up like a rag doll and flung him violently to the other side of the roof. He landed on his back beside Sergeant Love.

Love thrust his hand into a gaping hole the size of a coke can in the left side of Hicks's chest to stem the streaming blood. Sniper Corporal Michael Morris and GPMG gunner Drummer Michael Williamson strapped on field dressings. Hicks was unconscious and had multiple shrapnel wounds to his head, torso, groin and legs. The three men fought to plug the holes so they could get him down from the tower.

In the midst of the carnage, Lance Corporal Proctor, standing up as if nothing had happened, continued to blast out burst after burst of 40mm high-explosive grenades from his Heckler and Koch GMG. Lance Corporal Goodship, covered in dust, battered, bleeding and still dazed, got himself back behind his GPMG and was sending streams of 7.62mm tracer into likely Taliban firing positions.

Love, Morris, Williamson and Sergeant Booth, the MFC, lowered Hicks down the makeshift ladder, burning their hands and legs on the hot steel rungs, heated up in the intense glare of the early afternoon sun.

Ormiston, who had managed to get his own battered and bruised body down to the ground, received Hicks at the bottom of the ladder, and they put him on a stretcher at the base of the tower. The medics went straight to work there, not wanting to waste time moving him to the medical room.

McCabe had regained consciousness up in the tower. He put a field dressing on his own leg, which was bleeding from multiple small shrapnel wounds. He wanted to stay at his post, but with his Javelin destroyed by the SPG-9, he was just in the way so reluctantly agreed to move down to the ground. There he saw Hicks and, with Sergeant Waters, helped to stem the bleeding in his groin, calf and thigh.

Peyton handed over the ANA soldier, whom he had stabilized as much as he was going to, slung the medical bergen over his shoulder and raced out of the medical centre to help with Hicks.

Sergeant Booth was kneeling beside Hicks, slapping him round the face. 'Sir, stay with us. Sir, can you hear me? Sir, stay with us, sir. Stay with us.' Lance Corporal Pearce, an RAMC medic, was fighting to stop the bleeding in Hicks's upper body. She briefed Peyton on what she had done so far as she worked to fix a HemCon bandage to the gash in his shoulder.

Peyton knelt down and looked at Hicks. He was conscious, his face was white, and he was covered in thick, light grey dust. There was blood everywhere. Lance Corporal Pearce had strapped an oxygen mask round his face. A blood pressure cuff was strapped round his upper arm, and a pulse oximeter clipped to one of his fingers. The two devices were connected up to a Propaq patient monitor, on the ground next to Hicks, a box about the size of a car battery that gives a read-out of blood pressure, pulse rate and oxygen levels.

Peyton quickly checked the readings. *Oxygen levels low: not surprising. Pulse is racing: his heart is working overtime to deal with the blood loss. Blood pressure is dangerously low. Fifty over thirty. That's the first thing I need to sort.*

Peyton knew what he had to do to bring up Hicks's blood pressure. He desperately needed fluids, and Peyton saw from the readings that he had capilliary shut-down. His veins were collapsed due to the massive amount of blood he had lost, so there was no chance of getting fluids into his body intravenously. Peyton took out an EZ-IO intraosseous kit from his bergen. The main part of the kit was a drill, about the size and shape of a battery-powered screwdriver, and it functioned in much the same way. He connected the intraosseous needle into the head of the drill. He wiped clean the area around Hicks's left knee and drilled into the inside of his tibia, just below the knee-cap. In two seconds he heard a click, as the needle automatically detached itself. He withdrew the drill, leaving the needle sticking about one centimetre out of the leg.

As he worked he told Booth to set up a fluid bag. He took the end of the giving set, a clear plastic tube fixed into the bag, and connected it to the needle.

'OK, Boothie, squeeze the bag and keep the pressure on it, keep the fluid flowing through.'

Peyton studied the Propaq readings. Hicks was getting oxygen, Lance Corporal Pearce had stemmed the worst of the bleeding, and the sodium-chloride-based Hartmann's solution that Booth was holding was now flowing into his body. With relief Peyton saw Hicks's blood pressure creep back up. He was beginning to stabilize.

Hicks tried to sit up and tore the mask away from his face. '*Get me back up there,*' he shouted, '*Get me back up!*'

Peyton pressed the mask on to him again and tried to push him down, but Hicks fought it off, 'Get me up to the tower, get me back up.'

Peyton turned to Booth. 'Boothie, keep that fluid going in. And keep talking to him. I don't care what you say. Say what you like. Just keep talking to him. You need to calm him down. That's the most important thing now.'

Peyton was amazed that Hicks didn't seem to be in any great pain. *That's the adrenalin at work,* he thought. *Thank God for that, we can't give him any morphine with his head injury, and with his breathing rate fluctuating so much, morphine would screw up his respiratory system as well.*

Peyton checked the Propaq readings again. Still bad, but now heading in the right direction. He thought that Hicks was as stable as he was going to get here at Inkerman and, assuming he got rapidly back to the hospital in Bastion, he stood a fighting chance of surviving these horrific wounds.

Word spread around the base that Hicks was seriously wounded. It was the worst news. He was loved by the soldiers, and they were depending on him to lead them through the most intense attack any of them had ever experienced.

Lieutenant Manie Olivier, 11 Platoon commander, took command of the base and the company. Enemy missiles and machine-gun bullets were still pouring into Inkerman. Ormiston, who was back in the tower, continued to direct fire, urgently trying to identify enemy weapon positions and attack them with direct and indirect fire.

While Olivier confirmed the MERT was on the way in, Sergeant Major Taylor set about organizing the CASEVAC. He said to Lance Corporal Michael Robinson, a section commander in 10 Platoon, 'Get a team together, get those two WMIKs and get the HLS secured. Report on the net when you're in position.'

'Sir, is the chopper going to come in with all this incoming?'

'Yes, it's going to try and get in. Now get some guys together and get it done.'

The HLS was just outside the compound back gate. Ignoring the fact that at least 50 per cent of all the incoming rockets and shells had landed in and around the HLS, Robinson grabbed a handful of C Company men and moved out into the enemy fire.

The sergeant major loaded Hicks and the horrifically wounded ANA soldier on to his quad bike and drove them down towards the HLS. It was dangerous, but there was nothing else for it. Hicks had to be got back to Bastion rapidly if he was going to have a chance of surviving. The other casualties, Sergeant Love, Lance Corporal Goodship, Private Stevens and Private McCabe, hobbled out to the HLS under their own steam.

Within a few minutes the Apaches roared into sight and loitered overhead, hunting for any sign of the enemy. The Chinook wasn't far behind. Taylor supervised the loading of the casualties, Pearce did a rapid handover of Hicks to the MERT doctor, and seconds later, hurling clouds of dust in every direction, the huge chopper was speeding back to Bastion.

In the FSG tower, Private Peter Howell, manning the remaining Javelin, continued to search the Green Zone with his CLU. Something caught his eye, a puff of smoke. He studied the area intently for a few moments till he was sure, then shouted above the deafening two-way gunfire and explosions, 'Sir, I can see smoke, straight across the Meean Rud wadi. Three thousand five hundred metres. I think it's their mortars.'

The JTAC, Sergeant Alex Potter, was standing next to Ormiston. Ormiston said, 'Can you get some guns on to that?'

Fifteen kilometres away in FOB Robinson, the men of 28/143 Battery Royal Artillery were standing by their three guns. When they received word on the battle group artillery net that troops were in contact within range of their howitzers, the artillerymen straight away stood to, ready for immediate response if a fire mission was ordered. They had spread cam-nets and ponchos above the rear parts of the guns, to try to achieve some respite from the searing heat.

Sergeant Potter transmitted the fire orders to the artillery command post, and instructions were barked out to the gun line. Jets of flame spewed out from the muzzles of the three L118 light guns as they hurled their 105mm high-explosive shells across the 15 kilometres of desert. Fifty seconds later the shells started to pound in around the Taliban weapon position in the Meean Rud wadi.

They weren't quite on target. Potter called in an order adjusting fire, and then a second volley of three rounds landed. Binoculars in one hand to check the point of impact, radio handset in the other, Potter hit his pressel and ordered the gunners at FOB Robinson, 'On target, fire for effect.'

The light guns did their brutal job, and within minutes the attack on Inkerman faltered then stopped altogether.

16

Later that afternoon, Lieutenant Colonel Carver sent Major Charlie Calder, commander of D Company, to take over at Inkerman until Messenger returned from R and R a week later. D (Cambridgeshire) Company had been split up at the start of the tour, with the Sniper, Anti-Tank, Machine-gun and Mortar Platoons formed into FSGs, allocated to the rifle companies. Recce Platoon usually worked directly for Carver, but its sections were sometimes temporarily grouped to the companies.

Without a company to run, Calder had been working as operational planning officer for the battle group and had been heavily involved in all of the major operations. Aside from the tragic circumstances that brought it about, Calder relished the opportunity to at last spend some time doing what every infantry officer wants to do most – command troops in battle.

Calder was well known to all of the senior men in the company, and many of the junior ranks. Royal Anglian blood coursed through his veins. He had entered the Royal Military Academy Sandhurst in 1987 and had served with the 1st Battalion since he was commissioned, with breaks only to attend courses and for staff postings. His father, Tony Calder, commanded the 1st Battalion in the 1980s and retired as a brigadier, and his grandfather, Major Johnny Calder, had fought in France in 1944 with the Suffolk Regiment, which later became part of the Royal Anglian Regiment.

With extensive operational experience in Iraq, Northern Ireland and the Balkans, Calder was a calm, level-headed and measured officer, and exactly the man the troops now needed at the helm to restore confidence and balance after the battering C Company had taken over the last couple of days.

When Inkerman was attacked Calder had been at Sangin DC, overseeing the battle group's reconstruction projects and liaising with the district governor, the ANA and the Afghan police. He was on the next available Chinook from Sangin and landed at Inkerman at 1600 hours.

He surveyed the battered base. Craters and missile debris littered the ground. Thin whisps of smoke were still gently rising from some of the shell holes. The Oshkosh tanker looked burnt out. The FSG tower was wrecked, with its sandbags flung all round the base, and the walls collapsed. Everywhere, soldiers were working to sort out the damage. A stench of cordite, explosives and burning permeated the whole place.

Calder conferred with Captain Ormiston, Lieutenant Olivier and Sergeant Major Taylor. They briefed him on the details of the attack and then he walked round the base, and was shown the damage that had been done and the enemy firing points. As he moved around, he stopped and spoke to many of the soldiers, giving them a word of reassurance and gauging their mood.

Calder sensed that although C Company and the fire support group had been hit hard over the past days, with the deaths of Lance Corporal Hawkins and Private Rawson, and the battering they had taken just a few hours earlier, they remained stoical, resilient and ready for action. He felt, however, that FSG Delta, which had taken the brunt of the casualties and had been in the austere and demanding conditions of Inkerman for two months without respite, should now rotate with Captain Mark Taylor's FSG Charlie at Nowzad, and straight away he arranged for their transfer.

Calder's priority was to assess and repair the damage to the FOB and to wrest the operational initiative from the Taliban. He requested additional mobile support, in the form of the Brigade Reconnaissance Force, to move north and probe and harry the enemy, taking the heat off Inkerman. The BRF, two platoons mounted in WMIKs, arrived that night. They were commanded by Major Mick Aston, who had handed over command of B Company when they left for Kajaki. After checking in with Calder, Aston led his force to the Putay area, 7 kilometres north of Inkerman.

Calder also wanted to beef up the company's fighting power on the ground and requested a squadron, or part of a squadron, of Mastiff heavy-armoured patrol vehicles, newly arrived in theatre.

Calder had been on patrol with Hicks in the Inkerman area a few days before, but he was now taking temporary command of the company and needed to get to know the men quickly. He visited the sangars and the admin areas, meeting and talking to commanders and soldiers.

Around midnight that night, Sergeant Matt Waters woke after a couple of hours' sleep and took over as duty watchkeeper in the Inkerman ops room. He was told word had recently come through that Captain Hicks had died of his wounds in Bastion. Waters was deeply shocked. Like everyone else, he had thought Hicks would make it. He stood up and walked outside into the warm and dusty night air and stood on his own for a few moments, his eyes moistening, before returning to his post.

Just twenty-four hours earlier, Hicks had sat in this ops room, writing a eulogy for Private Tony Rawson. Now it was Waters's turn to do the same for his commander and friend, and he concluded with the words: 'Dave will be sorely missed by all in C (Essex) Company and across the Battalion. He was a true star.'

Among the eulogies by Hicks's comrades C Company soldier Private Benjamin Emmett wrote, 'Captain Hicks was a very hard-working and understanding Second in Command. He was a funny, caring man and would always put a smile on your face. He was always willing to give advice and would never put you down. He always had time for everyone from private soldiers to the company commander. He will be missed greatly by all that knew him.'

17

Over the next few days Calder directed the reorganization of Inkerman's defences. He was assisted by Captain Dave Haggar, an officer attached from the 2nd Battalion, who was sent by Carver to take over Hicks's role as company 2IC and ops officer and remained with C Company for the rest of the tour.

The base was attacked again and again during the following week by 107mm rockets, RPGs and smallarms. Further casualties were inflicted in these attacks. A Grenadier Guards soldier, a member of the OMLT working with the ANA in Inkerman, sustained a shrapnel wound to the head and eventually lost his eye. And a member of the Royal Artillery Fire Support Team received shrapnel wounds to the legs.

As in the previous attacks, the Taliban fire was accurate, and their firing positions difficult to identify. If confirmation were needed, this demonstrated again that a numerically strong, hard-core group of Taliban fighters had been brought into the area. Calder realized that he had to hit back at them and somehow throw them on to the defensive.

The Mastiffs that he had asked for arrived at Inkerman two days after the attack that killed Hicks. Commanded by Major Nick Cowie and crewed by Royal Armoured Corps soldiers from Falcon Squadron, 2nd Royal Tank Regiment, the Mastiffs provided protected movement and heavy firepower for the infantry troops.

Initially Calder deployed the large and aggressive-looking vehicles, operating without infantry, to probe around the desert and on the fringes of the Green Zone 5 or 6 kilometres to the north of Inkerman. Their arrival shocked the Taliban, who had not seen such machines in the area before. Calder decided to use the Mastiffs to deploy his men out of Inkerman and drop them off in the desert so that they could patrol on foot into the Green Zone; they would then provide heavy fire support. Before the first patrol, a Mastiff was allocated to each section, and the men gathered at the vehicle to be shown around by the RTR crewmen.

One of the most heavily armoured troop-carriers used by the Army, the 6x6 Mastiff looks like a large armoured truck. Carrying up to eight troops, the vehicle protects against smallarms, landmines and improvised explosive devices. It features a mine-protected V-shaped steel hull that directs the blast away from under the vehicle. It has blast run-flat tyres, shock-mounted explosive attenuating seats and internal spall liners. It is fitted with Bowman radios. It carries GPMG, .50 cal heavy machine-gun and grenade machine-guns. American designed, the vehicle was modified from the US Marine Corps Cougar armoured patrol vehicles. Thermal imaging equipment allows drivers to operate closed down under armour, by day and night. Powered by the Caterpillar C-7 diesel engine yielding up to 330 shp of power, the vehicle can cruise at almost 90 kilometres per hour at ranges of around 1,200 kilometres on the road.

On Thursday 16 August, Calder led a patrol north to Putay. He took with him 10 Platoon under Sergeant Waters, an ANA platoon and Falcon Squadron's Mastiffs. The patrol moved out of Inkerman in the oppressive heat of the late morning. For once, the temperature wasn't a problem for the men of C Company. The Mastiffs were fitted with dual air-conditioning systems, and the troops were amazed to find air con in Afghanistan that actually worked. The more world-weary soldiers immediately speculated about how long it would take before the systems broke down.

As soon as they left the FOB and moved through the desert, the Taliban radio net came alive, and Calder was told by his interpreter that they were unusually excited and became increasingly apprehensive as they gave a running commentary on the column's movements.

Calder had planned that the troops would be dropped at three locations in the desert, patrol on foot into the Green Zone to check and clear specific compounds, marry back up with the vehicles and move on. The first two operations went without incident. During compound searches the troops found evidence of Taliban activity, including equipment such as RPG boosters and AK47 magazines. At the final location, Falcon Squadron dropped off 10 Platoon and, with the ANA troops remaining mounted, moved up to the high ground to provide overwatch. Waters led the platoon into a group of compounds astride the 611 on the outskirts of Putay. They were in the desert just to the west of the Green Zone. There was no one around, no sign of life.

The interpreter with the Mastiffs on the high ground reported radio chatter. The Taliban were reporting the dismounted troops' and the vehicles' activity and discussing their plan to ambush the British soldiers. 'If the green eyes come close, we hit them. We will hit them with the big thing.'

Calder speculated on what the 'big thing' might be – the SPG-9 they had used against Inkerman perhaps?

18

Machine-gun fire rattled in towards 10 Platoon from a compound 600 metres into the Green Zone. Waters's men returned fire, and on the high ground the Mastiff gunners opened up with their machine-guns and GMGs.

Falcon Squadron leader, Major Nick Cowie, radioed Calder on the company net: 'Hello, Metal Zero Alpha, this is Titanium Zero Alpha. There seems to be a clear route from the desert to the compound that's causing you trouble. Would you like my callsign to take Metal Two Zero down there? Over.'

Calder looked at the ground. A golden opportunity to take the enemy by surprise and to hit them hard. He replied, 'Metal Zero Alpha, roger, good idea. Let's move immediately.'

The Mastiff troop leader that would take 10 Platoon in drove rapidly to Waters's compound and dismounted. Calder quickly gave orders to him and Waters. '10 Platoon will assault the compound, clear through and destroy any enemy within.' He turned to the Mastiff troop leader. 'I want you to get them right up to the compound. Move as fast as you can. Then stay in intimate support. The other Mastiffs will remain on the high ground and provide fire support from there.'

Within minutes Waters had given a lightning set of battle orders to his men in an irrigation ditch, and they mounted up ready to assault. There was a smile on the face of every 10 Platoon soldier, as they sensed they were about to give out to the enemy more than they had been getting from him.

As 10 Platoon were getting into the vehicles, the interpreter reported further enemy radio traffic. 'The green eyes are moving away now, they are driving back to their camp. Do not fire. Let them go.'

Mounted in the Falcon Squadron leader's Mastiff, Calder was amused. He thought, *You couldn't do this very often, especially in the Green Zone, or they would quickly work out how to destroy the vehicles. But this hasn't happened before. Shock and awe, I think the Americans would call it.*

The mastiffs formed up, three abreast and the fourth just behind, with the squadron leader and Calder behind that. A classic armoured infantry assault formation, pointing towards the target compound 300 metres across the open desert, on the edge of the Green Zone. On the radio, the Mastiff troop leader, standing in the turret of the centre vehicle, gave the countdown to his other vehicles, 'Five. Four. Three. Two. One. Move now, move now.'

The drivers slammed their feet down on the accelerators, and the heavy vehicles lumbered forward. They moved fast, but not at breakneck speed, as the infantrymen in the back would be bounced from floor to ceiling as the vehicles crashed over the rocky and uneven desert.

Even at this speed it was a hard enough ride in the back. As they moved, the .50 cal and GMG gunners in the Mastiff turrets opened up on the compound, sending in devastating fire. They were blasting at the walls and all round the building, spraying lead and explosives into likely enemy firing positions beside the compound.

As they got closer, the Taliban opened up from compounds right and left with PKM machine-guns and AK47 assault rifles. A heavy weight of fire rained down on the Mastiffs, but it was futile, with no possibility of penetration against such heavy armour.

Inside the vehicles, the C Company soldiers were getting a running commentary from the vehicle commanders on the internal speakers, and they could see the other Mastiffs and the desert fly past on the monitors, which showed pictures provided by external cameras mounted on each side of the vehicles.

The Mastiffs on the high ground identified enemy firing positions and possible firing positions and laid down withering fire on the Taliban with their GMGs and machine-guns.

Two hundred metres out, the charging Mastiffs concentrated their fire on the wooden compound doors, blasting and splintering them into small pieces.

Ten metres from the badly smashed-up compound, the troop commander yelled into his radio, 'Stop – debus!'

The drivers jammed on the brakes, and the troops flung open the double doors in the rear of the Mastiffs. As Waters leapt to the ground, he remembered the many times he had been through this drill, jumping out of Warrior armoured vehicles in Canada, Germany and Bosnia as a young soldier in the 2nd Battalion's famed Point Company.

The Mastiffs were still blazing away at the compound, and immediately checked firing as Lance Corporal Robinson led his section forward of the vehicles and into the compound. His men lobbed in high-explosive grenades and then rushed straight in with rifles and machine-guns blazing – attacking at state red.

As they went, the Mastiffs reversed back, then moved into position to cover left and right of the compounds, ready to cut down escaping enemy.

Robinson's section broke through a series of small huts inside the compound, grenading and shooting as they went. As they moved through, decimating everything in their path, a Minimi gunner with 10

Platoon's reserve section, still outside the compound, saw a man carrying an AK47, running for his life out of the right-hand side of the compound. He was making for a nearby irrigation ditch, but the gunner cut him down with a twenty-round burst. At the same time two more Taliban escaping from the left of the compound were blown to pieces by a lethal blast from a Mastiff machine-gun. On the high ground, the fire support Mastiffs identified more Taliban fighters trying to escape down an irrigation ditch, and with their machine-guns cut down seven of them as they ran.

Waters ordered Lance Corporal Thomas's section, stacked up against the wall outside, to move in through Robinson's men and clear the central dwelling area, which was within a further walled area of the compound. They hurled grenades, broke down the door and raced in firing.

Then there came the dreaded cry, 'Man down, man down. Medic!'

Not again, thought Waters, *please – not again*.

Corporal Tim Ferrand, acting platoon sergeant, rushed forward into the compound. Private Luke Harris was in one of the small smoke-filled inner rooms, clutching his bleeding leg and shouting in pain. Ferrand checked him out and then clapped him on the back. 'Just a bit of glass, Luke, you've not been shot. Get back in there, boy.'

Blasting into the room, firing automatic, Harris's bullets had shattered a glass bottle, and a chunk had been hurled back at him, ripping a gash into his leg. Normally cause for concern. Right now, relief that it wasn't a bullet. Crack on and worry about it later.

After a few minute the section commanders were reporting, 'Compound clear.'

Calder, with his Tac, which had been behind Waters's reserve section, walked into the compound. He was smiling. 'Well done, Sergeant Waters. Good job. Now please get your men to thoroughly search every room, see if there is anything here of intelligence value.'

The 10 Platoon soldiers found several photos of bearded men in kurtas posing with AK47s, PKMs and RPG launchers. They also found water and warm bread. They had clearly interrupted the Taliban fighters as they were tucking into their lunch. They had taken them completely by surprise. Seeing C Company mount up in their Mastiffs, the fighters had expected them to be heading back to Inkerman.

They were not used to being assaulted by infantry mounted in heavy armour. They were used to soldiers on foot approaching their ambush positions. They would fire at them from multiple well-concealed positions, stand and fight for as long as it was safe to do so and then escape through cut-outs and mouse-holes in compound walls and then down well-recced irrigation ditches, moving away to set up the next ambush or reappear innocently as farmers tilling their land. But now for the first time, and the last for some of the fighters, they had experienced the shocking impact of a Mastiff attack.

C Company's morale soared. Within a week of the worst attack that Inkerman had experienced, leaving Hicks dead and several others wounded, they had hit back decisively at the Taliban, killing at least ten of their number.

Darkest Day: 23–24 August 2007

I

Just before B Company deployed to Kajaki at the end of July, Major Mick Aston had handed over as company commander to Major Tony Borgnis. The two officers had been students at the Staff College together, and several years before Borgnis had handed over to Aston as operations officer of the battalion. Borgnis arrived in Helmand following a two-year staff job in the UK. With the exception of courses and postings, Borgnis had served with the 1st Battalion throughout his fourteen-year military career, which included operational tours in Bosnia, Belfast and Londonderry.

Extremely fit, aggressive in battle, approachable and determined, Borgnis had been intent on joing the Army since he was a boy. There was military tradition in the family. A great grandfather served in the Boer War, and his grandfather, the highly decorated Major General Anthony Deane-Drummond, fought at Arnhem and in Italy during the Second World War, and after the war commanded the 22nd Special Air Service Regiment in Malaya and Oman. When his grandson left for Helmand, the general's only advice was 'Look after your soldiers,' a sentiment that remained at the forefront of Borgnis's mind.

B Company patrolled from their base, COP Zeebrugge, in company strength almost every day, pushing back the forward Taliban lines further and further from the Kajaki Dam and its hydroelectricity station. The majority of the patrols resulted in savage contacts with the enemy.

On 23 August, the company were preparing for yet another fighting patrol. Just after ten in the morning, Lieutenant George Seal-Coon, Sergeant Michael Woodrow and the NCOs of 7 Platoon were sitting in the briefing area next to the ops room in Zeebrugge. The room was hot, although the building's stone construction gave some mitigation from the otherwise relentless heat of the Afghan summer. They were waiting for Corporal Stu Parker, who liked to emphasize his self-appointed position as senior section commander by being the last into the room.

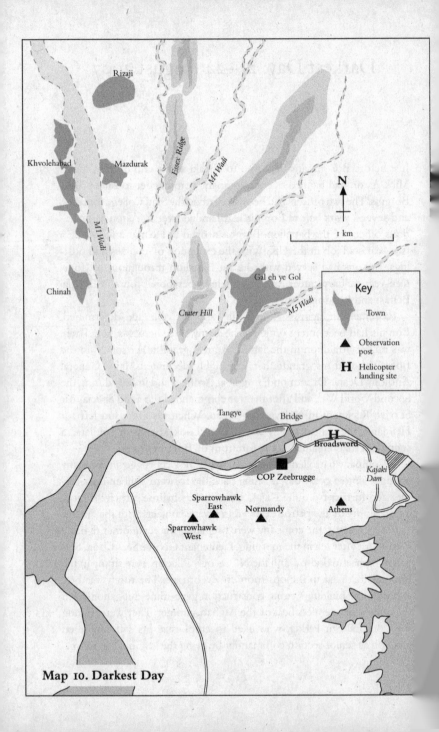

Map 10. Darkest Day

'Glad you could make it, Corporal P. Sorry if we got you up,' said Seal-Coon as Parker strolled in.

'That's OK, sir, you could have started without me. I probably knew the plan before you did anyway, boss: you know how the OC likes to confide in me when planning his ops.'

Woodrow shook his head. He and Parker went back a long way, and he had given up on him years ago.

Seal-Coon, with a show of exasperation that Parker enjoyed, made a start. 'You all know in outline what's happening from the warning order I issued. The OC gave me orders yesterday. It's a pretty much routine patrol, but the big difference is we're going out at 1600 hours this afternoon.'

This was a break from the pattern at Kajaki, where company-strength fighting patrols usually deployed from the base in the early hours of the morning. Major Borgnis wanted to vary the routine, to keep the enemy off guard. The frequency of patrolling in a relatively small area meant that significantly varying routes was difficult to achieve. There were only so many options. Timing was about all they had to play with to make their activities less predictable.

Seal-Coon continued. 'Task org within the platoon – Corporal Mann is off on R and R, so I'm moving Corporal Veal from your section, Corporal P, to command 3 Section. OK?'

'Not a problem,' said Parker, 'I'll use Josh Lee as my 2IC.'

'OK, good. He could probably do with the responsibility, good experience for his NCOs' cadre when we get back. Private O'Dell will move into platoon HQ and take over as 51mm mortar man from Barke, who is leaving for the UK today. We'll have a medic attached to the platoon plus engineers and a terp.

'Company task org. The patrol will be commanded by the OC. We and 6 Platoon will be on the ground plus the FSG. There will also be an ANA platoon. 5 Platoon will remain in overwatch from the Peaks. The OC will also be using the UAV detachment for surveillance. We have two F15s allocated for part of the patrol.'

The men were always happy to hear that US Air Force F15 Eagle tactical fighter jets were working with them. The pilots of the F15 squadron would always get a handle on the ground situation very quickly and were very effective at rapid and accurate bombing runs – extremely reassuring when things got sticky.

Seal-Coon continued, now reading from his notes taken at Borgnis's orders. 'Within the overall purpose of pushing back the enemy lines, the company commander's intent is to conduct a company clearance of Merzie and Mazdurak, to a limit of exploitation on the 812 northing, north of Mazdurak.'

He looked around. 'This is further than we or C Company before us have pushed before.'

He continued reading. 'As always the company commander intends to defeat any identified enemy forces with overwhelming use of direct and indirect fire assets. The company main effort is to find the enemy sniper in Khvolehabad or Rizaji and, once positively identified, to destroy him with all available combat power.'

Ever since the company had arrived at Kajaki, Major Borgnis had been concerned about a Taliban sniper who was operating in the area. They were building up a pattern of his activity. He seemed to be getting better and more accurate – edging nearer to the point where he would kill a member of the company. So far he hadn't hit anyone, but it had been a close thing on several occasions.

During one clearance patrol in a compound on the way to Khvolehabad, Private Ronnie Barker was moving up on to the roof to provide cover. A single shot rang out and impacted in the wall just inches from his head. A short time later, Seal-Coon's platoon deployed a sniper themselves, and as he crawled into position another shot splashed into the wall immediately above his body. Accurate fire like that caused the company to pull back rather than risk losing a soldier. On virtually every patrol they conducted now, they were getting held up by the sniper, making it increasingly difficult to maintain pressure on the Taliban, which was necessary to the objective of keeping them away from the dam.

Borgnis believed there was just one sniper, as sometimes they would take accurate fire from one location, sometimes from another, but never at the same time. During several patrols they had specifically set out to find the sniper, and by a process of elimination had worked out that he most often operated from Compound 469 in the village of Khvolehabad, across the wadi from Mazdurak.

They could not figure out what type of weapon was being used. The sniper seemed to be engaging over ranges from 400 to about 1,000 metres. It could have been a Russian-designed 7.62mm Dragunov sniper rifle, a high-velocity weapon with a killing range up to 3,800 metres. Readily available to the Taliban, in the right hands the Dragunov could easily pin down an entire company.

There was speculation also about the possibility of various other weapons, perhaps heavier calibre. On one patrol, Private Thrumble had dug a large-calibre bullet head out of a compound wall. It was unusual, more closely resembling a 20mm round from an A10 cannon than a normal smallarms bullet. But if it had been fired by an A10 they would have expected to find dozens more bullet heads and splash marks around the area. There were none. Borgnis had the bullet sent back to Bastion for examination by the Weapons Intelligence Section.

The sniper appeared at different points on the battlefield, regardless of the location of the main Taliban forces. They had found some of his skilfully concealed firing positions. He used tunnels to slip from one to another, and his escape routes were impossible to spot from the air.

Using classic counter-sniper tactics, on each patrol Borgnis deployed Lance Corporal Teddy Ruecker and his sniper team into firing positions. If he showed himself, they would be able to engage the enemy marksman from a number of different angles. They engaged likely firing positions with mortars, artillery and air. During one operation they discovered human faeces and a recently killed snake in a hide that they thought might be his.

Despite their efforts so far to triangulate the sniper's fire, and to track him, they made little progress. They were up against an excellent sniper, clearly well trained, perhaps by a regular army: their speculation included Iran or Pakistan, and even the possibility that he was a veteran of the mujahideen campaign against the Soviets.

2

By 1045 hours Seal-Coon had finished his orders, and the section commanders passed the information on to their men in their own briefing sessions. Most of the essential pre-patrol administration had been completed the day before, and all that remained was final weapons preparation, redistribution of ammo and radio checks. After all that was complete the troops had the standard Kajaki diet of noodles or rice for lunch and then snatched a few hours relaxation or sleep before deploying.

Private Richie Barke, the 51mm mortar man who had been instrumental in saving Mac the medic's life at Heyderabad back in May, was doing the rounds, saying goodbye to his mates in the company. At twenty-four, with six years' service under his belt, he was an old soldier in the youthful B Company and had decided to leave the Army. He was flying out of Zeebrugge that afternoon and would be back in the UK a few days later.

He walked into Private Foster's room. Several of the lads, wearing shorts and flip flops, were sitting on their beds chatting. Foster was alone on his bed, peering into his PSP, grinning to himself and clearly enjoying what he was looking at.

'What's that you're watching, Fozzie?' said Barke.

Foster looked up and then straight back at the screen, 'Eh?'

'What are you watching?'

'Oh it's just a film called *13 Going on 30*. Brought it back from R and R.'

'You what?' said Barke, amused. He knew what the film was about, because he'd watched it himself but wasn't about to admit it. 'That's a little girl's film. You're watching a girl's film. You're supposed to be a big tough soldier now, what're you doing watching a girl's film?'

'What're you talking about?' said Foster, looking up.

'Come on, lads, we can't have this,' said Barke, appealing to the others in the room. 'He must have got all soft during his R and R.'

With that they all piled on top of Foster, dragging him away from the PSP, grinding knuckles into his head, pulling his hair and poking him in the ribs. Foster managed to wriggle out from the bottom of the heap of soldiers and ran off into the next room, craftily booting Barke as he went.

Josh Lee and several other soldiers were watching a DVD in one corner. Breathless from his exertions next door, Foster sat down on Thrumble's bed and looked around the smoke-filled room.

'Thrumble, I'd forgotten what a nutter you are,' he said, surveying the room which was hung with plastic seventies disco banners showing silhouetted dancing figures wearing flares. A glitter ball dangled from the ceiling.

'Shut up, Foz,' said Thrumble, who was oiling his GPMG for the second time that morning, 'or I'll give you a bolt with the old cattle prod.'

Thrumble's mum, Pearl, had sent out the disco banners and lots of other weird things. She'd also sent an electric fly swatter. Characteristically,

Thrumble had modified it, breaking off the net and using the exposed circuit to give his mates an electric shock whenever the mood took him.

Barke came in and sat on the bed next to Foster. 'I suppose your sister lent you that film, did she? I'll probably go and see her when I'm back in Harlow.' Barke and Foster were from the same Essex town.

'Forget it, Rich, you're not going anywhere near her. None of you squads are. So forget all about it.'

'What was her name again?'

'You'll never find out her name so don't even bother to try.' He clipped Barke across the top of the head.

Foster adored his sister and was always very protective. The other lads, as always, seized on this to wind him up. And it worked every time. He quickly changed the subject. 'Did I tell you how many cheese sandwiches I had on R and R? Unbelievable. I've only been back a day and I'm desperate for one now instead of all this crappy noodles and rice.'

'Foz, it'll be worth leaving all you lot here just so I don't have to listen to you and your cheese sandwiches all the time. Can't you change the record?'

'Send us some sarnies out, will you, Rich? You haven't got a job sorted out yet, have you? Tell you what, why don't you get a job in a sandwich shop then you can keep me supplied.'

'Give it a rest. You want me to work in a sandwich shop just so I can keep you fed? I don't think so. Anyway I have got a job fixed, pretty much. There's this old boy that used to be CO of the battalion a few years back. He's taking on ex soldiers in some security thing in London. I'll probably go and do that.'

'I wish I was you, mate,' said Thrumble. 'I can't wait to get back to see my mum and dad and my brothers. I don't blame you for going. Good luck to you, mate.'

'Thrumble, you love it out here, you'll never leave the Army. We could never separate you from that GPMG of yours.'

'Yeah, that's probably true. I expect I'll stick with it. I was talking to Stevie Veal about doing an NCOs' cadre when we get back. But I still can't wait to get home and see my mum and dad.'

Barke stood up. 'Better say goodbye to the rest of the lads. The chopper's not supposed to be here for a couple of hours, but you know what the crabs are like; they'll probably call in about ten minutes and tell us we're late.'

Thrumble jumped up. 'Richie, before you go, you've got to see this. I haven't shown you the latest headcam video of Pingu, have I? Josh, eject that crap you're watching there, and put this disc in. It's brilliant, the best yet.'

He looked at Private Sloane. 'You've got to see this too, Pingu mate, you're the star of the show. We can't watch it without you.'

Thrumble often took headcam footage of Sloane on patrol. Sloane had an unfortunate ability to always trip in potholes, or fall over low walls or ledges. He rarely managed to stay on his feet for long, and the troops likened him to Cristiano Ronaldo, the Manchester United player who also seemed to spend most of his time on the deck.

Thrumble constantly, almost unceasingly, ragged Sloane. The only respite Sloane ever got was when Thrumble's attention was turned to his other mate, Guardsman Hogg, or to his beloved machine-gun. But woe betide any other soldier, whoever they were, who attempted to have a go at Sloane. Thrumble had been Sloane's close friend in training, and he was not fair game to anybody else.

The video over, Barke tried again to get out of the room. As departure time grew closer, he was getting increasingly guilty about leaving his mates. It was an odd feeling, almost of letting them down, even though Barke had more than pulled his weight during the tour and was well liked and respected throughout the platoon. But they had all been through so much together in the last few months. He said to Private O'Dell, who had taken over his role in platoon HQ, 'OD, make sure you take care of that fifty-one. I'm not as crazy about my weapon as Thrumble, but it's given us some good service out here. Hope you get on OK with it.'

He shook hands with everyone in the room, and as he walked out he said awkwardly, 'Look, I'll be in Pirbright when you get back, and then we all need to get on the piss. Good luck, lads, and keep your heads down. You all need to come back in one piece.'

He looked into the room Stu Parker shared with Sergeant Woodrow. Parker was watching *The Bourne Identity* on Woodrow's PSP. 'Stu, your face is a bit red. You been sunbathing again?'

'No,' said Parker, 'got up a bit late this morning, and the sun was burning my head.'

Barke laughed. He knew that each night Parker picked up his camp-bed and carried it outside to sleep. He couldn't stand Woodrow's incessant snoring.

They shook hands. 'Well, cheers then, Stu, good luck for the rest of the tour. I'll see you back in Pirbright. Look after the lads for me.'

Outside the block Private Troy McLure, stripped to the waist, in shorts and trainers, was furiously doing press-ups, the sun beating down on his back.

'All right, Troy?' said Barke.

McLure stood up, pouring sweat. 'What's up, Rich?'

'I'm just going round saying goodbye. Probably see you before I go, but I want to make sure I get everyone.

'Anyway good luck, mate. Hope it all works out for you. Hope you get in the SAS and all that. Don't know why I'm saying that, I'll be seeing you in a couple of months back at Pirbright.'

'OK, Rich, see you later. Take care.'

McLure sprung back on to his hands and toes. As he resumed his press-ups Barke squeezed his right calf hard. McLure turned his face up to Barke with a grin. 'You know that doesn't work any more, Rich. You can't wind me up with that.' He winked. 'Or do you just enjoy it? Something you want to tell me?'

Barke laughed and walked away. When McLure first arrived the other men in the platoon quickly found out that he hated anyone touching him. In the manner of soldiers everywhere they then mercilessly wound him up at every opportunity. This had continued into the tour, but recently, to the annoyance of Barke and his mates, McLure had realized that it was best to ignore them rather than react every time they fooled about.

3

There was a resupply of rations, water, ammunition and other stores that afternoon, flown in by Chinook from Bastion, and it had arrived later than planned. The CQMS needed the troops to help shift the vast weight of gear off the HLS into the stores, so the patrol's departure was delayed.

As he was waiting to move out, Parker plugged into his iPod and listened to Dire Straits' 'Brothers in Arms', the song he normally switched on before going out on patrol.

Before they left Zeebrugge, Private Luke Geater was chatting with Troy McLure. Both were from Ipswich. Geater was a school friend of one of McLure's brothers and had only got to know Troy since joining the Army, but they had become close mates. As Geater left he said, 'Only three months now, mate. Three months and we'll be sunning it up in Tenerife. By the pool. With a beer or three.'

McLure nodded and smiled. They touched fists and Geater said, 'Stay safe, Aaron, see you later, bruv.'

Geater, with 6 Platoon, moved out of the base first. It was just before 1630 hours. The sun was bright and the temperature a stifling 40 degrees. With the standard battle load of 36 kilos of gear, the men were pouring sweat before they even left the gates of Zeebrugge.

Company Tac followed 6 Platoon out, and then Parker's section led 7 Platoon from the base. Parker waved at the Afghan soldiers guarding the outer gates and got barely a flicker of interest in return.

They were heading back into enemy territory. Across the river they entered a sort of no-man's-land between COP Zeebrugge and the Taliban. As if the heat wasn't bad enough, Foster was having real problems settling into his prized new Lowe Seeker desert boots.

'Just because you've got the same boots as me, Fozzie old mate, don't think you're going to step into my shoes,' said Parker, 'especially with a daft walk like that. You look like one of those gangly teenagers whose legs are too long for their body.'

Despite their difference in rank and age, Foster always gave back as good as he got, sometimes retaliating with a joke about how his commander had taken some years out as a civvie and perhaps, at thirty, should have stayed that way.

'You're getting a bit too old for this game, Parky. Want a hand with your kit?'

Parker liked and admired the nineteen-year-old. Foster had developed an excellent sense for the ground and the enemy threat, so was always point man, leading the section on patrol.

Fifteen minutes later the company emerged from Tangye and immediately became more alert, even though they were overwatched by the company's observation posts, armed with .50 cal machine-guns and GPMGs, and could call for fire at any time from the three-barrel 81mm mortar section back in Zeebrugge.

Parker took a break from the ongoing exchange with Foster to watch as Sergeant Major Ivan Snow's FSG drove their four WMIKs on to the high ground a few metres away. With the FSG were Lance Corporals

Teddy Ruecker and Jamie Carter, the sniper pair. Their task was to scan ahead, looking for the enemy sniper.

By now everyone was pouring sweat but trying hard to conserve water, something they had got used to in the three months of relentless patrolling in the Green Zone.

Parker's section halted in the dirt of a familiar wadi. Six metres deep in parts, and flanked with covering foliage, it had been specified by the company commander as the FUP for the thrust into Mazdurak. The company was now deep into enemy territory. 7 Platoon were to secure the FUP to enable 6 Platoon to attack. Parker deployed his men into fire positions to observe for enemy activity.

Lieutenant Seal-Coon moved forward to join Parker's section and took up a position beside McLure. Although they hadn't walked far, the oppressive heat was taking it out of them. Seal-Coon looked across at McLure. 'How's it going, Troy, you OK?'

McLure grinned back. 'Great, boss, no problem.'

Seal-Coon was amazed that McLure barely seemed to have broken into a sweat. He was one of the few who weren't breathless. He was super-fit and someone you could depend on, no matter what. One of the younger soldiers in the company, he had performed brilliantly in Helmand, and Seal-Coon considered him to be a man with great potential.

Though this was a place of relative safety, there was the constant fear of mines. Private Matt Woollard of C Company had lost a leg close by when he stepped on a mine four months earlier.

And somewhere in the relentless grey of the Afghan landscape was that sniper.

Parker and his section watched 6 Platoon move through the wadi, closely followed by Borgnis and the half dozen men of Company Tac HQ. As they moved up on to the high gound, they hard-targeted towards Mazdurak, running across 500 metres of deadly open terrain.

'Three Zero Alpha, this is Zero Alpha.' After so long Seal-Coon found it hard to get used to the callsign Zero Alpha being used by anyone but Mick Aston with his Antipodean drawl. But he and the other men in B Company had immediately gained confidence in their new OC's leadership. Borgnis was just as aggressive as Aston and had already proved himself to be every bit as competent a commander.

'Three Zero Alpha, send, over,' he replied.

'As soon as Two Zero get into the first compounds in Mazdurak, start moving your callsign forward and push in right behind them.'

Seal-Coon acknowledged and then called across to Parker, 'OK, Parky, you heard that from the OC. Get your lads ready to move.'

A couple of minutes later, Parker said, 'Fozzie, up you get, you know where you're going. As soon as you get over the lip of the wadi, start running.'

Foster wasn't too concerned about this move over the open ground. 6 Platoon and Company Tac had pushed across without a problem, and he knew the FSG was watching carefully from Essex Ridge, scrutinizing the surrounding area for enemy and ready to fire a devastating volley should any fighters appear. But although he was very fit, running 500 metres across this terrain, in this heat, with this kit, was still a nightmare.

It was now 1800 hours. Still broad daylight. As the section, blowing hard and sweating heavily, got within a couple of hundred metres of the compounds, a long burst of AK47 fire shattered the early-evening calm.

They kept running. It wasn't aimed at them. It was 6 Platoon that were in contact – from Khvolehabad Compound 469. Within seconds shells slammed into the forward enemy positions as Sergeant Ben Browning, acting as 6 Platoon commander, called in a mortar fire mission.

At the same time, Snow's fire support group started taking incoming RPG air-bursts up on Essex Ridge. Seven had exploded in rapid succession, and Snow and his men were returning fire with their GPMGs and heavy machine-guns. The RPG fire was followed immediately by rifle and machine-gun bullets, landing accurately in and around the FSG's position.

Snow's group was being outgunned, and it wouldn't be long before they started taking casualties.

4

Sergeant Major Snow radioed Major Borgnis. 'Heavy fire from Rizaji. Have identified at least four separate firing points. Am returning fire, but we need some compounds hit by air.'

'Roger,' said Borgnis, 'I'm on to that. Keep putting down fire, and I'll sort it out soonest.'

Borgnis and his Tac were in a compound on the outskirts of Mazdurak, just behind 6 Platoon. With Borgnis were his signaller Corporal Jimmy Naylor, Corporal Wilsher, the MFC, Captain Hay, the FST commander, the OC of the UAV detachment, a soldier from the company intelligence section and a visiting captain from the Operational Training and Advisory Group who was out from the UK to update himself on current ops. A key member of the team was the company JTAC, Royal Artillery Sergeant 'Reggie' Perrin. Borgnis and Perrin were confirming on their maps the enemy compounds that needed to be hit from the air.

From the time the company had left Zeebrugge, Perrin, using callsign Widow Seven Six, had been talking to Dude Zero Five, giving constant updates on the ground situation as the F15 Eagle circled 6,000 metres above the troops, standing by for target details. The minute the Taliban attacked, Perrin contacted the F15 commander to confirm they were still in comms.

The JTAC transmitted the 'nine liner', a standard NATO instruction giving details of enemy strengths and locations and the exact positions of friendly forces.

As 6 Platoon and the FSG continued to exchange fire with the enemy to the south, Seal-Coon's 7 Platoon cleared through the northern half of Mazdurak. They moved fast, but knew the Taliban well enough to be wary of their likely efforts to outflank them and get in behind, using the rat-runs that criss-crossed between the compounds. In a few minutes they reached the western edge of the village, overlooking Khvolehabad.

Seal-Coon had been moving with Parker's section. Parker said, 'Sir, there's a compound just down there that I've been on before. Compound 248. From the roof you get excellent fields of fire across into Khvolehabad and Chinah.'

They would be exposed to enemy fire as they ran through a narrow alleyway and down a slope. Seal-Coon called Browning on the company net. 'Hello, Two Zero Alpha, this is Three Zero Alpha. Be aware I'm moving into compound 248 to your left. Can you give me covering fire as I move in?'

6 Platoon opened up with a series of heavy blasts of machine-gun and rifle fire, and Parker led the way to the compound. Seal-Coon deployed the rest of the platoon around the area to provide protection against Taliban infiltration.

Parker positioned Private Sloane at the entrance to compound 248 to act as link-man. The rest of the section moved in and dashed towards the single-storey building inside. As the others raced up an exposed set of steps to the roof, Foster took up a fire position in the lower part of the building, immediately putting down several bursts of covering fire.

Parker pulled his men back to the rear of the roof, where there was some cover from the massive corrugated bumps on top of the building. He positioned the two machine-gunners, McClure with his Minimi and Thrumble with his GPMG, on either side of the firing line, leaving himself and Lee in the centre with their rifles.

Thrumble opened up with a long, lethally accurate burst of fire from Mary, his machine-gun. Within minutes he had fired 600 rounds at the enemy positions in Khvolehabad. McLure was keeping pace with his Minimi, firing streams of tracer towards the Taliban's treeline. Lee wanted to engage with the UGL attached to his SA80 rifle, but the enemy were out of range. Lee and Parker decided to improvise by 'lobbing' the grenades at a higher angle than usual and dropping them on to the enemy position, mortar style. Lee fired the grenades with Parker, using binoculars, correcting the elevation to get him on target. After four rounds they were hitting the enemy 800 metres away. Lee then let loose ten rounds in succession, pounding the target area with the 40mm high-explosive grenades.

Thousands of metres above Dude Zero Five prepared to release a 500-pound bomb.

As he blasted away with his Minimi, McClure shouted, 'This is awesome, this is awesome.'

Seal-Coon climbed on to the roof and lay down beside Parker, who immediately briefed him. 'The enemy is forward left 800 metres in the edge of the compounds. I reckon ten to twelve of them.'

Seal-Coon looked through his binoculars. Mortar rounds, called in by Browning, were still exploding in the area, but they were landing beyond the enemy positions. Seal-Coon radioed the MFC, giving adjustments to bring the fire in more accurately.

'Well done, Corporal P.' He clapped Parker on the shoulder and crawled back to the rear edge of the roof, where he could keep an eye on the rest of the 7 Platoon, as well as Parker's section. He leant over and called down to Barker in the adjacent compound, 'Ronnie, get your section to check out the rat-runs coming into this compound and get eyes on the approaches into here from Rizaji. That's where they'll be coming from if they try to flank us.'

The voice of company signaller Corporal Jimmy Naylor came on the radio. 'Charlie Charlie One. This is Two One Alpha. Bomb on the ground figures four zero. Out.'

Parker switched on his headcam to record the explosion and shouted to his men, 'Bomb on ground forty seconds.'

Seal-Coon checked his map. He knew where the bomb would be landing – compound 8 in Rizaji, about 1,000 metres away from their position. He had seen plenty of bombs drop before, but it was always spectacular. And it gave a certain satisfaction to know that the people that were trying to kill you and your mates were being dealt a deadly blow from above.

Just over a minute earlier and hundreds of metres away Lance Corporal Jason Tower, attached to Snow's FSG, was engaging the Taliban with his GPMG. Bullets were chopping up the ground feet away from him, and when another soldier said, 'Air's being dropped on the enemy,' Tower was too busy to acknowledge.

In the WMIKs the .50 cal gunners were putting down heavy fire, beginning to hit the enemy. An RPG hit the hillside a few feet away.

Somebody shouted, 'Air dropping on them in two minutes.'

Then, 'Sixty seconds...'

Then, 'Thirty...'

Tower and the other members of the FSG continued to engage but began looking for the bomb. Some had their cameras out. Tower saw the aircraft overhead.

He saw a flash and heard an enormous explosion. A huge mushroom cloud started to form.

'That's landed in the wrong place,' he yelled. 'That's where our guys are...'

The radio crackled. 'There's casualties...'

5

The 500-pound bomb exploded at 1828 hours, less than 3 metres from Parker's section. The end wall of the compound collapsed, reduced to a fine dust. The shock wave from the explosion could be felt by the men of the fire support group 100 metres higher and a kilometre away from the point of impact.

Parker did not hear the bomb fall through the air or the explosion as it detonated. He felt an immense force closing in on him, then lost consciousness.

When he came round the atmosphere was black. He fought to get air into his lungs. He couldn't see anything and he couldn't breathe. His eyes and throat were filled with dust and thick acrid smoke. It felt as if his head had been hit by a sledgehammer. He had a high-pitched whine in his ears. He tried to move and felt bone grating on bone in his right leg. His thumb was flapping about. All of his clothes had been blown off, along with his body armour and helmet. He had shrapnel in his foot.

He had landed on top of Josh Lee. Lee never lost consciousness. He didn't see the bomb but he heard it come in – a loud whoosh – then it landed just in front of him.

Lee shouted, 'Troy was there…' He started pointing and shouting 'Troy was there, Troy was there…'

Everything had gone quiet; he'd been deafened by the bomb. He could hardly see anything. He put his hand up to his eye; it felt as if it wasn't there. It felt as if his entire face wasn't there. Parker was lying on top of him. He started shouting, 'Find my eye! Where's my eye?'

Parker was dripping blood into his one working eye. His arms looked like freshly planed wood. His shirt was hanging off, and he lay there in his boots and boxer shorts. His body armour and helmet had disappeared. Enemy machine-gun fire raked across what was left of their rooftop position.

Lee folded his arms around Parker and started trying to pull them both off the roof. It was better than getting shot.

As the bomb landed Seal-Coon heard a whoosh and a terrifying explosion. There was a red flash, and he felt an intense heat surge over him. The shock wave slammed into his back, knocked the air out of him and smashed him into the roof. Everything went black.

The next thing he knew there was light again, but smoke and dust were everywhere, so thick he couldn't see his hand in front of his face.

Disorientated, his immediate thought was that one of the company's mortar bombs had landed on the building. He tried to get on the net to order the mortars to check firing, but the radio, which had been on his back, no longer worked. Looking around at the way the dust and smoke was moving he thought the mortar had hit Ronnie Barker's section below. He called down and asked if they were OK. Barker, dazed, shouted something back. At least he was alive.

Seal-Coon picked up his own crushed body and looked to see if his arms and legs were still there. He wasn't sure. He staggered forward to where Parker's section had been. Through the dust and smoke he saw Parker, and Lee holding on to him, clothes blasted away or shredded, both groaning. He shouted, 'Medic! Medic!'

Thrumble, motionless, was hanging half over the edge of the partially destroyed building.

McLure also lay still, the chest plate from his body armour blown away and his kit strewn about.

He went over to McLure and shook his shoulder, desperate for a response. 'Troy, Troy, Troy.'

He looked up and saw Sergeant Woodrow, on the ground, reach up to check Thrumble's pulse. Woodrow shook his head and then he and Private O'Dell lowered him down to them.

'Medic, medic. Four casualties. Two responsive. Two non-responsive,' Seal-Coon yelled as loudly as he could.

Bullets were still landing around them, but, still dazed, he only half registered them. He went back to Parker and Lee and pulled them apart. Lee's legs were black, covered in blood, dust and dirt, and he was bleeding from the left eye. Seal-Coon dragged him across the roof, hands under his armpits, and passed him down to Sergeant Woodrow below.

He went back for Parker and dragged him across. He was dead weight, unconscious and immobile. As Seal-Coon pulled him, he banged Parker's leg, and the corporal moaned loudly. It really hurt him. Seal-Coon cursed himself for inflicting even more pain on one of his soldiers who was so terribly wounded but at the same time thought to himself, *At least I know he's alive*.

Private Barker, who had been close to the explosion and had been knocked to the ground by its force, checked Parker's wounds. He was bleeding from the mouth. Barker realized he had bitten through his tongue and ignored that. He was having difficulty breathing. His ribs were black and looked broken. His arms and legs were badly burnt,

355

and his leg seemed to be broken. Barker placed him carefully on a lightweight stretcher and, using bandages, tied his bad leg to his good one, to act as a splint.

Having sorted him out as best he could, Barker and three other soldiers carried him to the sergeant major's quad.

Seal-Coon had returned to the rooftop, still under fire, for McLure. His lower arm was gone. There was no arterial bleeding, and no sign of consciousness, but he quickly put on a tourniquet anyway. Just in case. And in hope.

He carried McLure across the roof and, as he got towards the edge, it collapsed under him. He tried to push McLure back on to the roof as he fell, but McLure landed on top of him in the rubble, knocking the air out of him.

A soldier was staring at McLure in horror. Seal-Coon shouted, 'Grab his legs,' and they carried him clear of the building and laid him on the ground.

6

Some men from 6 Platoon had moved in to help. Team medics from both platoons were hard at work moving the casualties away from the line of fire and getting them ready for evacuation. Someone said to Seal-Coon, 'Thrumble's dead.'

Private Luke Geater was one of the 6 Platoon soldiers who came to help. He placed Thrumble's body on a stretcher and covered him up. He saw another body being brought down and ran across to help. He was shocked and saddened at seeing Thrumble's dead body and didn't really want to see who this was. Without looking at the corpse, he just helped carry the stretcher. Then Geater noticed a tattoo on his right arm, and thought, *No, no, it can't be.* He had recognized McLure's tattoo, but tried desperately to blank the possibility from his mind. *It is not Aaron*, he told himself. But he knew it was. His eyes filled up, and he almost broke down. He was distraught. But he immediately got a grip of himself. *I've got a job to do. I'm supposed to be section 2IC, I can't let the blokes see me crack. Not now of all times.* He covered McLure's body with another field stretcher. Then he called the section to his position and checked they were all present, ready to move.

Sergeant Woodrow had climbed on to the roof with Lance Corporal Daniel Knowles, checking the place out to make sure there were no more casualties and collecting up weapons and maps. The Taliban were still firing towards them, and the men of 6 Platoon were blasting down a heavy weight of fire to cover the extraction of the casualties.

Seal-Coon ordered the soldiers to move back, following the stretcher bearers. Woodrow did a head check.

'Where's Fozzie?' asked Seal-Coon.

One of the soldiers said, 'He's already been taken back.'

Another soldier said, 'He's dead, I saw him being taken back.'

Seal-Coon was utterly devastated. He already knew Thrumble and McLure were dead. Now Foster too. And Lee and Parker were in a horrific condition.

Lee was dazed and confused. He suddenly realized he didn't have his body armour on. He thought, *Wandering around Afghanistan in a pair of boxers is probably not the best idea...*

As 7 Platoon soldiers carried him away, he kept saying, 'Go back and find my eye...'

The stretcher party were struggling to manoeuvre him over walls, across ditches and through mouse-holes in the compound walls. It was all too slow. Private Pryke, who had only recently joined the battalion, just grabbed hold of him, took him off the stretcher and dashed more than 200 metres across rough and open ground to place him on the trailer of the company sergeant major's quad bike.

But Lee's immediate problems were still not over. As the quad drew close to the medical RV it swerved to avoid Taliban bullets, went out of control and flipped over, throwing Lee on to the ground. Disorientated, Lee managed to stagger the last few feet to the RV.

The medic was Captain Pete Hall, a no-nonsense nursing officer who had served as a junior soldier in the Falklands and risen through the ranks. Hall calmly told Lee to sit down, and Lance Corporal Cooledge injected him with morphine. It was then that Lee started to realize the extent of his injuries. His face was badly broken up, with his left eye sunk far behind the socket. There were shrapnel wounds all over his body. He had severe burns, worst on his arms and legs.

As he drifted into drug-induced semi-consciousness, pulling on a fake Pine Light, Lee was joined by Teddy Ruecker. With other members of the FSG, he had been summoned down from Essex Ridge to help with casualties. As he held Lee's hand the injured private said, 'I can't see. I can't see. Who's that? Who's there?'

'Josh, it's Teddy.'

'Teddy, don't leave me, mate…'

The IRT Chinook was hovering overhead at Zeebrugge, waiting for clearance to land.

Ruecker said, 'I'm not leaving you, Josh. You're going to be all right. You're going to get through this…'

Parker was next. Hall took one look at him and waived the rule about not giving morphine to anyone with a chest or head injury. He would be dead unless they operated within the hour. He had a broken right tibia. Both lungs had been punctured and burnt. His pancreas, stomach and kidneys had been torn by the blast. He had lacerations to his left hand, burns all over his body, shrapnel wounds, perforated ear drums and damage to his left eye.

Both men were carried to a waiting Pinzgauer.

They were now in severe pain, despite the morphine, but the vehicle was forced to go at snail's pace. For Parker, even the slightest movement was life-threatening.

The MERT Chinook commander radioed Borgnis, 'I have only enough fuel for ten minutes more on station, then I will have to return to Bastion.'

Borgnis knew that if the helicopter had to depart before it picked up the casualties it would be another hour or more before it could return. They were in the worst kind of Catch-22 situation. If the vehicle carrying Parker moved too fast, he would almost certainly die. If he didn't get back to Bastion rapidly for an operation he would also die.

Borgnis radioed the Pinzgauer commander, an RMP corporal, telling him to increase speed and get the casualties to the HLS as soon as possible. The corporal replied, 'I am under express orders from One Four Alpha not to move any faster.'

One Four Alpha was Hall's callsign. 'Roger out, said Borgnis, utterly confident that Hall would have weighed all the factors and made the best possible decision.

With the Chinook pilot flying to the absolute limit of his endurance time, the Pinzgauer somehow made it. Ruecker helped carry Lee on to the Chinook, and he realized for the first time that the bomb had killed some of his mates. He saw John Thrumble and Troy McLure, on stretchers on the floor of the helicopter. He took a moment to say goodbye.

Borgnis ordered the rest of the company back towards Zeebrugge. As the men moved back through his position, he had a word of encouragement for each soldier: 'Keep your heads up, lads, well done, keep moving now.'

6 Platoon, leading the way, came under fire as they crossed the open ground beyond Mazdurak. The FSG hammered fire into likely enemy positions, and Browning and Woodrow got their 51mm mortar men to lay down a smokescreen between them and the enemy to conceal movement.

Seal-Coon moved up and down the line of soldiers as they patrolled through the wadi. 'Keep spread out now, lads, watch your spacing, cover your arcs.'

As Lance Corporal James Murphy went by, he squinted at Seal-Coon in the moonlight, still covered in dust and McLure's blood, and said, 'Boss, are you OK?'

'Yes thanks, Murph, I'm OK.'

He wasn't, and he fought not to break down.

7

When he got into Zeebrugge at 2100 hours Seal-Coon went direct to the medical sergeant to confirm who had been evacuated. 'Parker and Lee both T One. Thrumble and McLure both T Four.'

'What about Foster?'

'Foster hasn't been evacuated. He wasn't among the casualties.'

Seal-Coon felt sick. He raced to the platoon accommodation and pulled Woodrow aside, 'Fozzie was not CASEVACed.'

Woodrow went through the accommodation. No Foster. Seal-Coon and Woodrow searched for Borgnis. Seal-Coon said, 'Sir, we haven't got Fozzie. We've done a head-check, sir, and, he's not here...He's not here...'

Borgnis's face dropped. He ordered Woodrow to conduct another head-check and an immediate search of the base.

If Foster is still out there – in enemy territory...All kinds of horrors raced through the company commander's mind.

'Whatever happens out there, we bring everybody home. Even the dead. We bring everybody back.' It had become Borgnis's mantra.

Woodrow returned within minutes to confirm that Foster was not in the base. Borgnis ordered the company back out to find him. They would have to be static in the heart of Taliban country – on the ground, probably for hours, at night.

Lieutenant Colonel Carver was allocated the Helmand Reaction Force to reinforce B Company. Based at Camp Bastion on one hour's notice to move, the HRF platoon was drawn on rotation from units across Task Force Helmand. One of Major Mick Aston's Brigade Reconnaissance Force platoons was taking its turn. Aston came to Carver's operations centre to offer assistance as soon as he heard his former company was in trouble. Five hundred metres from the operations centre a Chinook was already standing by with rotors turning.

B Company's sergeant major, Tim Newton, had arrived at Camp Bastion from Kajaki the previous day, on the first leg of his return to England for R and R. He knew his men needed him with them on the ground at this time of crisis, so he got his kit together and flew back out with the HRF.

A Nimrod MR2 surveillance aircraft from NATO Regional Command South and a US Predator unmanned surveillance aircraft were put on standby. The battle group operations staff were assembling specialist search and detection equipment and operators to deploy if necessary. Carver also planned additional reinforcements from the battle group, including his Tac HQ, to bolster security if the search for Foster went on into daylight.

At 2138 hours, just over half an hour after they had got back into Zeebrugge, Sergeant Major Snow's FSG deployed back out to Essex Ridge to provide overwatch for the search. Close behind, 6 Platoon, travelling in Pinzgauers, drove towards Mazdurak. Seal-Coon and Woodrow, together with Private Perkins, the platoon radio operator who had last seen Foster firing from the ground floor of the compound, accompanied them. Moving troops by vehicle at night in this terrain was a gamble, but Borgnis demanded speed. He had just been told that communications intercepts showed Taliban fighters discussing the discovery of an electronic device in the area the bomb had landed. He now knew the enemy was on the ground, almost certainly close to Private Foster.

On the peaks 300 metres above Zeebrugge, 5 Platoon scanned the area for enemy activity, and, as 6 Platoon deployed, two Apaches arrived on station, buzzing Mazdurak as a show of strength to scare off the enemy.

Within half an hour Seal-Coon led a section of 6 Platoon into the compound. The air was thick with the smell of explosives. Sergeant Ben Browning, commander of 6 Platoon, deployed his other two sections into close protection.

The searchers started to move large lumps of rubble from the demolished building where Foster had been positioned. They then dug carefully through the fine dust with their hands. They were in full moonlit view of the Taliban positions just 350 metres away. Borgnis, taking his turn with the spade, thought, *This could all get very nasty*. His only consolation was the sound of Apaches overhead.

Two hours later the HRF arrived and were tasked to assist the exhausted 6 Platoon digging through the rubble. With the HRF came Sergeant Major Newton. Borgnis had never been so pleased to see anyone in his life. Newton said, 'Hello, sir, you all right?'

'No, Sergeant Major, not really.'

Newton looked around. It was a grim scene, soldiers digging in the moonlight with the smell of explosives lingering on the air. He moved to the spot where they were working and heard Seal-Coon's voice. 'Is that you, George?' he said.

Newton had never called an officer by his first name before, and he wasn't quite sure why he did now.

Minutes later Lance Corporal Kieran Hunt from 6 Platoon uncovered a green Camelbak clip of the kind Foster had carried. Soon afterwards they uncovered Robert Foster's lifeless body. His rifle was still slung across his shoulder, and his daysack was on his back.

B Company's operations log betrayed none of the emotion felt by the soldiers on the ground: 'At 0205 hours 1 x T4 casualty FO0423 was recovered from the rubble of compound 248.'

Everybody went silent. Some braced their backs and brought their heels together, coming spontaneously to attention.

The soldiers of the HRF prepared to place Private Foster into a body bag. But Company Sergeant Major Newton stepped forward and said quietly, 'Don't you dare put one of my men into a body bag. Put him on a stretcher. He came here as a soldier, and he will leave as a soldier.'

The commanding officer of the US Air Force F15 squadron phoned Zeebrugge later that day. He was extremely emotional and told Borgnis how much he and his squadron regretted what had happened. Borgnis said, 'You should be aware, sir, that nobody here blames your aircrew. Whatever happened, and whatever the outcome of the inquiries, my men know how much they owe to your pilots. You have always been there for us, and your planes have saved many of my soldiers' lives. I have spoken to the men in my company this morning, and that is their view too.'

Expecting recrimination, the American was astonished at what he heard. He told Borgnis that his words would mean a great deal to his pilots. Borgnis said, 'Please pass them on. And tell them we are looking forward to having a Dude callsign on station next time we're in trouble on patrol.'

Snipers: 24–28 August 2007

A few hours after Private Foster's body was recovered from the ruined compound in Mazdurak, 25 kilometres south Major Phil Messenger led a C Company patrol out of FOB Inkerman. Messenger had returned from R and R the day after Calder's Mastiff attack on 16 August, and Calder had handed C Company over to him and flown to Bastion.

In the oppressive late-morning heat, with Lieutenant Sam Perrin's 10 Platoon in the lead, the company pushed rapidly across the open field between Inkerman and the start of the Green Zone. They were within sight and range of the base's sangars, but always crossed this area at speed – no infantryman likes being in the open for any longer than is absolutely necessary.

Once across they were in a deep, empty irrigation ditch, which provided cover as they moved further into the Green Zone. Messenger spoke on the net: 'All stations this is Zero Alpha. Be aware that so far there has been no enemy radio chatter. It is just possible we have got out of Inkerman without being picked up by them. Ensure you move with the greatest possible stealth. We'll see how far we can get without them IDing us.'

It had never happened before. By this point on every other patrol, the Taliban radios would have come alive with excited chatter, as fighters warned each other of the movement of British troops. Messenger considered two possible options. For some reason the enemy might have slipped up and let their guard drop. Or they might have twigged to the intercepts and wanted to increase the chances of surprise if they had an ambush ready for C Company. A sniper pair, Lance Corporal Tom Mann and Private Dan Gent, were moving with 10 Platoon. Messenger usually deployed the snipers with whichever platoon was leading the company, and, as the platoons switched roles, he would shift them accordingly. Conventionally one member of a sniper pair would be equipped with a sniper rifle and the other with an automatic weapon to provide back-up. But as the snipers were working within the protection provided by the company, both had sniper rifles – Mann carried a .338 long-range rifle and Gent the smaller and less powerful 7.62mm L96.

The previous afternoon, Mann had spent several hours preparing his equipment. Every few weeks, he carried out the time-consuming task of redoing the camouflage to make his kit blend in. Every sniper had his own methods and ideas to give himself that extra edge over the enemy that could make all the difference. Gent had filled a bucket with mud and water and carefully mixed the two into a gritty, paint-like slurry. He had previously tried to acquire desert vehicle paint, but was told none was available – 'dues out' in the time-honoured quartermasters' parlance, in other words: 'you're not getting any'. He reckoned his own technique worked better anyway, blending in more effectively than the artificial stuff. He then taped up his rifle, spotting scope and laser range finder with sleeping bag repair tape that he had scrounged when the CQMS wasn't looking. The tape was made of a green fabric, just what he needed to absorb his camouflage mix. With his hands, he then carefully rubbed the slurry into the tape, making sure it didn't get into any of the apertures that could either jam his weapon or obscure his vision. It dried almost immediately under the baking sun, and he looked at it with satisfaction – exactly the same shade as the dirt on the ground and the walls of the compounds. From his webbing he took a small green plastic box, the size of a thick credit card. This was the issued camouflage cream – dark brown, light brown and green – designed for the face and arms, but rarely used in Afghanistan. He streaked the cream over the top of the now dried dirt and water slurry, creating a series of jagged lines and blotches to break up the shape of the rifle and the other equipment.

Mann was the consummate sniper. He took huge pride in what he did and went to enormous lengths to be the best that he could be. He had wanted to do this since watching the Tom Berenger film *Sniper* as a little boy. Always a good shot, he had been in the regional shooting team when he was an Army Cadet. During his basic training at Catterick, Royal Anglian soldiers had visited to show the recruits the different weapon systems they would use when they got to the battalion. All Mann wanted to do was get his hands on the sniper rifle.

When he got to the battalion in 2003 and was posted to B Company, his first question was: 'When can I do a sniper course?' His commanders had other ideas and were keen for him to spend as much time as possible as a Saxon vehicle driver. Over the next three years he made himself a nuisance to his platoon commander, platoon sergeant and company sergeant major, constantly belly-aching about getting on to a sniper course.

Eventually they'd had enough, and he was put on a course at the beginning of 2006, after returning from Iraq. Students with him on the course at Pirbright and Brecon included Alex Hawkins, Oliver Bailey, Dean Bailey and Teddy Ruecker. It was demanding, both physically and mentally, but Mann loved every minute of it. He worked as hard as he could and came top. He considered the greatest achievement of his life to that point was being handed the sniper badge, something he had been desperate to gain for so long.

2

Gent was happy to be patrolling with 10 Platoon. He knew and respected Sergeant Armon, who had himself been a battalion sniper. Armon understood how to get the best use out of a sniper pair and was a good laugh with it. And he thought Perrin, the platoon commander, was an outstanding officer. He knew exactly what he was doing, never panicked whatever was going on, kept a good grip on his men, but was also close to them and approachable.

Half an hour after crossing Route 611 outside Inkerman, 10 Platoon were wading through ditches full of water up to their thighs. Gent was at the front, and Mann was moving near the rear of the platoon with Sergeant Steve Armon. Armon said, 'If we see any targets, Tom, pass that 338 straight over to me, I'll take the shot.'

'Not a hope, Sarge,' Mann smiled. 'You don't seriously think I'm going to be carrying this thing round just so you can fire it, do you?'

'Yeah, I do. You make a good gun-bearer for a real shooter.'

The platoon, spread out in a snake along the ditch, suddenly stopped moving, and the soldiers automatically took up fire positions left and right. Word came back that the point man had seen movement ahead.

Mann splashed forward along the ditch to join Gent, who was crouched down with Lieutenant Perrin looking intently across the field. 'Three blokes, Tom, over by those compounds. Look like civvies,' said Gent.

Perrin said, 'Yes they do. But I haven't seen any civvies in this area for ages. I'm surprised they're here unless they're up to something they shouldn't be.'

Mann looked towards them. They were 700 to 800 metres away, across an open field, the other side of a second irrigation ditch. They seemed to be doing some kind of work around a collection of compounds and trees beyond the ditch. They were making no attempt to conceal themselves, and some were wearing white kurtas as opposed to the darker colours favoured by fighters trying to blend in. Whatever they were up to they obviously hadn't spotted 10 Platoon.

Major Messenger came forward and spoke to Perrin. He looked at the men through his SUSAT sight and said, 'Yeah, I agree, they look like civvies, though goodness knows what they're doing here. We'll move on but keep an eye on them as we go. Try not to let them see us so, if they are involved, they won't let anyone else know we're here. I still haven't heard any radio chatter.'

Perrin pushed 10 Platoon forward. They reached a bend in the irrigation ditch, and beside the ditch there was a high compound wall. They again went firm to check out the group of men, the C Company soldiers taking up low fire positions.

Mann removed his daysack and, wedging himself against a tree growing in the bank, took out the Leupold x40 spotting scope he had so carefully camouflaged the previous day. The scope came in a box with a tripod, which was bulky, and with all the water and ammo that had to be carried, Mann never bothered with it.

The bend in the ditch had brought them slightly closer to the group of men, who were now about 600 metres away. At that range Mann could see the figures very clearly through the 30cm-long Leupold. There were more of them, moving about. He counted six. He trained the scope on a man in a white kurta with a grey waistcoat and black Afghan-style flat round cap. He looked quite young and unusually didn't have a beard. The others were moving about around him. *Could he be a sentry? If he was he wasn't doing a very good job!* The men were partially obscured by trees and undergrowth, and the bank of the far irrigation ditch, and he could not make out what they were doing. They seemed to be carrying things from the compound and placing them outside.

He looked back at the man in white. He could make out something on his shoulder, which appeared to be draped over by a white cloth, a sheet, or maybe even part of the kurta. Whatever it was it was smooth and elongated – and about the right length for an AK47. The hair stood up on the back of his neck. *It can't be. But if it is, this is a gift.*

He whispered to Perrin, 'Sir, I think one of those guys has got an AK. I can't quite see it, but it looks like it to me.'

Mann carried on watching. He was in an ideal position. With his head up over the ditch, against the background of the compound wall he was less likely to be silhouetted than in the open. And the shadow cast by the trees lining the ditch gave added concealment.

As Mann peered through the scope, the cloth dropped away from the object and he could clearly see the glint of an AK47 assault rifle, with magazine fitted. Adrenalin surged into his bloodstream and he fought to contain his excitement and stay calm.

He told Perrin, who in a low voice briefed the company commander on the radio.

'Engage,' replied Messenger.

Ten metres to Perrin's right, Gent, who had been watching the position through the times 25 Schmidt and Bender sniper scope on his rifle, said in a low voice, 'Tom, one of those punters has got a radio in his hand.'

Quietly, calmly, everything started to happen at once as C Company geared up for a contact – for once on their own terms.

Messenger said to his MFC, 'Get the mortars ready to fire. I want a fire mission in behind those compounds on my command. We will fire it the minute 10 Platoon start engaging. But not before. Understood?'

The MFC was immediately on the mortar net, relaying instructions, and back in Inkerman the three 81mm mortar teams set the bearing and elevation to hit the rear of the compound, which had previously been registered as a mortar target. Like the troops on the ground, the mortar men were excited that they were about to initiate a contact rather than respond to an enemy ambush.

Perrin passed the word along the platoon: 'The snipers will take them out. No one is to fire unless I order it. If we all fire, it will create obscuration and make the snipers' job more difficult.' He knew his men were well disciplined and professional, but he also knew that every man in 10 Platoon would be itching to take a shot.

Gent took out his laser rangefinder. He could have accurately estimated the range but wanted to leave as little as possible to chance. This was a rare opportunity to ambush the Taliban, and he did not want it to go wrong. Added to the need to kill the enemy, he was aware that the whole of C Company would be watching.

The laser range finder looked like a large pair of binoculars, and Mann had coated them too with his camouflage slurry. He put the device to his eyes and pressed the button on top. A red square appeared in the centre of the right-hand eye piece. Mann moved the square on to the man in the white kurta with the AK47 and released the button, shooting a laser pulse straight at him. Seconds later a small red number appeared in the lower part of the eyepiece: 600. 'Six hundred metres,' he hissed at Gent, returning the rangefinder into his daysack.

Gent nodded, pushed his own daysack up the bank, and, lying flat, wrapped himself round it into a solid fire position. Mann stowed his Leupold scope back into his daysack, ready to move immediately if anything went wrong. With his back supported by the tree, he got himself into an awkward but steady fire position, sitting cross-legged, with the .338 bipod legs resting on the baked-hard dirt on the lip of the ditch. He undid his chin strap and pushed his helmet on to the back of his head to raise it away from the weapon sight.

Sergeant Armon had come forward, and said, 'Tom, we'll do a coordinated shoot, OK?'

'Roger, Sarge.'

'Tom, Dan. I'll give "standby, standby, fire". Thumbs up when you're both ready.'

Mann hissed across to Gent, 'Dan. Listen. I'll take the man on the left in the white kurta. You take the one on the right in blue. After that they'll be running everywhere, so just shoot anything you can see.'

'Roger that,' said Gent.

Mann had already chambered a .338 Lapua Magnum bullet. He looked at his personal shooting data, which was taped to the left side of his rifle butt. Through experience every sniper knows the precise personal range adjustment that must be made to the scope of his own weapon, and the Royal Anglian snipers had added to this by getting localized atmospheric data from the Marines when they took over. He then clicked in the adjustment using the drum on the top of his scope.

He didn't think there was any wind at all, but double-checked. Looking carefully at the weeds in the field in front of him he saw there was no movement, and the same further up in the tops of the tallest trees. There was no sign of distortion in the heat shimmer either, so he checked the drum on the right side of the sight was at zero – no lateral adjustment.

He slipped forward the safety catch to the left of the rifle's bolt assembly, then looked through the sight picture in his Schmidt and Bender times 25 sniper scope. His target was still standing, facing to the right, sideways on, AK47 down by his side. Mann brought the cross-hairs on to the centre of the man's shoulder. If he had been firing the L96, he would have gone for a head shot, to guarantee a kill. With the much more powerful .338 Lapua Magnum that would also be virtually guaranteed if he got him anywhere in the torso, and going for the shoulders gave a better chance of hitting. If his aim was slightly high he would get him in the head, if low he would hit the chest.

He gave Armon the thumbs-up and out of the corner of his eye saw Gent do the same. Armon gave the pair a moment to settle down. This was almost it. Mann had used his sniper skills in many contacts before, up in Kajaki. But none was like this. The odds were stacked in his favour now, and if he failed it would be his fault alone. But he knew he wasn't going to fail.

He calmed himself and got control of his breathing. He would do this by the book. Exactly by the book. Contrary to myth a good sniper will never hold his breath. If you hold your breath you strain and your body becomes uncomfortable, leading to a miss at longer ranges. You use natural breathing, and you shoot between breaths.

Armon said, 'Stand by.'

Mann breathed in and took up the first trigger pressure.

'Stand by.'

He breathed out.

'Fire.'

He did not squeeze the trigger with his finger. If you do that it can pull the hand slightly, which jerks the rifle and can lead to a miss. He squeezed with his whole hand and the rifle jerked back into his shoulder. Three-quarters of a second later the .338 bullet ripped open the upper body of the man with the AK47; he was flung back and crumpled to the ground in a heap.

Gent fired at precisely the same moment but missed. He could not afford to curse himself, but quickly adjusted his sight and fired again, sending a 7.62mm black spot bullet into the shoulder of his target, who dropped to the ground.

There was panic among the group of Taliban. They picked up rifles and RPGs from the ground and were running in every direction, like ants in a nest that had been kicked over. Mann calmly continued to engage. He was concentrating totally on his task, but behind him he heard the interpreter, with his radio scanner, shouting that the Taliban net had suddenly come alive.

A fighter holding an AK47 ran up the bank of the distant irrigation ditch. Gent caught him squarely in the chest with his third shot, and he did a spectacular back flip into the ditch.

As the two snipers continued to hit the enemy, they heard explosions from Inkerman, and seconds later crump-crump-crump, crump-crump-crump as the three mortar teams in the base bombarded the area behind the compounds with high-explosive 81mm shells, cutting off any escape.

While the mortars continued to explode, throwing up clouds of dust and smoke, all activity stopped around the compounds. Mann and Gent remained in their fire positions, scanning the area for any sign of movement.

'OK, lads,' said Armon after a few minutes. 'I reckon that's it.'

While the rest of C Company kept their rifles and machine-guns trained on the area round the compounds, the two snipers slid back down the bank. Armon said, 'Well done, lads, good shooting. Tom, you got four, and Dan, you got two.

'I reckon that was all of them, unless maybe one or two somehow got away, but I doubt it.

'Glad you learnt some of the stuff I taught you, Tom, I never thought you'd be able to get them at 600 with a 338. Thought I might have to step in.'

Mann smiled but was on too much of a high to make any retort.

3

Back at Inkerman later that day, Mann and Gent were briefed that, when the shooting began, a Taliban fighter in the compound had been screaming into the radio that they were pinned down by accurate fire and needed reinforcements. Suddenly the radio went dead, and, despite calls from other Taliban fighters, there was no response from the compound.

The radio callsign that had been used was Farouk, believed by the Royal Anglians to be an important Taliban leader. Not much was known about him, but two days before he was killed he had travelled back into the area of Inkerman from Musa Qalah, perhaps with instructions for a further operation. Farouk had been linked by intelligence to a known Taliban HVI, or 'high-value individual', named Haji Qalam. Farouk was thought to have been behind many of the recent attacks, perhaps including the mortar and rocket attack on Inkerman thirteen days earlier that killed Captain Hicks and wounded several others. It was also assessed as possible that he had been involved in the attacks that resulted in the deaths of Lance Corporal Hawkins and Private Rawson.

The Taliban fighters were caught off guard and didn't manage to fire a single shot in return. It was not clear exactly what the group had been doing, but assessment of their activity and the proximity to Inkerman suggested it was possible that they were preparing another indirect fire attack on the base. Whatever the truth, the number and ferocity of attacks against Inkerman, which had continued for the previous two weeks, now dramatically reduced.

At around the same time as Lance Corporal Mann and Private Gent were dealing with Farouk and his team of fighters, Private Oliver Bailey, one of the A Company snipers, was having an altogether different form of contact 7 kilometres away, south of Sangin.

A Company had mounted a patrol to prevent Taliban interference with the distribution of US humanitarian aid to the people of Sangin. FSG Alpha was moving through the Green Zone, about 800 metres south of Sangin DC, with 3 Platoon. A section patrolling to the rear of the FSG came into contact. The FSG went firm behind a partially demolished wall next to a cornfield. They were in close country, and Bailey had his .338 sniper rifle in his left hand and his Browning pistol, ready to fire, in his right. Knowing how adept the Taliban were at infiltrating round the flanks, Bailey moved forward to make sure the enemy weren't approaching beyond a corner in the wall directly to their front. Private Clay Donnachie and Drummer Richard Railton covered him.

Suddenly a fighter popped up from behind the wall with an RPG, right beside Bailey. Bailey smacked him straight in the face with his pistol, then, moving back, fired a full magazine of 9mm bullets into him as he collapsed, dropping into the cornfield. As Bailey moved backwards, Donnachie fired at the fighter with his rifle.

A short distance along the wall a second fighter raised his head and fired an RPG. It smashed into a tree right beside the soldiers but didn't explode. Donnachie fired at him but got a stoppage, and Railton opened up with his GPMG from the hip, ripping the man apart.

Another RPG missile whizzed past them, fired from within the cornfield, and exploded further down the track, narrowly missing FSG Corporal Gavin Watts. Donnachie lobbed a hand grenade over the wall and rushed forward, spraying the cornfield with his SA80 on automatic. Lance Corporal Terry Findley and his section ran to assist and with two Minimis and a GPMG blasted hundreds of bullets into the cornfield.

Bailey couldn't believe what had happened. This was the second time since arriving in Helmand that he, a sniper, had ended up killing a Taliban fighter at close range with his pistol. The first time was right at the start of the tour as he was moving through the compounds of Sorkhani, at Nowzad, on Friday 13 April.

4

A few days later, on Tuesday 28 August, the bodies of Privates Foster, Thrumble and McClure, killed in the accidental air strike near Kajaki, were repatriated to the UK following a ramp ceremony in Camp Bastion. Their platoon commander, Lieutenant George Seal-Coon, who had briefly returned to Bastion for medical checks after the battering he took from the 500-pound bomb that killed his three soldiers, carried the Colour.

It is against military protocol for Colours to be on parade during such a ceremony, unless the deceased is a commissioned officer. But Lieutenant Colonel Carver took the view that honouring his dead soldiers with the Colours that embodied the fighting heart and soul of the battalion was more important than observance of regulations born in a now outdated era. To Carver, his soldiers' lives were every bit as important as those of his officers. The Queen's and Regimental Colours, emblazoned with the battle honours of the regiment's 300-year history, were on parade at the ramp ceremony for every Royal Anglian officer and soldier killed in Afghanistan.

The night before the ceremony, Regimental Sergeant Major Ian Robinson paid a private visit to the three dead men in the Camp Bastion mortuary. Unknown to anybody else Robinson made a point of being the last person to see the body of every soldier before the coffin lid was sealed and they left the battalion for ever. Robinson paused for a few moments beside each soldier, whispered a quiet goodbye on behalf of their comrades and ruffled each man's hair. A final human contact with the regimental family with whom they had been through so much.

At the precise time of the ramp ceremony, B Company held their own memorial service for their three dead comrades, up on the hillside above Kajaki, looking across to the spot in Mazdurak where they died. Dusk was gathering as Major Borgnis read out eulogies for each of the three men that he had prepared the day after they were killed.

Captain Dave Robinson, the company 2IC, spoke the exhortation:

They shall grow not old, as we that are left grow old:
Age shall not weary them, nor the years condemn.
At the going down of the sun and in the morning
We will remember them.

With barely a dry eye among the group of tough, battle-hardened infantrymen, the soldiers responded, 'We will remember them.'

There was a brief pause and then a lone American F15 Eagle flew directly towards them, fired its flares in salute to the three dead soldiers and soared upwards across the Peaks.

The 81mm mortar section in Zeebrugge then fired a star shell to mark the start of two minutes' silence. During the silence the mortars shot three more star shells into the sky, one each for Privates Robert Foster, Aaron McLure and John Thrumble.

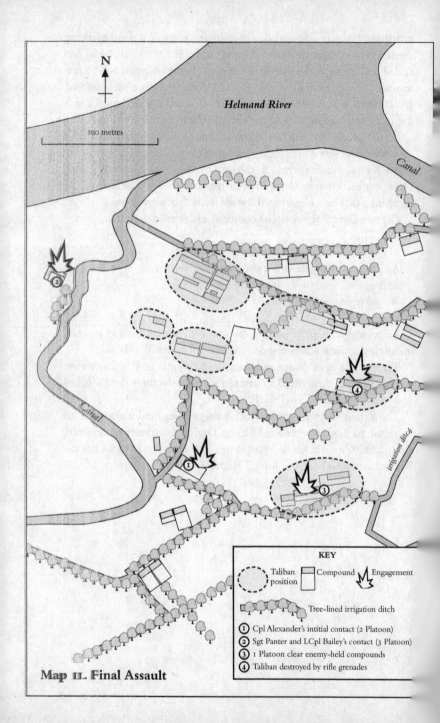

N

Helmand River

100 metres

Canal

Canal

irrigation ditch

KEY

Taliban position Compound Engagement

Tree-lined irrigation ditch

1 Cpl Alexander's intitial contact (2 Platoon)
2 Sgt Panter and LCpl Bailey's contact (3 Platoon)
3 1 Platoon clear enemy-held compounds
4 Taliban destroyed by rifle grenades

Map II. Final Assault

Final Assault: 29 August–1 September 2007

Major Calder's Mastiff assault, a series of subsequent offensive operations led by Major Messenger and the killing of Farouk and his team by Lance Corporal Mann and Private Gent, had all damaged the Taliban's offensive capability. But the effects were only temporary, and there were continuing signs of a further Taliban build-up in the area, threatening the security of Sangin and reconstruction efforts in the town and district.

Lieutenant Colonel Carver realized that another battle group offensive against the Taliban in the Helmand River valley north-east of Sangin was going to be needed. He was determined to prevent the Taliban gathering enough strength to lay waste again to the town, destroying the remarkable reconstruction and confidence-building work that had been accomplished by A Company since the end of Operation Lastay Kulang back at the beginning of June.

It was now late August, and Carver also had in mind that 40 Commando Royal Marines would be arriving in just a few weeks to take over from the Royal Anglians in Helmand. He did not want to throw a newly arrived unit straight into the deep end. They needed a chance to find their feet in the demanding battle zone around Sangin. Clearing the hard-core Taliban out and knocking them off balance before the marines arrived would at least buy some time for them. Carver wanted the operation to be complete before they arrived.

Carver and his staff planned an offensive in which A and C Companies would clear the valley from south to north, driving the Taliban into a block provided by the Estonian armoured infantry company and the Brigade Recce Force. The Recce Platoon, with a powerful armoured group of Viking vehicles and Mastiffs, would screen exits from the Green Zone into the desert on the east side, preventing enemy reinforcement and dealing with any Taliban attempting to escape in that direction. C Squadron of the Light Dragoons, allocated by Task Force

Helmand to the Royal Anglian Battle Group for this operation, would carry out the same function on the west flank of the advance, operating on the other side of the Helmand River.

D-Day for Operation Palk Ghar, which Carver expected to be the Royal Anglians' final battle group offensive of the tour, was planned for 30 August.

Carver's intention was to mount the entire infantry operation on foot, to increase the element of surprise, with A Company carrying out a demanding approach march to bring them up to a start point near Inkerman. From there the company would advance north through the Green Zone with C Company on their right. Carver believed that several crossing points on the Helmand River would be heavily defended by the Taliban, and would have to be cleared.

Major Biddick had kept A Company at the peak of fitness throughout the tour. Much of this came naturally through the endless, grinding foot patrols, sweating through desert and Green Zone under huge weights in the soaring summer temperatures. But he made sure fitness levels were kept topped up by running around the base, doing circuits on the improvised gyms the troops had put together and by boxing training. Biddick made it absolutely clear to his men that weak links would not deploy on operations. They would become a liability to the rest of the company, and he wasn't prepared to risk the life of a Chinook crew and MERT team with a CASEVAC into the Green Zone for a heat casualty that could have been prevented by a higher level of fitness. He knew Operation Palk Ghar was going be one of the most physically demanding tasks he would ask his men to undertake, and he wanted to be certain everyone was up to it. Despite months of acclimatization, heat illness was still a threat that loomed large, and he didn't want men on this operation who were not physically up to it.

His greatest concern was for soldiers who had twisted ankles or were recovering from other patrol injuries. He knew that every man in the company would try to conceal an injury rather than be left back in the DC while his mates were out facing the enemy. Biddick admired the bond of loyalty that this represented but he also knew that it could put other men's lives at risk. As they had learnt in the last five months, evacuating just one casualty – be it from enemy action, accidental injury or heat illness – was extremely manpower intensive and sometimes caused patrols to be curtailed or abandoned.

Biddick's solution, as for previous operations, was to conduct physical fitness tests for the whole company before they deployed. As in everything, he led from the front and was the first to undergo the demanding exercises. The men hated being put through their paces in this way, and those who had the slightest leg or ankle problem dreaded the prospect of failure. That would mean staying behind in the sangars, and was seen by them as letting their mates down.

Private Kane Hornigold was extremely worried when he was called forward to do the test. He had just arrived in Helmand, having flown out from the battalion's Rear Party in Pirbright just three days after his eighteenth birthday. Sergeant Major Stephen Clark, the Rear Party sergeant major, had been glad to see the back of him. Since he had arrived from Catterick Hornigold had done nothing except pester him about getting out to Afghanistan.

However often Clark explained it, Hornigold never seemed to understand that until he was eighteen he simply wasn't deploying – it was government policy. Hornigold had been beside himself. The mates who had passed out of training with him, who were all a bit older, were now in theatre. He was terrified the battalion would come back before he had the chance to get out and do some fighting alongside them.

Palk Ghar was going to be his first operation. And this test was the first hurdle he would face in the battalion. He was physically very fit and had worked hard to get even fitter while being forced to wait in Pirbright between the time he passed out of Catterick and joing his company in Sangin. But he didn't know what to expect. The idea that he might fail the test made him shudder. There was no way he could live that down at the start of his military service. And even worse was the thought he might not be allowed to deploy on Op Palk Ghar. He didn't voice his concerns to anybody, partly because he didn't yet really know anybody in Sangin. His mates from training had gone to other companies, and it takes time to settle into a platoon, even on operations. But Sergeant Holmes, his platoon sergeant, noticed the concern on his face, and said, 'Don't worry about it, Hornigold, I'll go through the test with you. Just keep with me and you'll have no problem getting round. Anyway, there's no way I'm letting you get off this op, I need you in Platoon HQ.'

Hornigold laughed nervously. Holmes's offer to go through the test with him had boosted his confidence, but he was still dreading it. In the event, it turned out to be the hardest physical test he had ever done.

The run seemed to be endless, wearing boots, combat trousers and T-shirt, round and round the Sangin DC circuit, at Biddick's pace. In fact it wasn't at Biddick's pace, because very few would have been able to achieve that. But it was fast. The squad kicked up dust as they ran, and Hornigold was half-choking on the fine Sangin sand that filled the air. The worst thing was the heat. He had never in his life experienced such oppressive, glaring heat, bearing down on him and giving him a headache even when he was standing still. It was almost unbearable even for the seasoned A Company soldiers who had been in Helmand for nearly five months. But Hornigold had arrived only four days earlier and hadn't had time to acclimatize. Somehow he kept up, and at the end, fighting for breath, pouring sweat down his already soaked T-shirt, he did his best to stay standing up when all he wanted to do was collapse in a heap on the dirt.

Biddick's words, 'Well done, Hornigold,' meant more to him than anything he could remember. He was elated. He still had to prove himself on operations under enemy fire, but at least he had made the team.

Biddick said to Holmes, 'Well done to you as well, Sergeant Holmes. I'm slightly surprised you made it, but I suppose young Hornigold carried you round.'

'Yeah, all right, sir, glad you could keep up too. Looked like you were struggling a bit towards the end there, sir.'

'Thanks, Sergeant H, I appreciate your concern.'

He looked at Hornigold and then turned again to Holmes. 'By the way that reminds me there was something I wanted to speak to you about.'

Holmes said to Hornigold, 'OK, lad, well done. Go and get yourself in the river and then get on with your admin.'

Biddick walked over to a shaded corner of the dusty base. 'It's actually about Hornigold. Do you remember a while back, before he actually arrived, you asked me if he could be posted to 1 Platoon so you could keep an eye on him, because he was related to you? Can't remember what you said – cousin or something, wasn't it? And you said he was special to you. I think they were the words you used. I can remember the conversation quite clearly, because you interrupted me while I was shaving one morning.'

Holmes seemed uncharacteristically nervous, looking from Biddick to the ground. 'Yes, sir, something like that, sir.'

'Yes, well, I happened to be chatting to young Hornigold yesterday when he was on stag and I mentioned the family connection. He didn't know what I was talking about. I'm sure there's a perfectly reasonable explanation, and I was just wondering what it was.'

Holmes couldn't be sure whether Biddick was smiling or not. He said, 'Yes, sir, I can explain, sir. I'm really sorry, sir…'

When he was back in his home town of Great Yarmouth on R and R in June, Holmes had gone to the Vauxhall dealership with his father to order a new car. Speaking to the salesman, Holmes's proud father mentioned that his son was in the Army, on leave from Afghanistan.

'Shut up, Dad, we're here to buy a car not tell war stories,' Holmes said.

But the dealer said, 'Oh, that's interesting, my son has just passed out of Catterick. He's a Royal Anglian. He's going out to Afghanistan himself soon. I'm really worried. I've heard they're all getting hurt because they're mixing it big time. I've seen it in the news.'

Holmes told him he too was a Royal Anglian.

Steve Hornigold, the dealer, stared at him. He begged Holmes to look after his son in Afghanistan. 'I just want to know that someone's looking out for him. He's looking forward to going out there. But I'm really, really worried about him. I'm sure it's not as bad as they say on the TV, but I am so worried.'

Holmes didn't want to tell Mr Hornigold the truth about what was going on in Helmand. The poor man, who obviously cared deeply for his son, would probably have a heart attack.

'I'll look after him,' said Holmes, understanding the desperation in Mr Hornigold's voice. He wondered how he was going to make good on this hasty promise. He had no idea whether young Hornigold would be posted to A, B, C or D Company. He could be going anywhere.

Mr Hornigold shook Holmes's hand, immense relief and gratitude on his face. He said, 'Thanks, mate, thanks so much. I'll tell you what, I'll take my commission off whatever you buy.'

Holmes finished his explanation to Biddick: 'Sir, I'm sorry I told you he was related. I couldn't think of anything else to say. It wasn't the money off the car – he didn't even say anything about that till I'd agreed to look after Kane. I just wanted to help him. He was so worried about his boy.'

Biddick tutted, but he was smiling. He had guessed this wasn't about a family relationship. He said, 'Well, I hope you got a good deal, Sergeant H. What car did you go for in the end?'

'It's a Vauxhall Zafira VXR, sir, a people carrier.'

Biddick laughed, 'Really? Settling down then, Sergeant H?'

'No, it's pretty sporty. A turbo. Anyway I need it now we've got another baby.'

Holmes went back to the finish of the run. Two more of his men, Privates Fabio Oliviero and Sam Hicks were just finishing their test. He slapped them on the back, 'Well done, lads. Get down to the river and get yourselves sorted.'

Oliviero, from Peterborough, was half Italian. He was a bright, confident soldier, who had the academic qualifications to be an officer. He considered applying for Sandhurst, but decided he wanted to experience life as a private soldier in the infantry. Straight from training in Catterick, in July 2004, he joined the battalion while they were deployed in Iraq.

Oliviero, normally upbeat and positive no matter what was going on, was on a downer. A few days earlier, Operation Minimise had been called in Sangin. That meant someone had been killed or seriously wounded. Whenever Minimise was invoked, non-operational phones, emails and texting systems were all deactivated. The idea was that the rumours that would inevitably spread around the battalion in these circumstances did not filter back to the UK, causing unnecessary alarm among family and friends back home.

Soon after Minimise was called, it became known among the troops in Sangin that casualties had been taken by B Company at Kajaki. Everyone knew people in B Company, and rumour and speculation about what had happened was rife. But it was not till days later that the details came out about the F15 attack that killed Privates Foster, McLure and Thrumble.

Oliviero had been in the same training platoon at Catterick as Thrumble, and they had been close, seeing a lot of each other in the battalion over the years since they passed out. He was devastated by the news of his mate's death.

The news from Kajaki also got Oliviero thinking about Operation Palk Ghar, due to begin in a few days. They would be going home in three or four weeks. Mixing with the Taliban in the Green Zone raised the stakes hugely. Was he going to die here in the last few weeks of the tour? Or any more of his mates? He couldn't bear the thought. He looked at Sam Hicks, washing his clothes in the river next to him. He was one of his closest mates. And that meant a lot in Helmand, where the nightmare of intensive, toe-to-toe combat bound infantrymen closer together even than brothers.

The two had been through so much together since that time on Friday 13 April when they had been up on a compound roof, exposed to intensive enemy fire, trying to support Sergeant Larry Holmes's withdrawal back to safety. They had looked out for one another ever since and had saved each other's skins a few times. Oliviero was full of admiration for the friend whom he had seen storming through Helmand over the past five months, breaking down doors and blasting his way into compounds. Hicks was often at point for the section, the platoon and frequently the whole company group. Oliviero thought he was one of the bravest men he had ever known.

Since the end of Operation Ghartse Ghar, A Company had been in Sangin. They had conducted security patrols by day and night throughout the town and surrounding areas, talking to the locals in the streets and in the teeming market place. These patrols were designed to deter and disrupt Taliban activities, and also to support reconstruction efforts, gain intelligence and protect the developing market economy in Sangin. Some people were indifferent, a few overtly hostile, but the majority had become increasingly friendly towards the Royal Anglian soldiers as they got used to them. Biddick had demanded that his men treat the locals with the utmost respect, and that they should do whatever they could to help them, whether during a minor incident in the street, in a reconstruction project, or in the event of a Taliban attack. This approach had paid off, and as the patrols moved through the town there would be lots of handshaking, waving and the exchange of friendly greetings. With interpreters, they could have conversations, but Oliviero and the other soldiers also learnt quickly how to communicate, make themselves understood and even have a laugh with the locals using signs and gestures.

Oliviero found the work rewarding. He had seen the market grow from virtually nothing when they arrived to the thriving district trading centre it had now become. He knew how much this meant to the locals. He also knew how tired the locals were of the fighting that had plagued their lives for so long, and how happy they mostly were that the Royal Anglians were there, doing their best to keep the peace.

But while A Company was patrolling and protecting Sangin, Oliviero and all of the other soldiers knew what was happening just a few kilometres north at FOB Inkerman. They heard the reports, the stories and the rumours of almost daily attacks and vicious contact battles. And with their own eyes and ears, in the distance, they saw the Apaches screaming down on to the Taliban around Inkerman, the F15s roaring overhead on their way to dump their deadly munitions, the distant rattle of heavy gunfire and the dull crump of C Company's and the Taliban's rockets and mortars pounding each other.

That was where Oliviero and all his mates really wanted to be. In the fight alongside C Company.

Operation Palk Ghar therefore brought mixed feelings. Oliviero was energized by the idea of getting into contact with the enemy again. It was what he had joined the Army to do, it was what he had trained for back in Pirbright and it was what he had become extremely good at in the hard experience of battle after battle before they arrived at Sangin. And there was that electric feeling of living by the skin of your teeth, where every single action and reaction could mean the difference between life and death, and the heady adrenalin rush as the first rocket streaked overhead or the first bullet cracked into the ground.

But then there was the worry in the back of his head about whether his or his mates' luck would run out in the last few weeks of the tour, the timeless concern of every soldier in the history of human conflict...

Two days later, on Wednesday 29 August, the men of 1 Platoon, with their medic and Royal Engineers attachments, were in Oliviero's room waiting for orders for Operation Palk Ghar. Ten by five metres, and home to ten soldiers, this was one of the larger rooms in the block and normally used for 1 Platoon's O Groups. They were on the top floor of a two-storey stone building, which bore many battle scars from the RPGs, 107mm rockets and gunfire that had peppered the base over the last year. There was no air conditioning to make the red-hot summer days bearable and no heating to take the edge off the sometimes freezing nights. The windows had no glass; some were sandbagged, others just gaping holes. On the roof was the sandbag and wriggly tin FSG tower, permanently manned by observers and machine-gunners.

Some of the camp beds had been pulled round to form a hollow square for the men to sit on during the orders. They were dressed in flip flops and shorts, sweating in the morning heat. Oliviero, wedged between Hicks and Private Sam Wills, had an irrational hatred of these O Groups. People always messed up his bedspace, and he was very particular about keeping tidy the few possessions he had with him – sleeping bag, mosquito net, daysack and personal equipment – an obsession that increased as the tour went on.

As Oliviero bickered with the other soldiers about football, women and how much they were abusing his bedspace, Sergeant Holmes shouted, 'All right now, shut up, you lot, listen in to the boss.'

The platoon commander, Lieutenant Nick Denning, walked in. He was the only member of the platoon in uniform and had come straight from Biddick's company O Group.

The room was silent. Everyone wanted to know what they were going to be doing. Rumours had flown around since the first mention of Operation Palk Ghar. The big one was it would be an advance all the way to Musa Qalah, to take on the Taliban stronghold there. What everyone wanted to know was how long the operation would go on. They were all thinking about Ghartse Ghar. They had been told they would be out for three days and came back two weeks later.

'Before I begin the orders properly, I'm just going to give you an outline,' Denning began. 'There has been significant Taliban reinfiltration into the Green Zone north-east of here since we kicked them out in Ghartse Ghar. That's why C Company have had so much crap up in Inkerman. We don't know how many enemy are there, but estimates range from four to six hundred. So a lot. And from C Company's experience, as well as other intelligence, it looks like many of them are hard-core fighters from Pakistan. Some have also come down from Musa Qalah.'

Oliviero and the other soldiers sat shaking their heads. He knew they would win the battle against the Taliban, but he also realized just how tough the fight was likely to be. And not long before the end of the tour ...

Denning continued, 'So we and C Company are going to push north into the same area as we did in Ghartse, and kill, capture or drive out all the Taliban in the Green Zone.'

Denning spent over an hour going through the details of the plan. He took questions, and finished off by saying, 'Lads, be sure of one thing: we are going to stick it all over the Taliban again. It isn't going to be easy, they are not going to like it and they aren't going to be a walkover. But I am totally confident we can all do the job, no problem. This is probably going to be the last big op we do on this tour, and while we're all together I want to wish you good luck. You've all done brilliantly so far, and I am really proud of everything you individually have achieved and what we have achieved as a platoon.'

When the orders were finished, the men started preparing for battle. Having painstakingly restored order to his bed space, Oliviero went through the routine he had been through a hundred times before. He cleaned his rifle and the underslung grenade launcher attached to it, carefully stripping down every working part, cleaning off the dust with a cloth and brush, lightly oiling the mechanism and the barrel.

Hornigold, who was helping Sergeant Holmes issue ammo, brought him a Claymore off-route anti-personnel mine to carry and a hundred rounds of spare 7.62mm link for the GPMG gunner. He cleaned every bullet and link and then emptied his magazines and bandoliers. He had eight magazines and two bandoliers, 540 rounds in total. He cleaned his 5.56mm ammunition with a rag. He then dismantled his magazines and cleaned the springs and the interior of the housing. He didn't want even the most minute piece of grit to increase the possibility of a stoppage just as he came face to face with an angry AK47-wielding Taliban fighter.

He checked and repacked the rest of his ammunition – twelve UGL high-explosive grenades, two L109 high-explosive hand grenades, a red phosphorous grenade and a smoke grenade.

He checked the items in his team medic's pack – two extra morphine syrettes, two extra field dressings and some bandages. He checked his own two morphine syrettes, two tourniquets and two first field dressings, and stowed them in the left-hand map pocket of the desert combat trousers that he had laid out on his camp-bed. He checked over and laid out on the bed his knee-pads and leather desert gloves.

He filled his two water bottles and Camelbak water pack from jerry cans – 5 litres in all. He packed the Camelbak into his daysack, along with his softee jacket, lightweight stretcher, infrared cyalume night sticks, miniflares, camera, and the 100 rounds of 7.62mm link. Somehow it all jammed in.

He cleaned and checked his infrared monocular night-viewing device and put it on top of the daysack. They would be leaving after dark that night, and he would fit it to his helmet just before they moved out. He checked over and dusted off his Osprey body armour – *20 kilograms of pain, but worth every ounce,* he thought.

He changed the batteries in his PRR radio, tested it and placed it beside his daysack.

Finally he stowed his magazines into his webbing along with two boil-in-the-bag meals, a pack of biscuits, some compo sweets and some sweets his mum had sent out. He checked his notebook and pens and his ammo state card. His section commander, Corporal Chris Brooks, would make him section 2IC if anything happened to Lance Corporal Sven Chatfield, and he would need that card for section ammo checks.

He made sure his bible was in his webbing. It had been issued to him when he joined the Army. Oliviero was a Roman Catholic and, although he did not consider himself 'overly religious', he always had a bible with him and occasionally read from it.

He also carried a gold Saint Christopher medallion in the front plate pouch of his body armour. It had been given to him by a family member, and his mum had told him to take it with him when he went to Afghanistan and to always carry it when he was on patrol. Oliviero knew better than to disobey his mum.

While he was sorting out his kit, Oliviero didn't speak to anyone else. All the other men were working pretty much in silence, going through the same routines. He was reflecting on what was to come, and what they had all done so far on this extraordinary tour. And he kept thinking about Private John Thrumble, and what a nightmare his poor parents must be going through now, back in their home in Essex.

3

Lieutenant George Seal-Coon's 7 Platoon from B Company, who had suffered the F15 bombing seven days earlier, had been temporarily moved to Sangin to provide the guard force during Operation Palk

Ghar. After he had finished packing his personal equipment, Oliviero bumped into Private Ronnie Barker, one of the 7 Platoon soldiers.

Barker had also been in the same training platoon at Catterick as Oliviero and Thrumble. Oliviero started to ask him what had happened. Barker said that it had been really bad, the worst thing that he had ever seen. Oliviero could see that Barker was still upset by the loss of three of his close mates and he knew he had been right there when it happened and had helped treat and evacuate them. Oliviero didn't press for any more details. He would no doubt learn the full facts soon enough.

The rest of the day was spent loading and unloading kit for the company sergeant major and doing various administrative tasks around the base. Oliviero tried to grab a few hours' sleep during the afternoon, but the stifling, airless heat ensured he only managed to doze off briefly once or twice.

Oliviero and Hicks went down to the front gate just before 2000 hours with the rest of the platoon, kitted up, ready to deploy. It was dark and there were no lights in the base, but there was a full moon, and a cloudless sky, crammed with bright stars. The whole company was there, all three platoons, the FSG dismounted from their vehicles, plus a platoon of the ANA that was attached to A Company for the operation.

Biddick was moving around the small gaggles of silent soldiers. He stopped at Oliviero's group. 'How're you doing, lads? All ready? It's going to be a tough few days. Keep your wits about you.'

When he had moved on, Oliviero whispered to Hicks, 'Hicksie, did you see Biddick? He loves this. He was made for war. He'd be lost doing anything else. He's a legend. Thank God he's leading us. If anyone can get us through this and back home safely it's Big Dom. I'd follow him anywhere.'

Hicks nodded in agreement.

Holmes walked around the men. Hornigold was right behind him, the platoon sergeant's runner. 'Lads, don't screw up. Use your skills and drills. I know it's near the end of the tour, but no complacency.'

Oliviero's section was leading the company north into the Green Zone, and Hicks was point man. Oliviero loaded a magazine on to his rifle, and Hicks fitted the belt of 5.56mm link to his Minimi. As they shuffled into line to move through the gate, Oliviero put his hand on

Hicks's shoulder and said, 'Hicksie, just watch it out there. I'm keeping my eye on you, mate.'

Hicks looked back at him, grinning. Oliviero could see he was happy and really up for whatever lay ahead.

Corporal Brooks, the section commander, followed Hicks out, and Oliviero moved behind him. Brooks was navigating the whole company through the night to their start point, using his map and compass and a Garmin GPS on his wrist. As they weaved their way through compound complexes and villages there were occasional stops to check navigation, or to wait for the rear elements to catch up.

In the compounds they encountered occasional groups of young men, gathered outside the walls, chatting. They checked them for weapons and carried on. All the way dogs were barking, howling and baying, close by and in the distance. There were domestic beasts, within compound walls, and packs of filthy, disease-ridden wild dogs prowling the night.

As they patrolled deeper and deeper into Taliban country, they used tracks when they could, and they were easy going. Cutting through the vegetation, they were frequently whipped in the face by tree branches and brambles. They moved round tall fields of corn, 3 metres high, and across the endless ditches, streams and canals that criss-crossed the whole of the route.

Everyone had got soaking wet up to their knees within ten minutes of leaving the DC as they waded across the first ditch. Soldiers tripped, slipped and fell on uneven, rutted ground, rocks and stick bridges. Falling with the enormous battle loads they were carrying was always a nightmare, with everyone dreading a wrenched knee or twisted ankle.

It was not too hot, but, moving fast and carrying between 30 and 45 kilos, every man was dripping sweat and constantly wiping the stinging salt water out of their eyes, as they patrolled forward, weapons at the ready, covering arcs.

One of Biddick's engineers was bitten by a spider soon after leaving the base. He was in pain and he had to be kept going. As they moved on, the medic monitored him to see if the bite was poisonous and whether he would go into shock. Of even greater concern to Biddick, his stand-in JTAC, who had arrived with the company just before they deployed, collapsed with heat exhaustion about 5 kilometres into the insertion march. They resuscitated him as rapidly as they could and kept him moving. Without a JTAC the company would have been combat ineffective. Finally the company went firm at 0115 hours, five hours after they had set out from the DC. They were just short of their line of departure. Ahead of time, Biddick allowed them to rest for a bit, with sentries deployed, keeping watch.

Oliviero sat down next to a compound, with Sam Hicks slumped next to him. He was soaked to the skin with ditchwater and sweat, his feet were killing him, his shoulders even worse, and he was exhausted. He swigged several mouthfuls of water, ate a biscuit and suddenly felt elated. He took off his boots, wrung out his sodden socks and put them and his boots back on. He refilled his Camelbak from his water bottle, strapped his daysack back on and dozed off sitting against a compound wall.

4

Oliviero woke up half an hour later. 2 Platoon started moving past. Rubbing his eyes, he remembered the plan. 1 Platoon would lead up to the line of departure, and then 2 Platoon would take over, and lead the company into the assault.

As he struggled to his feet, Hicks and he propping each other up, in the dark he could make out Corporal Ryan Alexander moving by, followed by Stevo and then the platoon commander, Lieutenant Graham Goodey.

Biddick's Tac followed 2 Platoon, and then Hicks led 1 Platoon forward along the same route. Oliviero felt happier now that his platoon was no longer point. He was less tense, there was less pressure. If you were at the front, you had to deal straight away with anything that came at you. And you were more likely to take casualties. He had mates in 2 Platoon, including the men he had just seen go by, and the last thing he wanted was for anything to happen to them. But it was not the same as if it happened to his own platoon.

The company continued to move forward without incident for three more hours. At 0530 they stopped, and 1 Platoon got into all-round defence in a field just short of a major irrigation canal. They were in open ground, near a bund-line. Oliviero gulped down some more water.

It was getting light, and he looked around at the rest of the lads. He could see in everyone's faces that they were feeling it as much as he was. They had been marching for nearly ten hours now. In a low voice he said to Hicks, 'Hicksie, that was the hardest night ever. Now we've got to go and do some fighting. I hope today goes well. Remember what I said back in the DC. Be careful.'

He ate a biscuit and a couple of sweets. Corporal Brooks said, 'Lads, 2 Platoon are leading. They are going to move in and clear this crossing point over the river. There's likely to be Taliban here, so there could be a fight. We'll be directly behind. 3 Platoon and the FSG are up on the west of the canal providing fire support. If anything happens, stand by for QBOs and react immediately. Well done so far. Now for the hard bit.'

A few minutes later, Oliviero was moving along beside a compound wall when suddenly, up ahead, there was a long, loud burst of machine-gun fire. He went down on one knee but couldn't see anything. *What the hell's going on? 2 Platoon must be in contact.*

Eight hundred metres forward, Private Anthony Glover, point man for 2 Platoon, moved round the corner of a compound wall. Directly in front of him, 200 metres away, in the open field, a Taliban fighter stood up, levelled a PKM machine-gun and, firing from the hip, blasted at Glover. Glover did a backward roll into cover behind the wall, as a second burst came his way.

His section commander, Corporal Ryan Alexander, pulled Glover back and crawled forward to see for himself. The fighter had disappeared. Alexander knew he wouldn't be on his own. He thought the enemy must be in the large compound, forward right. An irrigation ditch led towards it. He ran back, with Glover, to his section. He thought, *We need to act fast here, try to get them by surprise.*

'Follow me,' he yelled to his men and led them back round the cover of the compound and into the ditch. He moved up the ditch, and was met by a blanket of fire, as several machine-guns opened up and RPGs exploded into the compound walls behind. He heard the splintering of wood as tree branches were ripped away by gunfire, several crashing on top of him. To the rear he heard shouting as one of the other sections, on the far side of the compound, came under fire.

Alexander couldn't make out the enemy firing points but worked out roughly where they would be and opened fire into the area with his

SA80. He crawled forward down the ditch, trying to get into a better position to observe. A fighter darted round the corner of one of the compounds to his front and fired an RPG straight at him. Alexander fired two quick shots at the fighter but missed, and the missile skimmed between him and Glover, a metre ahead, and exploded behind them.

Glover was firing towards the enemy compound, and enemy bullets started pouring in from the left. Alexander again couldn't find the firing point, but directed his Minimi gunner to open up into the general area.

Further left, Alexander now heard firing coming from 3 Platoon's area. He heard on the radio that they were engaging a group of Taliban who had been moving towards his own position. *Well done, Si*, he thought, *I owe you one*, knowing that Sergeant Si Panter, commanding the platoon, would be cutting the enemy to pieces.

On the left, in 3 Platoon's area, sniper Private Oliver Bailey was on a compound roof with four other soldiers. Two RPGs whizzed low over their heads. Bailey saw smoke from the firing points, 200 metres away, and directed Private Ben Roberts, a 3 Platoon GPMG gunner, and Private Jemail McLeod, a Minimi gunner, to return fire. Bailey crawled forward to get a better view and saw an RPG gunner, 200 metres away in a woodline. He was aiming towards Alexander's platoon, off to the right. Bailey was too exposed to get into a fire position, so talked Roberts on to the fighter, directing his arc of tracer straight at the man like a hose. The fighter crumpled into the ground before he got his missile off.

Bullets started hitting the roof, heavy automatic fire. Roberts and two of the other soldiers jumped on the ground. McLeod and Bailey continued to fire. McLeod said, 'This is getting very close.'

Bullets were licking around them, but Bailey said, 'Don't worry, I'll tell you when it's close. Keep firing.'

Seconds later a bullet punched into the compound roof right between them, and Bailey said, 'OK, that's close, let's go.'

The two jumped to the ground.

Forward of the compound, FSG Corporal Gav Watts and Lance Corporal David Evans were pinned down by heavy fire behind a small rut in the ground. The other men of 3 Platoon and the FSG were in firing points around the compound. They were unable to identify the enemy positions firing at the two FSG soldiers, but were firing into likely cover.

Sergeant Si Panter said to Bailey, 'There's only one place you can see anything from, that's up on that roof. Get back up there with your sniper rifle, boy. I'll give you a leg up.'

Bailey crawled across the compound roof, thick with dust. Keeping low, trying not to draw attention to himself, he laid his magazines out in front of him. Using the sniper scope on his .338 long-range rifle, Bailey scanned for enemy. He couldn't identify any firing points, so started firing into windows and doorways, possible enemy positions.

A sudden movement caught his eye. A compound roof, 300 metres to the right, in front of 2 Platoon. Bailey swung his scope on to it. Stacked on the roof were huge bundles of dried poppy stalks. Beside one of the bundles, a Taliban fighter, wearing a dark kurta, was kneeling up, holding a PKM machine-gun. Bailey could clearly make out the bipod, and the man seemed to be pulling the working parts to the rear, as if he was trying to clear a stoppage. Bailey adjusted his sights, took aim and fired. *Missed.* He knew he had the right settings. He knew he had the right point of aim. *Why did it miss, or is this bloke bullet-proof?* He fired again. The fighter fell forward on to his machine-gun and then crumpled into a ball on the roof. He didn't move. Bailey kept him in his sights, watching to see if he got up. He doubted he would, not with a .338 bullet in him.

He detected movement on the left-hand side of the compound wall and slowly moved his sight to it. Another fighter, wearing a light-coloured kurta, AK47 slung over his shoulder, was climbing up the wall, pulling himself on to the roof. He walked across to where the other man lay, put his hands under the dead fighter's armpits and started dragging him towards the edge of the roof. He dropped the corpse to the ground. Bailey fired, and the second fighter followed his comrade down, head first.

Heavy fire was still streaming towards the two FSG soldiers in the open. Below him, Bailey heard Colour Sergeant Faupel, the FSG commander, shout to them, 'Gav! Gav! You're going to have to run for it. Drop your daysacks off. When I give rapid fire, get up and run back here. Stand by. Stand by. Raaaapid – fire!'

The enemy compound and the treelines round it were hit by a wall of fire, as all the FSG and 3 Platoon machine-gunners and riflemen opened up. From the roof, Bailey joined in, cranking off his .338 rounds into windows and doors.

The Taliban fire slowed significantly but did not stop, and the two FSG men got up and ran, bullets cracking around them, and somehow made it back behind the compound wall.

5

After Bailey killed the two fighters on their compound roof, all enemy fire into Alexander's position ceased. Behind him, the other section in the platoon was still in contact, and the firefight continued with 3 Platoon and the FSG on the left. On the net, Alexander heard Biddick, calm as ever, say, 'All stations, this is Zero Alpha. Orders. Two Zero remain in current location and suppress the enemy. One Zero are to move forward and assault the enemy compound forward right of Two Zero. Three Zero are to continue to provide fire support from current position. One Zero Alpha, acknowledge, over.'

Lieutenant Denning said, 'Roger out,' and Oliviero watched as he gave rapid orders to the three section commanders. Then Brooks was back with the section. 'OK, lads, we're going to move through the ditch and assault the compounds to the right, two hundred metres away.' He indicated a complex of three dark brown compounds. The men nodded, confirming they knew where they were going. '2 Platoon were contacted from there. Don't know enemy strength. As a platoon we will clear all of the compounds. 2 Platoon will give fire support from their current location, as will 3 Platoon, further left.' He pointed out the other platoon positions. 'Order of march from here is Davies's section, Field's section, then us.'

They moved into the ditch. Members of 2 Platoon were in fire positions near the bank, providing cover. The water was chest height, and the men waded along, holding rifles and machine-guns above their heads. Oliviero fought against the strong current and the tree branches, tangled roots and brambles, struggling to move forward with the sludgy mud at the bottom of the ditch sucking his boots in.

As they battled along the ditch, an Apache sat overhead, and they heard the thunderous rapid clatter of its 30mm gun as it blasted enemy further in depth.

The platoon reached a point just short of the compound, and Corporal Davies's section clawed their way out of the ditch and moved up to assault the first compound, attacking at state red. Oliviero, still in the ditch, heard the ear-splitting blast of a bar-mine exploding into the wall, then two grenades and the rattle of smallarms fire as Davies's men entered the building.

Oliviero was now out of the ditch, water pouring from his daysack and dripping from his trousers and shirt, and Brooks stacked the section up against the compound wall. Davies's men were clearing the place room by room, and Oliviero could hear the muffled rifle fire within.

The engineers set up a bar-mine for entry into the next compound. Oliviero and Private Craig Broom, Assault Team 1, were poised to rush in. The charge refused to function. Brooks cursed then moved quickly to the corner. 'No explosive entry. We'll go in through the entrance round this corner. Hicksie, push past the entry.'

Hicks, carrying his Minimi, ran forward to secure the far side and protect the assault team from enemy attack. Brooks shouted, 'Assault Team 1, move in now. I'm right behind.'

Oliviero and Private Craig Broom ran up to the compound entrance. The entry was blocked by stacks of dried opium poppy stalks, piled up to close it off. With one hand pointing his rifle into the entryway, Oliviero pulled the stalks away. He was worried. Too exposed.

Broom fired into the room, as Oliviero dived over the top of the poppy stalks and rolled through into the compound. Immediately he knelt up and started blasting bullets all round the courtyard area. Broom dived in. The two sprayed a hut on the left and checked it. Clear. The pair raced from room to room, firing into each one.

They moved back into the middle of the open courtyard, and Oliviero heard the whoosh of an RPG just above his head. He was thrown to the ground, deafened by the blast and battered by lumps of baked dirt as it exploded against the far wall. The explosion was colossal, far greater than any other RPG impact. By an amazing fluke, the warhead had exploded precisely where the defective bar-mine was positioned, causing it to detonate at the same time.

Dazed, bruised and disorientated, Oliviero picked himself up. There was a mush in his ears, as if he was under water, but from outside the compound he could make out muffled cries of 'Medic! Medic!' He couldn't see anything. The compound was full of dust and smoke. He thought, *Where's Broomie?* Broom had been nearer the point the

RPG exploded. He was horror-stricken. He called, 'Broomie! Broomie!' There was no answer. *God don't let him be dead. Please.*

The dust began to settle, and he could now begin to see the outline of the compound. He saw Broom picking himself up, unsteady on his feet.

Oliviero moved over to him. The two men were totally covered in thick, brown dust from head to foot. They looked at each other. They said nothing, but Oliviero knew Broom was thinking exactly the same thing as he was: *How did we survive that?*

Broom started laughing. Oliviero thought, *What the hell is he laughing about?* Then he was laughing himself.

Brooks and the rest of the section rushed in through the entrance-way. Brooks said to Oliviero and Broom. 'You two OK? Thought you'd been clobbered.'

Without further ceremony, he allocated fire positions and arcs to the section, who filed past, staring at Oliviero and Broom as if they were ghosts. Oliviero thought, *Covered in all this dust we probably look something like ghosts anyway. We nearly were.*

Biddick had walked in behind Brooks and was conferring with Captain Charlie Harmer, his FST commander. Oliviero looked at him, as ever cool, calm and collected. He thought, *Biddick at the front, what a surprise, always at the front.*

Biddick half-grinned, 'Hello, Oliviero. You having a good war?' and then he and his men left the compound.

He's probably taking point now, thought Oliviero. He dropped to one knee, drank some water and reloaded his magazines from the spare ammo in his bandolier.

Brooks, positioned on a small platform that gave a view over the compound wall, together with Private Scott Hardy, his GPMG gunner, yelled, 'There's enemy over there.'

As Hardy opened up with his gun, Hicks leapt on to the shelf and got his Minimi firing almost the second he was up there.

Brooks called, 'Ollie, up here with your UGL.'

Oliviero clambered up, squeezing on to the now overcrowded platform. Bullets were pinging into the compound wall below. Hardy and Hicks were blazing away with their guns, tracer pouring towards a group of trees.

Pointing with his arm, Brooks shouted above the clatter of gunfire, 'Ollie, ten o'clock, one hundred and fifty metres, trees, two enemy.'

Oliviero's UGL was loaded. He looked through his SUSAT sight to confirm the target and could just make out one fighter, between the trees, firing from behind a bund-line. At that range he had to fire indirect. He flipped up the black plastic foresight, recessed into a bracket on the left-hand side of the UGL, near the rifle muzzle. He flipped up the rear sight, also black plastic, about 10 centimetres long, further back on the bracket. He leant against the compound wall, right hand on the rifle pistol grip, left hand on the forward UGL pistol grip, resting the base of his UGL on the wall to give a stable firing platform. With his left thumb, he pressed down the safety catch from 'safe' to 'fire'. He placed the point at the top of the foresight on to the target and lined up the white 200-metre graduation on the left of the rear sight. The weapon was now aligned at 45 degrees to the ground. With his left hand he pressed the UGL pistol grip. The weapon jerked back into his shoulder, there was a deep thud and the UGL flew over the treeline. *Missed – reload.*

He didn't have time to scold himself but, dropping to one knee, banged straight into the reload drills. He pressed up the barrel release catch in front of the UGL trigger guard, and the barrel swivelled to the left. He held the rifle up to the vertical, and the empty case, like a large green plastic bottle cap, dropped at his feet. He took another grenade from his chest bandolier and pushed it into the breach, then clicked the barrel shut.

The gunners were still rattling fire into the trees, and enemy fire was still crunching into the compound wall and zipping overhead. Oliviero got back into his firing position, this time selecting 150 metres, and fired again. The grenade exploded with a loud blast, kicking up a cloud of smoke and dust. It was right in the centre of the clump of trees.

Brooks was ecstatic. He clapped Oliviero on the back, 'Quality, quality.'

6

The enemy fighters had been firing from behind a deep bund-line, and the machine-gunners had been unable to get them. After Oliviero's grenade hit, there was no further fire from the trees. He had killed them both.

Lieutenant Denning moved the whole platoon into the compounds that had just been cleared, and he and Sergeant Holmes positioned themselves with Brooks's section. The Apaches had spotted Taliban withdrawing from the area, moving around a group of compounds several hundred metres away. Biddick ordered them to engage.

One of the Apaches hovered above Oliviero's compound. It was so low that Holmes thought he could almost reach up and touch it. The noise from the engines was deafening, but Holmes and his men were elated. An attack helicopter that close in the middle of Taliban country was a real confidence boost.

On the net, Biddick, relaying a message from the Apache pilot, said, 'All stations, this is Zero Alpha, Ugly callsign now engaging with flechette rounds.'

Holmes looked up and saw smoke coming out of the Apache guns, then heard the deafening sound of the chaingun blasting at the Taliban. It sounded like a pneumatic drill as the machine sent burst after burst of deadly flechette canisters into the enemy-held compound.

Biddick said, 'Ugly about to fire Hellfire.'

There was a sudden whoosh as the Hellfire missile flew towards the enemy, and then a distant explosion as it smashed in through the compound wall. Holmes watched the aircraft hover sideways, and he could clearly see the American pilot, pulling the Apache upwards, circling away, looking for further targets.

The Apaches continued to engage Taliban in compounds and in the open and then moved off, standing by for further tasking. Biddick sent the ANA platoon forward to check and clear the compounds that the Apaches had engaged, and they found several dead bodies and numerous blood trails.

Biddick tasked 2 Platoon to clear the area of trees that Oliviero had engaged with his UGL, and Corporal Alexander reported on the radio that he had found two bodies, blown apart by Oliviero's grenade, as well as two further blood trails.

It was now late morning, and 1 Platoon remained in the compound while the clearances continued. Holmes got around the men. 'Make sure you drink plenty. Have something to eat now, while we've got a pause. Have a boily or something.'

As he walked round the men, Holmes squeezed down a revolting bag of corned beef, covered in melted lard that had heated up in his webbing and was lukewarm. Some of the men were too exhausted to bother eating, but Holmes made sure they did. 'Why aren't you eating? I know it's disgusting, but eat. Think of the thousands of calories you are using up. You've got to replace it. I'm not having any of you going down.'

Holmes was always mindful of Biddick's warning to the platoon sergeants before every operation: 'If any of your men go down because they haven't drunk enough or eaten enough, I'll be coming to you for answers.'

Holmes had Hornigold, acting as his runner, moving around the compound, checking ammo states with the section 2ICs and helping to redistribute bullets, grenades and belts of machine-gun link. He was impressed by Hornigold, the youngest soldier in the battalion, and a strong, tough and fit lad. He had just been in his first contact and for the first time in his young life had been shot at, witnessed RPGs exploding near by, bullets flying in every direction and attack helicopters firing rockets into the enemy from just a few metres overhead. Holmes sat beside him in the compound and said, 'Well done, Kane, mate, you survived your first contact. You've got to survive all the rest too, because your dad's going to sort me out with my new car if I get you back alive. Believe me, mate, you're worth a few quid to me.'

He winked at Hornigold. Then the company was on the move again, advancing with the Helmand River on the left and C Company on the right. All through the day, the fearless Private Sam Hicks led 1 Platoon, and often the whole company, across the battlefield and into contact after contact. During the advance, on Hornigold's first day of battle, he saw a Taliban fighter concealed in a tree to his front and unhesitatingly fired a full magazine of thirty rounds from his SA80.

Throughout the day Biddick's platoons had frequent firefights with the Taliban as they cleared through what seemed like an endless network of compounds; crawling through the undergrowth, wading along irrigation ditches. The men were so utterly exhausted that some of them even fell asleep firing their weapons during contacts. There were many close shaves, as sections were ambushed at point blank range, from compounds and across cornfields. They replied with 81mm fire from the battalion's Mortar Platoon. And when the attack helicopters departed, Biddick and his FST commander, Captain Charlie Harmer, used to devastating effect a troop of Royal Artillery 105 light guns deployed in the desert.

With the heat still intense, but the shadows lengthening, at 1800 hours Biddick ordered the company to go firm in a night harbour area near the river.

7

After several hours spent helping Sergeant Holmes haul supplies dropped by Chinook to the troops in the harbour area, Oliviero finally got his head down at about midnight. He only managed two hours' sleep before being shaken back to life for his turn at sentry duty. He was on stag with Private Dan Burgess, one of the section Minimi gunners. Watching their arcs through nightsights, the two men whispered to each other to keep themselves awake. Oliviero was glad to chat: it was the first conversation he'd had with anyone since leaving Sangin. They discussed how the day had gone, what tomorrow might bring and what they hoped for the future. They spoke about the often-discussed and never-realized rumour of ice cream when they got back to Sangin, about football, about the new rumour that they would be marching all the way to Musa Qalah. And about the other rumour that they would be in the Green Zone for ever.

Five months earlier, on Friday 13 April, both men had been under heavy fire on a compound roof in their first contact of the tour, blasting away at the Taliban to help Sergeant Holmes and his section get to safety. They had been through so much since that day: endless patrolling around the ruins of Sangin, marching across the desert, battling through the Green Zone, being ambushed, firing bullets back at the Taliban.

After his close shave just a few hours earlier, Oliviero was now convinced he was going to make it to the end of the tour. 'You know, Dan,' he hissed, 'I can't believe we haven't got a scratch with all those bullets and RPGs fired at us since we got out here. How have we got away with it?'

Burgess shrugged. 'God knows. I suppose we were just lucky, mate.'

Oliviero whispered, 'I wish all our lads had been as lucky as us. I was in the same platoon in training as John Thrumble. I was Chris Gray's mentor when he first joined the battalion, and I was on the NCOs' cadre with Skinny Murph and George Davey. Great, great lads, all of them.'

'Yeah I know, and Daz Bonner . . . I still can't believe he's dead.'

The two soldiers lay in sad and silent thought for a few minutes, all the while intently scanning their arcs, then Burgess whispered, 'I'd love some Taliban to try and infiltrate into here now, I'd proper mince 'em up.' He gripped his machine-gun tightly.

Oliviero grinned. 'I'd hate to be them, Dan, mate. I've seen you firing that LMG too often. Anyway, a lot of our lads may have been killed and wounded – and I'd give anything, anything at all, to have them back. But when I think about them, I always remind myself that we've smashed the Taliban a lot worse than they've smashed us.'

After Action Review

I

Private Oliviero was right. The Royal Anglian Battle Group, together with their air- and ground-based offensive support forces, 'smashed the Taliban' very hard. In addition to the engagements related in the forego-ing pages, the Royal Anglian companies fought many, many battles throughout their six-month tour, destroying the enemy in substantial numbers. Despite frequently stiff Taliban resistance, no Royal Anglians were killed in any of these other battles. Many, however, were shot and blown up during firefights; and many more suffered broken bones, espe-cially ankles, heat exhaustion and various other debilitating illnesses.

Lieutenant Colonel Carver estimated that the battle group killed forty Taliban during Operation Palk Ghar. After the operation, attacks against Sangin reduced but did not end, and the Taliban remained determined to strike at the local population, the representatives of the government and the British troops. But their ability to do so had been further degraded, and Major Biddick and his men continued to patrol aggressively throughout the town and surrounding country to further deny the enemy freedom of action. Despite A Company's efforts, towards the end of September a suicide bomb attack against the gover-nor's bodyguard resulted in the death of an Afghan police officer and the wounding of another. Two days later an IED on Route 611 just outside the town killed three Afghan National Army soldiers.

To the north, over many weeks following the most intensive phase of attacks against Inkerman in July, Major Messenger and C Company fought numerous tough battles in the desert and Green Zone near the base. One such action involved the whole Royal Anglian Sniper Pla-toon, brought together under a battle group operation codenamed Palk Law, after the actor Jude Law, who played a sniper in the Second World War film *Enemy at the Gates*.

Not far from FOB Inkerman, the snipers took up fire positions in a vantage point overlooking the Green Zone while Major Messenger led

C Company forward to flush out a Taliban IED team. As the company advanced, the enemy began to extract and were engaged by the L96 and long-range rifles of the Sniper Platoon. During the ensuing firefight, C Company and the snipers killed at least twelve Taliban fighters.

Around Kajaki, Major Borgnis and B Company continued to battle the Taliban right up until the Royal Anglians handed over responsibility for Northern Helmand to 40 Commando, Royal Marines. During the last month of the tour there was a significant increase in the level and ferocity of enemy activity in the Kajaki area of operations. Borgnis felt the Taliban wanted to have a final hard push before the traditional fighting season came to an end and they settled in for a less active winter.

On Saturday 6 October, after most of the battle group had begun heading home, B Company were patrolling in the area of Mazdurak, the scene of so many previous battles involving the Royal Anglians. Borgnis's men were attacked on three sides with an astonishing weight of fire by Taliban from twenty separate positions, interconnected by tunnels and trench systems.

The fighting was intense, and Borgnis ordered counter-strikes from the guided multiple launch rocket system, nicknamed the '70-kilometre sniper'. GMLRS, based 50 kilometres away in FOB Robinson, had arrived in August and could deliver a GPS-guided 200-pound high-explosive warhead to its target, at up to 70 kilometres, with pinpoint accuracy. To enable B Company's extraction under fire, Borgnis called in a US B1 bomber, which dropped eight 2,000-pound bombs and six 500-pound bombs on the enemy. The aircraft used up its entire payload of munitions. This rarely occurs and therefore has a special name in the US Air Force: 'Winchestering'. The name comes from the First World War, when a biplane pilot would reach for his Winchester repeating rifle after he ran out of machine-gun bullets in a dog fight. Borgnis estimated that thirteen Taliban had been killed during the battle, which was the Royal Anglians' last major combat action in Helmand.

2

By the time Lieutenant Colonel Carver handed over to the Royal Marines' commanding officer in early October, the Royal Anglian Battle Group had fought more than 350 violent close-quarter battles. On average, every soldier was involved in at least forty serious engagements with the Taliban. They had fired more than a million bullets and 22,000 artillery and mortar shells. They had thrown over 500 hand grenades and launched more than 7,000 rifle grenades at the enemy. And they had called in over 200,000 pounds of air-delivered munitions.

Carver estimated that more than 1,000 Taliban fighters had been killed during the battle group's operations. But neither he, Brigadier Lorimer nor any of the Royal Anglian commanders considered body count to be the measure of success in Helmand. Under Lorimer's concept for Task Force Helmand, all security operations in the province were in support of the government of Afghanistan, and were executed to set the conditions for improved governance, reconstruction and economic development. Both Lorimer and Carver recognized that vital to any success in these areas was an improved sense of safety and security among the population of Helmand: key components in the 'battle for consent'.

When the battle group deployed, together with the rest of Lorimer's brigade, the so-called Taliban spring offensive was due, according to intelligence reports and the Taliban's own propaganda. There was a noticeable increase in Taliban attacks as they prepared to give the British forces a bloody nose. Lorimer and Carver had other ideas. They recognized that to stand any chance of improving security for the people they had to switch tactics and take the fight to the enemy. There were insufficient forces available to hold any significant area of ground, but, by entering and staying in the Green Zone for extended periods, the battle group denied the Taliban the freedom they needed for their own 'spring offensive'. Having seized the upper hand in this way, the Royal Anglians – and Task Force Helmand as a whole – retained the initiative for the whole of the six-month tour, remaining on the offensive throughout.

For the Taliban in Helmand, this was tactically devastating. Having failed to overcome the hard-fought defences of platoon bases in Helmand during 2006, and unable to counter the offensive strikes into their own strongholds in 2007, they increasingly came to realize that they could not win in face-to-face confrontation with NATO forces. The attrition the Taliban suffered during 2007 was a major factor in their shift towards greater – but not exclusive – use of mines, roadside bombs and other improvised explosive devices.

Of equal importance, Task Force Helmand's offensive operations sought to demonstrate to the local communities that the British forces meant business, were able to protect them to a substantial extent and could provide an alternative to Taliban intimidation.

The Royal Anglian Battle Group's operations led to real improvements in safety and prosperity for the people in Sangin and Gereshk and the surrounding districts. Towards the beginning of the deployment, Operation Silicon and its aftermath had denied the Taliban freedom to attack, kill and intimidate the population of Gereshk. President Karzai said, 'If we fail in Sangin we will fail in Afghanistan.' And for most of the tour, the security and reconstruction of Sangin was the Royal Anglians' priority. The three major battle group operations in the Helmand River valley north-east of the town, the establishment of FOB Inkerman and the extensive security activity in and around Sangin resulted in its transformation.

Until the US-led Operation Silver, launched as the Royal Anglians deployed into Helmand, Sangin had endured almost a year under siege. When the battle group arrived it was a virtual ghost town. Six months later, many of the residents had returned, and the vitally important bazaar was flourishing once again. A range of development projects had been initiated, including irrigation, repair of electricity transformers, constructing wells, opening schools and clinics and clearing bomb damage. Following a lengthy battle with the system, a few days after Operation Palk Ghar ended, Carver succeeded in gaining the release of $104,500 of humanitarian relief cash to pay families in Sangin whose homes had been destroyed in fighting. The payments, made by Biddick, represented a milestone in the struggle to gain the consent and confidence of the community.

Over the six-month period, there was an increasing sense of hope and optimism among the people of Sangin, and in the community across the district. But despite everything they did on reconstruction and development, Carver and Biddick felt their efforts represented only a drop in the ocean compared to what was really needed, and throughout the tour it was a cause of constant frustration that more resources and energy were not made available by Allied governments for these vital lines of operation.

The Royal Anglian Battle Group achieved significant success at the strategically important Kajaki Dam. Relentless aggressive patrolling by first C then B Company had pushed the Taliban front line at Kajaki further and further back, leaving the dam itself and the hydroelectricity-generating plant virtually immune to interference from the Taliban. The Royal

Anglians' example was followed by successive units, and less than a year after the battalion left Helmand, the vital third generator was brought in by road, an achievement that will enable the hydroelectricity station to supply electric power to most of Helmand and Kandahar provinces.

Following the tour, Brigadier Lorimer said of the Royal Anglians: 'The officers and soldiers of the Royal Anglian Battle Group were quite superb during the summer of 2007. They knew that it was going to be a tough operational deployment, and their training and preparation for the six-month tour were comprehensive and rigorous. In Helmand Province, they had a sharp focus and a desire to maintain the pressure on the enemy. They were agile, controlled and disciplined. Despite taking casualties, they cracked on in their efforts to make northern Helmand a better place. They had a terrific regimental ethos and esprit de corps which affected everyone who worked with them.

'The soldiers of The 1st Battalion The Royal Anglian Regiment represented the British infantry at its best, exuding all those essential qualities that have been so important over the years: courage, determination, dedication to duty, humility, patience and forbearance; and all done with a wry smile and a sense of humour. In short, the Royal Anglian Battle Group was a fantastic group of professional soldiers, who rose to the challenge in 2007 and who should be justifiably proud of what they achieved. I am exceptionally proud to have commanded them.'

3

Every Royal Anglian who was in Helmand can testify to the chaos and confusion of war. According to a well-known military adage, 'no plan ever survives contact with the enemy'. It is difficult enough to manoeuvre large numbers of troops and vehicles across treacherous and inhospitable terrain, sometimes by night, in dust storms, rain or searing heat; in armoured vehicles with limited external vision; against near-impossible time-lines; and coordinating with neighbouring forces, ground attack aircraft, helicopters, artillery, engineers and logistic support. But the complexities and potential for confusion are hugely increased when the enemy is trying to prevent you from doing it by killing you and blowing up your vehicles and equipment.

Piled on top of this are the limits of reconnaissance and the frequent inaccuracy or incompleteness of the intelligence picture, sometimes brought about by the enemy's own operational security, deception and disinformation, sometimes by lack of resources or inadequacy of collection systems. For every intelligence success such as the one achieved by Captain Tom Coleman in Sangin, there are a hundred disappointments. In close combat even the most technologically sophisticated weapons, surveillance systems and communications devices can and frequently do fail. The Royal Anglians' repeated experience of failure at the critical moment of their state-of-the-art combat radios is a case in point. Messages are sometimes not transmitted, not received, or garbled. Precision-guided munitions don't always hit the target they are supposed to and sometimes explode when they shouldn't or don't explode when they should. Especially in close infantry combat, the concept of the precise, surgical strike is more often pipe dream than practical reality. The Helmand environment, especially the Green Zone, also served to diminish the advantages of technology, frequently putting the Royal Anglians and Taliban on equal terms during the close fighting.

Then there is perceptual distortion, common in combat situations, which can lead a commander or soldier to comprehend events in a way that is different from reality. The stresses and fears of battle, tiredness and the body's natural chemical reactions, including production of adrenalin, can lead to excluding or intensifying sounds, tunnel vision, temporary paralysis, events appearing to move faster or more slowly than they actually are, loss, reduction or distortion of memory and distracting thoughts. These affect different people in different ways and can add to the confusion and chaos of battle.

Amid the disorientation, the smoke, the fire, the explosions, the ear-piercing rattle of bullets, the screams of the wounded, the incomplete intelligence picture and the failure of technology, commanders and soldiers must work on to achieve their mission, no matter how hard it gets. Commanders in particular must plan, decide and act in a way that will avoid unnecessary danger, risk and loss of life to their own men and to the civilian population. These calculations and decisions become doubly difficult when fighting a tough, wily, skilful enemy, one minute shooting at you or setting a landmine to blow up your vehicle, the next tilling the land while waving or smiling or chatting to you, dressed indistinguishably from the population.

To quote Major Biddick: 'As a commander you are surrounded by your men yet are totally alone. You have the NATO military arsenal at your disposal, but the most useful weapons are the rifle and the bayonet. You have to kill the enemy knowing that you will then need to shake hands and win the consent of the family in the compound that he is occupying. You haven't slept for two days, you are shattered, you are wet with sweat and the chaos of battle reigns all about you. There are no computers; on your map with your pen you must compute the locations and intentions of the enemy, your flanking forces, the unpredictable ANA, their OMLT and fourteen of your own callsigns. You must do this immediately because the CO needs a SITREP, your company group need a situation brief to orient them, and your FST commander is about to bring in fast air, helicopters and mortars, and needs to know that the danger-close fire missions – which all fire missions were in the Green Zone – are not going to kill your men. You must assess the situation and give the go in seconds to secure the initiative.

'The advantage for the commander of all this is that it makes you forget the eighty pounds on your back, the water in the ditch that is up to your waist, and the sweat and dirt that streams constantly into your eyes. The battle manifests itself as a wall of noise that surrounds you, interspersed with the infantryman's most detested sound – incoming bullets cracking above, to the side and below your head.'

In the kind of high-intensity combat faced by the Royal Anglians in Helmand, success can only be achieved, chaos can only be controlled, and dangers can only be overcome by commanders who are fearlessly aggressive and know how to seize the initiative, imposing their own brand of order on events by surprise, momentum, pace, speed and shock action. Indecision, uncertainty, delay and timidity can lower the morale of the troops and lead to disaster. This is why Major Dominic Biddick pushed to attack Habibollah Kalay during Operation Silicon, why Major Phil Messenger forced his way into the Taliban stronghold of Mazdurak, why Major Mick Aston was determined to hunt down the enemy fighters in Katowzay during Operation Ghartse Ghar, and why Major Tony Borgnis Winchestered a B1 bomber to support his company's extraction from Mazdurak in the closing shots of the tour.

The chaos and friction of battle frequently leads to incidents of so-called 'friendly fire' or 'blue on blue'. The tragic F15 strike that accidentally killed three of B Company's bravest men in August 2007 stands out. There were other, less catastrophic, incidents of friendly fire during the Royal Anglians' tour, as there have been on every combat tour in Afghanistan and Iraq and every conflict, ancient and modern, including both world wars, Korea, the Falklands campaign, Northern Ireland, the Balkans and the Gulf War. The more intensive the combat, the more often friendly fire incidents will occur. When analysing the chaos, the confusion and the ebb and flow of battle, it is astonishing that more such incidents do not take place. But the effect on morale of friendly fire can be significantly greater than death or injury caused by enemy fire. Modern surveillance, target acquisition, fire control, geo-locational and communications systems help reduce the risk, but, as with other areas of combat, technology will never completely do away with friendly fire incidents, however desirable that would be.

4

While significantly lower than the blood cost to their opponents, the price of their six-month tour had also been high for the Royal Anglians. Nine killed and fifty-seven wounded in action. The homecoming for the dead was always poignant. Hours after the emotional ramp ceremonies when the battalion said goodbye to their dead comrades at Camp Bastion, close families gathered for the arrival of their loved ones at Brize Norton. The funeral of every Royal Anglian soldier was packed; people were standing in the aisles, and crowds assembled outside. Serving soldiers, from General Sir John McColl, Colonel of the Regiment, downwards, gathered at churches and crematoriums across the country, as did retired officers and soldiers. The sense of regimental loyalty, incomprehensible to those who have not served, drew them close.

Many a battle-hardened combat-suited infantryman, rarely given to displays of emotion, could be seen with tears running down his cheeks, alongside boys just out of their teens, some wearing football shirts or tracksuits and trainers, others in unfamiliar dark suits or ill-fitting jackets and black ties. These were the shocked school friends, who only months earlier had been messing about in the classroom, listening to loud music or boozing illegally with the occupant of the Union Flag-draped coffin.

Corporal Daz Bonner's funeral was one of the largest. At the wake afterwards, the British Legion hall was packed with soldiers and former soldiers from both of the battalions he had served in. Major Dave Goude, who had been regimental sergeant major of the 2nd Battalion, observed that this was the first time in living memory that large numbers of troops from the 1st and 2nd Battalions had been together with drink taken and there hadn't been a fight.

The funerals of John Thrumble, Robert Foster and Aaron McLure, killed together by an accidental bombardment at Mazdurak, were each attended by the families of the others. Private Josh Lee, still very ill and under heavy medication, discharged himself from hospital to be at the funerals of the friends who died alongside him. Corporal Stu Parker, their section commander, couldn't make it; he lay silent in a coma at Selly Oak Hospital.

Many of the more seriously wounded will pay the price of the fighting in Helmand for the rest of their lives. Those who survived did so thanks to the excellent battlefield first aid, often administered by their mates, the speedy helicopter evacuation and the first-rate medical treatment at Bastion field hospital. But some will not be able to lead a normal life again and will never get back to full fitness, including Private Matt Woollard, who lost his right leg to a mine near Kajaki; Private Simon Peacock, who was blown up by a missile in Mazdurak; Lance Corporal Dean Bailey, who was permanently deafened in the Sangin ambush and sustained serious wounds to his shoulder and hand; Corporal Mac McLaughlan, the medic shot in the stomach at Heyderabad; Sergeant Keith Nieves, badly burnt by a minestrike on the way to FOB Robinson; Private Jason Thompson, who was blown up by a rocket-propelled grenade at Katowzay; and Corporal Stuart Parker, who sustained severe blast injuries in the F15 bombing at Mazdurak.

Others suffered psychological scarring. Many killed a man for the first time and saw their mates blown apart right beside them. Most witnessed horrors that few civilians will ever have to see. For some of these, the effects have already begun to emerge. For some others, the nightmares will inevitably begin at a point in the future, with untold consequences.

Every member of the battalion felt keenly the loss of each of their nine comrades killed in action. Every Royal Anglian who was in Helmand had the intense compassion for the dead and wounded that only exists among those who know that it could just as easily have been them. Private Oliviero's words, 'I'd give anything, anything at all to have them back', reflect the sentiments of every Royal Anglian soldier that served in Afghanistan.

Soldiers in Helmand who were worried about their wounded mates flown back to the UK, the wounded soldiers themselves, their families and the families of Royal Anglians killed in action all had a most remarkable pillar of strength upon which to lean: Major Dean Stefanetti. Commander of the Rear Party, Stefanetti masterminded every aspect of the military response at home to the deaths of Royal Anglian soldiers in Afghanistan and made himself personally responsible for the wellbeing of the battalion's wounded and the care of their families. The standards and levels of service that he set for himself, and those under his command, far exceeded anything laid down in the book and were testament to the strength of regimental pride, spirit and devotion in this renowned former regimental sergeant major.

Few Royal Anglians spent much time dwelling on whether or not it was worth it. During more than 300 interviews for this book it was clear that virtually every soldier of every rank understood the declared purpose of British military operations in Afghanistan, explained to them by their commanders – to prevent extremists from re-establishing a base in the country from where they could plan or organize terrorist attacks against the West, including the UK. Private Oliviero rationalized the operation in simple terms: his sister was using the London Underground at the time of the July 2005 bombings; she could so easily have been a casualty; it was his duty to fight to prevent that kind of danger.

Most said they would go back and do it all over again if they had the chance, including many who had been wounded. One of these was Corporal Stu Parker, whose injuries will forever prevent him from overseas deployments. There were almost as many motives as there were soldiers who said they would go back. But in simple terms they boil down to three main views: 'I want to stand up for my country and protect the people of this country'; 'If my mates and my battalion go, I am going'; 'It's the job I volunteered to do, I trained to do, and I enjoy doing'.

∫

The story of the Royal Anglians' tour in Helmand is the story of modern British youth. Despite their frequent dismissal as 'the PlayStation generation', the conflict in Afghanistan proved once again that the innate spirit and moral fibre of our young people has remained undiminished down the centuries. To quote Sergeant Larry Holmes, 'Eighteen-year-old soldiers that play a computer game all their life proved to me that they could walk for forty-eight hours and fight all day in the heat. I looked at them and I thought, what's it going to take to break these blokes? You smash them all day and night and they keep going. Give them a cigarette and a brew and they'll be off again.'

Infantry commanders – from fire team upwards – have it tough. They must always think and plan ahead, enforce standards, navigate their way across the battlefield and make difficult, often life-or-death, decisions. The loneliness of command is not a cliché but a reality, and the higher up you are the lonelier it gets. But according to Corporal Stuart Parker, section commander in B Company, 'In some ways the hardest job is being a private. And they're the ones who normally get the least recognition. They are often in the dark about what's going on; they usually get ordered to do the most boring, tedious duties like sangar sentry and fatigues; and they are more often than not in the most dangerous positions as the company advances to ambush.' Like Robert Foster, Parker's point man until he was killed at Mazdurak, the majority of privates in the Royal Anglian Regiment were in their late teens, or sometimes their very early twenties. Their commanders, from Lieutenant Colonel Carver downwards, praised them for their bravery, aggression, robustness and dependability – in all of which they exceeded even the very high expectations set by the battalion.

Every generation of British soldiers believes wrongly that the young men of the generations that follow lack the physical and mental robustness and the fortitude of their own. The courage, determination, resilience and fighting spirit shown by the soldiers of The 1st Battalion The Royal Anglian Regiment in 2007 was no less than that of their direct regimental predecessors at the Battle of Minden in 1759, the stand at Gandamack in north-east Afghanistan in 1842 and the storming of Sword Beach on D-Day, 6 June 1944. In this context, Dr Duncan Anderson, a military historian who spent several weeks on operations with the Royal Anglians in 2007, said, 'At company level in Helmand I thought the fight I witnessed was indistinguishable from that experienced by the Americans in July and August 1944, facing a highly efficient, highly competent enemy in the Normandy bocage.

The Royal Anglians' story is also the story of the British Army's historic regimental system, evolved and perfected down the years. It was the regimental system that welded and shaped the raw material, some forged by council estates, care homes, sink schools and frequent visits to the police station, probation officer or social services into the powerful fighting unit that proved equal to every challenge, and able to withstand any setback. In common with other infantry regiments in the British Army, most Royal Anglian soldiers remain members of the same battalion throughout their career – whether four years, twenty-two years or longer. Some are temporarily posted to headquarters and training establishments, but most will return to their battalion after a couple of years away. They live together, work together, drink together, fight together – and sometimes get arrested together. The close relationships thus developed over many years, extending up and down the ranks, make for a close-knit, family regiment, with friendship, understanding, trust and loyalty that are essential to effectiveness in combat. For many young soldiers in the twenty-first century, their battalion is the first real family they have ever known.

Every soldier knows he plays a vital role in his battalion, which is understood, respected and appreciated by his fellow soldiers and by his commanders. He knows his mates will look after him, as will his officers, NCOs and warrant officers. And when away on operations, the battalion and regimental welfare system will be tuned up to make sure that his family is properly looked after should anything happen to him.

You won't hear a Royal Anglian soldier boast about how in Afghanistan his battalion fought harder, had higher standards of fitness, was tougher or more robust than any other. It is for other regiments to worry about how 'gung ho' or 'hard-core' they are. The Royal Anglian soldier knows what he did and what his mates did, and he knows also – though he is unlikely to admit it – that soldiers from other regiments would probably have done the same thing in much the same way had they been at that place at that time.

With over 300 years of distinguished conduct in battle behind them, as well as an Army-wide reputation for being a no-nonsense, professional and warlike regiment without airs or graces, Royal Anglian soldiers have never thought they had anything to prove. According to Corporal Ryan Alexander, however, 'This did not make us complacent or over-confident in Afghanistan. In fact the opposite is true. Our priority was to get the job done as best we could. I think one of the most obvious characteristics of Royal Anglian battalions is being very self-critical. We are always looking to see how we can improve our effectiveness and do things better next time, even if we succeeded this time.

Our traditions are important to us, but we never let them get in the way of operational effectiveness. If they do, it's time for a new tradition!'

This approach helps to account for the Royal Anglians' success in Helmand in 2007. Their soldiers were not afraid to fight hard one minute and engage with the locals the next – despite knowing that the very locals they were talking to could well have been among those who had been attacking them. In the words of Regimental Sergeant Major Ian Robinson, 'Our soldiers could assault through a village with the massive amount of violence you have to use to do it and then calmly go back in and discuss sorting out reconstruction projects with the local people.'

6

The defining virtues of the Royal Anglians' tour in Helmand in 2007 were courage and offensive spirit. These qualities are closely linked, but offensive spirit – the determination to attack, to move forward, to close with the enemy, to take the initiative, to dictate the pace – is more than anything the result of the leadership and example set by commanders. Lieutenant Colonel Carver and Regimental Sergeant Major Robinson set the tone for the battle group's aggressive approach during the twelve months' training prior to deployment, and they and the company commanders carried it through right to the end of the six-month deployment.

Courage, on the other hand, while influenced by the actions of commanders, and the consequent overall morale of a platoon, company or battalion, is very much an individual and a personal attribute. Why did Lance Corporal Boyle run through what he believed to be a minefield to give first aid to Private Woollard? Why did Corporal Brown lead his section into the teeth of enemy fire to rescue Private Gordon and Guardsman Harrison? Why did Lance Corporal Ruecker run through an ambush zone thick with enemy bullets to save Lance Corporal Bailey? Why did Private Barker charge into machine-gun fire to drag Corporal McLaughlan to safety?

There were many other feats of uncommon valour by Royal Anglian officers and soldiers, only some of which have been described in this book. And of course the very acts of patrolling in territory where ambush was inevitable, or running forward towards the enemy under fire – daily events in the lives of most Royal Anglian infantrymen – themselves require courage of an order that most people will never be called upon to muster.

Why did these men risk their lives in this way? After six months of intensive combat, most soldiers seemed surprised when asked the question. 'What else would I do?', 'What else could I do?', 'It's what being a soldier is about', 'You just did it'.

So were these men without fear? Most admitted readily to being afraid in almost every battle, and sometimes utterly terrified. Others avoided the issue. The reality is that virtually everybody who faces the danger that these soldiers faced on an almost daily basis is afraid, whether they are prepared to admit it or not. And that fact makes their actions in combat truly courageous, because without fear there can be no courage.

The remarkable courage of the Royal Anglians was the result of many influences and motivations. But, as in battles throughout history, most soldiers stood up and moved forward under fire ultimately because they weren't prepared to let their mates down. They were all in it together.

Some will find it hard to fully understand the actions of C Company in the aftermath of Private Tony Rawson's death at Regay. Why did Corporal Willan, Private Garrett and Private Cain, and many other soldiers in the company group, risk their lives to recover Private Rawson's dead body under enemy fire over many hundreds of metres of gruelling terrain and in searing heat conditions? The answer is simple: no one gets left behind. Ever. This tragic yet uplifting episode encapsulates the spirit of comradeship among infantry soldiers in battle. If your mate needs someone to watch his back or his flank, if he needs to be rescued from enemy fire, if he is wounded and needs to be dragged to safety, then you will do it, however much effort it takes, whatever the danger you face. And if he is killed you will make sure his body gets back so that his family can give him a decent funeral. You will not leave him. You hope – you know – that if you need help in desperate circumstances yourself, your mates will do the same for you.

But there was more to it even than this extraordinary mutual reliance. The shared dangers, hardships and horrors of close infantry combat create a closeness, a respect and an iron bond of comradeship that has no equivalent in any other human conditions. Private Kenny Meighan, point man in A Company, summed it up by referring to the eight-man rifle section of which he was a member: 'I went to Afghanistan with seven mates and came back with seven brothers.'

Honours and Awards

The following members of The 1st Battalion The Royal Anglian Regiment were recognized in the operational awards list immediately following the tour in Afghanistan.

Distinguished Service Order
Lieutenant Colonel Stuart Carver

Military Cross
Lance Corporal Levi Ashby
Major Michael Aston
Major Dominic Biddick MBE
Captain David Hicks
Corporal Robert Moore
Lance Corporal Oliver Ruecker

Queen's Gallantry Medal
Private Luke Nadriva

**Mention in Dispatches
(for operational gallantry)**
Sergeant Steve Armon
Major Philip Messenger
Warrant Officer Class 2 Kevin Main
Warrant Officer Class 2
   Timothy Newton
Sergeant Simon Panter

**Queen's Commendation for
Valuable Service**
Captain Phillip Blanchfield

Joint Commander's Commendations
Lance Corporal Mark Armstrong
Private Oliver Bailey

Corporal Andrew Brown
Private Matthew Duffy
Private Derwin Edwards
Private Anthony Freeman
Private Jordan Gibbs
Lieutenant Graham Goodey
Private Matthew Johnson
Private Josh Lee
Private Fabio Oliviero
Lieutenant Samuel Perrin
Corporal Ian Peyton
Lance Corporal Alistair Proctor
Corporal William Roberts
Captain George Seal-Coon

**Commander British Forces
Commendations**
Corporal Ryan Alexander
Staff Sergeant John Beighton
Captain Mark Bevin
Sergeant Dale Booth
Lance Corporal Matthew Boyle
Private Thomas Brace
Lance Corporal Ian Brown
Sergeant William Browning
Sergeant Michael Butcher
Corporal James Davies
Lance Corporal Karl Ehret
Sergeant Adrian Evans
Corporal Darren Farrugia
Colour Sergeant Andrew Faupel
Corporal Shaun Fosker

Sergeant Stuart Gardner
Corporal Simon Goodchild
Private Christopher Gray
Corporal Ashley Hill
Sergeant Christopher Holmes
Private Martin Hughes
Gunner Thomas Hughes
Corporal Dean Johnson
Lance Corporal John King
Private Harrison McCabe
Private Stephen Moore
Colour Sergeant Stephen Neal
Private Clinton Odell
Captain Oliver Ormiston
Sergeant Edward Owen
Corporal Stuart Parker
Drummer Dean Prior

Warrant officer Class 2
    Peter Ramm
Lance Corporal Michael Robinson
Lieutenant Bjorn Rose
Private Neil Sayce
Warrant Officer Class 2 James Self
Private Allen Sheppard
Staff Sergeant Graham Shorthouse
Captain Robert Smit
Captain Paul Steel
Captain Mark Taylor
Corporal Peter Toynton
Lance Corporal Antony Warwick
Sergeant Matthew Waters
Captain Andrew Wilde
Private Michael Williamson
Private Robert Wright

The following members of The 1st Battalion The Royal Anglian Regiment were recognized in subsequent honours lists, for their contribution to the battalion's Afghanistan tour.

**Member of the Most Excellent Order
of the British Empire**
Captain Ian John Robinson (formerly
    regimental sergeant major)
Major Dean Stefanetti

Order of Battle

Key

AGC: Adjutant General's Corps.

APTC: Army Physical Training Corps.

Coldm Gds: Coldstream Guards.

ETS: Education and Training Services.

Gib Regt: Gibraltar Regiment.

Gren Gds: Grenadier Guards.

Int Corps: Intelligence Corps.

PWRR: Princess of Wales's Royal Regiment.

R Irish: Royal Irish Regiment.

R Signals: Royal Signals.

RAChD: Royal Army Chaplains' Department.

RAMC: Royal Army Medical Corps.

REME: Royal Electrical and Mechanical Engineers.

Rifles: The Rifles (infantry regiment).

RLC: Royal Logistic Corps.

RRF: Royal Regiment of Fusiliers.

Scots: Royal Regiment of Scotland.

SPS: Staff and Personnel Support.

Yorks: Yorkshire Regiment.

Commanding Officer:
Lt Col. SW Carver

Regimental Sergeant Major: WO1 Robinson IJ

A (Norfolk) Company
Company Headquarters

Maj DSJ Biddick MBE

Capt GDR Hudson

Capt PR Steel

Lt D Pozo
(Gib Regt)

WO2 Main K

WO2 Smith S

Sgt Manning AE
(PWRR)

Cpl Bell C

Cpl Bonner DW
(Killed in Action)

Cpl Hannam TRD
(R Sigs)

Cpl Thompson AT
(Australian Army)

Cpl Walker M

LCpl Morfitt DJ

LCpl Duckett JM

Pte Dodds O

Pte Graves A

Pte Holt T

Pte Ranns RS

Pte Simons

Pte Sivewright C

Pte Theobald G

Pte Turner BN

1 Platoon

Lt NGV Denning

Sgt Holmes CJ

Cpl Brooks CA

Cpl Davies JR

Cpl Field SR

LCpl Chatfield SPM

LCpl Coleby PJ

LCpl Murray DP

Pte Broom C

Pte Brown AJ

Pte Burgess DA

Pte Chapman GJ

Pte Charlesworth M

Pte Ellis BE

Pte Gillasbey ALP
(Gib Regt)

Pte Hardy SH

Pte Harrison CA

Pte Hill CA

Pte Holden L (Gib Regt)

Pte Hornigold KH

Pte Hicks SD

Pte Mathieson S

Pte Meighan KJ

Pte Oliviero F

Pte Pozo NPR (Gib Regt)

Pte Redford S

Pte Richardson RM
Pte Rolph IJ
Pte Slater M
Pte Taylor AR
Pte Williams JD
Pte Wills SJ

2 Platoon

Lt GJ Goodey
2Lt HJ Willies
Sgt Butcher MJ
Cpl Alexander RC
Cpl Hazell CG
Cpl Sawasdee N (RRF)
LCpl Johnson T
LCpl Mercer NA
  (Gren Gds)
LCpl Penwright OP
  (Gren Gds)
LCpl van der Merwe WJ
Pte Bigmore MS
Pte Bowman JA
Pte Brace TD
Pte Carter C
Pte Chumbley LA
Gdsm Crook DK
  (Gren Gds)
Pte Fisher CL
Pte Flegg DF
Pte Glover AR
Gdsm Harrison CA
  (Gren Gds)
Pte Hassell NF
Gdsm Hastings L
  (Gren Gds)
Pte Illsley SE
Pte Johnson AJ
Gdsm Keeley KJ
  (Gren Gds)
Gdsm Lee OT
  (Gren Gds)
Pte Marano J

Pte Ndego MN
Pte Nicholls SM
Pte Njie ML
Pte Okotie OT
Pte Smith KAG
Pte Smits SPD
Pte Stephens MTC
Gdsm Tipping B
  (Gren Gds)
Pte Ward ALW
Pte Whaites N

3 Platoon

Lt BES Rose
Sgt Panter SI
Cpl Moore RW
LCpl Findley T
LCpl Fish TA
LCpl Garner DA
LCpl Green PJ
LCpl Kisby CS (Yorks)
LCpl Marley NA
Pte Appleton M
Pte Bridges MJ
Pte Burkard AET
Pte Casey PJ
Pte Clarke AS
Pte Cowley TR
Pte Copperwheat AJ
Pte Croft T
Pte Duffy NJT
Pte Feltham B
Pte Flanagan DA
Pte Giles CS
Pte Goodwin C
Pte Gray C
  (Killed in Action)
Pte Hammond MP
Pte Jarrad DK
Pte Johnson GP
Pte Jones RC
Pte Leonardi MP

Pte McLeod JAA
Pte Osborn TJ
Pte Roberts BL
Pte Ryan TJP
Pte Scrivener BD
Pte Stringer M
Pte Symonds LA
Pte Ward AJ

FSG A

CSgt Faupel A
Cpl Meadows LG
Cpl Smith PA
Cpl Watts G
LCpl Evans AM
LCpl Flight MC
LCpl Magee B
LCpl Silvey RW
LCpl Terry AJ
LCpl Willian M
Pte Bailey OJ
Pte Burrnell CM
Dmr Deigan RA
Pte Donnachie CJ
Pte Long JL
Pte Mason DAK
Dmr Pegrum RN
Dmr Railton JB
Pte Wallace DW

B (Suffolk) Company
Company Headquarters

Maj M Aston
Maj AHC Borgnis
Capt DJ Robinson
WO2 Newton TR
CSgt Shand CS
Sgt Hartland C
Cpl Dickenson MJ
  (R Sigs)
Cpl Naylor JMH

LCpl Jackson N
LCpl Lambell JS
LCpl Stuczynski DG
  (Gren Gds)
Pte Coram CEJ
Pte Haldenby J
Pte Handley R
Pte McCluskey PJ
Pte McIlroy IS
Pte O' Dell CM
Pte Whatley TS

5 Platoon

2Lt BJ Howes
CSgt Nieves K
Sgt Canepa R (Gib Regt)
Cpl Mason TB
Cpl Thorne SJ
LCpl Blewett BW
LCpl Cooledge AD
LCpl Davey G
  (Killed in Action)
LCpl McCall R
LCpl Swindells SJ
  (Yorks)
LCpl Tower J
Pte Anderson MD
Pte Arnott RT
Pte Corless SA
Pte Cox TA
Pte Galliano MR
  (Gib Regt)
Pte George CJ
Pte Heirsher J
Pte Hill JP
Pte Humphrey BJ
Pte Lingley M
Pte Lizzi SM
Pte McKendrick C
Pte Monks C
Pte Nadriva LC
Pte Rix J

Pte Rogers SM
Pte Rushen-Smith P
Pte Scott JS
Pte Shea D
Pte Shirley CB
Pte Sheppard AJ
Pte Smith 70 D
Pte Waghorne GA
Pte White GA

6 Platoon

Capt DN Broomfield
2Lt MO Driver
Sgt Browning WB
Sgt Owen JE
Cpl Adlington JW
Cpl George G
Cpl Murphy J
LCpl Ashby LD
LCpl Hunt KJ
LCpl Kennedy P
LCpl Murphy J
Pte Archer AF
Pte Battison PMR
  (Gib Regt)
Pte Bradbury M
Pte Bramman SC
Pte Day MS
Pte Dickerson PJ
Pte Down CL
Pte Drane AP
Pte Geater LJ
Pte Green RC
Pte Greenland DR
Pte Hare OH
Pte Harper S
Pte Harrison RF
Pte Hastings RF
Pte Hill DJ
Pte Hlubi Y
Pte Kushinga S
Pte Lee NA

Pte Lowe GJ
Pte Muley J
Pte Perry J
Pte Purcell T
Pte Rogers AJ
Pte Sample D
Pte Thompson J
Pte Wanjau E
Pte Watson L
Pte Whatley TS
Pte White B

7 Platoon

Lt GEB Seal-Coon
Lt Luff AK
Sgt Martin S
Sgt Woodrow ML
Cpl Murphy J
Cpl Parker SW
LCpl Knowles DAH
LCpl Lockley JA
  (Gren Gds)
Lcpl Mann GS
  (Gren Gds)
LCpl Veal SP
Pte Barke RW
Pte Barker AJ
Pte Booth JL
Pte Cress JDC
Gdsm Davidson M
  (Gren Gds)
Pte Doherty RJ
Pte Dowd SL
Pte Ensinger ML
Pte Foster R
  (Killed in Action)
Gdsm Freiss
  (Gren Gds)
Pte Gillmore P
Pte Goddard D
Gdsm Heavens
  (Gren Gds)

Gdsm Hogg ST
  (Gren Gds)
Pte Lee JO
Pte Lewis J
Pte McClure A
  (Killed in Action)
Pte Medlock JC
Pte Merlo AL
Pte Nurse GA
Pte Pearson MA
Pte Perkins KD
Pte Porter D
Pte Sloan ARR
Pte Smith 14 MJ
Gdsm Thomas BD
  (Gren Gds)
Gdsm Thomas ME
  (Gren Gds)
Pte Thrumble J
  (Killed in Action)

FSG B

WO2 Snow IJ
Cpl Toynton PM
LCpl Auckland MP
LCpl Bailey D
LCpl Carter JC
LCpl Dowles AJ
LCpl Farrar A
LCpl Owusu GO
LCpl Ruecker OS
Pte Carruthers MC
Dmr Curtis KP
Pte Davis JP
Pte Fryer SC
Pte Lambell JS
Pte McKelvie A
Pte Read G
Pte Strike IK
Pte Tanner
  Tremaine JJ
Pte Turner BK

C (Essex) Company
Company Headquarters

Maj PJ Messenger
Capt DC Hicks
  (Killed in Action)
Capt DJ Haggar
Lt J Titchener
  (PWRR)
WO2 Ramm PA
CSgt Culshaw P
Sgt Duffy JG
Cpl Fosker S
Cpl Seager DJ (R Sigs)
LCpl Baxter NS
LCpl Ehret KH
LCpl James BL
LCpl Stuczynski PA
  (Gren Gds)
LCpl Walker LE
LCpl Wilson R
Pte Athorn LD
Pte Cobb SD
Pte Emmett BJ
Pte Ford TM
Pte Juby SP
Pte Langton A
Pte Trussler SJL

9 Platoon

Lt TA Clarke
Sgt Hassan JR
Cpl Everitt MP
Cpl Johnson A (RRF)
Cpl Milam (PWRR)
LCpl Aldridge RV
LCpl Kerrin ARP
LCpl Kirby AK
Pte Dexter MS
Pte Dunster JJ
Pte Gamadze AS
Pte Ghazalli SJ
Pte Harman A

Pte Hill JF
Pte Hines DG
Pte Jacks MA
Pte Johnson MW
Pte Khan MTS
Pte Hilton B
Pte Holland RJW
Pte Howard SL
Pte Tomlin S
Pte Wells W

10 Platoon

Lt SED Perrin
Sgt Armon S
Cpl Brown A
Cpl Ferrand TL
Cpl Pindar AN
LCpl Drinkwater WG
LCpl Howe AJ
LCpl Smith NAJ
  (Gren Gds)
LCpl Thomas GD
  (Gren Gds)
Pte Alden W
Gdsm Bangham CJ
  (Gren Gds)
Pte Bayley CA
Pte Becala MS
Pte Brace NB
Pte Brown DB
Pte Cooper LB
Gdsm Emery CR
  (Gren Gds)
Pte Facal KJF
Gdsm Foxall LA
  (Gren Gds)
Pte Garner EW
Pte Gibbs J
Pte Gordon CR
Pte Gough BAA
Pte Harris L
Pte Harris SL

Gdsm Harrison AEB
(Gren Gds)
Pte Hyett ML
Pte Jeary RP
Gdsm Jones DA
(Gren Gds)
Pte Kent PM
Pte Langridge G
Gdsm Matai JB
(Gren Gds)
Pte McDermott S
Pte Murray SE
Pte Pritchard JM
Pte Spanton BR
Pte Stevenson IJ
Pte Thompson J
Pte Wright CD
Pte Wright P

11 Platoon

Lt HJJ Olivier (R Sigs)
2Lt C Powell
Sgt Waters M
Cpl Farrugia DJ
Cpl Thomson KR (Scots)
Cpl Townsend NG (Rifles)
Cpl Willan M
LCpl Lake B
LCpl Watson DW
Pte Bates D
Pte Blowes DDJ
Pte Bonnell JJ
Pte Budd JD
Pte Cain M
Pte Cumberbatch CWD
Pte Davitt CA
Pte Garrett SM
Pte Jones RA
Pte Joseph D
Pte Kemp JAK
Pte O'Connor LK
Pte Olen LM

Pte Palmer A
Pte Peacock SM
Pte Rawson TA
(Killed in Action)
Pte Sellers MN
Pte Snow J
Pte Thorpe CS
Pte Todd RM
Pte Vaughan TDC
Pte Walker SD
Pte Webb CS
Pte Woollard MD

FSG C

Capt MOG Taylor
Sgt Head ST
Cpl Eastwood M
Cpl Gayler LD
LCpl Chadwick DW
LCpl Corner E
LCpl Henty SR
LCpl Highton KJ
LCpl Mann TM
LCpl McPhee SM
LCpl Mercer S
LCpl Robinson ML
Dmr Armstrong FS
Pte Casburn A
Dmr Gent DT
Dmr Meiring D
Pte Moore SP
Dmr Prior DA
Dmr Seymour D
Dmr Wright RJ

D (Cambridgeshire) Company
Company Headquarters

Maj CS Calder
WO2 Taylor T
CSgt Hopkin C

Cpl Groves LL
Cpl Moore MJ
Cpl Nicholls MB
Pte Pudwell AJ

Recce Platoon

Capt APT Wilde
Sgt Hill JJ
Sgt Thurston A
Cpl Hill AR
Cpl Kearney PM
Cpl Eggleton JS
Cpl Ling DW
Cpl Roberts WJ
Cpl Vickery R
LCpl Cadman DP
LCpl Eggleton PMG
LCpl Green JM
LCpl Pimm S
LCpl Ryan J
Pte Boyle C
Pte Brown A
Pte Cook N
Pte Cooper WP
Pte Freeman ADA
Pte Greenfield WJ
Pte Hancock GM
Pte Hautfleisch GUR
Pte Mazariel SC
Pte Prior WM
Pte Rowley JA
Pte Sawyer MJ
Pte Webster PA
Pte Worsley CD

Mortar Platoon

Capt PMJ Kelly
CSgt Grice JA
Sgt Booth DS
Sgt Duggan B
Sgt Evans AM
Sgt Tinkler AP

Cpl Baker BJ
Cpl Duncan AN
Cpl Fay DJ
Cpl Johnson D
Cpl Mataceva A
Cpl Smith BI
Cpl Wilsher MI
LCpl Grange Cook D
LCpl Jackson NJ
LCpl Kingsey MJ
LCpl Owens D
LCpl Warwick T
Pte Ablett GA
Pte Alford D
Pte Brooks JC
Pte Browne SR
Pte Carruthers MC
Pte Dare RA
Pte Dean B
Pte Dowsett DJ
Pte Edwards DL
Pte Fox TC
Pte Frampton TS
Pte Gould WJ
Pte Green JM
Pte Griffiths MS
Pte Jakes M
Pte Johnson JG (PWRR)
Pte Kneller C
Pte Lappage JS
Pte Malembe KV
Pte McLaughlin RH
Pte Penny S
Pte Perridge M (PWRR)
Pte Reynolds KL
Pte Rogers WV
Pte Saumi S
Pte Sessions N
Pte Sianakevi R
Pte Smith ATH
Pty Taylor RI
Pte Tyrell ML

Pte Van Hinsberg D
Pte Wade B
Gdsm Bulivou TDN
  (Gren Gds)
Gdsm Goggin JD
  (Gren Gds)
Gdsm Mann AJ
  (Gren Gds)
Gdsm Mati ET (Gren Gds)
Gdsm Mulholland RM
  (Gren Gds)
Gdsm Pendlebury GM
  (Gren Gds)

FSG D

Capt OB Ormiston
Sgt Love NJ
Cpl Metcalf SH
Cpl Morris MJ
LCpl Goodship IW
LCpl Hawkins A
  (Killed in Action)
LCpl King J
LCpl Proctor AM
LCpl Rouse C
Dmr Cucciniello MJ
Pte Henning PL
Pte Howell PJ
Pte McCabe HR
Pte Prinns RL
Pte Saunders-Jones DC
Pte Smith MJ
Dmr Stephens WN
Pte Ward DF
Dmr Williamson MN

Echelon Company
Battalion Headquarters

Maj HR Bell (PWRR)
Maj RC Barrett (AGC)
  (SPS)

Maj FR Landrigin (AGC)
  (ETS)
Maj IL Hall
Maj MA Nicholas
Capt MJ Bevin
Capt AJ Buxton
Capt AM Firmin (AGC)
  (ETS)
Capt K Fisher
  (R Sigs)
Capt DJ Glover
Capt PC Moxey
Ch4 AE Strachan
  (RAChD)
Capt RA Smit
Capt RA Wicks (Coldm
  Gds)
Lt GR Cromie
  (R Irish)
Lt AK Luff (RLC)
WO2 Coleing DGF
  (Gib Regt)
WO2 Self JE
Sgt Hodgson J (AGC)
  (SPS)
Cpl Durdle BA (AGC)
  (SPS)
Cpl McGowan Griffin VC
  (AGC) (SPS)
LCpl Oaks GD (AGC)
  (SPS)
Pte Fairclough LM
Pte Harris Barnett WR
  (AGC) (SPS)

Echelon Company HQ

Capt PN Blanchfield
WO2 Freeman MA
CSgt Collins IL
Cpl Jackson S
Cpl McDonald RDG
LCpl Bale O

Quartermaster's Department

WO2 Granfield D
WO2 Jay L
CSgt Holly D (PWRR)
Sgt Hardy A
Sgt Magee K
Sgt Richardson I
Cpl Brown N
Cpl Gomer W
LCpl Bale O
Pte Tuttle C

Rover Group

Sgt Waddell SM
    (APTC)
Cpl Buff DL
Cpl Heal MJ
Cpl Rayfield I
LCpl Mayer B
LCpl Murton T
LCpl Warner GJ
Pte Mavin CR

Regimental Aid Post

Maj AD Tredget
    (RAMC)
Cpl Clarke DAV (RAMC)
Cpl Horn SC
Cpl Lewis S (RAMC)
Cpl McLaughlan RB
Cpl Peyton IJ
LCpl Boyle M
LCpl Linsley S (RAMC)
Pte O'Reilly L
Pte Quick TQ

Intelligence Cell

Capt TGBP Coleman
2Lt HJ Briscoe (Int Corp)
CSgt Neal S

Sgt Gardner S
Sgt Wallis C
Cpl Guy A
Cpl Wood RL
Pte Himfen J
Pte Hood M
Pte Long T

Communications and Information Systems Platoon

Capt AI Maclay
WO2 Rackham MR
CSgt Stringer G
Sgt Mitchell DJ
Sgt Rumsey SJ
Sgt Scott GP (R Sigs)
Cpl Cartwright G
Cpl Cole W
Cpl Haley NP (R Sigs)
Cpl Heal MJ
Cpl Overton C LD
LCpl Elgumaty HI
    (R Sigs)
LCpl Ellis L
LCpl Freebairn C
LCpl Reilly L
Pte Bowyer MA
Sig Callaghan A (R Sigs)
Pte Garcia RL
Pte Hughes M
Sig Kane J (R Sigs)
Pte Kerner S
Pte Mavin CR
Pte Patmore R
Pte Turner DB

Mechanical Transport Platoon

Capt T Jones
CSgt Neal T
Sgt Penny C

Cpl Chandler DW
Cpl Goodchild S
Cpl Griffiths J
Cpl Lomas GJ
LCpl Jones TW
LCpl Murton T
LCpl Stevens SD
Pte Andrews L
Pte Cartwright G
Pte Donner TID
Pte Howard S
Pte Kenny E
Pte Lawrence B
Pte Pearson M
Pte Sayce NA
Pte Wymark TCG
Pte Roberts B

Light Aid Detachment (REME)

Capt DJ Fallowfield
WO2 Southall JJ
SSgt Shorthouse G
Sgt Horrocks A
Sgt Roberts GP
Cpl Camp SE
Cpl Tshuma ZW
LCpl Armstrong MW
LCpl Brown AD
LCpl Evans D
LCpl Keen RA
LCpl Henson RJ
LCpl Masiwini D
LCpl Weatherall TC
Cfn Bird S
Cfn Cadd BM
Cfn Curtis LJ
Cfn Healey C
Cfn Madams A
Cfn Tate G
Cfn Watson MDN
Cfn Wilkes B

Catering Platoon (RLC)

WO2 (RCWO) Beal DP
SSgt Oldfield RM
Sgt Swinney TT
Cpl Freeman MJ
Cpl Jordan S
Cpl Langdon MR
Cpl Standen DS
LCpl Powell SA
LCpl Sawyer C
LCpl Watkinson D
Pte Boila L
Pte Daniels AGI
Pte Gurung D
Pte Gurung I
Pte Mall J
Pte Mensa F
Pte Owen-Bridge L
Pte Qiutakira SN

Rear Party (Pirbright) Company Headquarters

Major DJ Stefanetti
Ch3 P Aldred
 (RAChD)
Capt DJ Glover
Capt G Leek
WO1 Buff AL
WO2 Clark S
Sgt Day MR
Cpl Filipo KT
Cpl Hogston DJ
Cpl Marshall MH
Cpl Williams RIJ
LCpl Owen DD
LCpl Phoenix SA
LCpl Skyers NC
Pte Bryant MPB
Pte Findley SD
Pte Flounders C
Pte McRoberts M

Pte Sullivian DJ
Pte Townsley JS
Pte Watkinson F

Families Office

CSgt Woods M
Cpl Franklin A
Pte Dindyal ADS
Pte Pemberton C
Pte Toublic GK

Regimental Career Management Office

CSgt Garvie A
Cpl Jones R
Pte Emmitt SP
Pte Jones LC

Mechanical Transport Detachment

Cpl McKenna JK
Cpl Pratt JI
LCpl Dennis SWJ
Pte Down C
Pte Firmin R
Pte Hubbard B
Pte James TD
Pte Lawrence B
Pte Neil AR
Pte Pearce JA
Pte Small A
Pte Sones MT
Pte Webster

Training Wing

CSgt Wright K
Sgt Johnson SM

Quartermaster's Department

Sgt Lovett L
Cpl Coding P

Light Aid Detachment (REME)

Cpl Poxon MPJ

Catering Platoon (RLC)

Sgt Hay A
Sgt Seal BA
Cpl Jordan S
LCpl Powell SA
Pte Webb CM

Guard Force

Cpl Cartwright GM
Cpl Debuc RP
LCpl Cornish PMG
LCpl Ferrand JWC
LCpl Jarvis NC
Pte Barritt DMT
Pte Carter C
Pte Coruchen
 MAGR
Pte Dodds O
Pte Fenn
Pte Fisher C
Pte Fletcher J
Pte Gilchrist T
Pte Graves A
Pte Green RC
Pte Johnson GP
Pte Jones DR
Pte Kent NPL
Pte Pearce
Pte Price GRW
Pte Pryke KJ
Pte Rayner SJ
Pte Redford SC
Pte Roberts SDL
Pte Shirley CB
Pte Tennyson K
Pte Thurlow BC
Pte Tilbury NR
Pte Wallis

Glossary of Military Terms

105mm light gun: British Army's standard light artillery gun, firing 105mm shells out to 16 kilometres. Either towed by *Pinzgauer* or airlifted by *Chinook*. Often referred to as '105'.

107: An 18.8kg 107mm rocket. Contains an 8.3kg TNT fragmentation warhead. Used by the Taliban in Afghanistan.

2IC: Second-in command.

.338: See *long-range rifle*.

.50 cal: Browning heavy machine-gun. Fires a half-inch-diameter (.50 calibre) bullet. Pronounced 'fifty cal' and normally mounted in *sangars* or on certain vehicles.

51mm mortar: Also referred to as the '51'. A hand-held mortar that fires high-explosive, smoke and illuminating shells out to 800 metres. Provides each rifle *platoon* its own indirect fire support. Normally controlled by the platoon sergeant.

5.56mm: Standard calibre of ammunition for the British Army SA80 rifle, light support weapon (*LSW*) and *Minimi*.

7.62mm: Standard calibre ammunition for *GPMG*. Also used by *PKM*.

81mm: British Army medium mortar. The main form of indirect fire support available to infantry troops in Afghanistan. Fires *HE*, smoke and illuminating rounds out to 5,650 metres.

A10: United States Air Force ground attack jet. Also known as the 'tank buster' or 'warthog'. Equipped with a 30mm Gatling gun and capable of delivering a variety of guided munitions.

AK47: Soviet-designed assault rifle, firing 7.62mm short round. Used by the *ANA* and the Taliban.

ANA: Afghan National Army.

Apache: AH64D attack helicopter. Used by NATO forces including British and American. Armed with rockets, Hellfire missiles and a 30mm cannon. Also referred to as 'AH'.

Asherman Chest Seal: A circular adhesive patch fitted with a one-way valve at the centre, allowing air to escape but not re-enter the wound. Designed to treat a sucking chest wound.

AT4: American 84mm shoulder-launched anti-tank weapon, capable of engaging targets out to 300 metres. Used also by British troops in Afghanistan.

B1B: US Air Force long-range bomber that carries a large payload of guided munitions.

bandolier: A rectangular-shaped nylon satchel, holding 150 5.56mm rounds in five individual pouches. Worn across the body by the use of a strap.

bar-mine: The L9 bar-mine is a plank-shaped anti-tank mine, 1.2 metres in length. Breaks into two halves if required. Half of a bar-mine is the standard charge used to gain explosive entry to a compound.

Browning Hi-Power pistol: 9mm semi-automatic pistol. The magazine holds thirteen rounds.

CASEVAC: Casualty evacuation.

Chinook: CH47 twin-rotored medium-lift helicopter. Used for troop movement, *CASEVAC* and logistics.

Claymore: Remotely initiated directional anti-personnel mine. Fires 700 ball bearings over a 100-metre radius.

CLU: Command launch unit, used to acquire targets and initiate *Javelin* anti-tank missiles. Can also be used for general surveillance purposes.

company: A rifle company consists of about 100 men, organized into three *platoons* and a headquarters element. Commanded by a major.

company group: An infantry *company* with attached combat assets such as engineers, artillery and *FSG*.

COP: Combat outpost.

CST: Close support tanker. The Oshkosh wheeled tanker, a highly mobile US-manufactured vehicle, in service with British forces, is used to transport up to 20,000 litres of fuel in Afghanistan.

CVRT: Combat vehicle reconnaissance (tracked). Tracked light-armoured reconnaissance vehicle. The *Scimitar* and *Spartan* variants are in use by British forces in Afghanistan.

CWS: Common weapon sight. Imaging intensifying night sight, normally fitted to infantry smallarms.

DC: District centre. Normally the centre of administration, police, etc. within the main town in an Afghan district, e.g. 'Sangin DC'.

ECM: Electronic counter-measures. Manpack or vehicle-mounted equipment designed to prevent the detonation of remote-controlled bombs and improvised explosive devices by jamming radio frequencies.

F15: US Air Force fighter jet.

F/A18: US Navy fighter jet.

FLET: Forward line of enemy troops.

FOB: Forward operating base.

FSG: Fire support group. Normally mounted in *WMIKs* and equipped with a mixture of heavy weapons, *Javelin*, *GMG*, *GPMG*, *.50 cal* and several snipers.

FST: Fire support team. Responsible for coordinating all mortar, artillery and air support for a sub-unit. Every *company group* in Helmand had an FST attached.

FUP: Forming-up place. A point on the ground in which a combat element, e.g. a *platoon* or *company*, deploys prior to conducting an advance or attack.

GMG: Grenade machine-gun. A belt-fed grenade launcher that fires 40mm HE grenades out to 2,000 metres. Normally mounted on a *WMIK* or in a *sangar*.

GPMG: General-purpose machine-gun. A 7.62mm belt-fed medium machine-gun. When fired in the light role with its bipod legs, can engage targets out to 800 metres. Each *section* is equipped with one GPMG.

GPS: Global positioning system.

HE: High-explosive.

Hesco: A large prefabricated cube made of steel welded mesh and lined with strong felt. Delivered flat-packed then filled with soil or sand. Used to protect *FOB*s and other static locations from weapons fire.

H-hour: The precise time when an attack or other operation begins.

HLS: Helicopter landing site. Can be a permanent location inside or outside a base or any area of ground where a helicopter can land. If not a permanent HLS, the ground is usually cleared by infantry troops to make sure there are no obstructions, dangerous debris, mines or other explosive devices.

Icom scanner: Hand-held radio scanner used to listen in on Taliban communication.

IED: Improvised explosive device.

IRT: Immediate response team, providing ground protection to a *MERT*.

Javelin: 127mm anti-tank 'fire and forget' missile, guided by an imaging infrared seeker and fired in conjunction with the *CLU*. Maximum range of 2,500 metres.

JOC: Joint operations centre.

JTAC: Joint terminal air controller is a member of the *FST*, responsible for coordinating air power in support of troops on the ground.

L109: Standard issued *HE* fragmentation hand grenade of the British Army.

L96 sniper rifle: 7.62mm sniper rifle, used by rifle platoon sharpshooters and sometimes by snipers. The weapon can achieve a first-round kill at 600 metres. It has an effective range of 900 metres and can provide harassing fire out to 1,100 metres.

L-Hour: In air assault operations, this is the pre-designated time that a helicopter or helicopter force lands on a target area, normally for an attack.

LMG: Light machine-gun; see *Minimi*.

long-range rifle: .338-inch calibre long-range rifle used by British Army snipers in Afghanistan. A trained sniper can achieve a first-round kill at 600 metres and harassing fire out to 1,100 metres using a x25 magnification scope. In Afghanistan some snipers fired harassing fire to 1,500 metres.

LSW: Light support weapon. Similar to an SA80 rifle but with a longer and stronger barrel, bipod legs and a modified rifle butt that allows a higher and more accurate rate of fire out to 600 metres.

MERT: Medical emergency response team.

MFC: Mortar fire controller. A member of the *FST*, responsible for calling in mortar fire for a company group or other military unit.

Minimi: A belt-fed 5.56mm light machine-gun capable of firing out to 400 metres. Each *section* is equipped with two Minimis.

NCO: Non-commissioned officer.

nine liner: A nine-point checklist providing a format for passing certain categories of operational information up the chain of command, usually by radio. There are separate 'nine liners' for CASEVAC and close air support requests.

OC: Officer commanding. Normally refers to a company commander.

O Group: Orders Group. The individuals that make up the command group and key specialists in a military unit. Also used to refer to the process of a commander delivering orders to his O Group.

OMLT: Operational mentoring and liaison team. A team of soldiers attached to the *ANA*.

PID: Positive identification of an enemy.

Pinzgauer or Pinz: A lightweight highly mobile off-road vehicle.

PKM: A Soviet-designed 7.62mm belt-fed light machine-gun, similar to the *GPMG*. Used by the *ANA* and the Taliban.

platoon: A group of approximately thirty soldiers with a lieutenant or second lieutenant in command. A sergeant normally acts as second in command. The platoon has a small headquarters element and is sub-divided into three *sections*.

PRC-354/355: Official designations for the British Army manpack radio. Capable of secure communications.

PRR: Personal role radio. Every man carries an insecure PRR operating on a *platoon* channel. Commanders also carry a *PRC-354/355*.

QBO: Quick battle orders. Rapid verbal orders by a commander to his men, giving only essential information, before launching an operation, e.g. an attack, when time is short. Often used when in contact or at close quarters with the enemy and there is no time for longer, more detailed orders.

RAMC: Royal Army Medical Corps. All British Army doctors, and many medics, in Afghanistan are from the RAMC. The Royal Anglians also used their own medics.

red phos: Red phosphorus hand grenade, used to create an instant smokescreen.

RESA: Royal Engineers search adviser.

REST: Royal Engineers search team.

RMP: Royal Military Police.

rocket-propelled grenade: In Afghanistan this normally refers to the Russian-designed RPG-7 shoulder-launched, man-portable weapon which is used to fire a warhead at distances above 20 metres. Warheads explode on impact or self-destruct between 800 and 900 metres, causing them to 'air burst'.

RPG, RPG-7: See *rocket-propelled grenade*.

RV: Rendezvous. A designated location where forces come together to conduct further operations or movement.

SA80: Standard British Army 5.56mm assault rifle.

sangar: A watchtower or bunker, the term originating in the North-west Frontier of Imperial India. In Afghanistan normally made from sandbags and *Hesco*.

sapper: Rank in the Royal Engineers, equivalent to a private.

Scimitar: A light-tracked reconnaissance vehicle from the *CVRT* family. Fitted with a 30mm Rarden cannon and coaxially mounted 7.62mm machine-gun. Used by the Recce Platoon of The 1st Battalion The Royal Anglian Regiment.

section: Sub-division of a *platoon* consisting of eight men. Commanded by a corporal, with a lance corporal as second in command.

SF: (1) Special Forces. (2) Sustained fire. This is a term used to describe high rates of machine-gun fire, often achieved using special tripod mounts and weapon sights to gain greater accuracy at high rates.

sharpshooter: Infantryman trained to use the *L96 sniper rifle* but not formally qualified as a sniper. Every *platoon* has a designated sharpshooter.

SITREP: Situation report.

Spartan: A light-tracked armoured personnel carrier of the CVRT family of vehicles. Equipped with a 7.62mm machine-gun.

SUSAT: Sight unit smallarms trilux. A x4 magnification sight fitted to the *SA80 rifle* and *LSW.* Limited night capability.

T1, T2, T3, T4: The triage system used to systematically sort casualties in order of priority for treatment and evacuation. T1 casualty requires immediate surgery or resuscitation. T2 possibly requires surgery. T3 is walking wounded and requires no immediate surgery. T4 is killed in action.

Tac or Tac HQ: An element of a larger headquarters consisting only of the personnel, vehicles and equipment essential to directly command an operation on the ground. This normally consists of the commander, radio operators and combat support specialists, e.g. JTAC and engineer commander. In Afghanistan, a Tac HQ is normally deployed at company level and above. The Tac HQ is mobile and will usually operate close behind forward combat troops.

TIC: Troops in contact. A term used to describe forces under fire or exchanging fire with the enemy. Declaration by a commander of a TIC will usually result in rapid allocation of air support and other assets to assist if required.

UAV: Unmanned air vehicle. A pilotless aircraft remotely controlled from the ground. Depending on the type of UAV, it can be fitted with cameras and other sensors and with weapons.

UGL: Under-slung grenade launcher. A 40mm grenade launcher that can be fitted to the *SA80 rifle.* Each *section* is normally equipped with two UGLs, each capable of firing *HE* grenades out to 350 metres, delivering a fragmentation effect against the enemy.

Vector: A six-wheeled armoured version of the *Pinzgauer.*

Viking: An armoured tracked articulated vehicle, crewed by a Royal Marines commander/gunner and driver, with room for a total of nine infantrymen in the forward and rear compartments.

Viper: Thermal imaging sight that can be fitted to the *SA80, GPMG* and *Minimi.*

WMIK: Pronounced 'Wimik'. Weapons mount installation kit. The name given to a Land Rover fitted to carry a *.50 cal* or *GMG* on the back and a *GPMG* in the commander's position. Used by the *FSG* as a mobile fire support platform.

Main Characters

All those listed below were members of The 1st Battalion The Royal Anglian Regiment unless otherwise stated.

Adlington, Joel. Corporal, section commander, 6 Platoon, B Company.

Alexander, Ryan. Corporal, section commander, 2 Platoon, A Company.

Armon, Steve. Sergeant, 10 Platoon sergeant, C Company.

Aston, Mick. Major, B Company commander until the end of July. 12 Brigade Recce Force commander from the end of July.

Bailey, Dean. Lance corporal, sniper, FSG B. Wounded in action.

Bailey, Oliver. Private, sniper, FSG A.

Barke, Richie. Private, 51mm mortarman, 7 Platoon, B Company.

Barker, Aaron. Private, rifleman and team medic, 7 Platoon, B Company.

Biddick, Dominic. Major, A Company commander.

Bonner, Darren. Corporal, signals detachment commander, A Company. Killed in action.

Borgnis, Tony. Major, B Company commander, end of July onwards.

Boyle, Matt. Lance Corporal, company medic, C Company.

Broomfield, Dave. Lieutenant, promoted captain on 11 June, 6 Platoon commander, B Company.

Brown, Andrew. Corporal, section commander, 10 Platoon, C Company.

Browning, Ben. Sergeant, 6 Platoon sergeant, B Company.

Burgess, Dan. Private, Minimi gunner, 1 Platoon, A Company.

Butcher, Michael. Sergeant, 2 Platoon sergeant, A Company.

Calder, Charlie. Major, D Company commander.

Carver, Stuart. Lieutenant colonel, Battle Group commander.

Clarke, Tom. Lieutenant, 9 Platoon commander, C Company.

Coleman, Tom. Captain, Battle Group intelligence officer.

Croft, Terry. Private, 3 Platoon, A Company.

Davey, George. Lance corporal, section 2IC, 5 Platoon, B Company. Killed in action.

Denning, Nick. Lieutenant, 1 Platoon commander, A Company.

Donnachie, Clay. Private, sniper, FSG A.

Duffy, Matt. Private, Minimi gunner and team medic, 3 Platoon, A Company.

Faupel, Andy. Colour sergeant, FSG A commander.

Ferrand, Tim. Corporal, section commander, 10 Platoon, C Company.

Fong, Ronald. Sapper, combat engineer, 8 Squadron, Royal Engineers.

Foster, Robert. Private, rifleman and point man, 7 Platoon, B Company. Killed in action.

Goodey, Graham. Lieutenant, 2 Platoon commander, A Company.

Goodman, Will. Captain, Viking troop commander, Royal Marines.

Gray, Chris. Private, Minimi gunner and point man, 3 Platoon, A Company. Killed in action.

Green, Ross. Private, GPMG gunner, 6 Platoon, B Company. Wounded in action.

Harmer, Charlie. Captain, A Company FST commander, 28/143 Battery, Royal Artillery.

Hawkins, Alex. Lance corporal, sniper, FSG D. Killed in action.

Hicks, David. Captain, B Company 2IC and operations officer. Killed in action.

Hill, Ashley. Corporal, section commander, Reconnaissance Platoon.

Hill, Jamie. Sergeant, Reconnaissance Platoon.

Holmes, Chris. Sergeant, 1 Platoon sergeant, A Company.

Howes, Ben. Lieutenant, 5 Platoon commander, B Company.

Lee, Josh. Private, rifleman and UGL gunner, 7 Platoon, B Company. Wounded in action.

Lorimer, John. Brigadier, commander Task Force Helmand. Late The Parachute Regiment.

Main, Kevin. Warrant officer class 2, A Company sergeant major.

McLure, Aaron. Private, Minimi gunner, 7 Platoon, B Company. Killed in action.

Meighan, Kenny. Private, rifleman and point man, 1 Platoon, A Company.

Messenger, Phil. Major, C company commander.

Moore, Robert. Corporal, section commander, 3 Platoon, A Company. Wounded in action.

Moxey, Phil. Captain, Battle Group operations officer.

Murphy, James. Corporal, section commander, 6 Platoon, B Company.

Nadriva, Luke. Private, 51mm mortar man, 5 Platoon, B Company.

Newton, Tim. Warrant officer class 2, B Company sergeant major.

Nieves, Keith. Sergeant, 5 Platoon sergeant, B Company. Wounded in action.

Olivier, Hermanus. Lieutenant, 11 Platoon commander, C Company. Royal Signals.

Oliviero, Fabio. Private, rifleman and UGL gunner, 1 Platoon, A Company.

Owen, James. Corporal, section commander, 6 Platoon, B Company.

Panter, Simon. Sergeant, 3 Platoon sergeant, A Company.

Parker, Stuart. Corporal, section commander, 7 Platoon, B Company. Wounded in action.

Perrin, Sam. Lieutenant, 10 Platoon commander, C Company.

Peyton, Ian. Corporal, company medic, attached to B and C Companies.

Ramm, Pete. Warrant officer class 2, C Company company sergeant major.

Rawson, Tony. Private, Minimi gunner, 11 Platoon, C Company. Killed in action.

Robinson, Dave. Captain, B Company 2IC and ops officer.

Robinson, Ian. Warrant officer class 1, Battle Group regimental sergeant major.

Rose, Bjorn. Lieutenant, 3 Platoon commander, A Company.

Ruecker, Oliver. Lance corporal, sniper and team medic, FSG B.

Seal-Coon, George. Lieutenant, 7 Platoon commander, B Company.

Snow, Ivan. Warrant officer class 2, FSG B commander.

Steel, Paul. Captain, A Company 2IC and ops officer.

Thompson, Jason. Private, rifleman and point man, 6 Platoon, B Company. Wounded in action.

Thrumble, John. Private, GPMG gunner, 7 Platoon, B Company. Killed in action.

Thurston, Al. Colour sergeant, Reconnaissance Platoon 2IC.

Townsend, Nick. Corporal, section commander, 11 Platoon, C Company.

Waters, Matt. Sergeant, 11 Platoon sergeant, C Company.

Wilde, Andy. Captain, Reconnaissance Platoon commander.

Willan, Matthew. Corporal, section commander, 11 Platoon, C Company.

Wilsher, Mark. Corporal, mortar fire controller, B Company.

Woodrow, Michael. Sergeant. 7 Platoon sergeant, B Company.

Woollard, Matt. Private, LSW gunner, 11 Platoon, C Company. Wounded in action.

Index

448

PENGUIN WORLD WAR II COLLECTION

FIRST LIGHT
GEOFFREY WELLUM

Two months before the outbreak of the Second World War, seventeen-year-old Geoffrey Wellum becomes a fighter pilot with the RAF . . .

Desperate to get in the air, he makes it through basic training to become the youngest Spitfire pilot in the prestigious 92 Squadron. Thrust into combat almost immediately, Wellum finds himself flying several sorties a day, caught up in terrifying dogfights with German Me 109s.

Over the coming months he and his fellow pilots play a crucial role in the Battle of Britain. But of the friends that take to the air alongside Wellum many never return.

PENGUIN WORLD WAR II COLLECTION

THE CRUEL SEA
NICHOLAS MONSARRAT

Based on the author's own vivid experiences, *The Cruel Sea* is the nail-biting story of the crew of HMS *Compass Rose*, a corvette assigned to protect convoys in World War Two.

Darting back and forth across the icy North Atlantic, *Compass Rose* played a deadly cat and mouse game with packs of German U-boats lying in wait beneath the ocean waves.

Packed with tension and vivid descriptions of agonizing U-boat hunts, this tale of the most bitter and chilling campaign of the war tells of ordinary, heroic men who had to face a brutal menace which would strike without warning from the deep . . .

PENGUIN WORLD WAR II
COLLECTION

TUMULT IN THE CLOUDS
JAMES GOODSON

Anglo-American James Goodson's war began on Sept 3rd 1939, when the *SS Athenia* was torpedoed and sank off the Hebrides. Surviving the sinking and distinguishing himself rescuing survivors, Goodson immediately signed on with the RAF. He was an American, but he wanted to fight.

Goodson flew Spitfires for the RAF before later joining his countrymen with the Fourth Fighter Group to get behind the controls of Thunderbolts and Mustangs where he became known as 'King of the Strafers'.

Chock full of breathtaking descriptions of aerial dogfights as well as the stories of others of the heroic 'few', *Tumult in the Clouds* is the ultimate story of War in the air, told by the one of the Second World War's outstanding fighter pilots.

PENGUIN WORLD WAR II COLLECTION

PANZER LEADER
HEINZ GUDERIAN

Heinz Guderian – master of the Blitzkrieg and father of modern tank warfare
– commanded the German XIX Army Corps as it rampaged across Poland in 1939.

Personally leading the devastating attack which traversed the Ardennes Forest
and broke through French lines, he was at the forefront of the race to the Channel
coast. Only Hitler's personal command to halt prevented Guderian's tanks and
troops turning Dunkirk into an Allied bloodbath.

Later commanding Panzergruppe 2 in Operation Barbarossa, Guderian's armoured
spearhead took Smolensk after fierce fighting and was poised to launch the final
assault on Moscow when he was ordered south to Kiev. In the battle that followed,
he helped encircle and capture over 600,000 Soviet troops after days of combat in
the most terrible conditions.

Panzer Leader is a searing firsthand account of the most effective fighting force in
modern history by the man who commanded it.

He just wanted a decent book to read ...

Not too much to ask, is it? It was in 1935 when Allen Lane, Managing Director of Bodley Head Publishers, stood on a platform at Exeter railway station looking for something good to read on his journey back to London. His choice was limited to popular magazines and poor-quality paperbacks – the same choice faced every day by the vast majority of readers, few of whom could afford hardbacks. Lane's disappointment and subsequent anger at the range of books generally available led him to found a company – and change the world.

'We believed in the existence in this country of a vast reading public for intelligent books at a low price, and staked everything on it'
Sir Allen Lane, 1902–1970, founder of Penguin Books

The quality paperback had arrived – and not just in bookshops. Lane was adamant that his Penguins should appear in chain stores and tobacconists, and should cost no more than a packet of cigarettes.

Reading habits (and cigarette prices) have changed since 1935, but Penguin still believes in publishing the best books for everybody to enjoy. We still believe that good design costs no more than bad design, and we still believe that quality books published passionately and responsibly make the world a better place.

So wherever you see the little bird – whether it's on a piece of prize-winning literary fiction or a celebrity autobiography, political tour de force or historical masterpiece, a serial-killer thriller, reference book, world classic or a piece of pure escapism – you can bet that it represents the very best that the genre has to offer.

Whatever you like to read – trust Penguin.